ACTION
AND
ORGANIZATION

ACTION AND ORGANIZATION:

An Introduction to Contemporary Political Science

ROBERT C. BONE

HARPER & ROW, PUBLISHERS
New York Evanston San Francisco London

Acknowledgments

Above all thanks are due to my wife whose unfailing faith, constant inspiration, and technical skills made this book possible. Nor should my students over the years at Florida State University be forgotten for their frank and trenchant reactions which were of much assistance in shaping and sharpening the concepts expressed in this book. Professional colleagues to whom I am much indebted are Dr. Thomas R. Dye, for his encouragement and comments over several years, and Dr. Joyotpaul Chaudhuri, for his helpful comments on Chapter 7.

At Harper & Row, Walter H. Lippincott, Jr., was endlessly patient, kind, and understanding. Nor would this book ever have seen daylight without the perceptive and expert guidance received from Firth Fabend and Rebecca Sacks. Finally, thanks are due to Gail Champion for her highly skilled and intelligent typing of the original manuscript. Needless to say, any and all sins of omission or commission are my personal responsibility.

Action and Organization: An Introduction to Contemporary Political Science

Standard Book Number: 06-040843-X

Library of Congress Catalog Card Number: 70-181546

PREFACE

The title of this book, *Action and Organization*, expresses the author's philosophy of how political science should be studied. The outstanding aspect of anything political is that it involves action. Further, this action is almost always consistent and systematic. So the logical way to understand and analyze it is as a separate and distinct pattern of regularly recurring relationships, i.e., as a system. This system exists to identify, process, and attempt to satisfy the political demands of a particular society.

Any demand is political if it requires action by the power-holding decision-makers involved in relation to an existing policy or personal situation. There are several points which need to be noted. First, the action which the decision-makers take may be no action at all. A decision not to act may have far more important effects than an affirmative decision. Second, the decision-makers involved need not occupy any official governmental position for the results of their action to have important political consequences. The refusal by a political party to endorse certain programs or to nominate a particular candidate may well be more important than any positive actions taken by governmental sources. (As used in this text, the term *governmental* describes the activities of those individuals and organizations legitimately monopolizing the right to determine universal policies for their society and to enforce their decisions.)

In the broadest sense, any action by any group is political if it has an effect on the power relationships of the individuals involved. Political conflict is concerned with a constant struggle for the control of power. When this occurs, as it usually does, as a regularly recurring pattern of relationships among the individuals and institutions involved, we can speak of a *political system*. Since struggles over power relationships occur in any type of group, in any complex society there are innumerable private political systems functioning simultaneously. The complex interaction of all these make up the public political system of a society.

Thus it is inaccurate to think of the political system of

a society as a single harmonious whole. Rather, there are numerous hierarchies of subsystems with widely differing values and objectives. The greater the differences among the political cultures of these subsystems, the greater the lack of consensus in the society at large and the more serious the stresses and strains put upon its effective functioning. The American political system is currently experiencing turmoil and upheaval because of a very serious lack of consensus on the rules of the political game; indeed some groups see it as no game but as a type of warfare.

But all this political activity cannot take place in a vacuum. Some sort of structural framework has to exist as a means of expression. So it is important to understand how these organizational structures first came into existence and why they function as they do. Although the concept of action is of prime importance, it is inextricably linked with organization. Just as action cannot occur without a supporting framework, neither can any organization function without reference to its particular environment. The role of environment in determining how organizations, or individuals for that matter, develop and act needs no comment. It is obvious that the types of cultures in any society affect the kinds of political systems there are, what demands are presented to them for solution, and how those demands are acted on.

It is the author's firm conviction that political culture is basic to an understanding of action and organization. Throughout the text emphasis has been placed on the way in which the varied cultural influences of both past and present shape the structure of institutions and the roles they play. How else, for example, can the dissimilar roles of the executive in the French, the American, and the Indian political systems be explained? How else can we understand why parliamentary democracy has functioned so admirably in Great Britain and so badly in Indonesia and Pakistan?

The reference to India, Indonesia, and Pakistan serves to introduce one more area of concern of this text: the political systems of the new nations, for contemporary political science is as much concerned with the political dynamics of the Asian and African peoples as with action and organization in the traditional Western European and American areas of interest. We now know that if political analysis and evaluation is to have any significance it must be in cross-cultural terms. For only in these terms can the differences and unique aspects in the functioning of theoretically identical political processes and structures be understood. The cultural factor determines the perceptions of what is expected from the political system.

It seems clear that the politics of our increasingly complex technological age will pose problems and challenges of an unprecedented character. We are already well into what has been called the "technetronic" age. The more complex society's problems become, the more they are the raw materials for political action. Technological development has brought about unprecedented pressures for the reallocation of power relationships. The mastery of technology for creative instead of destructive ends is the great political challenge of our time. This challenge has never been better summarized than by the great scientist and social thinker René Dubos: "Modern industrial civilization can only survive if it makes quality of living rather than quantity of production its goals."

The individuals who in the early twenty-first century must provide the solutions to these problems are the political-science students of the 1970s. If even to a small degree this text can help them to build the foundation for understanding these problems, the author will rest content. In all the long history of mankind the study and analysis of political action and organization has never been more necessary than in these closing decades of the twentieth century.

R.C.B.

Tallahassee, Florida
October, 1971

PART ONE
THE FRAMEWORK FOR STUDYING POLITICAL SCIENCE

THE PROBLEMS OF THE WORLD WE LIVE IN

1

The major concern of political science is the study and analysis of the political action and organization of the contemporary world. But this does not mean that political scientists are therefore indifferent to either the future or the past. Any contemporary political system operates in terms of the way in which it has developed over a long period of time, and the influences of both the past and the present have to be taken into account to make any conjectures about the future.

To achieve this understanding, political science draws on the other social sciences. Traditional political science was more closely linked to history than to any other academic discipline; contemporary political scientists draw more inspiration from sociology than from any other source. Indeed, political sociology has become a rapidly growing area of great importance in modern political science. Political science draws on various sources in order to find an effective way to study and analyze contemporary political problems. To understand why political science attacks these problems in the ways that it does (its *methodologies*) it is necessary to have some general idea about the political problems of the world in which we live.

In the first place, in our crisis-ridden contemporary world virtually every problem that confronts us is political. In the study and analysis of these problems, which, because of their complexity and universality, can be attacked and possibly solved only in terms of governmental, i.e., official action, it is important to determine not only what official action has already been taken, and through what sort of institutional mechanisms, but also the ways and means by which these problems were brought initially within the sphere of governmental attention and action. In this connection, we have to investigate a number of important questions: How were these problems first identified? What were the roles played by interest groups and political parties in bringing them to public attention? Why were these groups and parties interested in doing so? How were the demands of these groups processed within the governmental system? What influences and pressures were responsible for the official action, or the lack of it, that ultimately disposed of the problems? What was the impact of these actions on the social environment in which the problems originated? Were the problems solved, simply made worse, or did the efforts at solution in themselves create a whole feedback of new problems that raised new issues and called for different organizational approaches?

MEDICARE AS A POLITICAL PROBLEM

An excellent example of this process is the issue of Medicare. For many years the desire for government-sponsored medical insurance for the aged was little more than a grumble overshadowed by more pressing demands being fed into the political system. Then, as the proportion of elderly people in our society mounted, as soaring costs made individual families either unable or unwilling to assume the costs of the medical expenses of their elderly members, the pressures for governmental action steadily increased. Elderly people became increasingly aware of the possibilities for governmental assistance, and their organized efforts to receive it were intensified. As the political parties and individual politicians became aware of the political support potential represented by these people, their willingness to listen and to take official action was increased.

To make a long story short, the result of this particular phase of the problem was the passage in 1966 of a bill to provide governmental assistance in financing medical care for the aged. But it is already obvious that the feedback effects from this solution to the problem have only begun. There will be mounting demands for programs to train the experts in geriatrics who will be needed. It is also clear that extensive government subsidizing of the rest homes will be necessary. And these problems and others which the solution of the basic issue of Medicare has brought to the top of the agenda will, in their turn, have a feedback effect which will create other new problems for political action.

WHY THE POLITICAL SYSTEM IS ALWAYS IN FLUX

The constant emergence of new problems demanding action and the constant struggle over which new problems should have priority or, for that matter, receive any consideration explain why the political system is always in a state of dynamic and often turbulent change. Even under the most ideal conditions, a panel of highly qualified experts would find it difficult to reach agreement on what priorities to give the various social and economic problems for which solutions are being demanded. In the United States now, for example, race is the most urgent problem for blacks, while such issues as ending the Vietnam war or conservation or population control are of lesser importance. On the other hand, in an agricultural state in the Midwest with a small black population, parity might be an issue of much greater relevancy.

The attention which any problem receives often has very little to do with its urgency, but rather with the force and intensity with which it is presented. Success or failure in getting action on a problem plays an important role in the attitude toward how effective the political system is. For those groups which almost always get action for their concerns, it is a highly efficient and satisfactory system. At the other extreme, there is no reason for those who lose consistently to feel loyalty toward the system or to praise its workings. We can tentatively say that a political system is functioning reasonably well when it provides some access to "a piece of the action" under peaceful and well-ordered conditions for almost all the groups in its society.

The degree to which the reverse is true can serve as a rough index of the health of any political system. If substantial groups feel shut out of meaningful participation, if those groups who have the greatest influence are able to practice a sort of negative decision-making and prevent certain problems from even being considered, as happened for so long with race relations in the South, then the system in question is likely to be in trouble. Substantial numbers of individuals are likely to feel alienated from the establishment and simply opt out of even trying to work through the system. Among American young people today, an indication of this is not so much that tiny minority that has turned to bombing buildings as the very substantial numbers converted to the drug culture with its credo of "tune in, turn on, and drop out," of passive personal withdrawal from the world, the system, and any kind of involvement with either social or political problems.

WHY POLITICAL ACTION IS EVERYWHERE

Why is it that, in our contemporary world, virtually all social and economic problems are but the raw materials for political action? In general terms, the answer to this is found in the very nature of the world in which we live and in the kinds of problems it creates. The most obvious characteristic of the modern world is that the human race has achieved technological and scientific triumphs undreamed of or regarded as impossible only a few generations back. In 1901, for example, the British writer H. G. Wells, often thought of as the first twentieth-century science-fiction writer, in a book predicting the scientific developments of the next hundred years, wrote, "I have said nothing in this chapter, devoted to locomotion, of the coming invention of flying. . . . I do not think it at all probable that aeronautics will ever come into play as a serious modification of transport and communication." Yet, by the time Wells died in 1945, aeronautics had become a commonplace and indispensable element of transport and communication; and the submarine, the invention of which Wells derided in that same book, had become so potent an instrument of warfare as to bring his own country to the brink of defeat in two world wars.

Since Wells's time, television, transistor radios, stereo phonographs, automatic car transmissions, air conditioning, jet planes, synthetic fabrics, plastics, and pop-top cans have affected the daily life of even the world's least technologically advanced and prosperous societies. And since World War II, a new and important development has occurred with the emergence of *cybernetics*. Increasingly in the 1970s we are becoming uneasily aware of the tremendous social and economic impact of what has been called the *cybernetic revolution*. The term was coined as early as 1947 by the mathematician Norbert Weiner to describe automation, the new science of communications and control of machines made possible by the development of high-speed computers, which themselves owe their origin to remarkable developments in the science of electronics within the last thirty years. The impact of cybernetics is felt in every area of existence, ranging from the broadest aspects of scientific, economic, social, and political problems to the narrow question of what sort of career choice to make. So significant has it become that students of cybernetics refer to it as the second Industrial Revolution and hold conferences to discuss the problems which it is thrusting upon the world.

But as impressive and even as miraculous as this and other developments have been, the harnessing of thermonuclear energy has been the most awesome and, in many ways, most terrifying achievement in the history of man's technological and scientific development. When the first atomic bomb was dropped on the city of Hiroshima on August 6, 1945, a completely new and disturbingly different era in the history of the human race began.

Before we list the major problems that these developments have created, suppose we ask why these problems are essentially political ones. The answer is really very simple. All of the problems of the post-Hiroshima period, the atomic age, the cybernetic revolution, or whatever one chooses to call it, are totally beyond the ability of any one individual or any group of private individuals to solve. If they can be solved at all, or even partially controlled, it can be only at the highest level of organized group action and effort, by an effective organization of all the available resources of society. This can be done only by government, which is to say, by the actions of that select body of individuals who have the right to determine universal policies for the whole society and to enforce their application.

THE CHANGING ROLE OF GOVERNMENT

This world-wide expectation that government will play an active role in coping with society's problems represents a considerable reversal of the role which government was expected to play in the period from the French Revolution of 1789 to the Great Depression of the 1930s. The dominant concept during that period was of the "passive state." When Tom Paine, the fiery publicist of the American Revolution, declared that "government, even in its best state, is but a necessary evil," he spoke not only for himself but for a viewpoint which dominated political thinking for a century and more.

The French Revolution brought to political power the middle class, Karl Marx's *bourgeoisie,* which in the course of the great economic and social transformation of the Industrial Revolution had already discovered the virtues of individual initiative and the possibilities of rising high and rapidly in the world as the result of hard work, shrewd business dealings, and personal daring. In the nineteenth century as the Industrial Revolution developed (quite literally) an ever-greater head of steam, this sense of exuberant optimism about the capability of the individual became sacred gospel under the name of *laissez faire.* In no country was this truer than in the United States, where everything from geography to social conditions seemed to make such a philosophy natural and inevitable.

In nineteenth-century Europe and the United States, there was a growing feeling with each new technological advance and scientific breakthrough that for the first time in his long existence man was becoming the master of his own destiny and that it was only a question of time until all the problems which faced him would be solved. When, for example, the American industrialist Andrew Carnegie created the Carnegie Endowment for International Peace in 1911, he was careful to stipulate that after a solution had been found for the problem of war, the trustees should then carefully consider the next most important problem to be tackled.

This feeling of optimism was not limited to the expectation of endless progress in technology and science. Economically and socially, also, it was believed that the possibilities for what modern sociologists call "upward mobility" were very much present if one had the ability to make use of them. Even in terms of the life of the average man in the Western world in the late nineteenth and early twentieth centuries, it could be statistically demonstrated that never before in history had the masses in any society enjoyed such creature comforts and rising standards.

In the same way, there seemed to be every reason for optimism in political terms. Here again, the prospect of unlimited progress was a foregone conclusion. There were many who agreed with James Mill (1773–1836), father of the British political economist John Stuart Mill, that reform of political representation, popular suffrage, and mass education represented the pillars on which an enduring edifice of constitutional democracy could be built. Implicit in this and in other optimistic viewpoints was the fundamental conviction, characteristic of liberal philosophy, that men in general were basically good and rational creatures who needed only to understand what was the right and logical action to take in order to do it.

Optimism about the future in general and the ability of each individual to cope with it left little need for active governmental participation in the lives of the people. The late nineteenth-century social philosopher Herbert Spencer defined the best state of political and social affairs as being "anarchy plus a policeman," and this, as we shall note later, was simply the logical development of a trend of thought which had been first popularized some two centuries earlier by John Locke, whose philosophy so greatly shaped the development of both the British and the American political systems.

Even in the time when Spencer's philosophy was dominant, however, it was not sufficient. On the surface, to be sure, the doctrine of individual self-sufficiency seemed to be working well, and in the United States, particularly, the role of government in society was a passive one. Developing a communications system, carrying the mails, maintaining contacts with foreign nations, collecting modest taxes, and preserving internal peace were the chief functions performed by government. But, as a number of perceptive social critics of that time pointed out, the Industrial Revolution, along with its remarkable achievements, had also created new and increasingly disturbing problems. In international terms, these came to a head with World War I, which pushed the nations of the world into a period of conflict the end of which is in the remote future. For many countries in the world, particularly the United States, the period of the Great Depression in the 1930s marked the shift from the passive to the active state in domestic affairs. Social and economic problems ceased to be manageable by restricted and private groups or individuals and instead became material for political processing and governmental action.

We will return to the shift this represented in terms of political philosophy, but, for the present, let us simply sketch the broad outlines of the post-World War II period by listing the major international and internal problems that characterize it. We turn first to the international problems, which challenge, indeed strain, the resources of even the world's most advanced and strongest political systems.

MAJOR INFLUENCES IN THE MODERN WORLD

There are three great concepts which dominate the international politics of our time: technology, nationalism, and, perhaps to a lesser degree, ideology. Of course, these three elements have always been present in the affairs of nations, but never before in history has their influence been quite so universal and disruptive as now. The late twentieth century, as we have noted, has seen the force and influence of technological development expand with far-reaching consequences on every aspect of political and social activity. Quite aside from the fashion in which this has influenced the workings of the internal political process in various nations, it has completely altered the whole nature and functioning of international politics.

Along with this has come the revival of nationalism as a virulent and powerful corrosive in world affairs at a time in history when there was high hope that nationalism as a dynamic force was dwindling in power and influence. World statesmen, communist revolutionaries, and well-intentioned internationalists have drastically miscalculated the continued strength and influence of nationalism. Indeed, in the years since World War II, we have seen the emergence of a completely new and different type of nationalism from that which the Western nations experienced in the nineteenth century. This new nationalism did not come into existence as a process of organic growth, as was the case in the Western world over a period of centuries. Rather, it was manufactured almost overnight in an effort to create a common focus for those widely disparate racial, religious, and tribal groups which so often find themselves trapped together within the political boundaries of a new nation as a result of those accidental and arbitrary divisions of territory, which took place in the nineteenth century among the colonial powers. The psychological characteristics of this manufactured nationalism are such that it has been a dynamic and highly explosive force in world affairs and seems likely to continue to be such. It has been particularly ironic that the sudden eruption of nationalism as a vital force in world politics occurred just at the period in history when it seemed that many old nationalistic countries were increasingly showing an interest in regional groupings and federations. In 1971, for example, the European Economic Community, composed of six nations of Western Europe, achieved new importance with the entrance of Great Britain as a new member. There also has been a trend toward federation in such areas as Southeast Asia where the Association of Southeast Asian Nations (ASEAN) has been formed for mutual cooperation.

Much more so than in the case of either technology or nationalism, it is difficult to evaluate the role played by ideology in world affairs. Long gone is the tenor of the 1950s when American spokesmen orated about "liberating" eastern Europe or "rolling back communism." On the other hand, Soviet spokesmen make very few references today to world victory for their ideas. Significantly their speeches on such occasions as the anniversary of the Bolshevik revolution are almost always concerned with the progress of *Russia* and the ability of the Red Army to defend it against aggression. Even communist China, with all its polemics about the "struggle against American imperialism," is clearly far more concerned with China's interests than with world revolution. As far as the United States and the Soviet Union are concerned, it seems doubtful if either country could whip up sufficient enthusiasm among its people for any sort of holy crusade to make the world safe for either democracy or communism. These two superpowers, simply by virtue of their world positions, will continue to spar warily with each other without much expectation on either side of being able to achieve dominance.

Writing in the 1830s, the astute French social thinker Alexis de Tocqueville referred to the United States and Russia as "marked out by the will of Heaven to sway the destinies of half the globe." But, for a number of reasons, this comment does not describe the world situation in the late twentieth century. For one thing, the traditional power center of Europe, with West Germany as its most dynamic element, has suddenly reappeared on the world scene after a long recuperation from the ravages of World War II. It seems highly problematical whether the much-discussed United States of Europe is likely to emerge in the predictable future but, this aside, it is clear that the revived nations of western Europe are not overly concerned about ideological allegiances in their dealings with either of the superpowers.

For that matter, it would be hard to find a better illustration of the dominant importance of nationalism and the relative unimportance of ideology than in the persistent and often threatening antagonism between the world's two great communist powers. Just as medieval power struggles were fought out in terms of who was really the best Christian, the Sino-Soviet conflict has expressed itself in ideological terms. But it is clear that for geographical reasons alone any powerful Russia and strong China would be in conflict.

Nor, in most cases, have the recently independent nations shown an inclination to base their participation in world affairs on ideological preferences. Here, too, nationalist interests have been a far more important factor. Ideology will continue to be invoked as justification for policy decisions, but how much as a convenience and how much in earnest is very much open to question.

CONTEMPORARY INTERNATIONAL CHARACTERISTICS

As important as technology and nationalism certainly are, and ideology may be, in shaping current world affairs, it is necessary to be more specific about the international characteristics of our age. This is the purpose of the ten propositions to which we now turn.

1. For several important reasons, the international issues at stake are no longer changes in the pecking order, as was the case in nineteenth-century Europe, or even the survival of any particular power or group of powers as in World War II, but rather the continued existence of world civilization and even of the human race itself.

One of the most obvious reasons for this is the development of thermonuclear weapons. In itself, the final character of such weapons is an incentive to their use. As the number of countries possessing nuclear weapons increases, the mirage of total victory by a preemptive first strike may well exercise a fatal fascination for power-hungry and scientifically unsophisticated leaders. It has been estimated by strategic-research institutions that the probability of such a "megawar" in the decade of the 1970s is from 10 to 40 percent, with casualties likely to range from 2 million to 2 billion.

In itself the development of thermonuclear weapons merely offers a means of expressing hostility at an unprecedented level, but for the causes we must look deeper. Above all, the unending mounting pressures of population growth seem the most obvious cause for continuing world turmoil and threat to human survival. In the last century, world population increased more than in the previous nineteen hundred years. In the late 1960s, the United Nations estimated world population at close to 4 billion, with a virtual doubling expected by the year 2000. If this does occur, and little is being done to prevent it, starvation on a worldwide scale seems inevitable. And the possibility always exists that various countries may turn to nuclear weapons in a desperate effort to get more resources for their people or to protect themselves against real or imagined outside threats.

2. The reduction of the decisive units of world politics since 1945 to two great superpowers means that their conflict or cooperation can, literally, determine the future of the world—or lack of it. For several hundred years, up to the end of World War II, there were from five to eight so-called Great Powers which dominated world politics, all of which were approximately equal in strength. No one, or even any two, of these Great Powers possessed the capability to dominate the others. Now all this is changed. In sheer military terms there are at present no countries or combination of countries which can check either the United States or the Soviet Union. For example, what prevented the start of World War III during the Cuban missile crisis was nothing that the UN or any nations of the world were able to do, but simply that Washington and Moscow were able to reach agreement with each other on how to settle it. Possibly sometime in the future, if it can sort out its internal troubles, communist China may become a third great superpower, although many experts on world affairs doubt that China has the basic resources to achieve this. Even more speculative is the possible emergence of a United States of Europe or possibly Japan as a fourth or fifth superpower. In the foreseeable future the focus of world politics will continue to rest with the Soviet Union and the United States.

3. Unique in world history is the lack of freedom of action by the superpowers which is a result of what we might call the standoff of thermonuclear terror. Neither power dares to make a sudden move, particularly since the Cuban missile crisis, for fear that it might start the final and fatal chain reaction. Thus, even in 1956, when the Soviet Union was faced with the revolt of its satellite states in Eastern Europe, the United States did nothing to aid the rebelling states; and in Vietnam the Soviet Union has given aid and assistance to the communist side only cautiously. Another interesting aspect of this fear of starting an uncontrollable, and fatal, chain reaction is the way in which the threshold of tolerance has risen steadily since World War II. In the nineteenth century if one of the great powers suffered any kind of insult to its honor or any harm to its citizens in some remote place in the world, it was almost routine to send at least a gunboat or often a military expedition to force amends. Now, with the hands of the superpowers tied by the fear of nuclear holocaust, even the burning of embassies or the utmost in insult and injury does not lead to the breaking of diplomatic relations.

We can perhaps best exemplify this raising of the threshold of tolerance by looking at what it took to start some of the important military conflicts of the last hundred years. In 1870, for example, France and Prussia went to war ostensibly because the Prussian king had been rude to the French ambassador. And the incident which started the chain reaction that sparked Word War I was the assassination of the Archduke of Austria.

In the case of the Franco-Prussian War and of World War I, of course, the basic causes were far more fundamental than an unkind word from a king or the murder of a single important person. In both cases there were long-enduring political and economic power rivalries. Both in 1870 and 1914 many leaders and most of the citizens of the countries concerned almost welcomed any reasonable excuse to achieve a "final" settlement. War, after all, was a matter for professionals which affected the lives of the population in general very little. This attitude prevailed until World War I taught the grim lesson of what modern war means. By World War II, however, the threshold of tolerance had risen to the point where it took the "assassination" of not just one man but two countries (Czechoslovakia and Poland) to start a general war. Since World War II, although we have lived in a constant state of crisis, the threshold of tolerance has become very high indeed. By any pre-World War II standards, either the Berlin Blockade of 1948 or the Korean War of 1950 could have been enough to start a general conflagration. But neither these nor the other numerous and equally dangerous incidents, including Vietnam, have forced the world across the threshold of tolerance.

4. As we are all aware, conflict is often characteristic of relations on the international as well as the personal level. Because of the technological impracticality of carrying on conflict in the old way, the cold war developed as a safer means of carrying on the conflict between rival ideological systems. A new era in world affairs seems to have opened in the 1970s, however. In January, 1970, Secretary of State Rogers spoke of the end of the cold war; and the next month in a "state of the world" message to Congress, President Nixon observed:

> The postwar period in international relations has ended. . . . Then we were confronted by a monolithic Communist world. Today, the nature of that world has changed—the power of individual Communist nations has grown, but international Communist unity has been shattered. . . .
>
> We will deal with the Communist countries on the basis of a precise understanding of what they are about in the world, and thus of what we can reasonably expect of them and ourselves. We will not become psychologically dependent on rapid or extravagant progress. Nor will we be discouraged by frustration or seeming failure. We must match our purpose with perseverance.[1]

[1]*Congressional Quarterly Weekly Report* 28 (February 20, 1970): 516, 540.

But even if we accept at face value the statements that the cold war is over, this does not mean that the U.S.-Soviet conflict has come to an end; an authority on the Soviet Union stated in an evaluation written for a Senate committee at the start of the 1970s:

> In the very long run the interests of the two superpowers are antagonistic, not only because of their ideological differences but because of the fact that they are rivals for primacy. This does not mean that they cannot reach a mutually profitable and long-lasting accomodation but not in the sense that they would ever be able to relax their guard completely or to base their relations on the, say, Canadian-American pattern.[2]

5. This means that all of the highly sophisticated psychological, cultural, economic, and guerrilla war techniques that have been developed over the past twenty years as a means for fighting the cold war will continue to present their problems. Foreign-aid programs, propaganda, and the like, continue to be part of the world we live in and major means for waging conflict.

6. Intermeshed with this cold war conflict, partly in it and partly out of it, is the struggle of the developing nations for political and economic status. Unique to the post-World War II period is the fact that for the first time in history all of the non-Western peoples are actively involved in world politics, not merely serving as passive pawns or spoils of war. There is no better indication of this than the growth in the number of sovereign nations in the world over the past fifty years. In 1918 there were 57 sovereign nations, in 1938 approximately 70, in 1950 the total had reached 80, and by 1971 it had increased to 146.

7. Although these new nations are relatively powerless compared with the United States or the Soviet Union, the sheer numbers of people they represent and the number of votes they control in such an international organization as the United Nations (70 Afro-Asian nations, for example, among the 131 United Nation members, as of 1972) make their friendship or, at least, neutrality important. Hence the constant efforts by the superpowers to woo them with economic aid and to sway them with propaganda.

8. The emergence of these new nations in itself guarantees that we will continue to live in a world of conflict and chaos because of the compulsive drive on the part of the non-Western peoples to achieve economic, political, and, above all, psychological parity with the advanced Western nations, and because of their desperate need to find solu-

[2]Professor Adam B. Ulam of Harvard University's Russian Research Center in a report written for the Senate subcommittee on national security. U.S. Congress, Senate Committee on Government Operations, *International Negotiation: Communist Doctrine and Soviet Diplomacy,* Committee Print, 91st Cong., 2nd sess. (Washington, D.C.: G.P.O., 1970), p. 2.

tions for their problems of poverty, population pressures, industrialization, education, and satisfactory regimes.

9. While it would be naive to think in terms of any such visionary concept as a world state, one solution to global chaos and conflict may be found in the emergence of regional federations where states which have much the same type of political system can join together. In such widely diverse areas as Western Europe, Central America, and Southeast Asia there have already been groping, although so far unsuccessful, efforts in this direction.

10. Finally, as the manufacture of thermonuclear weapons becomes increasingly cheap, these devices become increasingly available to even the poorest countries. The possession of even one thermonuclear bomb makes all the relative concepts of national power that have applied for the last four hundred years quite meaningless. In this connection you may remember seeing the movie or reading the book *On the Beach,* which is the story of the last six months of the human race before radioactive fallout finally destroys the survivors. In one scene, some of the characters are trying to decide whether World War III started when the Albanians, or was it the Egyptians, dropped the one hydrogen bomb they had. In the end it really didn't matter, for this action had started the chain reaction to disaster. In the early 1970s there seems to be at least a possibility that the United States and the Soviet Union might be able to work together to prevent the further spread of nuclear weapons. But even if the two superpowers are able to achieve such accord, it is doubtful if even they could enforce a ban against the bomb, particularly since neither France nor China was among the 60 signatories to the 1968 nuclear antiproliferation treaty. For the future, as in the present, control of thermonuclear energy seems destined to remain as the most threatening and difficult of all the international challenges.

INTERNAL PROBLEMS IN THE POST-WORLD WAR II PERIOD

There are those who would argue that there are no internal problems as such since a political assassination in America is capable of setting off student riots in Paris or Tokyo and numerous cities in between. As blurred and debatable as the boundary between international and internal problems may be, it is nevertheless convenient to make the distinction.

Once made, however, a further distinction has to be recognized within the category of internal problems: the distinction between the internal problems of those two groups of nation states which we can designate respectively as the Developed and the Developing Nations. As we have noted, one of the most unprecedented and complex developments of the postwar period has been the disintegration of the great colonial empires and the subsequent tripling of the number of sovereign states. The main difference between the Developed and the Developing nations is that the former are highly industrialized, technologically developed, and socially stable societies, and the latter are largely unindustrialized, technologically underdeveloped, and socially unstable societies. While the two groups share certain problems common to all political entities, there are enough problems peculiar to each to make separate listings meaningful.

Problems of the Developed Nations

Let us turn, then, to the problems faced by the first category of nations, the old or developed ones.

Perhaps one of the most authoritative statements compiled of the problems faced by a highly developed, technological society was the 1960 Report of the President's Commission on National Goals.[3] Allowing for obvious national differences, the problems facing American society in the 1970s are not unlike those confronted by any other society at a similar level of technological and social development.

1. One of the main problems of a technological society is how to preserve and foster the "maximum development" of each individual's capabilities and "widen the range and effectiveness of opportunities for individual choice" which seem to be increasingly restricted by the political, social, and economic pressures for conformity. Unless the society is able to do this, more and more individuals will withdraw from participation in either the political system or the society in general, thus weakening them still further.

2. Directly involved with this first concern is the need for equality of opportunity, regardless of race, color, sex, or creed. This applies alike to economic, social, and political aspects of participation.

3. Important to the goal of maximum mass participation in the life of the society is an effective communications process. Ironically, the technological possibilities that exist in this connection can be a difficult barrier in themselves; and far from the medium's facilitating the delivery of the message, it may well obscure it, or make the means involved an end in itself. This communications problem does not have anything to do with whether or not a society is democratic or totalitarian. In a mass technological society of any type, the communications process is the most important single element in the functioning of the political system.

[3]The report was published under the title *Goals for Americans* for the American Assembly of Columbia University by Prentice-Hall, Englewood Cliffs, N.J., 1960.

4. In any technological society, education is a matter of major concern. Illiterate peasants cannot read the directions to operate machines; secondary-school graduates cannot do research in astrophysics. For that matter, effective communication with the illiterate is not possible. The problem of the quantity and quality of the educational system is large indeed.

5. Scientific and cultural development and expansion must be consistently encouraged. How this is to be done is an important problem in the creative orientation of an advanced technological society.

6. Along with scientific and cultural development is the need for constant economic growth. Such growth is necessary to maintain reasonably full employment and provide jobs for the new additions to the labor force which occur every year, to improve the standard of living, and to provide competitive economic strength for the whole society.

7. Closely related to this need for constant economic growth is the frustrating problem of technological change. This problem relates directly to a number of others, such as employment, education, conversion of industry, industrial relations, the allocation of social benefits, and the like.

8. Agriculture is a notable example of an area of activity drastically affected by the challenge of rapid technological change. Since subsistence farming is a negligible element in the agricultural organization of an advanced society, the problem of how to deal with agricultural unemployment, overproduction, market fluctuation, the demand–supply equilibrium, and the role of agriculture in the whole economic-social framework is a vital and challenging one.

9. How to control the monster of urbanization which our great industrial societies have produced is a problem of utmost urgency for all advanced societies. In this connection, the problems of the slums, of urban renewal, and of city and regional planning to produce a balanced socioeconomic pattern are crucial.

10. This, in turn, leads directly to the problems involved in the health and welfare issues. This is not only a matter of such obvious issues as providing the doctors, nurses, and other personnel plus the clinics and hospitals necessary to insure adequate medical care for all elements of the population, particularly the aged, the young, and the economically deprived. It is also directly related to such problems as providing pure water, pure air, and recreational facilities.

Problems of the Developing Nations

In the list that follows an effort has been made merely to suggest the nature of the problems facing the developing nations without going into detail.

1. If there is any one most important problem which the new nations all share, it is the *search for identity.* You, as

an individual just newly arrived as an adult, should understand this very well. You know where you came from, and you are aware and sometimes justifiably resentful of the forces that have influenced and shaped your development. But the question is What is the real you? Who are you now? And where do you go from here? This is precisely the bewildering, perplexing, and usually frustrating dilemma in which the various peoples of the new nations find themselves involved. In a large number of cases, purely by the accident of conquest, peoples with widely divergent heritages have suddenly found themselves included within the boundaries of a new independent nation with the necessity of discovering a consensus, a reasonable basis for living together, and a common loyalty, or seeing all their hopes and aspirations dissolve into anarchy and bloody civil war. In the late 1960s Nigeria, once regarded as the most promising among all the new African nations, was a grim example of precisely this. Nigeria and the other new nations, if they are to survive, must create a sense of common identity and of accepted political and social goals for their diverse peoples. Whether they can do this is in many cases open to doubt.

Frequently the effort to create some focus for integration has resulted in attempts to manufacture a new kind of nationalism notable for its ideological intensity and its hostility and suspicion toward all foreign influences—particularly those from the West.

2. About equal in importance to this search for identity is the need for economic development. No government can long endure if it is unable to satisfy its people's desire for a better standard of living. Industrial development is a necessity in the creation of a modern state. Here, once again, the new nations find themselves up against a series of seemingly insoluble problems. How can they accomplish such development in a few brief years, as they must, when Western Europe had a century to do it? Where is the necessary heavy capital investment going to come from? Domestic sources are insufficient, and there are not enough foreign investors willing to take the risks involved. Further, even if there were, many of the developing countries fear the growth of a kind of neo-colonialism or economic imperialism which would re-establish Western control and automatically reject such assistance as too dangerous to their continued independence.

3. The problem of economic development leads directly into the equally difficult choice of a governmental system. When they gained independence, all of the new nations modeled their governmental systems on some variation of a Western pattern, usually the European parliamentary system. By the late 1960s, with the outstanding exception of India, many of these states had come under some type of

authoritarian rule, usually by the military. Although only a few have shown an inclination toward totalitarianism, it is clear that the leaders of these countries had given up hope of being able to achieve their economic goals through voluntary cooperation in a constitutional democracy. But the problem of what type of governmental system is most suited for the country in question was simply postponed, not solved.

4. Both governmental and economic development are conditioned by the goals of the leaders of developing countries and by how they interpret the actions of the outside world. When their outlook is highly systematized and claims to have universal application with its parts consistently fitting together, we can term it an *ideology*. Once more the search for identity enters into the picture. For the problem is how to combine the many frequently contradictory elements in the native heritage of a country with one of the ideologies of the contemporary world. Most of the leaders of the new nations, partly because they equate capitalism with colonialism, are sympathetic to socialist ideas. But this does not mean the socialism of either Moscow or Peking. Instead there are efforts to formulate an Indian or Arab or Burmese or African socialism. The cloudiness of these concepts has made it difficult to use them to draw up any political or social blueprints for development.

5. The way in which they view the world has made it difficult for the leaders to communicate with their own people, if indeed the technical means even exist. Frequently, in the new nations, the leadership at the national level is composed of a small group of Western-educated individuals who feel far more at home in London or Paris than in the villages of their own country. The different way in which the peasants and the national leaders look at the world is often further complicated by the fact that, quite literally, they may not even speak each other's language. In an effort to overcome such a barrier as this, the Indian national radio finds it necessary to broadcast its program in at least fourteen languages. But here again, for countries so poor as India and with such low literacy rates, the problem arises of how many "average" men have access to a radio or can read or afford to buy a newspaper. Further the government radio talks to, not with, the masses. In most cases there is no shared basis of understanding from which to build.

6. Another aspect of the communication problem is that there are simply not enough competent and trained people. This is particularly true in the functioning, or lack of it, of the machinery of government. There is a lack of trained administrators to make things work properly, with the result that the best of decisions and policies at the top never filter down to the working level where they could affect the lives of the common people.

7. All new nations face an imposing (and discouraging) array of social problems which, if they can be solved at all, or even kept under control, require *political* action. Population control, the assimilation of ethnic and religious minorities, modernization of agriculture, creation of modern educational systems, reform of traditional social customs, the involvement of the masses of the people in political activity, and even the question of which language shall be given official status as the national language are only some of the most pressing ones.

CONCLUSION

In this chapter we have surveyed briefly the various challenges, both international and domestic, which confront the political systems of the late twentieth century. One has only to glance at the disturbing headlines in any daily paper to realize the complexity and magnitude of these problems. World statesmen and national leaders are engaged in an urgent search to find fresh approaches and answers to them.

It is not surprising that the same urgency is present in the basic effort simply to understand and analyze these problems. The result is that the post-World War II period has witnessed sweeping changes in the very nature and methodology of those academic disciplines most immediately concerned with defining, explaining, and solving political and social problems. This group of disciplines, usually called the social sciences, includes anthropology, economics, geography, political science, psychology, and sociology.

Perhaps more than any other, political science has been forced to rethink most of its basic assumptions in an effort to cope with contemporary political challenges. In part, this was because political science had lagged behind both economics and sociology in trying to develop a satisfactory methodology for analyzing and explaining contemporary problems.

The need for political science to find expanded and creative techniques with universal application has been intensified by the emergence of the new nations from their colonial status. It has become necessary to search for the common political factors underlying a wide variety of forms and diverse cultural backgrounds. The unspoken assumptions of traditional political science as to how and why political action occurs are no longer valid. The "world" of political science is no longer composed solely of Western Europe and North America. Rather, it must now function on a global basis if it is to function at all.

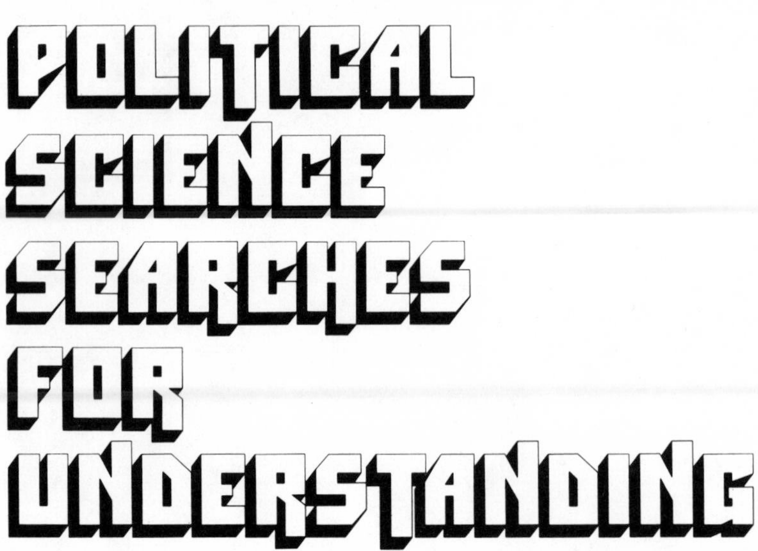
POLITICAL
SCIENCE
SEARCHES
FOR
UNDERSTANDING

At the beginning of Chapter 1, there is a reference to *methodologies,* the descriptive term for the various techniques used by political science in dealing with its subject matter. Because this is an important term in the vocabularies of all the social sciences, it is necessary to define it in some detail. Usually the term is employed in the singular. A methodology may be defined as an approach comprising a coherent set of basic assumptions and analytical techniques intended to clarify and explain the problem under consideration. If a methodology cannot explain what has been done or might be done, then it is useless. It is only an intellectual tool, a means, never an end in itself.

One of the major problems with which political science is confronted is to find an acceptable methodology without becoming so obsessed with this search that it becomes an end in itself. A frequently justified criticism on the part of the traditionalists is that the modernists or *behavioralists* are frequently so involved in bitter arguments over what implements should go into the tool kit that they never get around to doing anything with them. Or, to put it more academically, they charge that many contemporary political scientists are so obsessed with the problems of methodological theory that they tend to forget that its only function is to serve as a tool for analyzing and explaining political affairs. In their defense, the behavioralists reply that at least they are trying, which is more than the traditionalists ever did.

There is much truth in this charge, for if political science is now confronted with all too many methodological schools fiercely competing for universal acceptance, in the past the very word *methodology* was alien to its vocabulary. Before we survey the methodological alternatives of the present, it will help our understanding if we take a look at the state of political science prior to World War II.

TRADITIONAL POLITICAL SCIENCE

Let us, first of all, list some general characteristics of traditional political science without, for the moment, trying to go into any detail of either analysis or explanation.

1. It was primarily historical and chronological in its approach.
2. It lacked either a general theory of politics or a methodology of its own and showed little interest in trying to develop any.
3. Its focus was principally on political and governmental institutions in an isolated and legalistic sense.
4. It was largely indifferent to the realities of political action (behavior) within the institutional structures.
5. It placed much emphasis on pure description in terms of the endless piling of fact on fact.
6. It had a highly optimistic and single-minded outlook on political development.
7. It was focused entirely on the Western, above all the American, political process.
8. There was always an intense, almost obsessive, concern with recommendations for civic betterment.

The explanation for the close affinity of political science with history can best be explained in terms of an historical review of the emergence of political science as an academic discipline. This came very late in the development of human thought. For two thousand years, from the time of Plato and Aristotle in the fourth century B.C. through the Middle Ages and, for that matter, the Renaissance, all of knowledge was regarded as forming a unitary whole. Although in the Middle Ages law, theology, and medicine became separate academic disciplines, all the rest of human knowledge was included under the heading of philosophy. It was not until the seventeenth century that a division into natural philosophy (the present natural sciences) and moral philosophy (the first appearance of our contemporary social sciences) took place. Only in the nineteenth century did economics and sociology and anthropology appear, with political science one of the very last of the social sciences to make even a modest claim to an independent status. It was as late as 1858, for example, that the first full-time professor of political science was appointed in the United States at Columbia University. Even in 1914 there were only thirty-eight independent departments of political science in American colleges and universities.

The reason for the laggard status of political science among the social sciences is a simple one. Like a pampered younger brother in a prosperous family, it didn't have to make any particular effort to survive. The other social sciences had more or less invented themselves, so that merely to justify their existences a vigorous display of creative effort was necessary. Political science, in contrast, had come into existence within the household of history, that highly respected and ancient craft which could trace its intellectual lineage back beyond even Aristotle and Plato to Herodotus in the fifth century B.C.

In its own right, of course, one area of political science, political philosophy, had maintained an active role in intellectual development from the time of Plato, but, for the rest, after Aristotle's brilliant inauguration of the study of comparative politics on an empirical basis, political science went into hibernation for centuries. Even in the nineteenth century, when political science began to make its first tentative gestures toward independent existence, its Siamese-twin relationship with history was not only accepted but gloried in. Axiomatic in the outlook of pre-World War II political scientists was the admonition of the distinguished British political scientist, Sir John Seeley, that "History without political science has no fruits; Political science without History has no roots."[1] Or, as the most prominent of late nineteenth-century American political scientists expressed it, "the two spheres so lap over one another and interpenetrate each other that they cannot be distinctly separated. . . . Separate them, and the one becomes a cripple, if not a corpse, the other a will-o'-the-wisp."[2] This relationship even found expression on the organizational level. While political science was sometimes joined in a single university department with economics or sociology, far more characteristic was its linkage with history in a department always significantly entitled "Department of History and Political Science."

In methodological terms, the result of this symbiotic relationship with history was the consistent and virtually universal acceptance of historical concepts as a basis for the organization of material. Even today this tendency is with us. It is quite probable that you have used at least one textbook in American government in which the opening chapters discussed the sources of the American constitutional tradition, the constitutional convention, and the political ideas of the founding fathers. The convenient availability of the historical method and the fact that it seemed quite sufficient for the purpose explain why traditional political scientists never thought it necessary to develop either a general theory of politics or a unique methodology.

This historical influence goes far to explain several

[1]John Seeley, *Introduction to Political Science* (London: 1896), p. 4.

[2]John W. Burgess as quoted by Albert Somit and Joseph Tanenhaus, *The Development of American Political Science* (Boston: Allyn & Bacon, 1967), p. 26.

other characteristics of traditional political science, particularly the acceptance of the idea that if enough facts were accumulated, they would speak for themselves without any interpretation being necessary. Historical influence, with its strong reliance on documentary sources, was also an important factor in the emphasis given to institutions and the lack of interest in or, more often, unawareness of actual political behavior within the institutional structure.

The Area Focus of Traditional Political Science

This treatment of both institutions and political behavior was also linked with the almost total focus on the Western, particularly the American, political process. The reason for this was that there was no other political process to study. More precisely, the only political process in the late nineteenth and early twentieth centuries worth studying was the Western, with its American subdivision as the most successful and most important example. All others were either quaint museum survivals or in process of transition to becoming Western-type constitutional democracies. As Lord Bryce, the most prominent political scientist of his time, expressed it in the preface of a book published shortly after World War I and appropriately entitled *Modern Democracies:*

> Within the last hundred years that now lie behind us what changes have passed upon the world! Nearly all of the monarchies of the Old World have turned into democracies. The States of the American Union have grown from thirteen to forty-eight. While twenty new republics have sprung up in the Western hemisphere, five new democracies have been developed out of colonies within the British dominions. There are now more than one hundred representative assemblies at work all over the earth legislating for self-governing communities; . . . the materials for a study of free governments have been and are accumulating so fast that the most diligent student cannot keep pace with the course of political evolution in more than a few out of these many countries.[3]

It was not surprising, given this triumphant sweep of democracy described so eloquently above, that its victory on a global scale was apparently but a question of time and that the whole pattern of political development seemed set on one inevitable course. It was obviously a waste of time to seek for other topics of study. And since the known and the familiar could be so well explained, seemingly at least, by tried and familar methods of analysis, there was little incentive for methodological experimentation.

[3]Lord Bryce, *Modern Democracies* (New York: Macmillan, 1921), 1:3–5.

The Civic Involvement Concern

The origin of the traditional concern with recommendations for civic betterment was the dominant role which political theory exercised for so long within the area of political science. At the very core of political theorizing from Plato to the present has been the creation of utopias, those model societies toward the realization of which all political activity should be directed. This served to give all political thinking a strongly normative focus; i.e., all political thought and action were thought to be directed to the achievement of the model society, the ultimate utopia.

The effect of this was that the political scientist found it very difficult to observe the same degree of detachment toward his subject matter as could the chemist or the biologist. The political scientist naturally approached his subject matter with a strong subjective feeling about what was good or bad, reactionary or progressive, and he had a compulsion to try to make sure that the "right side" won. Almost routinely, political science writings before World War II included recommendations for civic betterment, and from the days of the Progressive Movement in the early twentieth century to the New Deal, political scientists were constantly involved in the politics of reform.

Although there were various efforts to create a "scientific" politics in the period between the two world wars, there was not enough urgency behind any of these reform movements to push them through to victory. In general, political scientists saw little need for any sweeping changes in operational philosophy or techniques until the accumulated pressures of the unprecedented problem of the postwar period and significant developments in the other social sciences forced them to do so. The first of these influences was discussed in Chapter 1. We can now note how developments in allied disciplines stimulated the still-continuing transformation in contemporary political science.

THE EMERGENCE OF BEHAVIORAL POLITICS

What is observed in political science at the present time is the last phase of a transformation which all the social sciences have been experiencing for some decades. In the period prior to World War II, social scientists increasingly attempted to apply the scientific method to the problems of their respective disciplines. Economists were perhaps most successful in this; the efforts of psychologists and sociologists largely bogged down in the accumulation of large masses of empirical data which they were not quite sure what to do with. In contrast, anthropologists concentrated more on developing new methodological approaches, several of which have exerted much influence on political science. Regardless of the particular emphasis involved, all these other social sciences had extensively explored the possibilities for new development before political science had even begun to move in these directions. The result was that when the behavioral movement began to sweep through the ranks of political science, it actually represented two reform movements occurring simultaneously.

In the late 1940s the other social sciences became seriously concerned with the question of what to do with scientific method once it had been used as a research tool. There were three aspects to this new development: (1) keen interest in the development of empirical theory, reducible to testable propositions, at all levels of scholarly investigation; (2) an attempt to discover dependable units of analysis which would be for the social sciences what particles of matter are for research in the natural sciences; and (3) a push toward the creation of a unified science concerned with all aspects of man's role in society.

In the course of pursuing this new concern, a group of scientists at the University of Chicago coined the term *behavioral sciences* in 1949. Allegedly they were motivated by a desire to find a term which could be used by both social and biological scientists and also one that would avoid any connection with the word *socialist*.

For political science the impact of the behavioral approach coincided with the first serious full-scale efforts to apply scientific method to the problems of the discipline. In microcosm, the upheaval produced was similar to the traumatic experience suffered by a newly developing nation attempting simultaneously to adjust to accumulated impacts of the French and the Industrial revolutions. In a sense, political science has been engaged in forging its working tools at the same time as it has been using them in clearing out new areas for theoretical development. Not surprisingly, this led to much confusion. So widespread was this confusion in the first phase of the assimilation of behavioralism that one observer commented, "One got the impression that the term served as a sort of umbrella, capacious enough to provide temporary shelter for a heterogenous group united only by dissatisfaction with traditional political science. . . ."[4]

The aims of the behavioral movement are as follows:

1. To make political science, as far as possible, capable of prediction and explanation in the realm of political happenings.
2. To employ research based on a theoretical framework which would give shape and coherence.

[4]Evron M. Kirkpatrick, "Impact of the Behavioral Approach," in *Essays on the Behavioral Study of Politics,* ed. Austin Ranney (Urbana: University of Illinois Press, 1962), p. 11.

3. To try to find some unit, comparable to the cell in biology, which was concretely identifiable and which would permit broad comparison.
4. To test all theoretical propositions by the collection and analysis of factual material.
5. To be concerned with only those theoretical propositions which lend themselves to this treatment.
6. To make use of all available mechanical facilities and advanced techniques, such as computers, statistical analysis, polling, and the like, that facilitate this process.
7. To emphasize that political activity is everywhere, not merely in terms of government, and that "the root is man."[5] By this is meant that all institutional activity is simply a combination of the political roles which various individuals are playing.

There is one common misapprehension about the behavioral movement which deserves to be noted. This is the impression that it proposes to ignore all the institutional and structural aspects of government which were the major concern of traditional political science. This is simply not the case. As one of the most prominent figures of the behavioral movement has expressed it, "The continuing institutional focus of political science remains at all levels the defining, and in a sense limiting, factor. This point, it seems to me, is the fundamental one."[6] It is not that behavioralists wish to ignore institutions, but rather that they view them as only a part and, at times, not even the most important part, of the whole subject matter of political study.

There is one other aspect to the behavioral view of institutions: Institutions apart from the people involved in their functioning are meaningless. Here again *action* is the key term. An institution is simply a system of action, and the action is carried on by a variety of people all performing the political roles which the nature of that institution requires. Hence, whether it be the Supreme Court or a legislative body or the presidency, an institution can best be understood in terms of how the people involved behave, and why.

Now what has been the effect of the behavioral persuasion on contemporary political science? It has already exerted important influence. Whether the behavioral approach will continue to expand its influence is subject to debate, but here are some of the results so far.

1. There has been a strenuous effort to develop a theoretical framework for conducting research.

[5]Heinz Eulau, *The Behavioral Persuasion in Politics* (New York Random House, 1964), p. 3.

[6]David Truman as quoted by Kirkpatrick, "Impact of the Behavioral Approach," p. 27.

2. This research has focused on the constant need to test theoretical hypotheses against reality.
3. In so doing, the use of technical facilities, notably computers, has become standard practice.
4. There is an increasingly interdisciplinary focus which draws on economics, psychology, biology, anthropology, and, above all, sociology.
5. A significant indication of this interdisciplinary focus is the creation of an entirely new political vocabulary which includes a large number of "loan words" taken from the other behavioral sciences.

By way of illustration, traditional political science talked of

> checks and balances, *jus soli,* divesting legislation, brokerage function, quota system, bloc voting, resulting powers, proportional representation, pressure group, sovereignty, dual federalism, lobbying, recall and referendum, Posdcorb, quasi-judicial agencies, concurrent majority, legislative court, Taylorism, state of nature, item vote, unit rule, and natural law.[7]

Contemporary political scientists, freely borrowing from the other behavioral sciences, deal in terms of

> boundary maintenance, bargaining, cognitive dissonance, community power structure, conflict resolution, conceptual framework, cross-pressures, decision-making, dysfunctional, factor analysis, feedback, Fortran, game theory, Guttman scaling, homeostasis, input-output, interaction, model multiple regression, multivariate analysis, nonparametric payoff, transation flow model, role simulation, political systems analysis, *t* test, unit record equipment, variance, and, of course, political socialization.[8]

The traditional terms, however, are still very much in use and seem likely to continue to be. One of the major problems of the new vocabulary has been that, as yet, there is no general agreement on what the terms mean. Various groups, like Humpty Dumpty in Lewis Carroll's *Through the Looking Glass,* have often made these terms mean what they want them to mean. The problems of definition are matched by the difficulties in trying to settle on one particular analytical approach.

APPROACHES TO CONTEMPORARY POLITICAL SCIENCE

Because there is no basic agreement, nor is there likely to be for some time to come, on any one approach to the study and analysis of political problems, it is important to have a general awareness of the strengths and weaknesses of the

[7] Somit and Tanenhaus, *Development of American Political Science,* pp. 190–191.

[8] *Ibid.,* p. 191.

most important approaches in current use. It will help in evaluating them if, first, we survey the concerns of political science.[9] One way to do this is to list the customary division of courses to be found in any sizeable department of political science or government. Your university or college catalogue tells you that for a major you must take so many hours distributed in the major areas of American government, comparative government, international politics, political theory, and public administration. But this listing tells you nothing of what political scientists are trying to investigate, of the sort of problems common to this wide array of subject matter.

Range of Subject Matter

Common to the analytical concerns of political scientists, whether in American government or in international politics, are the following topics: (1) description, (2) pattern maintenance, (3) patterns of control, (4) goals and goal attainment, and (5) patterns of change.

The first of these terms, *description,* needs no explanation. While the details involved can be somewhat more elaborate than may appear at the surface, everyone is well aware of what the word means. By *pattern maintenance* is meant the procedures and actions necessary to keep a political system or institution operating in its accustomed fashion. By *patterns of control* is meant who runs things and how. Or, in more academic terms, patterns of control are concerned with the possession and exercise of political power. The term *goals and goal attainment* means the study of where a political system is going, how it proposes to get there, and what are the likely results. Finally, *patterns of change* involves the examination of the wide range of problems created by the diverse possibilities for peaceful or violent change.

As we have commented, *description* is not quite so simple and self-explanatory a term as it sounds. Description is basic to everything else. Unless you are aware of the dimensions and nature of a problem, it is impossible to go further. To take a homely illustration, with all of the miraculous resources of modern medicine at his command, your physician can do nothing until he has gone through that familiar ritual of having you tell him where it hurts and how it feels. Description serves to indicate the broad outlines of the problem and to offer a basis for classifica-

[9]This entire section relies heavily on Oran R. Young, *Systems of Political Science,* Foundations of Modern Political Science Series (Englewood Cliffs, N.J.: Prentice-Hall, 1968). This brief, brilliant monograph affords an excellent introduction to an understanding of the methodologies of contemporary political science. In most respects I have followed both its terminology and its evaluations.

tion and for the application of the *theory of categorization.* This theory is the basis for much of the comparative analysis in political science. Its basic proposition is very simply that systems or structures which resemble each other in some respects are likely to do so in other respects. In short, the more comparative description that you engage in, the more similarities you are likely to find. Another important purpose of description is to distinguish between a political entity and its environment and the way in which the interaction patterns operate. Then, focusing on the political structure or system itself, description can point up the important aspects of internal organization, the way the various parts are put together, the differences between them, and whether they are loosely or tightly structured.

Under pattern maintenance, consideration is given to such questions as stability and equilibrium, patterns and types of political conflict, conflict resolution, and questions involving such factors as legitimacy, authority, and the procedures by which an official stamp of approval is given to these last two factors. Patterns of control offer some rather complex problems for analysis. This is particularly true in connection with power and influence, which make up the most important element under this heading. In connection with these factors, it is necessary to ask: How widely does any particular manifestation of power and influence extend? What degree of control is exerted? How are decisions enforced? Has the power and influence involved already reached its maximum influence? Or does it have potential for further development? Also involved in the analysis of patterns of control are such topics as the way in which political resources for control are utilized, the relationships between expertise and the formulation of control patterns, and, finally, the role of political elites and the ways they interact.

Goals and goal attainments are the motivations for both the maintenance and the control of political patterns. The most obvious basic goal, both in prospect and realization, for any political system is, of course, survival. But also involved in this category are such factors as the priorities among goals, the price that has to be paid to achieve them, and, to a degree, the utilization of political functions for successful outcomes. Perhaps most importantly, the role of policies and policy-making in connection with the achievement of goals comes under this heading. For those who regard the political system as a process for the attempted solution of the problems which face a society, the chief concern of political science should be the study of goals and goal attainments. Under the headings policies and policy-making come the study and analysis of such topics as alternative policies, consequences of adopting or rejecting a particular set of policies, the priority ranking of various possible policies, the analysis of the differences between the objective analysis of the possible outcome of any policy, and the policy-maker's often too hopeful expectation of the probable results.

The fifth and last of the analytical concerns of political science, that of patterns of change, has been an extremely important topic in the political world of the postwar period and yet one which, particularly in connection with destructive change, still largely lacks a satisfactory methodological framework for study and analysis. Change is as much an inevitability in political matters as in individual human lives. As for individuals, sometimes it is gradual, sometimes it is abrupt, if not revolutionary. And sometimes its results are constructive and sometimes they are destructive. Under the constructive aspects of patterns of change we can note such variations as evolution, transition, expansion, growth, and, in connection with the new nations, that tremendously important topic *modernization.* In fact so much attention has been devoted in recent years to the problems of modernization of the developing nations that this has virtually become an independent area of its own rather than a subdivision of a subdivision. Under the destructive aspects of change are such problem areas as revolutions, crises, stresses and strains, disruptions, decay and decline, and, as a terminal result, dissolution of a political system. This, then, is the range of subject matter with which approaches to analysis must deal.

Functions of Analysis

Any approach to analysis serves three functions. These are *perception, organization,* and *communication.* By perception is meant how the observer of any political problem understands it. If you have ever had a class in journalism, you have probably been exposed to that often-used teaching device of staging some dramatic episode and then having the members of the class write about what they have seen. Invariably the descriptions vary widely because the perceptions of the various members of the class have been conditioned by individual social and cultural frames of reference. In the same fashion, although quite deliberately rather than accidentally, when an observer turns to the first step of the description of a political development, the particular approach to analysis which he has adopted as his guide serves to screen out certain aspects of his observation as irrelevant, note others as of secondary importance, and focus close attention on yet others as of prime importance. What factors are regarded as irrelevant or of secondary or of primary importance depends on the particular approach to analysis being used. This is how an approach helps make a selective choice of the otherwise overwhelming mass of factors involved in the initial function of perception.

Equally important is the way in which an analytical approach can aid in the organization of what has been perceived. In this connection, it does the following: (1) sorts out the huge mass of perceived material into its proper subdivisions, (2) distinguishes the important variables of the analytical scheme so that the material can be organized around them, (3) ranks the material in order of importance, and (4) furnishes the hypotheses (unproved theories) as to how the material is related.

In an approach to analysis, communication serves to provide the adherents of any particular approach with a common language and frame of reference for discussion and analysis. The important element here is that this common language provides a set of concepts and a vocabulary which make possible the description and analysis of highly complex political phenomena. This is beyond the capability of everyday vocabulary and demands its own specialized verbal "shorthand" for meaningful explanation and hypothesizing.

Now that we have taken a look at the requirements which subject matter places upon any approach to analysis and have noted the functions that an approach must serve, we are in a better position to understand and evaluate the strengths and weaknesses of the most important contemporary approaches. One reason that there is no single dominant contemporary approach to analysis is that no single one is equally strong in all of the necessary areas of analysis and explanation. This raises certain problems in using the various approaches, as we shall see later. But first, let us look at the significant approaches to analysis in contemporary political science. The most important categories of approach are *group theory, decision-making, and systems analysis.* I have used the term *categories* because in all cases, and particularly in connection with decision-making and systems analysis, there is more than one variation on the basic theme.

GROUP THEORY

Group theory represented the first swell of the behavioral tidal wave that has since flooded political science. This concept was put forward in 1908 by Arthur F. Bentley, a sociologist turned journalist, who "was certainly one of behaviorism's earliest and most explicit, if not explosive, pioneers."[10] Nor did he escape the customary fate of pioneers. His highly readable *Process of Government,* now recognized as a classic work in the emergence of modern

[10]Arthur F. Bentley, *The Process of Government*, ed. Peter H. Odegard (Cambridge, Mass.: Harvard University Press, 1967), p. xiv.

political science, was largely forgotten for almost forty years. It was not until the late 1940s that Bentley's concepts provided the inspiration for a later generation of group theories of which David Truman's is probably the most outstanding.[11]

Group theory originated as a reaction against the emphasis which traditional political science laid on a formal and static institutional approach. Bentley put forward the concept of society as composed of a "complex of groups" in constant dynamic interaction with each other. He defines a group as

> a certain portion of the men of a society, taken, however, not as a physical mass cut off from other masses of men, but as a mass activity, which does not preclude the men who participate in it from participating likewise in many other group activities. . . . It is always so many men, acting or tending toward action—that is, in various stages of action. Group and group activity are equivalent terms with just a little difference of emphasis. . . .

Activity, in Bentley's definition, includes thoughts, feelings, intentions, and ideas. Groups are brought into existence by the desire to advance a shared "interest." As Bentley expresses it, "There is no group without its interest. An interest . . . is the equivalent of a group."

The political process is but the story of the endless kaleidoscopic interaction among groups and the subgroups that make them up as they struggle to advance their various interests. But this is not that state of "warre, as is of every man, against every man" of which the seventeenth-century English political philosopher Thomas Hobbes spoke, for there are a number of mitigating circumstances.

First of all, government plays a mediating role. Then there is the check provided by the competing interests of other groups. Further, since there is overlapping membership in various groups under normal circumstances, individuals are unlikely to give such total loyalty to any one group that it will be able to dominate completely all the others. There are two more factors which tend to lessen the prospects of ruthless group conflict. For one thing, in a fashion similar to the balance-of-power concept in international politics, if one group should be able to enlist its members in an all-out power drive, it is likely to find that it has automatically created active opposition from a number of previously inactive or latent groups. In addition, both the balance and the intensity of conflict will be powerfully influenced in the direction of moderation by what Bentley termed the "habit background" in which the group activity operates. This background is created by the fact

[11]See David Truman, *The Governmental Process* (New York: Knopf, 1964).

that group activity rests "in a great sea of social life, of which it is but a slight modulation." Implicit is the belief that the "great sea of social life" is a placid and soothing influence.

However much the various interpretations in group theory differ, government is but a microcosm of the group and subgroup struggles in society at large. Its function is to serve as a moderator and to provide a carefully supervised playing field upon which group competition can take place. All things political involve the exercise of power to adjust group conflict.

The emphasis which group theory places on the action concept and on "government [as] a certain network of activities" would entitle Bentley to respect as a pioneer of modern political science. But there are two more points which add to his status in this connection. First of all, very much in tune with the preoccupations of contemporary political science are Bentley's intense interest in methodological problems and his effort to create a blueprint for a comprehensive research design. As he phrased it in a one-sentence preface, "This Book is an Attempt to Fashion a Tool." Another very modern aspect is his insistence on the need for empirical research:

> . . . The raw material of government cannot be found in the lawbooks. . . .
>
> It cannot be found in the "law" behind the lawbooks, except as this is taken to mean the actual functioning of the people—
>
> It cannot be found in the proceedings of constitutional conventions, nor in the arguments and discussions surrounding them. . . .
>
> It cannot be found in essays, addresses, appeals, and diatribes on tyranny and democracy. All that the world has ever produced in this way cannot do more than point out to us where the raw material may be found.
>
> It cannot be found in the "character of the people," in their specific "feelings" or "thoughts," in their "hearts" or "minds." All these are hypotheses or dreams.
>
> The raw material can be found only in the actually performed legislating-administering-adjudicating activities of the nation and in the streams and currents of activity that gather among the people and rush into these spheres.[12]

The fact that Bentley's statement today sounds obvious is an indication of how far political science has developed since he first made it in 1908 when it was received with cold snubs and scathing ridicule.

Measured against the five analytical concerns of political scientists discussed at the beginning of this section, group theory comes out well on several counts. To that initial and very basic process of description it is able to offer a number of new concepts and categories which afford fresh

[12]Bentley, *Process of Government*, pp. 179–180.

insights and new bases for comparative analysis. Bentley, for example, included a chapter on "The Classification of Governments" in which he derided the meaninglessness of the old classifications and suggested the possibilities inherent in group theory.

In relation to both pattern maintenance and patterns of control, group theory is more suggestive than definitive. In neither case does it spell any very concrete concepts. Goals and goal attainment are highly important in group theory. Indeed, goal attainment for the realization of interests is the most dynamic factor in the whole universe of group theory. But the concern is with getting there. Group theory is very little concerned with why the particular goal is important or what its particular elements are.

With the emphasis that group theory lays on action and process, patterns of change are obviously objects of prime concern. But there is an important limitation involved here. Its concern is only with what we have termed the problems of constructive change, and even within this category it operates on the assumption of the essential stability of the broad outlines of the system. Change is in terms of the shifting power balance among groups as they strive to advance their interests and achieve their goals.

We can best state the criticisms of group theory by first listing and then briefly discussing them. Some major criticisms made of group theory are:

1. It treats groups as though they were entities in their own right.
2. It fails to explain why groups have the energy to act.
3. It lays too much emphasis on activity without explaining it.
4. It offers no real explanation of the how and why of political actions.
5. It is too vague in definitions of terms.
6. It applies only to a developed political system.

Critics of group theory charge that in reifying groups (that is, treating them as if they were things) it loses sight of the fact that they are actually composed of individual human beings. Not only does this cut off the possibilities for valuable insight but leads directly into the second point. If the group is going to carry on the struggle and do it all, why should any one individual member exert himself? But, if the individual members do not act, then the group can accomplish nothing. By reifying the group, say the critics, the theory loses the ability to explain how the action on which it lays such emphasis can possibly occur and to explain the vital factors of emotional and intangible reactions.

Critics of group theory go on to charge that group theory focuses so exclusively on groups and their interactions that it says nothing about society in general and offers no explanations for the how and why of the way things are except for a vague mention of the influence exerted by the "habit background." Connected with both this point and the fifth criticism is the charge that group theory doesn't really define satisfactorily such an important term as *government* or, for that matter, any of the basic concepts of political science.

Criticism that group theory has dubious value in terms of the developing nations might be considered the most damaging of all. For an economically developed, politically and socially sophisticated plural society like that of the United States or of the Western European countries, group theory may have something to offer, the critics say; but for totalitarian societies, societies in conflict, societies where American-type groups are nonexistent or unimportant, it can contribute little, if anything, to analysis and understanding. In spite of all these criticisms, group theory has much appeal and many creative possibilities.

Decision-Making

From the emphasis placed by Bentley and his disciples on the group, we turn to the opposite pole represented by the decision-makers of all varieties with their emphasis on the individual. Decision-making is the best known, though in certain ways the least successful, of all the new approaches of political science. The term itself, as have few others, has come into wide popular usage. A variety of nonacademic individuals from politicians to journalists refer routinely to decision-makers and the decision-making process. But within political science itself, as one of its proponents notes, "there has been no rush of graduate students to expand its propositions in Ph.D. dissertations and no accumulation of case studies utilizing its categories . . . the approach as such has tended to disappear from sight."[13]

Because of this peculiar situation, before we survey its principal characteristics we will look at some criticisms leveled at the decision-making concept. To put one of the major criticisms as colloquially as possible, decision-making can lay no real claim to being a theory. It lacks any "if–then" hypotheses, by which is meant any sort of propositions which assume that *if* certain conditions are present, *then* it is logical to assume that certain results will occur. The decision-making approach identified the existence of various factors and relationships, often at complicated and tedious length, without ever trying to explain how and why they hung together. All too often, decision-making has been

[13]James N. Rosenau, "Premises and Promises of Decision-Making Analysis," in *Contemporary Political Analysis*, ed. James C. Charlesworth (New York: Free Press, 1967), p. 207.

studied as an individual case in isolation from the political environment surrounding it. This has resulted in an inability to explain the *why* of the decision-making process although the *how* has often been outlined in redundant detail.

Communications Theory. One of the most important variations of the decision-making approach has been in terms of analysis based on communications theory and cybernetics with Karl Deutsch as its leading spokesman. The main emphasis of this approach, as suggested earlier, is on the mechanics of how decisions are made rather than being concerned with either cause or effect.

Because of this concern with the flow process and its close relationship to recent scientific development, communications theory stresses the creation of models to show how the decision-making process occurs. A simplified version of one of Deutsch's presentations is given in Figure 1.[14] If you see a resemblance to the operation of a complicated electric power system, you are quite correct. Indeed, one of the major charges by critics is that communications theory much too literally applies an engineering analysis to human behavior and treats individuals as though they were but programmed machines.

Even the vocabulary of the communications approach bears this out. There is much usage of such terms as *receptors, decision centers, implementation orders, effectors, load capacity, lag, gain, lead, and combinatorial capacity,* which until recently at least, have been far more familiar to the engineer than to the political scientist. It has been observed that "the approach as set forth by Deutsch generates a powerful thrust toward the effort to operationalize hypotheses and to engage in quantitative analysis."[15]

Once again let us measure the strengths and weaknesses of this approach against our list of analytical concerns. Within its limits, it is strong in the area of description. Indeed, because of its quantitative bent, communications theory has a tendency to accumulate masses of data without relation to what is actually pertinent. But even here, as Oran R. Young put it, its technical origins often lead to the treatment of political matters "in terms far from common sense or lexically accepted meaning."

In the area of pattern maintenance, utilizing the idea of a continuing flow of activity, communications theory has substituted the idea of *equilibrium* for stability. Control patterns are a particularly strong point of communications analysis. Like group theory it has a mixed approach to the problems of change. Both theories are well equipped to analyze constructive change. Communications theory deals

[14]Adapted from Karl Deutsch, *The Nerves of Government* (New York: Free Press, 1963). Copyright © 1963 by The Free Press of Glencoe, a Division of The Macmillan Company. Reprinted with permission.

[15]Young, *Systems of Political Science,* p. 56.

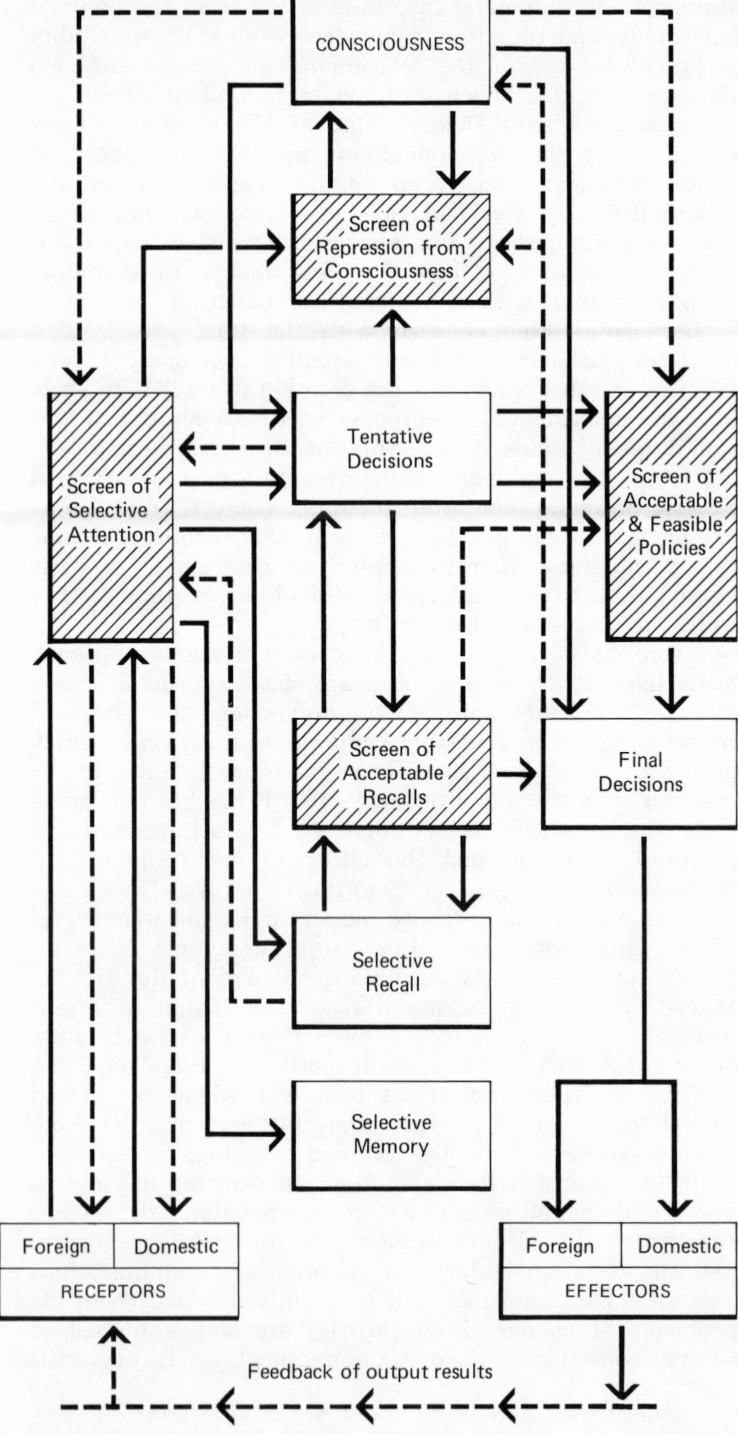

Figure 1
The Decision-Making Process

with it in terms of *breakdown* and *overload* of the regularly functioning system. Goals and goal attainment are simply objectives which explain why the flow process is taking place. Their justification or purpose is of little concern.

The major criticisms made of Deutsch's concept of communications are these:

1. It is essentially an engineering approach modeled on the performance of machines rather than of human beings.
2. It is too much focused on how action is taking place rather than on why and what the results will be.
3. It is so much concerned with quantitative analysis of data that it ignores quality and overlooks the significance of the information.
4. Not only is communications theory overly concerned with model building to the detriment of actual research but, because of their mechanistic origins, its models are too neat and too systematic to portray any aspect of the human condition.
5. This leads directly into a criticism of communications theory in general: It makes no allowances for the emotional vagaries of human nature and the frequent fuzziness of approach, but paints an unrealistic picture of consistently rational actions and machine-like precision.

Distributive Analysis. The most popular version of decision-making is that of Harold Lasswell, who posed the famous question "Who gets what, when, how?" Lasswell is the creator of "distributive analysis" in political science. Central to Lasswell's analysis are the concepts of influence and power and how they are exercised by the influential and powerful throughout society. These two factors, which are very closely related in Lasswell's thinking, are conditioned by a number of key variables and value categories involving *scope, weight, domain, coercion, persuasion,* and an elaborate classification of *deference* and *welfare values* evaluated in terms of *indulgences* and *deprivations.*

Along with his other elaborate classifications, Lasswell outlines a seven-step process for decision-making. For him the basic unit is the individual, and groups are simply aggregations of individuals whose interpersonal contacts are motivated by such factors as *symbols, political myths, ideologies, utopias, mores, patterns of perspectives, and attitudes.* Highly important in the exercise of power and influence are what Lasswell terms practices which are "all ways by which elites are recruited and trained, all the forms observed in policy-making and administration."[16] Finally,

[16]Harold Lasswell, *Politics: Who Gets What, When, How* (New York: McGraw-Hill, 1936).

Lasswell distinguishes between the *manipulative* and the *contemplative* approach to analysis. Essentially the distinction is between research done to discover how to produce changes in the political process and that carried out simply for the purposes of scholarly comprehension. His own personal emphasis has always been very much in terms of the first category.

In relation to the five analytical concerns of the political scientist, the distributive approach has these characteristics: (1) description—it has much to offer for those who know how to manipulate its complex categories; (2) pattern maintenance—it is weak in this area; (3) patterns of control—obviously the strongest point of all, since this is what the distribution of power approach is all about; (4) goals and goal achievement—again a point of strength in relation to the elaborate analysis of values as motivating factors in political action; and (5) change—focuses primarily on the problems and possibilities of constructive change but little on those of destructive change. As with group theory and Deutsch's decision-making, prime focus is on constructive and evolutionary aspects rather than on destructive and revolutionary possibilities.

It is possible to summarize the major objections to the distributive analysis approach briefly since some of them are almost self-evident.

1. The theory is too detailed and wide-ranging to be really useful.
2. This makes it difficult, if not impossible, to focus research.
3. Therefore, the would-be researcher must either be prepared to take the time and have the endurance to sift through a vast mass of material or resign himself to a purely superficial approach.
4. Moreover, as in the case of group theory, there is much danger of reification in connection with the various concepts and units of analysis; this leads to losing sight of the original objectives of the investigation.
5. Finally, the theory is so concerned with the study of the powerful and the influential that it cannot adjust to the analysis of mass political activity.

SYSTEMS THEORY

While Lasswell's distributive analysis draws on psychological sources and group theory on sociological sources, systems theory had its origins in the natural sciences. Its originators were concerned with the increasingly narrow specialization that was overtaking the various divisions of the natural sciences. They sought to find a unifying element which would offer a broader perspective for creative analysis. In the period after World War II, this crystallized around the concept of *systems,* which the German biologist Von Bertalanffy defined as "a set of elements standing in interaction."[17] To date there has been no fully developed effort to apply general systems theory to political analysis. For the future it probably offers much possibility for integrating political science with the other behavioral sciences and for creating an analytical scheme applicable alike to the social and the natural sciences.

It has become fashionable to talk about the systems approach, and the popularity of the term derives largely from offshoots of the general systems theory of which the two most widely known are *structural-functionalism* and *input-output analysis.*

Structure-Functional Analysis. Originating in the work of anthropologists early in the century, structural-functional analysis has come to political science by way of sociology.[18] For reasons that will shortly become clear, structural-functionalism has been used most in the area of comparative politics. As with all versions of systems theory, it begins with the concept of a definable unit operating within a recognizable setting. The basic theoretical proposition is that in all social systems certain basic functions have to be performed. The prime question for inquiry is what structures in the system under analysis perform these functions and how.

A *function* is defined as a regularly recurring pattern of action (behavior) carried on for the preservation and advancement of the system. The opposite of a function is a *dysfunction,* which is an action detrimental to the existence and growth of the system. A certain degree of dysfunction is inevitable in the operation of any pattern of action. To take a familiar illustration, think for a moment about an automobile. It has a very obvious system with an easily recognizable structure, regularly repeating certain functions necessary for continued and smooth operation. But we accept as inevitable that along with the production of these desirable functions there will also be various dysfunctions produced, such as carbon deposits on the valves, sludge in the lubrication system, and so on. No functioning process, whether mechanical, social, or political, is altogether without its dysfunctional aspects.

The appeals of structural-functional analysis for com-

[17]Von Bertalanffy, "General Systems Theory," *General Systems* 1 (1956): 3.

[18]Not surprisingly the major statements of the theory are by sociologists. See Marion Levy, Jr., *The Structure of Society* (Princeton, N.J.: Princeton University Press, 1952); and Robert K. Merton, *Social Theory and Social Structure* (New York: Free Press, 1957).

parative politics are particularly clear in connection with its approach to the concept of structure. Traditional political scientists were frequently confused and frustrated when they attempted to operate in the comparative area. They began analysis from the neat and clearly recognizable outlines of the structural organization of the American or British governmental systems. Where these structures were not present, it was assumed that the functions they performed in the American and British systems were likewise lacking. Hence the popular nineteenth-century delusion about the existence of "stateless" societies which lacked "government."[19] The result of this approach was that traditional political scientists were unable to, and felt no need to, function outside the familiar area of Western governmental systems. It was only when the demanding imperatives of the postwar period made a broadening of horizons not only desirable but necessary that comparative government increasingly reoriented itself as comparative politics. At that point political scientists turned to the methodological developments of the companion behavioral sciences, such as the structural-functional approach, for assistance in studying and analyzing non-Western political systems.

One of the most helpful assumptions of structural-functional theory in this connection is what Young calls "the concept of structural substitutibility." It accepts the basic proposition that the performance of certain essential functions is necessary for the continuance of any system.[20] But the means, the structures through which these functions are performed, may vary considerably from one system to another, depending on the way in which they are shaped by the particular culture of the system in question.

In connection with the five categories of political analysis, we can evaluate structural-functional analysis as follows. In the area of description, particularly for comparative purposes, it is quite strong. The focus of the approach on the necessary functions for continuance of a system and the ways in which they are expressed is directly related to the analysis of pattern maintenance. Except indirectly, however, structural-functional analysis has little to contribute to an understanding of either patterns of control or goals and goal attainment. By the very nature of its basic emphasis on how functions occur and in what way, it is clear that it has even less to contribute to an understanding

[19]Karl Marx was so misled by this error that he based his whole theory of history on the proposition that society began in a stateless condition and that the state originated as an instrument of oppression which would "wither away" with the abolition of private property.

[20]What constitutes essential functions for survival is clearly a topic for much discussion and debate. Levy, in chapter 4 of *The Structure of Society,* on a quite abstract basis, lists ten functions necessary for the survival of any and all social systems.

of any aspect of patterns of change than either group theory or any variety of decision-making theory.

Structural-functionalism has frequently come under strong criticism, particularly from sociologists who have had considerable experience with it by now. The major criticisms leveled against it are as follows.

1. It has, what might be termed, a procrustean approach. (The original Procrustes was a Greek robber of ancient legend who killed his victims by stretching them out or crushing them down to fit into a bed frame which was always the wrong size for the particular individual involved.) This criticism is somewhat exaggerated, but since to fit any proposed research into its methodological approach a judgment has to be made that it is possible to treat it as a system, critics contend that the advocates of the approach often insist on seeing a systemic relationship when none actually exists.

2. Focusing on the way things are rather than on the various possibilities frequently leads to acceptance of the obvious explanation rather than a search for other alternatives. For example, the mere fact that a particular structure carries out a certain function leads almost automatically (and often incorrectly) to the conclusion that this is why the structure came into existence in the first place. Thus, there is seemingly no reason to investigate alternative structures for the expression of the same functions. This particular emphasis of structural-functionalism leads to overlooking the fact that it may well have been pure accident that the structure in question was used in the first place.

3. Related to the above is the implicit assumption that structures exist because they serve a function. On the contrary, it is always possible that they are either archaic survivals or even actively dysfunctional.

4. The emphasis of structural-functional analysis on the way things are can lead to an unquestioning assumption of stability and an incapacity to deal with the challenges of change, particularly of a swift or violent character.

5. When this last criticism is phased in ideological terms, it leads to these charges: structural-functionalism has a strong bias towards the status quo and its research tends to support the existing order of things because it would not be present in the first place unless it were capable of performing the necessary functions for social survival. This is reminiscent of the German philosopher Hegel, who said, "The real is the rational and the rational is the real." In other words, what exists is logical and right, and it is logical and right because it exists.

Input-Output Analysis. David Easton's name is frequently mentioned in connection with contemporary political science. Easton has the distinction of having developed a systemic approach that is unique because it was developed originally for purposes of political analysis rather than shaped from one of the other social sciences.[21] Easton's basic concept is that of a political system, as one of the subsystems of a society, operating within an environment.

We have already defined a political system as having certain characteristics: (1) it is a *system* because it has a regularly recurring pattern of relationships among the actors, i.e., the individuals and institutions, involved; (2) it is *the* system for its particular society because it is universally accepted and unquestioningly authoritative; and (3) it is *political* because it is concerned with the satisfaction of those needs of society which are beyond the scope of nongovernmental capabilities for solution. For a particular system to exist at all it must, in Easton's terms, have boundaries that mark off its particular type of activities from all others. What is included within the boundaries of a political system, says Easton, are "all those actions more or less directly related to the making of binding decisions for a society."[22]

The units involved in this are *inputs* and *outputs.* Inputs break down into *demands* and *supports.*

Demands are requests for action on those needs of society which can be dealt with only by government. In Easton's words, "A demand may be defined as an expression of opinion that an authoritative allocation with regard to a particular subject matter should or should not be made by those responsible for doing so." There are two types of demands, those which are generated by the environment and those which originate within the political system itself.

The demand for governmental assistance for the sick and aged, which we cited in Chapter 1, is an example of the first of these types, whereas the issue of "one man, one vote" is an example of the second type of demand. A great deal of intensive activity occurs between the first muttering of a grumble and the thundering of a demand for action by the political system. There occurs not only the automatic processing of demands but also a weeding out of the most urgent from the merely desirable. This process of selection is as much a part of the functioning of the political system as is the conversion process it performs.

[21]The most important of Easton's writings are *The Political System* (New York: Knopf, 1953), *A Framework for Political Analysis* (Englewood Cliffs, N.J.: Prentice-Hall, 1965), and *A Systems Analysis of Political Life* (New York: Wiley, 1965).

[22]David Easton, "An Approach to the Analysis of Political Systems," *World Politics* 9 (April 1957): 87. Easton later defined a *system* as "any set of variables regardless of the relationship among them." David Easton, ed., *Varieties of Political Thought* (Englewood Cliffs, N.J.: Prentice-Hall, 1966), p. 147. He argues that this relieves the necessity to determine whether or not a system is really a system and that the only question to be answered in terms of any "set selected as a system to be analyzed" is: "Does it help us to understand and explain some aspect of human behavior of concern to us?"

Supports are what make both the selection and processing of demands possible. Easton makes an important distinction between *overt* and *covert* support. Overt support means exactly what the term implies, i.e., any open and direct action such as an interest group would take to advance its demands. As you can see, it has to be *actively* expressed to exist at all. The contrary is true of covert support, which means simply an attitude or a sentiment that is not hostile or even unfavorable. Perhaps the most important example of the way in which covert support makes the functioning of any political system possible is the factor of *acceptance.* No political system can function on the basis of force alone. Nor can it operate in the face of passive resistance. It can operate only if there is acceptance (i.e., covert support) of its rule and norms, and such overt support as the willingness to pay taxes so that the government can function. Both kinds of support flow simultaneously and both are important for the continued functioning of the *political community,* the *regime,* and the *government.* The *political community* is composed of all those individuals who regard themselves as participating members of the political system. The term *regime* includes both the constitutional concepts and the organizational means by which they are put into effect. The meaning of the term *government* needs no explanation.

It would be pointless to attempt an analysis of how much covert and overt support any one of the three elements has at any given time. But we can well ask ourselves: Why give a political system any kind of support in the first place? The answer to this lies in Easton's concept of outputs.

Outputs are the ultimate result of demands which have survived from their first feeble beginnings to move successfully through the political system. An output is "a political decision or policy." It constitutes an inducement for the members of the political community to actively support the existing political system, or at least to continue to accept it. As in the old proverb about the equal effectiveness of the carrot and the stick, inducements may be either positive or negative. Individuals support the political system because they are pleased with its rewards or afraid of its punishment, or, more true to life, from a combination of these reasons.

In the long run, support for a political system is dependent on a continuing feedback from a sufficiently satisfying output both as to quantity and quality. But like great athletes, political systems have their off days. It is the long-term average performance that counts. An established reputation goes a long way toward serving as a support mechanism, even though there may be a lengthy period of slump. Neither an individual nor a system can operate indefinitely

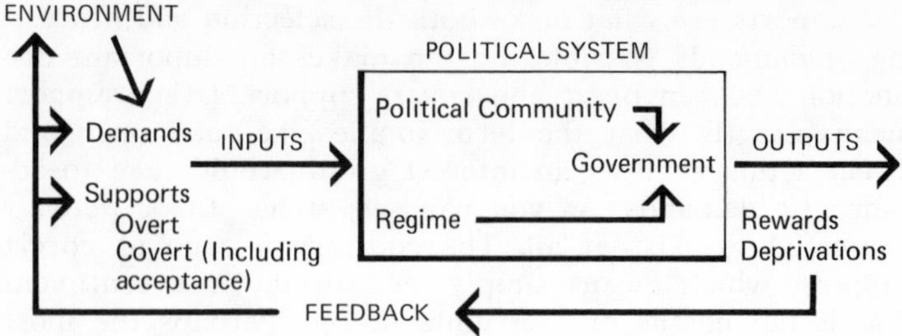

Figure 2
The Political System

on the basis of past successes, but those with a reservoir of proven achievement have a much better chance of surviving slump periods when there is no feedback from satisfying outputs. We shall see explicit illustrations of this in our discussion of the future of constitutional democracy.

The Easton-type input-output analysis is shown in Figure 2.[23] How does input-output analysis stack up in terms of the five analytical factors? It is excellent as a technique for comparative analysis since it is focused on an overview of entire political systems and has an inclusive set of concepts and categories which facilitate comparison. An even stronger aspect of input-output analysis is its dynamic approach to the problems of pattern maintenance and its awareness of the importance of the problems of stress, disturbance, regulation, and planned reorientation of system goals. Its weakest points are in the areas of patterns of control and goals and goal attainment. Because its fundamental concern is with the survival of a political system, the problems of breakdown or disruption are of little concern to input-output analysis. Goals and goal attainment are merely subpoints under pattern maintenance. As with the other approaches, there is a mixture of strength and weakness in connection with patterns of change. Once again, the basic factor in analysis is that the continuation of the fundamental structure of the system is assumed. Within these limits, however, input-output analysis has much to offer. As Easton stresses,

> It is the fact that persistence may include the idea of change that makes it vital and necessary to differentiate this concept from that of systems maintenance. . . . Systems analysis delves into a theory that explains the capacities of a system to persist, not to maintain itself as this would be normally understood. It seeks a theory of persistence, not of self-maintenance or equilibrium.

[23]Adapted from Easton, "An Approach to the Analysis . . ." *Ibid.*, p. 384. Copyright © 1957 by Princeton University Press.

Its weakness is that it has little to say about revolutionary change. Almost of necessity, the basic assumption is that the system will continue to be recognizable, and that any change that occurs will be of an evolutionary nature.

The major criticisms made of input-output analysis are:

1. It is focused on the dubious proposition that the problems of system persistence are the most important subjects for political analysis.

2. Without saying so, it really is concerned with the political system only at the *national* level. Easton himself makes this very clear when he says,

> I shall refer to the internal political systems of groups and organizations as *parapolitical systems* and retain the concept "political system" for political life in the more inclusive unit being analyzed, namely, in a society. . . . Parapolitical systems are concerned only with problems of authoritative allocations within the group.

This is a narrower view of political activity than many contemporary political scientists are prepared to accept. Not only is it limited in terms of internal political analysis; it is also little concerned with interactions *among* political systems so that its utility in the analysis of international politics is minimal.

3. As in the case of decision-making analysis, some critics feel that the focus of input-output analysis on the politically active members of any society tend to give it an elitist orientation that short-circuits its potential for providing any general theory of politics.

4. Related to this is the criticism that this means there is an automatic bias toward the status quo although, as we have noted change, except in revolutionary terms, and the redirection of goals are accepted as normal aspects of the system's dynamics.

5. Once again, as in the case of structural-functional analysis, the Procrustean charge is leveled. Linked with this is the criticism that input-output analysis is too theoretical to be applicable in practice.

CONCLUSION

It is clear that there is no such thing as an ideal or even an approximately ideal approach to political analysis. To return to five-factor analysis, we evaluate the points of strength and weakness in the various approaches in Table 1.

This attempt at evaluation is obviously not completely satisfactory, because to use such terms as *weak, strong,* and *satisfactory* is both vague and "unscientific." But it does, at least, weight the relative usefulness of each approach. It is important to remember that both the skill

Table 1
Principal Analytical Approaches Evaluated

Factor	Group theory	Decision-making	Structural-functional	Input-output
Description	Strong	Strong	Strong	Strong
Pattern maintenance	Weak	Strong (D) Weak (L)	Strong	Strong
Patterns of control	Weak	Satis-factory (D) Strong (L)	Weak	Weak
Goals & goal attainment	Strong	Weak (D) Strong (L)	Weak	Weak
Patterns of change	Satis-factory (but)	Satis-factory (but)	Satis-factory (but)	Satis-factory (but)

NOTE: The *D* refers to Deutsch's version of decision-making, and the *L* to Lasswell's.

with which any particular approach is applied and how much at home any researcher feels with it will determine how effective it is. None of the four approaches offers more than a rough explanation of the problems of breakdown, upheaval, and revolutionary change, so the over-all effectiveness in analyzing patterns of change must be classified as "satisfactory, but." In any problem of political analysis, inflexible adherence to any one approach is not likely to produce meaningful or important results. Researchers who are unable to shift gears all too often are guilty of selecting their research to fit the approach or methodology rather than deciding what topics need to be investigated and then selecting the approach that promises the best results. Political scientists strongly dedicated to the behavioral approach have been particularly guilty of this, especially those committed to the development of a so-called scientific politics by the application of a quantitative approach. It often seems that their first concern has been whether the research can be reduced to mathematical formulae or put on computer cards rather than whether it is worthwhile and timely.

This text is organized, broadly speaking, within the general input-output approach, because, in the writer's opinion, it is the best approach for presenting an organized and systematic introduction to political science within the action and organization philosophy. The concept of system and the vocabulary that goes with it is the framework within which we shall work in the chapters that follow.

One further aspect of our theoretical framework should be examined. No political system operates in a vacuum. Indeed, one of Easton's basic propositions is the importance of the concept of boundary maintenance between the political system and its environment. But, on the other hand, the form of a political system is strongly affected by the environment from which it has originated. The concept of *total environment* is complex and far-reaching indeed. Aside from the international (*extrasocietal*) environment, the domestic (*intrasocietal*) environment is shaped by such factors as geography, climate, soil fertility, and natural resources, all of which comprise the ecological system of a society. These factors play a significant role in determining the type of political system of any society.

More directly influential in the shaping of the political system, however, are the various aspects of the society's social system. In this category, Easton singles out the cultural, social, economic, and demographic subsystems. Taken together, these comprise the environmental influences with the most direct bearing on the political system. These elements exert the major influence on the shaping of the culture of a society of which the political culture is a subsystem. Perhaps the simplest definition of culture is to term it, as H. V. Wiseman has, "part of the common orientation of two or more people." This common orientation is composed of three elements: knowledge of and belief in the realities of the physical and social world and values shared, in varying degrees. Within the framework of a culture, these are the facts, even though they may differ substantially from the facts of another culture. It is on this basis that evaluations are made and actions taken.

The beliefs and values shared by the members of a particular culture go far to determine what they consider to constitute their particular set of facts about the world. Because we Americans assume that a popularly elected government represents the best expression of the values of our democratic faith, we regard it as a fact that any other type of regime is automatically undesirable. In terms of the influences which have shaped their political culture, however, Russians or Spaniards would consider this not a fact but a dubious assumption at best.

Based on our perception of the facts, all of us have certain beliefs and values as to how a government should operate and what its goals should be. The total of these elements constitutes our political culture. What we are doing, of course, is simply applying to political matters the overall beliefs and values of our general culture. The nature of that culture cannot be understood without an awareness of the forces that have shaped its development over a long period of time in the past. Consideration has to be given to the influence of geographic, demographic, economic, religious, and other social and political factors, and the interactions of these have to be evaluated in their historical perspective.

The nineteenth-century poet Alfred, Lord Tennyson, has one of his characters soliloquize, "I am a part of all that I have met." As true as this is of individuals, it is even more true of political systems. None came into existence fully formed. Instead, their present form represents the culmination of a long process of development. In the course of that development a wide variety of political, social, and economic forces affected the way in which the various elements of the political system coalesced. This is why it is necessary to be as concerned with the nature of the environment in which the political system functions as with the individual elements and the workings of the system itself.

It is important to realize, however, that very seldom is only one political culture involved. It has long been commonplace, for example, to attribute French political turbulence to the clash of competing and hostile political cultures. On the other hand, the lack of crucial issues in American politics was regarded as the result of a homogeneous and universally accepted political culture. That this is no longer the case in the 1970s is becoming increasingly obvious. Clearly there is no longer a single general culture or homogeneous political culture. If these developments continue, it is clear that American political life is likely to be increasingly characterized by conflict over goals rather than by mere disagreements over methods.

PART TWO
THE ACTION ELEMENTS OF POLITICS

THE ROLE OF INTEREST GROUPS IN THE POLITICAL SYSTEM

No political system can endure long if it is not capable of processing the demands for *action* made upon it by its particular society. In Chapter 2 we characterized demands as being the raw materials which the political system needs to operate. In Chapter 1 we spoke of how dissatisfaction or grumbles sometimes develop into vigorous demands if several factors are present. First of all, if a grumble is not to begin and end in the hot air of aimless discussion, it must express a widely shared, deeply felt, and continuing dissatisfaction with some aspect of contemporary society. But this in itself is not enough.

Organization is a second and equally important factor. Even the strongest grumbles cannot develop into successful demands unless they have strong and expertly organized support. This is why the role played by interest groups in any political system is one of major importance.

WHAT IS AN INTEREST GROUP?

By the term *interest group* we mean *a combination of individuals involved in political action to make their objectives priority items in society's authoritative allocation of values, without the group itself necessarily assuming formal control of the governmental process.*

Some students of interest groups make a distinction between interest groups and pressure groups or lobbies on the grounds that there is a distinction between persuasion and pressure. This distinction, however, is not really meaningful, because, however gently or subtly applied, any variety of persuasion represents some kind of pressure. So, for our purposes, the terms *interest* and *pressure* groups will be used interchangeably. The dictionary defines a lobby as "a group of persons who conduct a campaign to influence members of a legislature to vote according to the group's special interest."

Lobbying, then, is one aspect of the wide range of activities carried on by interest groups. Without support and activity outside the legislative sphere, a lobby would have no power to influence decisions.

In traditional American thought about interest groups, it is always assumed that they are voluntary associations which every individual is free to join or not, according to his personal inclinations. Some definitions of an interest group include this idea of voluntary participation as an essential element. But such is not always the case. For example, even through he might prefer to be independent, a small merchant or factory worker is likely to find life much easier if he joins his trade association or union.

An illustration of the often-compulsory nature of interest-group membership was afforded early in 1971 when the conservative editor and columnist William F. Buckley, Jr., filed suit challenging the constitutionality of the requirement that he join the American Federation of Television and Radio Artists in order to appear regularly on radio and television. Buckley was quoted in a press conference:

> It is my opinion that the requirement that an individual pay dues to a private organization in order to work is a modern writ of indenture; the requirement that he do the same in order to express an opinion over the public airways involves an act of coercion by a private organization operating under government sanction.

Modern Political Action

Political action is another term that can no longer be taken for granted. In the Western world, at least until recent years, political action by an interest group consisted of letter-writing campaigns, newspaper advertisements, petitions to elected officials with the maximum possible number of names signed to them, mass meetings and parades in support of the particular cause, the lobbying of legislators, and threats of bloc voting. But in the 1970s, in widely separated areas of the world where until recently such techniques would have been regarded as unthinkable, political action by interest groups has come to include murder, kidnapping of foreign diplomats, the hijacking of international airliners, and the bombing or threat of bombing of public buildings. Regardless of the method employed, however, it remains true that the objective of an interest group is not the official *control* of power, but rather the *shaping* or *directing* of how power is employed

Where Are Interest Groups Found?

The perception of where interest groups are to be found has changed as dramatically as the conception of political action. As we noted in Chapter 2, Bentley's *Process of Gov-*

ernment (1908) represented the first effort to view interest groups as a legitimate aspect of the political process, but it was not until the 1950s that interest groups were recognized as other than uniquely American phenomena. When European scholars first examined them, they were regarded as peculiar to political life in constitutional democracies. It was thought that interest groups flourished best when there was a long-standing tradition of freedom of expression, a plural society, and a well-established implicit belief that both political parties and official sources could be made responsive to properly articulated demands.

We now realize that interest groups exist in all political systems, even in totalitarian states. In the communist regimes, for example, all factions within *the* party were officially banned in 1921 as dangerous sources of subversive activity, yet analysts of Soviet affairs have broken down the membership of the Central Committee into such categories as "party officials," "state and economic representatives," "military officers," and so on. Although it is most unlikely that competing interest groups in the Soviet government desire any fundamental changes in Soviet society, it does seem clear that they have strong and separate interests which give rise to a constant struggle for control of the party apparatus as a means of shaping governmental policy. Besides the ruling-elite interest groups in the U.S.S.R., we catch occasional and fleeting glimpses of oppositional interest groups, mostly composed of antiestablishment intellectuals. So furtive are their activities, however, and so quickly are they suppressed by the regime, that it is impossible to evaluate their intentions or gauge their strength. But the mere fact that they exist is further proof of the universality of interest groups in even the most theoretically monolithic of societies.

It would be difficult to envisage a more dramatic and violent instance of interest-group conflict carried to the extreme than that afforded in recent years by communist China, where the Leninist prescription for monolithic unity is supposedly the guiding principle. During the so-called Great Proletarian Revolution of 1966–1969, interest-group conflict escalated almost to the level of civil war. The well-authenticated bloody conflicts between the Red Guard and the foes of Chairman Mao revealed, in a much starker fashion than has been true of the Soviet Union since the 1920s, that interest groups are present in all political cultures. One of the most interesting aspects of the Cultural Revolution in China has been the apparent position of dominance it has given the army as the one interest group possessing a coherent program and the force to implement it. We shall speak of the role of armed forces as interest groups when we discuss the functioning of interest groups in the political cultures of the new nations.

In the new developing nations, interest groups are still

largely unstudied phenomena. But the scarcity of easily organized data, the still-fluctuating nature of the political systems, and their different bases for affiliation have made research difficult if not impossible. In the mixed political cultures involved, interest groups comprise a wide spectrum of varied types ranging from such modern and sophisticated examples as trade unions and business interests to tribal, regional, and religious groups.

How Interest Groups Function

Regardless of the types of interest groups involved in any political system, all are influenced by certain common factors which determine how they function. As outlined by Professor Eckstein in his study of the British Medical Association, the determinants of interest-group activities are:

1. The Form of Their Activities. By this is meant that the way in which interest groups function is shaped by such influences as the form of the governmental structure, with particular reference to where the decisive policy decisions are made and the receptivity of the political system to interest-group activity.

2. Their Intensity and Scope. These two factors describe: (a) the dedication and persistence with which a group pursues its goals and (b) the "number and variety of groups engaged in politics." Shaping these factors are such influences as the degree of legitimacy groups have, the particular program goals, and the ability of the system to fulfill group demands.

3. Their Effectiveness. This conditioning factor of group activity needs little comment. The financial resources a group has, its geographical distribution, the percentage of potential clientele it can mobilize, the expertise of its leadership, and the relations it has with the official decision-makers are all obvious and important determinants of effectiveness, along with, of course, the factor of intensity of purpose mentioned in point two.[1]

The ways in which interest groups seek to express themselves in terms of these conditioning factors should provide insight into the political process as a whole. "For example," comments Gabriel Almond, "French business associations are different from the American in that they do not engage openly and on a large scale in public 'informational' activities. This may reflect a general condition of fragmentation in political communication in France, a condition of distrust and alienation among interests."[2]

[1]Harry Eckstein, *Pressure Group Politics* (London: Allen and Unwin, 1960).

[2]Gabriel A. Almond, "Research Note: A Comparative Study of Interest Groups and the Political Process," *American Political Science Review* 52 (March 1958): 274.

SITUATIONAL AND ATTITUDINAL INTEREST GROUPS

Broadly speaking, it is possible to divide interest groups into two major categories. Very probably no interest group fits completely into either category, but in general terms its major focus will be predominantly in one or the other. The two categories can be called the *situational* and the *attitudinal.*

In the first category can be placed all interest groups primarily concerned with the defense and improvement of the particular situation in which its members find themselves. The interests of such a group are nonideological, specific, and utilitarian. The AFL-CIO is a prime example from American political culture. Its justification for existence is the defense and improvement of the position of its members in economic and social terms. It is basically concerned with higher wages, shorter hours, improved social legislation, and so on. But this does not prevent it from issuing statements on national policy from time to time, even in areas so far removed from its primary concerns as American policy in Southeast Asia, Presidential politics, recognition of communist China, and other such attitudinal issues.

An attitudinal interest group, on the other hand, tends to be primarily ideological, diffuse, and somewhat utopian in its outlook. Its motivation comes from an idealistic concern for the general welfare, a conviction as to how this can be improved, and often a considerable degree of alienation on the part of its members. Whatever the particular combination of motives involved, such a group wants to improve society either by piecemeal reforms or sweeping revolutionary change. Examples in contemporary American society of such groups are the various organizations mobilized to end the war in Vietnam, to protect the environment, to influence U.S. foreign policy, and so on. It is a significant indication of far-reaching changes in social thinking that one of the foremost spokesmen for such an attitudinal interest group, Ralph Nader, famous for his one-man crusade for automobile safety, has become a widely admired public figure.

In the previous paragraph the term *mobilized* was used to describe how attitudinal groups are formed, for quite aside from their differences in objectives and attitudes, there is an obvious contrast between the operational techniques of situational and attitudinal interest groups. Situational groups have usually been around for a long time and expect to continue into the indefinite future. Time is seldom crucial. Nor, for that matter, are they usually stirred by crisis issues which must be dealt with immediately if not sooner. Such a group is concerned, rather, with the continuing protection and promotion of long-range interests.

As a result, the methods utilized to influence public opinion and the relevant decision-makers are intended to achieve cumulative rather than shock effect. The presentation of a consistently favorable public image, the continued cultivation of key decision-makers, the utilization of the traditional techniques of legislative lobbying—all these methods characterize the approaches of situational interest groups.

In contrast are the methods employed by attitudinal interest groups. By their very nature they are concerned with crisis situations which call for action now. Further they have usually come into existence only quite recently as a result of a perceived threat, and, in contrast to situational interest groups, they do not anticipate continuing into the indefinite future. Once it has either accomplished its program to solve the crisis or come to feel hopelessly frustrated in so doing, the attitudinal interest group dissolves or reorganizes in a new form with a different focus. These expectations are reflected in the techniques employed by attitudinal groups. For such groups nothing is more important than time. In the briefest possible period the group must make its existence widely known, attract the largest possible following, and somehow force a decision from the establishment favorable to its objectives. In military terms, it must mobilize its forces for maximum and immediate victory rather than wage a low-keyed war of attrition.

To this end such groups must utilize the ultimate in shock tactics. These include all types of confrontation techniques, ranging from the merely sensational to the brutally violent, from sit-ins, pouring of animal blood on draft files, disrupting opposition meetings, and harassing public officials to such extreme tactics as political assassination, the bombing of public buildings, the hijacking of international aircraft, and the kidnapping of ranking officials.

One further difference between situational and associational interest groups is in the roles played by their rank-and-file members. There is little in the regular activities of a situational interest group to inspire high emotion or induce mass involvement on the part of its members. Its activities are carried out by its permanent staff with their expert knowledge of public relations and how best to influence official decision-makers. The role of the average member, except in rare instances, tends to be one of providing financial aid or other relatively passive support.

In contrast, no one is likely to join an attitudinal interest group unless he has an emotional involvement with the cause and a desire to do something personally about the problem. This sense of emotional involvement generates a concern on the part of the rank and file about the right policy to follow and the way to carry it out that the executive secretary of a situational interest group would find an intolerable intrusion into his own area of responsibility. The executive secretary of an associational group, if it has one, is seldom in office long enough to acquire any sense of proprietorship over the affairs of the group. In many cases he was probably elected at a mass meeting for an indefinite term, subject to instant recall. In short, to make a simplified generalization, situational interest groups are usually characterized by the *passivity* of their general membership, while associational groups function in terms of their members' *activity.*

Structural Typology

Interest groups can also be described in terms of the structural forms in which these groups express themselves. One of the most promising efforts to provide a sufficiently inclusive typology of structural organization for interest groups in all types of political systems has been offered by Professor James Coleman. All political systems, he notes, have ways of "articulating interests, claims, demands for political action." The structures which serve these purposes and the style of their performance are important in determining the boundary between the political system and the society at large. Developing this proposition further, he suggests that "four main types of structures may be involved in interest articulation: (1) institutional interest groups, (2) nonassociational interest groups, (3) anomic interest groups, and (4) associational interest groups."[3]

Coleman classifies *institutional* interest groups as involving "phenomena occurring with such organizations as legislatures, political executives, armies, bureaucracies, churches, and the like." Although these organizations do not have interest representation as their prime function, "as corporate bodies or through groups with them (such as legislative blocs, officer cliques, higher or lower clergy or religious orders, departments, skill groups, and ideological cliques in bureaucracies)," they may express either their own interests or those of other groups in the society.

Nonassociational interest groups comprise "kinship and lineage groups, ethnic, regional, religious, status, and class groups which articulate interests informally and intermittently, through individuals, cliques, family and religious heads, and the like." The same operational style is characteristic of institutional interest groups, a typical example of which is "a formally organized body made up of professionally employed officials or employees, with another function," with interest-group activity either an intermit-

[3]Gabriel A. Almond and James S. Coleman, *The Politics of the Developing Areas* (Princeton, N.J.: Princeton University Press, 1960), p. 33.

tent affair or with the parent organization serving as "a base of operations for a clique or subgroup" consistently involved in interest-group activity.

Coleman's category of *associational* interest groups includes "trades unions, organizations of businessmen or industrialists, ethnic associations, associations organized by religious denominations, civic groups, and the like." Unlike the other categories, the organization and promotion of a particular interest is the sole reason for such a group's existence.

Most interesting in Coleman's classification, and of obvious timeliness in understanding an important aspect of contemporary interest-group expression, is his category of *anomic* interest groups. These are characterized by:

> more or less spontaneous breakthroughs into the political system from the society, such as riots and demonstrations. Their distinguishing characteristic is their relative structural and functional ability. We use the term "relative" advisedly, since riots and demonstrations may be deliberately organized and controlled. But even when organized and controlled they have the potentiality of exceeding limits and norms and disturbing or even changing the political system.[4]

We have now discussed two possible ways of classifying interest groups: (1) in terms of their general character and objectives and (2) in terms of their types of structural organization. Although no direct correlation is possible, we can approximately combine the two analytical schemes in this fashion:

By its very nature an anomic interest group is in the attitudinal category. Men who want increased social-security benefits or legislation concerned with retirement pensions are seldom stirred to rioting and violence. Rather, as both student and ghetto anomic outbursts have shown, riots and violence have their roots in a deeply felt and long-endured sense of injustice and deprivation. On the other hand, an associational interest group is solidly in the situational category. The group's reasons for existence are to manipulate situational issues and problems. Now and again it may find itself involved on attitudinal issues, but this is an exception from its normal operational pattern. The surest and shortest route to disaster for an associational interest group would be to become too involved in pursuing attitudinal issues.

Institutional and nonassociational interest groups fall

[4]*Ibid.*, p. 34.

more logically in the middle of the spectrum. An institutional interest group, for example, could be composed of civil servants engaged in the most traditional type of lobbying for budget increases. Or it could be a fanatical group of military officers sworn to protect the national honor, even to the extent of armed revolt or political assassination. The Japanese army officers' corps in the years before World War II is an example of this latter group. Nonassociational groups, depending upon the issues and emotions involved, may fall into either the attitudinal or situational categories.

THE POLITICAL SYSTEM FRAMEWORK

Regardless of the general character of their structural organization, all interest groups obviously function within the frame of reference of a particular political system. The characteristics of the political system determine how the groups function. Adhering in broad outline to the typology of political systems outlined by Professor Almond, we will briefly survey interest groups in terms of the following categories of political systems:

1. Anglo-American
2. Integrated Continental European
3. Fragmented Continental European
4. Totalitarian
5. Developing Nations[5]

INTEREST GROUPS IN THE ANGLO-AMERICAN POLITICAL SYSTEM

Professor Almond lists the cultural characteristics of the Anglo-American political system as follows:

1. Most people involved in the system share a common viewpoint on ends and means, however much the emphasis may vary on any one particular aspect.
2. Rational calculation, bargaining, and trial-and-error testing of policies are accepted operational techniques.
3. Pluralism in values produces strongly differentiated

[5]Gabriel A. Almond, "Comparative Political Systems," *Journal of Politics* 18 (August, 1956): 391–403. In this article Almond discusses these political systems in a different sequence. I have rearranged the order to provide a more logical transitional sequence. Almond uses only the general heading of "Continental European." For greater clarity I have used the two categories of Continental Europe which he employs in his previously cited *American Political Science Review* "Research Note" article. The terms *Integrated* and *Fragmented* are my addition, however, as is the use of the phrase *Developing Nations* instead of Almond's term *Pre-Industrial.* The reason for this latter change will be explained in the text.

though stable roles on the official, political, and interest levels.

4. While interdependent, all of these units are autonomous, organized, and administered by full-time, professional officials.
5. As Bentley pointed out, there is a constant interplay among the competing units which prevents an overwhelming concentration of either power or influence.

A sixth important characteristic of Anglo-American political culture is the large number of citizens who have a strong feeling of political effectiveness, who believe that they can bring about desired changes in the state of affairs. In the United States, 66 percent of citizens from a selected sample felt that they could do something to change an unjust law on either a national or a local level. For Great Britain the figure was 56 percent. By way of contrast, 33 percent of Germans, 33 percent of Mexicans, and 27 percent of Italians felt that they could be effective in this fashion.[6]

How do these characteristics of the political system shape the role of interest groups? First of all, the prevalence of a common viewpoint on ends and means does not imply social homogeneity in either Great Britain or the United States. It simply means that most groups accept the system as it is, have no desire to bring about revolutionary changes, and expect to continue working within its existing framework. But within this frame of reference the competition among groups for a piece of the action can be, and usually is, both intense and consistent.

Given this widespread acceptance of the status quo, it is not surprising that Anglo-American interest groups are predominantly situational in character with the defense or improvement of the economic position of their members a major concern. In 1969, for example, of 647 lobbyists registered with Congress, at least 73 percent were in this category. Ostensibly the 35 foundations, 83 citizens' groups, and 51 registered individuals were self-proclaimed champions of various attitudinal causes. But in their cases, also, strong elements of situational interest concerns were present. Comparable statistics are not available for Great Britain, but S. E. Finer, a pioneer researcher on British interest groups, requires four pages to list those situational groups representing industry, commerce, labor, and professionals and only a page for civic, religious, and "Recreational, Cultural, and Educational" associations.[7] Here again it is obvious that the groups in the latter category are

[6]Gabriel A. Almond and Sidney Verba, *The Civic Culture* (Boston: Little, Brown, 1965), p. 173.

[7]S. E. Finer, "Interest Groups and the Political Process in Great Britain," in *Interest Groups on Four Continents,* ed. Henry W. Ehrmann (Pittsburgh, Pa.: University of Pittsburgh Press, 1958), pp. 117–144; in particular, pp. 118–124.

likely to be motivated by a considerable degree of self-interest.

Given the complex web of interests in such highly developed technological societies as the United States and Great Britain, it is to be expected that institutional and associational interest groups will be predominant, particularly since the high degree of mobility and eroded status loyalties characteristic of these societies greatly reduce the role of nonassociational groups. Anomic interest groups arise sporadically in any society.

It is also to be expected that English and American interest groups function in terms of Almond's other points, too. By its very nature, modern industrial society demands an ethos of rational calculation, a willingness to adjust conflicting viewpoints in order to preserve the fragile technological structure, and the constant testing of hypotheses. Its complexity necessitates long and intensive specialization to master special skills. As a result of this early and long career-oriented conditioning, the individuals involved almost automatically come to be a full-time interest group in their own right. But again, the delicate interdependence of such a society's interest groups demands cooperative effort and basic restraint, which act to prevent any one group from becoming overwhelmingly dominant.

We have been viewing the roles of Anglo-American interest groups within a single framework. But clearly, however closely related they are, differences do exist. Let us now briefly survey the differences.

Role of Government and Parties in the Anglo-American System

The activities of American and British interest groups are substantially conditioned by the formal structure of government and the nature of the political parties in these two countries. The most obvious difference between the American, Australian, and Canadian governmental structures and that of the British is the difference between federal and unitary systems. The federal system with its separate but coordinate focuses of governmental authority provides for a separation of powers. British constitutional structure, by way of contrast, concentrates the ultimate decision-making authority in the national government, and, increasingly in recent years, the effective exercise of that authority in the national executive branch.

The activities of American educational interest groups for example, have been traditionally limited because of exclusive state jurisdiction in their field. But in recent years, as the federal government has become an important factor in the financing of state educational systems, this has become less and less so, particularly in connection with the racial integration of state school systems. Black attitudinal interest groups, working through the powers of the Department of Health, Education, and Welfare to grant or withhold essential funds to state and local school systems, have been able to make highly effective use of national political power to overcome state and local opposition to change in an area in which the state and local communities theoretically have exclusive jurisdiction.

The reasons are obvious for the differences between American and British interest groups as a result of their respective political systems—regional dispersion of power under the federal system and its national concentration under a unitary system. Less obvious are the reasons for their different focuses of interest on the national levels. Fundamentally this is caused by differences in the party systems. In the American case, the constitutional separation of powers, the existence of two separate but equal legislative bodies, the great importance of the committees and their control over the budgetary process, and the lack of party discipline which makes most senators and representatives not only open to individual persuasion but concerned about assuring themselves of the widest possible support at the next election—all explain why national interest groups tend to focus attention on the Congress. In terms of financial aid and support at the polls, such powerful situational interest groups as the AFL-CIO and the American Medical Association and such attitudinal groups as the American Legion and various religious groups are able to exert very powerful leverage.

But the role of interest groups is enhanced considerably by their opportunities for a second and a third chance to modify policy. If a group is unable to persuade Congress of the correctness of its goals, there is always the possibility of influencing administrators to interpret the legislation to achieve the same ends. If this attempt is unsuccessful, it may be possible to present a persuasive enough case to the judicial branch to get the offending legislation ruled unconstitutional.

The possibilities available for interest-group action go far to explain how outdated is the traditional picture of the lobbyist as a jovial gentleman with a briefcase full of hundred dollar bills, a list of friendly young ladies, and a "hospitality room" which never runs dry. That personality and skill in human relations are still important, however, is attested to by the number of former congressmen and military officers who, after retirement, became the Washington representatives for interests concerned with legislation or defense policy.

But more important is the front man's ability, once access to powerful decision-makers is gained, to present a convincing case. Regardless of personality and contacts, it is probably no exaggeration to say that behind every successful Washington interest-group representative is a well-trained and efficient staff of research specialists who can document their group's case impressively enough to cause their equivalents on the congressional staffs and in the government departments and agencies to pass it along with a favorable recommendation to the policy-makers they advise. The need for expertise in interest-group presentation before judicial bodies is obvious: Justice Thurgood Marshall, for example, won his Supreme Court appointment in part as a result of his brilliant record in pleading civil rights cases for the National Association for the Advancement of Colored People.

Importance of Finances and Grass-Roots Support

But neither the best of high-level contacts, the most brilliant of persuaders, nor the most efficient of research staffs can carry the day for a group unless it is able to muster a significant degree of grass-roots support and financial muscle. The most haunting fear of any elected official is that he may not get re-elected. To get re-elected he needs money and votes, and the knowledge that in his home district there is strong grass-roots support for some measure which a particular lobbyist is pushing is usually a powerful influence on him. Lester Milbraith quotes one experienced Washington lobbyist as saying:

> I'm convinced that the grass-roots support is the important thing rather than my contacts. I know this from my experience on the Hill where I've been on the receiving end. I can go up and explain the technical end of the thing, but it's the grass roots that lets the members of Congress know who is behind it. I would give 75 percent to the grass roots.[8]

There does not seem to be any consistent correlation between achievement of goals and the amount of money an interest group spends. In 1965, for example, in an all-out effort to block the passage of Medicare, the American Medical Association increased its lobbying appropriation from approximately $45,000 in 1964 to an impressive $1,156,000. And year in, year out, the AFL-CIO has been one of the top lobbying spenders in an equally unsuccessful campaign to bring about repeal of the Taft-Hartley Act, which for almost twenty years now has been anathema to organized labor.

American interest groups operate in a political culture that paradoxically views them with disapproval, yet offers them unique opportunities for influence. Traditionally, American political culture has stressed the romantic illusion of a face-to-face relationship between the citizen and a government which exists simply to carry out his will. In this perspective, interest groups could be said to frustrate

[8]Lester Milbraith, *The Washington Lobbyists* (Chicago: Rand McNally, 1963), pp. 238–239.

the will of the democratic majority and instead substitute for it the selfish and possibly sinister programs of interests harmful to the people at large.

There are several comments to be made about this. The traditional concept of the role of government as passive has offered a unique opportunity for interest groups. Reaction not action was government's role. That when the people spoke, the government responded—but not before—is part of the mythology that colored the American's thinking about his government. The same was true of political parties. In this idealized view of political institutions, the role of parties was not to initiate policy but to wait for demands that something be done and then offer solutions.

Another idealized concept is that of a constantly concerned and informed citizenry, but this again is a creature of myth and legend, as both public-opinion polls and routinely low voting-participation confirm. Approximately 60 percent of American voters participate in presidential elections, and at off-year congressional and gubernatorial elections little more than 40 percent of those eligible vote. Studies show that consistently one-third of the U.S. population is indifferent to political activity; an even smaller percentage is consistently actively involved.[9] In the early 1970s, whatever the reasons, the politics of apathy set a new record. In the New York Democratic primary, after weeks of the most intensive publicity, only one in four Democratic voters went to the polls.

Under these circumstances, interest groups are offered an inviting political vacuum to fill. It is they who, by default, become the voice of the people. Traditionally, American interest groups have provided the input of demands for action by both the political parties and the governmental machinery. Further, by their informed awareness of the issues, they have served not only to clarify issues but to compel a study of them which otherwise would be lacking. Even today when we are so accustomed to the concept of the active state, interest groups continue to mould and sharpen the definition of issues. Harmon Zeigler concludes that "the existence of an abundance of pressure groups is natural and healthy for a democracy."[10]

New Attitudinal Groups

The most striking development among American interest groups in recent years has been the growing prominence of a new type of attitudinal group inspired by mounting

[9]See Thomas R. Dye, Lee S. Greene, and George S. Parthomos, *American Government: Theory, Structure and Process* (Belmont, Calif.: Wadsworth, 1969), pp. 157–158.

[10]Harmon Zeigler, *Interest Groups in American Society* (Belmont, Calif.: Wadsworth, 1964), p. 39.

public concern over threats of pollution from an expanding technological society. What these groups lack in finances and lobbying expertise they more than compensate for in the enthusiasm and dedication of their highly involved members. If their faith has not quite been able to move mountains, it has demonstrated dramatically that it can stop canals. Perhaps the biggest single success of the new breed of attitudinal interest groups was their ability to end construction, by Presidential order early in 1971, of the Cross-Florida Barge Canal after nine years of work, the expenditure of $50,000,000, and in spite of the adamant opposition of the hitherto-unstoppable Army Corps of Engineers and powerful business interests. The fight against the canal began in 1962 when concerned members of a local branch of the Audubon Society began a campaign initially intended only to reroute the canal in order to preserve the natural beauty of an unspoiled river.

Until the late 1960s the fight seemed hopeless, although the original small group had grown to statewide proportions. But in 1969, aided by the surge of public concern over environmental problems, the Florida Defenders of the Environment, the newly formed Conservation '70s, and the Environmental Defense Fund of New York initiated court action to restrain the construction. That same year the Florida Department of Air and Water Pollution damned the canal as "the most devastating project ever undertaken in Florida." Impressed by the political power the conservation groups had come to represent, the Florida Senate Committee on Natural Resources voted unanimously in 1970 for an investigation of the desirability of the canal, and Secretary of the Interior Walter Hickel urged that work on the canal be suspended for fifteen months so the environmental impact of the project could be studied. So dynamic were the anticanal groups that 81 percent of the candidates in Florida's 1970 elections felt it prudent to declare themselves against the canal. The climax to this long and brilliantly conducted struggle was the Presidential order of January 19, 1971, halting all construction—apparently permanently.

During the same period, another amateur group also demonstrated the potency of the new type of attitudinal interest group. In 1960 the Army Corps of Engineers estimated that the area of San Francisco Bay, one of the world's largest and most beautiful natural harbors, had been reduced by a third, from 680 to 400 square miles, by land developers. Alarmed by reports that the city of Berkeley proposed to double its size by filling in 2000 bay acres, Catherine Kerr, the wife of the then president of the University of California, and two friends began in 1962 what seemed as hopeless a fight as that of the opponents of the Florida barge canal.

The developmental pattern was much the same as in the Florida case. Initially a Save San Francisco Bay Association was formed. The 700 letters soliciting membership in the association produced an amazing 600 replies. In 1963 the association persuaded the University of California's Institute of Governmental Studies to make a comprehensive study of the future development of the bay. The reports impressively documented conclusions on the bad effects of the proposed Berkeley fill and led to its defeat in a city election referendum.

From then until 1969, the association concentrated its efforts on the state level to bring about the creation of a Bay Conservation and Development Commission. With the aid of such other conservation groups as the Sierra Club, the Save the Redwoods League, and the Audubon Society, the association was able to mount a skillfully organized campaign which culminated in 1969 with the presentation to the California legislature of 3.4 miles of petitions demanding action to save the bay. As in the Florida case, opposition from business interest groups was intense. In spite of this, the group's efforts were crowned with success in 1969 when the Bay Conservation and Development Commission was approved by the legislature.[11]

It is apparent that in the 1970s probably the most important American attitudinal interest groups will be those concerned with the problem of ecology and conservation, which suddenly have a new political appeal. Senator Gaylord Nelson, for example, a long-time advocate of conservation measures, is quoted as saying that in 1966 no other member of the Senate or House was willing to join him in sponsoring a bill to regulate the use of DDT, but in 1969 "dozens of senators and congressmen wanted to be cosponsors." Also in 1969 a bill creating a Council on Environmental Quality in the White House, which a few years earlier would have undoubtedly died in committee, passed without opposition. The President's action in 1971 on the Cross-Florida Barge Canal is sufficient indication that this new type of attitudinal interest group has become a political force to be reckoned with.

Differing Styles of American-British Groups

We can conclude our survey of the general character of American and British interest groups by noting some of the important differences in their styles of operation. American interest groups have always operated under a stigma, but in Great Britain quite the contrary is true.

[11]This summary of the San Francisco Bay conservation struggle is based on Judson Gooding, "Victory on San Francisco Bay," *Fortune* (February 1970): 147, 157–158.

The reason for this, it has been suggested, lies in the continued British acceptance of the medieval concept of society as composed of corporate groups rather than of separate individuals. Thus group activity seems not only logical but natural. It has long been a commonplace and a respected aspect of the British political system. A number of political scientists point to this fact to explain the late development of interest-group studies in Great Britain. In operational terms this has resulted in an intermingling of interest-group and governmental activity to an extent that by American views would be nothing less than scandalous.

More than one American politician has had a promising national career ruined by the disclosure, usually in glaring headlines, that he was being subsidized by an interest group to represent its affairs. In Great Britain it is quite customary for Members of Parliament to receive both a regular salary and often assistance in their campaign expenses in return for representing an interest group's viewpoint. Eckstein comments that more than a hundred MP's receive such payments from labor unions.[12] Many other MP's are themselves either active, former, or honorary interest-group members regularly involved in protecting their group's affairs.

One of the most striking examples of this has been the role of the Cooperative movement within the Labour party. In 1917 the Cooperative movement officially formed its own party but soon found it necessary to cooperate with Labour to elect any candidates. Although its parliamentary members are subject to Labour party discipline, they are officially designated as Labour-Co-op representatives and have as their primary aim the furtherance of the Cooperative interests. Most closely approximating the American role of the lobbyist are the parliamentary agents, usually law firms rather than single individuals. In contrast to the suspicious scrutiny this arouses in the American political system, constant and close cooperation between bureaucrats and interest-group representatives is not only tolerated but encouraged.

Eckstein lists four variations of the relationship between interest groups and government: (1) formal interest-group deputations and negotiating committees, (2) informal semisocial contacts, (3) representation on government committees concerned with their affairs, and (4) most unusual of all by American standards, interest groups not only

[12]All of the material in this section is based on Harry Eckstein, "The British Political System," in *Patterns of Government*, ed. Samuel H. Beer and Adam B. Ulam, 2nd ed. (New York: Random House, 1962), pp. 170–175. See also Samuel H. Beer, "Group Representation in Britain and the United States," in *Comparative Politics*, ed. Roy C. Macridis and Bernard F. Brown, 3rd ed. (Homewood, Ill.: Dorsey, 1968), pp. 240–248.

helping to determine government policy but actually to administer it.

In both the American and the British systems, interest groups have ample scope and opportunity to function with as much intensity as their financial and personnel resources permit. In both systems they are able to operate, though in different ways, with a considerable degree of effectiveness. In both countries, even among the attitudinal interest groups, technical expertise in public relations and communications has become a necessity for effective interest-group functioning.

There is one last point of similarity between American and British interest groups which sets them apart from interest groups in several of the other political systems with which we are concerned. In neither system do any interest groups, singly or in combination, control any political party.

It is true, of course, that the British Labour party was created by the trades-union movement. When added to this is the fact of the Labour-Cooperative coalition, it does not seem inappropriate to describe the party as "in large degree an association of pressure groups." The British Conservative party has always been generally considered the party of the business and financial establishment. In the United States, of course, the Democratic party and the Republican party have had, respectively, a pro-labor and pro-business orientation, but in neither Britain nor America have the interest groups concerned actually controlled the respective parties. Given the alternating-majority pattern of both British and American politics, for the sake of their own survival, neither of the two major parties in either political system dares permit interest-group control, for only if they are able to appeal effectively to that increasingly important uncommitted group of voters can they hope to achieve victory. The various traditional interest groups certainly exert major influence in their respective parties; but, unlike the situation in fragmented party systems, they do not dominate.

INTEREST GROUPS IN THE INTEGRATED CONTINENTAL EUROPEAN SYSTEM

The interest groups in some European political systems share many of the characteristics of their Anglo-American counterparts. Perhaps the West German system has moved the closest of all in recent years to the Anglo-American system, while Finland probably lies at the other end of the spectrum. The other countries in the integrated continental European political systems include the Scandinavian countries, the Benelux group (Belgium, Netherlands,

Luxembourg), Austria, and Switzerland. In short, with the exception of Italy and France, all the countries of Western Europe can be included in this integrated category.

We can characterize the integrated European political systems as sharing, in varying degrees, the following properties:

1. An evenness of social and economic development that has prevented the emergence of such bitter regional antagonisms as that between northern and southern Italy
2. A widespread acceptance of the structural and functional aspects of the existing political system
3. Long-existing and sufficiently serious social and philosophical divisions to prevent the either/or aggregation of political interests characteristic of the Anglo-American system
4. A "live and let live" tradition and a consensus sufficient that stable government and opposition coalitions can be formed, but often only after long and hard bargaining
5. Differentiated and nonpolitical bureaucracies, and political parties and interest groups with a degree of penetration and interrelationship.

German Interest Groups

One of the most interesting developments in German politics since the establishment of the Bonn Republic in 1948 has been the increasingly close approximation to the Anglo-American pattern, particularly to the British pattern of two major parties with a smaller third party occasionally holding the balance of power. As in other highly developed nations, West German interest groups have increasingly become larger, less numerous, and more situational in character. The two major parties, particularly the Christian Democrats with their wide range of social support, have developed in the Anglo-American pattern, becoming coalitions of interest groups which have to be balanced off and synthesized. This integrating of group demands has been facilitated by the fact that the impressive social and economic progress of West Germany has not been limited to any one area or social group. It is obvious that men are far more ready to compromise demands on a full stomach than when there is a sense of material desperation and psychological frustration.

Also in the Anglo-American traditional pattern is the acceptance of the idea that politics is a bargaining process rather than a guerrilla war against "evil" opponents with total victory or defeat as the only goals. There is apparently, in contrast to prewar German or traditional French practice, a willingness to see group interest in relation to overall social and political concerns and to function in terms of the rules of the game. Feelings of economic and social well-being plus the grim memories of the failure of the First German Republic (1919–1933) have been influential factors in this outlook.

In addition to the customary practice of contributing to party funds, German interest groups, like the British, try to get their members elected to the Bundestag. It is estimated that consistently since the emergence of the Bonn Republic approximately 35 percent of Christian Democratic deputies and about 25 percent of Social Democratic representatives have been interest-group representatives. A variety of business groups have dominated among the interest-group spokesmen elected on the Christian Democrat list, while trade unions are represented in the roles of the Social Democratic members.

Again, similar to British practice, various government ministries have advisory bodies composed of representatives from the interest groups affected by the ministry in question. Akin to American practice is the two-way flow between government and business, with high bureaucratic officials recruited from business and ranking civil servants leaving to take better paying jobs in industry. The traditional German respect for expertise and the numerous opportunities to exert influence have given German interest groups more influence over policy formation than either their British or French counterparts. In many ways the functioning of German interest groups is more akin to the American situation than to its European counterparts.

Scandinavian Interest Groups

The Scandinavian countries, Finland aside, are notable for the unity of their political cultures. Both socially and economically, there has been a remarkable degree of uniform development. The resulting political systems are little concerned with ideological divisions but strongly focused on situational goals. Further, the struggle to achieve the goals of the various interest groups functions within an atmosphere of consensus and trust in the good intentions of the other actors involved.

Nothing illustrates this better than the lack of concern in the Scandinavian political systems over the existence of large and centrally controlled interest groups. Unlike the uneasiness which they inspire in other political systems, including the American, the existence of such groups is accepted as quite normal and natural. Sweden offers the most complete illustration of this since virtually all of its gainfully employed are members of various interest groups, with the major labor organization representing about half of the total labor force.

As in Germany, it is customary for Scandinavian political parties to accept interest-group representatives as candidates in an effort to attract the largest possible independent vote. Also well-established in the Scandinavian countries is the constant consultation in policy decisions between governmental agencies and concerned interest groups. In Sweden, for example, a major role is played in this respect by royal commissions which draw their members from a wide assortment of groups. The reports of these commissions represent an important consensus on policy from a number of sources. Also characteristic of Swedish practice is the soliciting of advisory memoranda on proposed policies from interest groups. These memoranda are important elements in the justification offered to the parliament for the proposed measures. One native student of Swedish interest groups considers that "due to their exceptional strength the organizations . . . constitute a kind of extra constitutional power balance system."[13]

The remarkably consensual role of the Scandinavian interest groups is best illustrated in the areas of labor relations and the functioning of the social security systems. In contrast to the virtual civil war which so often exists between employer and labor interest groups elsewhere, in all three Scandinavian countries there are long-standing procedures for the routine settlement of labor disputes.

INTEREST GROUPS IN THE FRAGMENTED CONTINENTAL EUROPEAN SYSTEM

In a number of respects, the characteristics of the fragmented Continental European systems are in direct contrast to those of the integrated political systems. The following traits characterize the fragmented systems:

1. There is an unevenness of social and political development which has led to a north–south division in Italy, and in France to conflicts between the primarily Catholic pre-1789 France of the old regime, the partially successful bourgeois political culture of the industrial revolution, and the unassimilated political culture of the industrial working class.

2. As a result, there is widespread alienation among these subcultures and general distrust and suspicion of the existing political system. Political roles in terms of the subculture constitute the important frame of reference.

[13]Niels Andren, *Modern Swedish Government* (Stockholm: Almquist & Wicksell, 1961), p. 20.

3. Social and political divisions even within the subcultures are deep and long standing, with groups viewing each other as enemies to the extent that bargaining and compromise are difficult if not impossible.

4. Government coalitions tend to be born in desperation, to operate in an atmosphere of constant suspicion, and to expire suddenly, with the legislatures serving as simply another battleground among the political parties and unmoderated interest groups.

5. Bureaucracies become infiltrated and lose their neutral, purely technical character. Interest groups often become either political parties or control parties. Conversely, political parties often control interest groups as ideological satellites.

French Interest Groups

Given these deep schisms and the subjective nature of political judgments, it is not surprising to find that, in the French political system, "public opinion does not consider an association or a group whose activity is considered praise-worthy as a pressure group."[14] In short, "*Our* group stands for the best interests of the nation as a whole, *their* group is concerned only with its own narrow, and probably disreputable, if not sinister, selfish interests."

This black and white evaluation of interest-group activity has been complicated still further by ideological and regional exclusiveness. Socialist, communist, and Catholic workers alike view factory owners as the natural enemy, but, on the other hand, the working-class groups themselves are ideologically impure in one way or another, thus making any unity impossible. For that matter, the feeling has been that within one's own subculture, there were groups simply not to be trusted.

French interest groups since the late nineteenth century have been characterized by both their extreme fragmentation and their inability to accomplish positive results. The weakness of the political parties and the unstable nature of governments under the Third and Fourth Republics have tended to give interest groups all too much opportunity for destructive political activity.

The inability of interest groups to achieve their demands through the political system probably goes far to explain the widespread and traditional role of anomic protest in the French system. Strikes and violent actions of all sorts have long been interest-group weapons. Peasant violence against governmental authority dates back to the chateau-burnings in the Middle Ages. Modern French farmers block-

[14]George E. Lavau, "Political Pressures by Interest Groups in France," in Ehrmann, *Interest Groups*, p. 61.

ade highways and push cars onto railroad tracks to dramatize their demands. Characteristically, the demands of French interest groups have always been stated in extreme terms that permitted no compromise.

Perhaps the most extreme examples of anomic violence in French interest-group activity have been the Poujadist movement of the mid-1950s, the emergence of the Army as an interest group in 1958 and 1961, and the student revolt of 1968. On numerous occasions, groups have launched strikes against taxes as a means of enforcing their demands, and this resistance has culminated at various times in tax collectors being literally tarred and feathered. After several years of particularly violent resistance by small shopkeepers to government efforts at more thorough tax collection, a small shopkeeper by the name of Pierre Poujade founded the Union of French Fraternity in 1955. On the simple platform of "pay no taxes," the union was able to elect fifty-two deputies in the 1956 elections. The Poujade movement very quickly destroyed itself through its own mindless excesses, but it mirrored an outlook of distrust and suspicion toward authority and all its works which has been characteristic before and since of interest-group attitudes in France.

Fragmented political systems such as the French and the Italian are characterized by an intermingling of situational and attitudinal interests. In Italy, for example, in late 1970 and early 1971, a rather routine dispute between two cities about which was to be designated the capital of the southern administrative region became a national issue dramatized by bloody rioting in Rome and elsewhere between communists and fascists.

In both France and Italy, situational interest groups have long played important roles in shaping public policy. In France, these groups have included, beside the labor unions, the Council of French Employers, the Confederation of Small and Medium-Sized Enterprises, the National Syndicate of Wine Growers, the National Association of Farmers' Syndicates, and the General Association of Beetgrowers.

Influence of Governmental Structure

Under the disorganized political systems of the French Third and Fourth Republics, the influence targets of these groups were widely dispersed. With power fluctuating so uncertainly, political parties, individual deputies, cabinet ministers, and the bureaucracy all had to be taken into consideration. Within the National Assembly, deputies sympathetic to an interest group worked to get their members on significant committees and to insure the appointment of sympathizers to key bureaucratic posts.

But little of this activity resulted in the winnowing out or synthesizing of the demands from the various interest groups. In the Third and Fourth Republics, most governments survived only by a few legislative votes. If even the smallest of the parliamentary groups in any coalition could be induced to withdraw its support, it was usually sufficient to bring the cabinet down. Thus, most interest groups were in a position to effect a negative vote on any measure they disliked simply by winning over support of one party in the government coalition. But the reverse of this was that no group was able to bring about any positive results for its measures. The result was a frustrating stalemate which contributed substantially to the tendency to anomic protest.

Individual deputies were able to survive only because of their personal relations with their constituents. Lacking that disciplined party support which enabled the British parliamentarian to act independently, the French deputy had no choice but to feed raw interest-group demands into the legislative process whether he agreed with them or not. When they were not buried in committee, the results bore little relation to any coherent program or any kind of thoughtful policy formulation.

The constitutional shift in power from the legislative to the executive branch which has taken place under the Fifth Republic has apparently brought about a reorientation of not only interest-group activity but also operational styles. Interest groups now must deal with a greatly strengthened executive and career bureaucracy rather than dispersed parties or isolated deputies. The result has been to introduce the technical experts who, very much in the American pattern, are able to talk to fellow experts or former colleagues in their own language. One student of interest groups under the Fifth Republic quotes a French observer as noting that "increasingly there is a dialogue between the 'men of the big lobbies' and the technocrats who speak the same language and usually come from the same class."[15] But, on the other hand, the groups unable financially or psychologically to adapt to the new circumstances or too closely allied with the now greatly weakened parties of the left—above all the trade unions—have lost influence as a result.

Unchanged under the Fifth Republic is the role played by special advisory councils to the various ministries, composed of the concerned interest groups. As in the case of the Fourth Republic, there exists a special advisory Economic and Social Council composed of representatives of the important situational interest groups and technical experts. But again, as in the case of the Fourth Republic, the interest groups have worked through either legislative

[15]Quoted by Bernard E. Brown, "Pressure Politics in the Fifth Republic," *Journal of Politics* 25 (August 1963): 525.

or executive channels with the result that the Economic and Social Council (intended to be the third house of parliament) has been little consulted and apparently has seldom exerted much influence in the development of either legislation or policy. A similar provision in the constitution of the Italian Republic has proven equally ineffective. This is only one reason why Italy and France are almost classic examples of a fragmented political system.

Italian Interest Groups

Professors Almond and Verba in their comparative survey of various political cultures have characterized Italian political culture as "one of relatively unrelieved political alienation and of social isolation and distrust."[16] In similar terms, the leading authority on Italian interest groups describes Italian political culture as "highly fragmented and isolative."[17] It is not surprising, then, to find that Italian interest groups involved in political activity are almost uncountable. Professor La Palombara estimates that "in Rome alone there are probably 3,000 different voluntary associations that might possibly intervene in the political process." Given the highly fragmented political culture in Italy, it is difficult, if not impossible, to place many of these organizations clearly in either the situational or the attitudinal category. Frequently both are involved.

Among the major categories of associational interest groups, La Palombara notes employer and industrial, professional, trade union, agricultural, veterans, Catholic, women, and various miscellaneous groupings. Although a number of these groups stress the fact that they are nonparty or nonpolitical, this more often than not is apparently to avoid being identified with any particular political party. But obviously, as in the case of France, there is "colonization" of interest groups by parties and the reverse of this in terms of interest groups largely dominating a particular party. Examples of the first situation are the communist and socialist domination of trade unions in both Italy and France while in Italy the Christian Democrats are particularly influential among women's groups.

La Palombara found that Italian associational interest groups are engaged in a variety of regular and constant interaction. Table 2 shows the results of a survey of 58 groups in connection with types and frequency of group interaction.

As La Palombara notes, the fact that 62 percent of those reporting have contact with other organizations does not belie the "unrelieved political alienation" or the "isolative"

[16]Almond and Verba, *Civic Culture,* p. 308.

[17]Joseph La Palombara, *Interest Groups in Italian Politics* (Princeton, N.J.: Princeton University Press, 1964), p. 55.

Table 2
Italian Interest-Group Interactions by Percentage (N = 58)

Type of contact	Often	Once in a while	Rarely	Never	Not reporting
Other organizations	62	28	7	0	3
Political parties	19	12	7	33	29
National conference	35	62	4	0	0
Local conferences	40	35	4	0	21
Public opinion organs	48	24	16	0	12
Parliamentary	50	11	15	8	16
Propaganda and publicity	61	11	7	5	16
Public administration	67	19	9	1	4
Local public bodies	54	19	11	0	16

NOTE: This table is adapted from Table 10 in La Palombara's *Interest Groups in Italian Politics*. Copyright © 1964, Princeton University Press.

character of Italian political life. Rather, he notes, the contacts for almost all the groups are routinely only with those in their own political subcultures. As far as political contacts are concerned, more than two-thirds of the groups report the most contacts with public administration.

A significant factor in this is the emergence of that positive state we spoke of in Chapter 1. As we noted, the impact of any piece of legislation is determined by the fashion in which the bureaucracy interpets and applies it. Given the widespread tendency to enact broadly authorizing legislation which simply delegates powers to the bureaucracy, administrators become a key target for interest-group pressures. Added to this, the widespread involvement of the modern state in every aspect of social welfare activity makes career civil servants not only powerful but omnipresent.

The pattern of access to the Italian bureaucracy, La Palombara suggests, "is *structured* rather than *fluid*." By this is meant that not all groups have equal access to the decision-makers and that actually, given the social composition of the bureaucracy, left-wing groups find it difficult and sometimes impossible to present their case. Illustrating that penetration of the bureaucracy characteristic of the fragmented political systems are the patron-client and "clan" relationships between government agencies and various interest groups, particularly those in the business and financial categories or within the sphere of influence of the long-dominant and Catholic-oriented Christian Democratic party.

The Army as Interest Group

It is an interesting aspect of political activity everywhere in the world today that military forces have become either active or potential factors in interest-group activity. Their presence is felt in every type of political system including the American. Their role, however, is no longer predominantly in terms of the traditional picture of tanks rumbling through the streets of the capital or civilian officials being ousted from their office at bayonet point. Far more commonplace now is the role of the army as a situational interest group, although one with unique means of persuasion available in any ultimate test of will. The interests of any army as an interest group in any industrialized or relatively technologically advanced society are very much concerned with achieving the maximum favorable possible allocation of values on its behalf. As we shall see in our discussion of the totalitarian political systems, this is as true for these systems as it is for any fragmented or developing political system.

INTEREST GROUPS IN THE TOTALITARIAN POLITICAL SYSTEM

Not so long ago to have talked of interest groups in the so-called totalitarian systems would have seemed a contradiction. For by definition a totalitarian system was one with only one party and/or one leader in absolute and unquestioned control of all policy decisions. No outside groups played any part in the political process. Even within the monolithic party, the will of the leader or the political bureau was arbitrarily determined and unquestioningly enforced. Based on ruthless force and unhindered terror, the power of totalitarian systems was obvious.

But as one of the earliest students of totalitarian systems pointed out thirty years ago, this impressive power has always had a peculiarly shapeless quality to it.[18] In both the Soviet and the German Nazi totalitarian regimes there has been formal authority without power as in the case of the official legislative bodies or the party congresses. The facade of authority and the reality of power have always been two different things. Where the reality was has always, however, been a major problem in any totalitarian system. In the Nazi system there was endless competition for power among different factions within the party and between the party itself, the secret police, the army officers' corps, the bureaucracy, big business interests, and the courtiers around Hitler. Under such conditions is can be argued that interest groups, particularly of an institutional and associational character, are as active behind the monolithic facade of a totalitarian system as they routinely are in societies where their presence is taken for granted.

[18]Franz Neumann, *Behemoth: The Structure and Practice of National Socialism* (New York: Oxford University Press, 1942), pp. 459 ff.

Latent Pluralism in the Soviet System

The world's most successful and longest-enduring totalitarian state, the Soviet Union, on the surface has been able to maintain a far greater semblance of regimented unity than ever was the case in Nazi Germany. Since the Tenth Party Congress of 1921, "factions" have been forbidden within the party and outright military discipline has been imposed since 1919.

But, although officially nonexistent for most of the life of the Soviet Union, "certain characteristics of the Soviet social and political systems are potentially or latently pluralistic."[19] Within the party itself it has long been commonplace to analyze policy developments in terms of the power struggle between the bureaucrats of the party apparatus, itself by no means a unified group, and the industrial managers supported by nonparty technocrats.[20] Khrushchev's ouster in 1964 made it clear that the party bureaucrats were still in control but, as the Soviet Union becomes increasingly a "technetronic" society, conflict between the industrial interest group and the party apparatus seems likely to intensify.[21]

One of the most interesting and potentially significant developments in the surfacing of Soviet interest groups, however, is the mounting public conflict between the party apparatus and the Soviet intellectual elite. Because of the Soviet Union's continuing competition with the United States, this group, particularly its scientific portion, has had a certain bargaining position which has given it some opportunity to express its desire for a freer society. In his illuminating discussion of the intellectual opposition in the Soviet Union, Professor Feuer says, "There are always some hopeful signs that the Scientific and Literary Oppositions are making real headway." Various observers, he notes, "conclude that it may be that some sections of the secret police and regime are starting to collaborate with the democratic Opposition: that we are seeing the beginnings of an intellectual secession of the bureaucracy."

[19]Frederick C. Barghoorn, *Politics in the USSR* (Boston: Little, Brown, 1966), p. 42.

[20]Representation on the Central Committee has long demonstrated this division. The Central Committee chosen by the Nineteenth Party Congress in 1952 was broken down, for example, into the categories of party apparatus (80), industrial-managerial (36), and other smaller representations including Armed Forces (19).

[21]Of necessity, the directors and technicians of an advanced industrial society must be innovators who function imaginatively within a pattern of rationality and pragmatism. In almost instinctively hostile contrast to this are the men of the party apparatus characterized by a "mediocratic simplicism, an absence of brilliance, a colorless anonymity, an absence of any impulse to dissent from a decision handed down from above." (Lewis S. Feuer, "The Intelligentsia in Opposition," *Problems of Communism* 19 [Nov./Dec. 1970]: 2.)

If this is so, the role of interest groups in the Soviet political system should become not only more important but also more obvious. There are those Russian and foreign observers who predict anomic interest-group movements of titanic proportions if there is an extensive breakdown of the regime's ability to control the masses. Russia has had a long history of its "unknown, anonymous masses" reacting "in a savage and bestial way" when government control weakened. One member of the literary opposition in a widely discussed book published in the West has predicted that if the Soviet Union should collapse in a war with China, "the horrors of the Russian revolutions of 1905–07 and 1917–20 will then seem simply like idyllic pictures."[22]

Roles of the Soviet and the Chinese Military

But of all the developments which have taken place in the Soviet Union and China in connection with the surfacing of interest groups in monolithic societies, none is more significant than the emergence of the armed forces. Party domination of the armed forces has long been an accepted truism of the Soviet political system. It still is apparently the case, but now a price has to be paid for it. In the late 1950s, with the acquiescence of his fellow officers, the party was able to remove the Soviet Union's greatest war hero, Marshall Zhukov, both from his position as Minister of Defense and from important party posts. Such an action was in the long-existing pattern of party-army relations which included Stalin's bloody and systematic destruction in 1937 of the officers' corps as a potential opposition interest group.

But by the late 1960s Thomas W. Wolfe, a specialist on the Soviet military, observed:

> There has been widespread speculation in recent years, especially since the invasion of Czechoslovakia in August, 1968, that the Soviet military leaders have acquired unprecedented influence in the policy councils of the Brezhnev-Kosygin regime. Some Western observers have even argued that there has been a major shift of political power to the Soviet marshals.[23]

However, Wolfe's conclusions were "that the Soviet military leadership—as a pressure group operating within the Soviet ruling elite—has acquired greater prestige and influence during the Brezhnev-Kosygin tenure than it enjoyed under Khrushchev." And, between party officials and military, "there are," he comments, "various intractable issues which generate continuing internal controversy and ten-

[22]Andrei Amalrik, *Will the Soviet Union Survive until 1984?* (New York: Harper & Row, 1970), p. 65.

[23]Thomas W. Wolfe, "Are the Generals Taking Over?" *Problems of Communism* 18 (July/Aug., Sept./Oct. 1969): 106.

sion." Splits within the party leadership itself give additional opportunities for exerting military influence. But although they have become an important interest group, the Soviet military has, until now, neither challenged the party's ultimate authority or seemingly wished to do so. Quite different is the role in which their counterparts in the Chinese Army have been cast.

In 1959, under the leadership of Chairman Mao's trusted lieutenant, Marshal Lin Piao, the military leadership was purged, although apparently not so violently as in the Soviet Union in 1937, of all ranking officers opposed to Chairman Mao's personal domination of the party. The result was to make the army into the chief source of Mao's power. Since the purge the army, rather than the party, has been publicized as the chief defender of revolutionary virtue and the thoughts of Chairman Mao. In 1965, for example, sufficient army recruits were inducted into the party to raise its membership to include one-third of the army's total strength as compared with approximately 1/33 of the population at large.[24]

If it had not been for the unique demands made upon the army by the crisis of the Great Proletarian Cultural Revolution of 1966–1969, in all probability it would have remained an important but party-dominated interest group like its Soviet counterpart. However, when Mao launched his frenzied effort in 1966 to rekindle the original spirit of revolutionary idealism and purge the party, the army became his major instrument. It was the army which provided the organization and transportation for the teenage Red Guards created by Mao in an effort to mount a counterforce to the party. Throughout this period the army played a major role, which was capped by the official designation of Marshal Lin Piao as Mao's successor at the Ninth Party Congress in 1969.

Finally, it was the army which brought the excesses of the Red Guard under control in early 1969 when its anomic violence threatened to destroy the industrial and political base which the army considered essential to its vital interests. As of 1971, it is estimated that 12 of the 21 members of the party's highest governing body are army officers as are more than 50 percent of the members of the Central Committee. In China the army has become the dominant interest group to an extent without precedent in a communist state for the same reasons as those which have made the military such an important factor in the political systems of the developing nations. The military as an interest

[24]These paragraphs are based on Franz Michael, "The Struggle for Power," *Problems of Communism* 16 (May/June 1969): 12–21. The figures on Army membership are taken from p. 19. The at-large percentage is based on a party membership of 20 million in a population of 750 million.

group has a vested concern in social stability and technological development. It also, as we have noted, has not only a sense of mission but an unparalleled ability to insure that its demands on the political system receive prompt and careful attention.

Yugoslavian Interest Groups

It is interesting but not surprising that the most extensive development of situational interest groups has occurred in the highly pragmatic Yugoslav system. One observer commented in 1969:

> The liberalization of the Yugoslav economy has been accompanied by a burgeoning of economic associations, regional pressure groups, industrial lobbies, and other special interest groups as complex and varied as those encountered in the West. Not only do these groups exist and vigorously defend their interests, but their activities are recognized and even encouraged in certain ways by the government.[25]

INTEREST GROUPS IN THE POLITICAL SYSTEMS OF THE DEVELOPING NATIONS

Only in very broad and general terms can we even try to list the characteristics of the political systems in the developing nations. But to a degree, they do have these aspects in common:

1. There is a complete lack of any consensus on ends and means with several or more subcultures engaged in a constant and often violent power struggle.
2. Political activity is largely an elitist affair with poor political communication while the masses constitute an unpredictable factor which may not intervene in a political situation or may completely transform it by anomic violence.
3. Policy-making is dominated by rigid ideological considerations and intense partisan concern.
4. There is no clear role differentiation in terms of who does what or through which means; political parties may actually be ethnic or clan groupings while the government bureaucracy is often only an appendage of one or more political parties.
5. Political action oscillates between evolutionary development and revolutionary upheaval with military rule or anarchic disintergration ever-present possibilities.

It is clear that an extraordinary variety of interest groups is present in such political systems. Possibly masquerading as modern political parties, traditional nonassoci-

[25]Paul Shoup, "The Evolution of a System," *Problems of Communism* 18 (July/Oct. 1969): 71.

ational interest groups attempt to forward their clan, caste, regional, ethnic, class, or clique interests. At the same time the modernized sections of the developing society will have produced various associational interest groups. Most likely in this connection will be the emergence of trade unions. The reasons go back to the development of the nationalist movements during the colonial period. The emergence of a trade-union movement in developing countries is not necessarily related to the level of industrialization achieved. In a number of countries during the colonial period large-scale agricultural enterprises developed which were devoted to producing export crops. The mass-labor forces involved were automatic targets for the first efforts of the various nationalist movements when they first began to expand. In developing nations as far removed as Peru, Kenya, and Malaysia these union movements have become important elements in the over-all political system. They have been a particularly attractive area of operation for dynamic and ambitious young leaders frustrated by the status or other restrictions of the traditional social structure.

As we commented earlier, anomic interest groups are more prevalent and play a more consistently important role in the political systems of the developing nations than in any others. They are always the threatening X factor in the background while their sudden and violent eruption often decides the issue. In Iraq in 1958 and Indonesia in 1966 it was this kind of group pressure which shaped the course of developments. The importance they have is an indication of the fragility and the high degree of malfunctioning of the political systems concerned.

Institutional interest groups, particularly as personified by the armed forces, play a highly important role in the political systems of the developing nations. We have already suggested some of the reasons for this. Of necessity, any armed forces are technologically minded and rationally oriented. Their leadership possesses an emotionally conditioned sense of unity and mission usually associated with religious or ideological inspiration. Finally, it should be emphasized, the armed forces as an interest group have unique means of exerting pressure.

More often than not the impetus for armed-forces action has come from one particular subgroup, that of the middle-grade and junior officers. For many in this group, the armed forces of the newly independent state have offered a unique opportunity for upward social mobility. It has offered one of the few—if not the only—opportunities to escape from the web of status and custom of the traditional social order. By training, the middle-grade and junior officers are an important, if not the dominant, section of the new "technical-executive intelligentsia."[26]

[26]John J. Johnson, ed., *The Role of the Military in Under-developed Countries* (Princeton, N.J.: Princeton University Press, 1962), p. 23.

This group functions simultaneously in both situational and attitudinal terms. Often the dominant factor seems to be its desire to protect its vested interest in the "authoritative allocation of values." But the frequently progressive and idealistic reform programs launched by this particular interest group bear witness to the other motivations involved.[27]

Much can be said about the future of interest groups in the developing nations. It seems certain, however, that the role of the armed forces will continue to be an important one. Only in the unlikely event that a high level of economic development and social adjustment is achieved will the armed forces cease to be a key element. Even if these developments should occur, American experience demonstrates that as a situational interest group the military still remains a factor to be reckoned with.

Anomic Interest Groups in Developed Societies

We have noted that anomic interest groups are important in the fragile political systems of the developing nations. In the long-existing and stable political systems of the highly developed nations they have often been considered obsolete.

But in such highly advanced countries as Japan, France and the United States recent events have demonstrated that this is not so. It is possible that the increasingly complex and frustrating character of modern society may be a fertile breeding ground for anomic interest groups. That such a sophisticated and technologically advanced society as our own breeds a sense of personal alienation and futility has often been commented on. Even in the very dawn of the industrial revolution, mobs of displaced handicraft workers (the Luddites) rose in anarchic frenzy to smash their hated machines.

Today it is not the workers but students, the most socially sensitive and acutely aware of spontaneous attitudinal interest groups, who are the likeliest source of anomic protest in the advanced societies. As in the case of the developing societies, the causes which produce their alienation do not seem likely to disappear, so it seems logical to expect that the expanding student population of the developed societies will continue to furnish one of the chief sources of manpower for anomic protest in the 1970s.

In the United States, an even more likely source of anomic protest is racial tension. Inevitably the explosive situations provoking racial protest will occur in spite of the best efforts to prevent them or the most sweeping reform programs. Anomic interest groups, in many countries throughout the world, may well continue to exemplify how

[27]This is an old tradition—from the Russian Decembrist revolt of 1825 through the Egyptian officers' revolt of 1881 to the more famous Egyptian coup of 1952 to the military coup in Uganda in January, 1971.

grumbles explode into demands which are not so much presented as flung at the political system for solution.

CONCLUSION

Throughout this chapter we have constantly referred to political parties as closely connected with interest groups. In the Anglo-American system the "normal" sequence is for political parties to pull together and order in terms of importance the demands of interest groups. Only the occasional and somewhat exotic interest group ever actually turns itself into a party in its own right, though in other systems, lacking the consensus of the Anglo-American, this is commonplace. Whatever the relationship or the interaction between interest groups and political parties, in any contemporary political system the two are always found together. It behooves us then to survey the nature and purpose of political parties.

THE POLITICAL PARTY: CHARACTERISTICS, FUNCTIONS, ORGANIZATION

It has been said that political parties are the lifeline of modern politics. It is taken for granted that any country which either is modern or wants to be so considered will channel its political life in terms of some type of party expression. The absence or suppression of parties is regarded as a mark of political backwardness or of retrogression in political development. Indeed, a list of the countries that have never had any kind of political parties would have a significant correlation with those nations that are generally regarded as the world's most underdeveloped (e.g., Andorra, Ethiopia, Kuwait, Yeman, etc.).

Of the 146 independent states in the world, only 41 are without some type of party organization. Of these latter, 19 have never known any modern party activity, and 22 represent suppressed party systems now replaced by some type of personalized dictatorial rule, usually military in character. But even in both types of nonparty states, the factor of party is important. For the reformers in the traditionalist states, the achievement of some type of party expression is desired as a status symbol for modernity. For the opposition in the dictatorships, return to party government means the restoration of normal political activity. La Palombara and Weiner summarize the role of political parties in the contemporary world as follows:

> The political party is a creature of modern and modernizing political systems. Whether one thinks of Anglo-American democracies or totalitarian systems such as the Soviet Union, Fascist Italy, and Nazi Germany; emergent African states in their earliest years of independent evolution or Latin American republics that have hobbled along for over a century; a mammoth excolonial area such as India groping toward democracy or an equally mammoth Communist power such as China seeking to mobilize a population through totalitarian methods, the political party in one form or another is omnipresent.[1]

[1]Joseph La Palombara and Myron Weiner, eds., *Political Parties and Political Development* (Princeton, N.J.: Princeton University Press, 1966), p. 3.

In this chapter we shall look at political parties in a contemporary perspective. To begin, let us define the term *political party.*

WHAT IS A POLITICAL PARTY?

Almost every writer on parties begins by lamenting the difficulty of defining the term. As one student put it, "It is one of the inconveniences of political science, and telling evidence of the essentially non-scientific nature of our discipline, that there are no neatly edged definitions for our most common terms, such as 'political party.'" One reason for this difficulty, as another source explains it, is that

> the term "political parties" emerged in the nineteenth century with the development of representative institutions and the expansion of the suffrage in Europe and the United States. It designated organizations whose goal was the capture of public office in electoral competition with one or more other parties. Subsequently the term "party" was extended to include political organizations not engaged in electoral competition: minor parties which had no realistic expectations of gaining office through appeals to the electorate, revolutionary organizations seeking to abolish competitive elections, and the governing groups in totalitarian states.[2]

Further complicating the problem of definition is the often-debated question of whether one-issue political parties are *really* parties or whether they are interest groups masquerading as parties. For instance, are the American Prohibition Party or the French Poujadists of the mid-1950s with their "pay-no-taxes" program really entitled to be regarded as political parties?

The eighteenth-century English statesman Edmund Burke defined a political party as "a body of men united for promoting by their joint endeavors the national interests upon some particular principle on which they all agreed." But this programmatic definition fails to specify either how the joint endeavors are to be carried out or structured. Burke's definition serves equally well to describe the activities of an interest group.

In contrast, a contemporary behavioralist defines a political party as a social group:

> It has an authority structure and . . . distinctive patterns of power distribution. It has a representative process, an electoral system, and subprocesses for recruiting leaders, defining goals, and resolving internal system conflict. Above all, the party

[2]Joseph A. Schlesinger, "Party Units" in "Parties, Political," *International Encyclopedia of the Social Sciences* (New York: Macmillan, 1968), 11:428.

is a decision-making system. . . . The political party, thus, conforms to the common characteristics of social groups.[3]

While this definition establishes the not very arguable proposition that a political party is an example of group activity, we are still far away from understanding its unique nature.

In more specific terms La Palombara and Weiner define a political party as having these characteristics:

> (1) continuity in organization—that is, an organization whose expected life span is not dependent on the life span of current leaders; (2) manifest and presumably permanent organization at the local level, with regularized communications and other relationships between local and national units; (3) self-conscious determination of leaders at both national and local levels to capture and to hold decision-making power alone or in coalition with others, not simply to influence the exercise of power, and (4) a concern on the part of the organization for seeking followers at the polls or in some manner striving for popular support.[4]

The first two points of this definition still do not help us distinguish between an interest group and a political party, but we begin to see, for the first time, the distinctive characteristics of a political party. Both interest group and political party are a combination of individuals involved in political action to make their objectives priority items in society's authoritative allocation of values, but the interest group does this *without the group itself necessarily assuming formal control of the governmental process.* In the phraseology of La Palombara and Weiner, its purpose is "simply to influence the exercise of power." The combination of individuals comprising a political party, on the other hand, seek to make their objectives priority items in society's authoritative allocation of values *by assuming formal control of the governmental process through placing its leaders in policy-making positions as a result of some sort of election procedures involving large numbers of voters.*

A political party, then, exists to get and keep control of power. To achieve this legitimately, a party today must use some type of electoral system to offer candidates for public office who are pledged to carry out the party's program. In competitive party systems, these candidates and the party's program are properly legitimized when accepted by the voters by even the slimmest margin. In noncompet-

[3]Samuel J. Eldersveld, *Political Parties: A Behavioral Analysis* (Chicago: Rand McNally, 1964), p. 1.

[4]La Palombara and Weiner, *Political Parties and Political Developments,* p. 6.

itive situations, where only one party offers its program and candidates for approval, there seems to be a compulsion on the part of the ruling party, long evidenced in the Soviet Union, to demonstrate that there is such near-unanimous acceptance of the party's claim to authority that any need for alternative choices is quite irrelevant.

On this basis we can accept as a political party any group which offers candidates for office and seeks the voters' endorsement of its election program. Whether the party is concerned with a single issue or an extensive program of issues is irrelevant. Whether it has a reasonable prospect of electing its candidates or none is also irrelevant. Its status as an official political party is not even affected by the fact that the sole purpose in going through the ritual of presenting candidates and offering an election platform is simply to exploit another area for long-range propaganda purposes having little to do with taking power by constitutional means. By our definition, however ritualistic or insincere the gesture, if a group presents candidates in an election, it qualifies as a political party.

To push this definition a step further, a group such as the Weathermen may regard its primary purpose as changing the social order by terror and violence, but if it formally contests elections, then it is a political party. If it does not, then it is a terrorist social group. The best actual illustration of this basic difference was afforded by the Communist party of the United States, which in 1944, as a contribution to United States-Soviet harmony, announced its withdrawal from the political arena by transforming itself into the American Communist Political Association dedicated, so it was said, entirely to a program of information and education.

To get and keep control of power, the group in question must have an organized structure, however inadequate it may be. So far, then, we have accepted three out of four of the characteristics of a political party set down by La Palombara and Weiner. Their first point, however, that a party must have "continuity in organization" with an existence "not dependent on the life span of current leaders," would exclude from the definition of a political party a number of bona fide parties, which, although their existence was brief, left their mark on their times.

For example, although it contested only one election, the French Poujadist movement of the mid-1950s was an important and disruptive force while it lasted. And in this country, who could rule out as a political party the American Independent Party, whose charismatic leader Governor Wallace of Alabama received almost 10 million votes in the presidential election of 1968?

To summarize, the following are the minimum characteristics which a social group must have to be considered a political party:

1. It must have some type of organizational structure.
2. It must offer candidates for elective office on the basis of a party program.
3. It must try to attract as much popular support as possible.

The Political Party as a Variable

A political party is a variable constantly playing three dynamic roles. It may be simultaneously an intervening, a dependent, and an independent variable, but the most obvious aspect of a political party's activities is in terms of its role as an *intervening* variable, for in this function it serves as the link between the official governmental structure and the general political community. In varying degree, depending on whether it is in office or in opposition, a party interprets government policy to its supporters and to the public at large. It also passes along to government the demands fed into the political system, and it is, or should be, constantly involved in testing public opinion for the purpose of calculating how to stay in office or how to get into office. Functioning as this type of variable, the party is the essential intervening link between government and the political community.

The fashion in which a political party is structured by its leaders to carry out this task and the style in which it does so are determined by the over-all character of the political culture in which the party functions. The nature of the governmental framework, the social divisions of the society, the cultural patterns which shape thought and action, and the laws and regulations affecting party action all constitute the independent variables which condition the party as a dependent variable.

In addition to its intervening and dependent roles, to some degree every party functions as an independent variable. It is not only "a system of meaningful and patterned activity within the larger society"; it is often a highly integrated subculture. As such it can be the original and dynamic source of actions which shape the nature of the whole society. Where there are two or more competing parties, the influence of any one party will be limited or moderated. But in those polities where one party is in a position to control the whole pattern of social and political order, it is often the independent variable which molds both government and society according to the blueprint of the party's program for achieving the just society. In Chapter 5 we shall discuss this type of party action in terms of the movement regimes.

The Functions of a Political Party

Keeping in mind the way in which the functions performed by any political party are influenced by the changing and interlocking variability of the roles it plays, we can detail these functions as follows:

1. Organization. The party provides a means for like-minded men to organize themselves systematically in order to make the maximum effort to get peaceful control of the machinery of government so as to carry out their party's program.

2. Issues. Whether it is competitive or monopolistic, no party lacks a program which allegedly offers solutions to all the pressing problems of its society. Priorities in the program are determined by the energy and expertise with which the interest groups concerned have made their cases. Not only by its aggregation of interest-group concerns but by assigning the issues an order of importance, the party insures some sort of orderly processing of demands.

In connection with issues, reference is often made to the party "educating the public." Certainly, it is as often a case of the public educating the party. Further, in those regimes where one party controls both government and society, there is usually but little objective "education" on the crucial issues. Rather there is a calculated and intensive effort to persuade or coerce the masses into accepting both the party's version of what are the crucial issues and the correct solutions.

3. Leaders. In any society the recruitment and selection of leaders is vital. If there is no systematic and structured procedure for their selection and replacement, the power struggle can either destroy the state involved, particularly if it is new and lacking in firm legitimacy, or so seriously weaken it that its eventual disintegration becomes inevitable. However varied the procedures involved, parties do recruit potential leaders and offer a peaceful means for their selection and replacement through some type of electoral process.

4. Legitimation. Governmental authority, as we have noted earlier, is simply the legitimate exercise of power. In a modern polity, it is government regulation which organizes the machinery to accomplish this. But, as noted in the preceding point, it is party which initially screens the potential power-wielders and presents them for the legitimation ritual.

5. Policy-Making. Here again, as in the case of legitimation, it is the factor of party which gives reality to the theoretical constitutional allocation of policy-making authority in the governmental structure. Party programs give coherence to legislation while party organization facilitates its passage. And it is party which makes it possible for

several hundred legislative representatives to conduct their official business with an acceptable degree of success.

6. Governmental Responsibility. Party control of the policy-making machinery of government provides public focus for praise or blame. Success and failure are explicable and controllable. They are the party's responsibility. In competitive party systems the dissatisfied citizen has an opportunity to "turn the rascals out." And in those political systems controlled by a movement-regime party, the party stays in power, but failures in, say, five-year plans or international negotiations are attributed to individual party members who are then purged for their alleged sabotage of the party's otherwise perfect solutions to the problem in question.

7. Modernization. In transitional societies the role performed by parties as a catalyst for modernization needs little comment. From the time of the economic and social planning inaugurated in the Soviet Union in the 1920s to the present, the party's vision for the future implemented by the dedicated enthusiasm and organizational discipline of its members has provided the necessary catalyst for the transformation of transitional societies. Especially in the new nations, the way in which the parties concerned cope with the problems of political development will have a significant effect on both parties and governments. As Weiner and La Palombara summarize it:

> How well governments deal with the crises of political development in the majority of the developing nations that now live under party governments (approximately 65 out of 83 countries) is in part affected by the character and performance of parties. In turn, the future of parties depends upon how successful they and their governments are in coping with the crisis of political development.[5]

DEGREES OF PARTY INVOLVEMENT

We have discussed the various roles in which a party may function as though the party had an individual life of its own, over and above the individuals who make it up. While it is convenient to talk of a party or an interest group in these terms, no group or organization exists or acts except through the individuals who comprise its membership. The degree of effectiveness with which any political party functions is in direct ratio not only to the number of its adherents but also to the intensity of support it receives from them. This is an important aspect of party existence which we must examine.

At the very start, there is an important point that should be kept in mind. This is the fundamental difference in the

[5]*Ibid.*, p. 435.

concept of party membership in the United States and most European and Afro-Asian countries.

Party Involvement in the United States

Membership in a party is more often than not simply a state of mind. If someone *says* or *feels* that he is a Democrat or a Republican, then he must be so counted. Even when there is need to make a public declaration of party adherence, usually in order to vote in a party primary, it is still the simplest of procedures. Nothing more is involved than going to the county voting registrar and simply asking to be enrolled as a Democrat or a Republican.

In their definition of what constitutes party membership, many American political scientists do not even regard the official act of registration as necessary. Rather, writes Austin Ranney:

> Whatever the differences in emphasis among the writers here in question, all of them are recognizably committed to what may be called the *ticket-voting* conception of party membership, according to which any citizen of the Republic who more or less regularly *votes* for the candidates of a given party must be deemed a full-fledged member of that party, with the same claim to an equal share in its decision-making processes as those who assume greater obligations toward the party and tender it greater services.[6]

In their authoritative study *Democracy and the American Party System,* Ranney and Kendall distinguish six circles of *involvement* within an American party. Beginning with the innermost circle and working out in ever-widening rings, they are: (1) leaders, (2) workers, (3) primary participants, (4) registrants, (5) regular supporters, and (6) occasional supporters.

The *leaders* are those who have the final say in party affairs, who personify the party for the general public. This group, says Ranney, includes "the candidates, the chairmen and members of party committees and conventions, and 'the bosses.'" The *workers* are the organization men who keep the party machinery functioning whether their motivation is patronage or a fascination with "the great game of politics." Together with the leaders they constitute the *cadre,* that relatively small group of experienced and skilled professionals who devote all or most of their energies to insure that an organization, whether it be a political party or a professional army, continues as a going concern. The fact that U.S. party *organization* essentially begins and ends with leaders and workers explains why, as

[6]Austin Ranney and Willmoore Kendall, *Democracy and the American Party System* (New York: Harcourt, Brace, Jovanovich, 1956), p. 202.

we shall discuss later, it is often appropriately referred to as a cadre-type system.

Ranney and Kendall's *partipants* are those who "in general participate in the party's nominating process—at least to the extent of ratifying or rejecting the candidates selected by the leaders and actively supported by the workers." *Registrants* are those who have felt strongly enough to place their party affiliation on public record so that they have the legal right to participate in party primaries, although Ranney notes that routinely only about 10 percent to 30 percent of all registered voters ever trouble to exercise this right.

The *regular supporters* correspond to *"ticket-voters,"* and the *occasional supporters* are voters who usually support their respective parties, except when they vote for opposition candidates or do not bother to vote at all. But, when asked to state political preference, they still classify themselves as Democratic or Republican.

European Party Involvement

Perhaps the best known description of the degrees of involvement in party activity in Western Europe is that given by Duverger in his classic *Political Parties.* He writes,

> Within parties in which no system of formal membership exists three concentric circles of participation can be distinguished. The widest comprises the *electors* who vote for the candidates put forward by the parties at local and national elections. . . . The second circle is made up of *supporters,* a vague term for a vague concept . . . the supporter is an elector, but more than an elector: he acknowledges that he favors the party; he defends it and sometimes he supports it financially; he even joins bodies ancillary to the party. The terms fellow-traveller and crypto-communist, often employed nowadays, designate supporters. Finally the third, the inmost circle, is composed of the *militants;* they consider themselves to be members of the party . . . they see to its organization and its operation; they direct its propaganda and its general activities. The "caucus-men" of the cadre parties are militants. In parties that have *members,* these constitute a fourth circle, intermediate between the last two: wider than the circle of militants, narrower than the circle of supporters: membership involves a greater degree of participation than the sympathy of the supporter, but less than militancy.[7]

There is obviously a certain correlation between Duverger's European-oriented typology of party involvement and Ranney's United States perspective. Ranney's occa-

[7]Maurice Duverger, *Political Parties,* trans. Barbara and Robert North (New York: Wiley, 1954), pp. 90–91. It is unfortunate that Duverger uses an illustration so closely linked to the communist party since any party may have its fellow-travelers.

sional and regular supporters correspond to Duverger's category of electors while his supporters correlate with Ranney's registrants and primary participants. Duverger's category of militants covers a broad stratum of party activity, which Ranney breaks down into workers and leaders.

The essential difference between the major United States parties and most European and Afro-Asian parties is that in the latter category, comprising most of the political parties in the world, the concept of membership has a precise and quantitatively definable meaning. For these parties, a member is someone who quite literally joined the party by visiting a party headquarters, enrolling himself as a member, receiving a numbered party membership card, and pledging to pay regular monthly dues for the support of the party as well as giving it consistent electoral support. There are, of course, as Duverger points out, "enormous differences that divide parties on the question of counting their membership." Some parties count as members anyone who has ever enrolled, while other parties define members as those who actively participate in party activities. Still others count as members only those who are current in their payments of party dues.

How alien the concept of party membership is to American political culture is demonstrated by the fact that if an American were to be referred to as a "card-carrying party member," most would infer that he must belong to the Communist party. In the European and Afro-Asian organizational framework, however, the chances are equally good that he might be a card-carrying member of the Catholic or Nationalist or Farmers parties.

ROOTS OF ANGLO-AMERICAN PARTY ORGANIZATION

Political parties developed in direct ratio to the growth of representative institutions and the development of mass democracy. In his examination of this process, Max Weber distinguished three stages in the emergence of modern parties: the "pure followings of the aristocracy" in the eighteenth century, the "parties of notables" under the limited-franchise conditions of the nineteenth century, and the highly structured party "machine" in the twentieth century as a result of the advent of *plebiscitarian* democracy.[8]

In different terms, but accepting the same general evolutionary pattern, Duverger sees the three-stage development of party organization as starting with a series of power struggles within the legislative branch among shifting and kaleidoscopic groups whose members were elected

[8]Max Weber, "Politics as a Vocation," in *From Max Weber: Essays in Sociology*, ed. C. Wright Mills and H. H. Gerth (New York: Oxford University Press, 1946), pp. 100–103.

on so narrow a franchise that only the most temporary and rudimentary of organization was needed to obtain office.[9] Then, with the first enlargement of the franchise, these parliamentary groups found it necessary to form electoral committees in order to mobilize support. Finally, with the advent of mass democracy, the modern party structure became necessary in order to organize the large numbers of voters. Both Weber's and Duverger's typologies are accurate enough descriptions of the developmental pattern for organized political activity in the United States, Great Britain, and, to a large extent, in the countries of Western Europe. However, as we shall see shortly, the relationship between the existence of legislative institutions, the gradual enlargement of the franchise, and the growth of party organization is by no means a universal explanation for the appearance of political parties, particularly in the new nations of Asia and Africa.

At a very early date in British political history, the idea of a representative assembly as the focus of governmental authority became the dominant element in constitutional development while elsewhere in Western Europe the so-called enlightened despots held sway. As early as the thirteenth century, for example, the recognizable outlines of the modern Anglo-American electoral system had already appeared. Members of the House of Commons were elected from single-member districts as a result of having been chosen by a larger number, though not necessarily a majority, of the qualified voters of that district than any other candidate.

From medieval times until the 1860s, very little effort was needed to organize election campaigns for Members of Parliament because of the small number of voters involved in proportion to the total population. As late as 1832, for example, just prior to the first extension of voting rights, less than half a million British citizens from a total population of about 14,000,000 owned sufficient property to have the right to vote. This meant that the voters in any individual election district might number a few hundred or, in extreme cases, since no reapportionment of voting districts had taken place since the fifteenth century, as few as two or three qualified property owners.

Weber's description of the members of the eighteenth-century House of Commons as "pure followings of the aristocracy" was aptly chosen, for the membership was

[9]In 1788, for example, a breakdown of the House of Commons divided its 557 members as follows: (1) Party of the Crown—185, (2) Party attached to Mr. Pitt—52, (3) (Four) Detached Parties supporting the Present Administration—43, (4) Independent or Unconnected Members of the House—108, (5) Opposition to the Present Administration (Parties attached to Mr. Fox and Lord North)—155, (6) Absentees and Neutrals—14. Quoted by Avery Leiserson, *Parties and Politics* (New York: Knopf, 1958), p. 59, n. 3.

composed of the relations or faithful clients of those great English aristocratic land-owning families who dominated political life well into the twentieth century. As much as the smallness of the electorate, the close social homogeneity of the Members of Parliament and their constituents explain the lack of any structured political activity. Everyone who was anyone in political life belonged almost literally to the same club. In the eighteenth and well into the nineteenth centuries, many a parliamentary "election" was decided well in advance by the members of the local establishment as they sat and talked it out over after-dinner port. Particularly in the eighteenth century, often the only name presented to the few hundred voters of a typical election district was that of the approved establishment candidate. Since no residence requirements were necessary for candidacy, the buying and selling of these "safe" seats was often a profitable sideline for those members of the local gentry who controlled them.

To describe this control of political activity by a self-appointed group of locally influential individuals, Duverger has adopted the political term *caucus:*

> The first characteristic of the caucus is its limited nature. It consists of a small number of members and seeks no expansion. . . . It does not readily admit members, for this limited group is also a closed group; you do not get into it simply because you desire to do so; membership is achieved only by a kind of tacit co-option or by formal nomination. In spite of this numerical weakness the caucus nevertheless wields great power. Its strength does not depend on the number of its members but on their quality. It is a group of notabilities chosen because of their influence.[10]

Perhaps the most vivid account of how a caucus functioned is provided by John Adams, who in 1763 penned a description in his journal of the fashion in which the notables of Boston stage-managed the political life of that city. Adams wrote:

> This day learned that the Caucus club meets at certain times in the garret of Tom Dawes, the Adjutant of the Boston regiment. . . . There they smoke tobacco till you cannot see from one end of the garret to the other. There they drink flip, I suppose, and they choose a moderator who puts questions to the vote regularly; and selectmen, assessors, collectors, firewards, *and representatives are regularly chosen before they are chosen in the town.*[11]

At the time, the property qualifications for voting in Massachusetts were little different from the requirements in Great Britain itself. It is worth remembering that historians estimate that so limited was the franchise in the

[10] Duverger, *Political Parties,* p. 18.

[11] Quoted by Ranney and Kendall, *Democracy and the Party System,* p. 101. (Italics are in original.)

United States in 1789 that approximately only one out of every fifteen adult American males was eligible to vote for the members of the various state constitutional conventions that adopted the Constitution.

The first enlargement of the franchise in Britain took place in 1832. In quantitative terms it was not particularly impressive, since it extended voting rights to only another 250,000 males, giving the right to vote to approximately one out of every six. It was not until the voting reforms of 1867 and 1885 that significant strides were made toward universal manhood suffrage. But not until 1918 did the last 25 percent of British adult males or any females receive the vote.

As quantitatively small as was the expansion of voting rights in 1832, it did represent a 50 percent increase in the voting public, and this required a more extensive system of organization than the old caucus system had provided. The result was a rapid growth between 1832 and 1867 of local registration associations primarily concerned with registering new voters and organizing campaigns. Their organization was a combination of the efforts of parliamentary representatives, local party notables, and interested organizations. In the period following the electoral reform act of 1867, these local associations were brought together by the two principal parties into a national federation governed by a national executive committee chosen at an annual conference.

The final step in the emergence of modern British party organization occurred in the twentieth century with the decline of the Liberal party and its replacement by the Labour party, which was based on the organizational system of *branches* composed of dues-paying members. "The branch," says Duverger, "is a Socialist invention." For the labor and socialist movements, experience in union organization preceded by some decades political participation on a national scale. Thus the organizational structure of unions with their central offices, locals, and collection of dues as the chief means of financing seemed obvious and logical for political activity when the time was finally ripe.

The superior efficiency of the new branch type of organization forced the old middle-class parties to adopt the same format in order to survive. Where there was a strong socialist movement, Duverger held, the adoption of the branch system was inevitable by both left and right. And, once again, the organizational development of British parties in the twentieth century appears to give credence to Duverger's thesis, for both the Labour and Conservative parties are organized on a branch basis. Between them they furnish the prototypes for one of the most complicated systems of branch organization in the world (the Labour party) and one of the simplest (the Conservative party).

Organization of the British Labour Party

The membership structure of the Labour Party reflects its origins in the union movement of the late nineteenth century. Its membership includes both trade unions as units and union members as individuals enrolled in the local party branches. Of the total membership, some 5.5 million members come from trade-union enrollment, with an additional 900,000 direct individual members. Not every trade union or every member of every trade union is affiliated with the Labour party. But in those unions whose executive committees have voted affiliation, unless the individual member indicates otherwise, a certain portion of his union dues are earmarked for Labour party contribution. Addi-

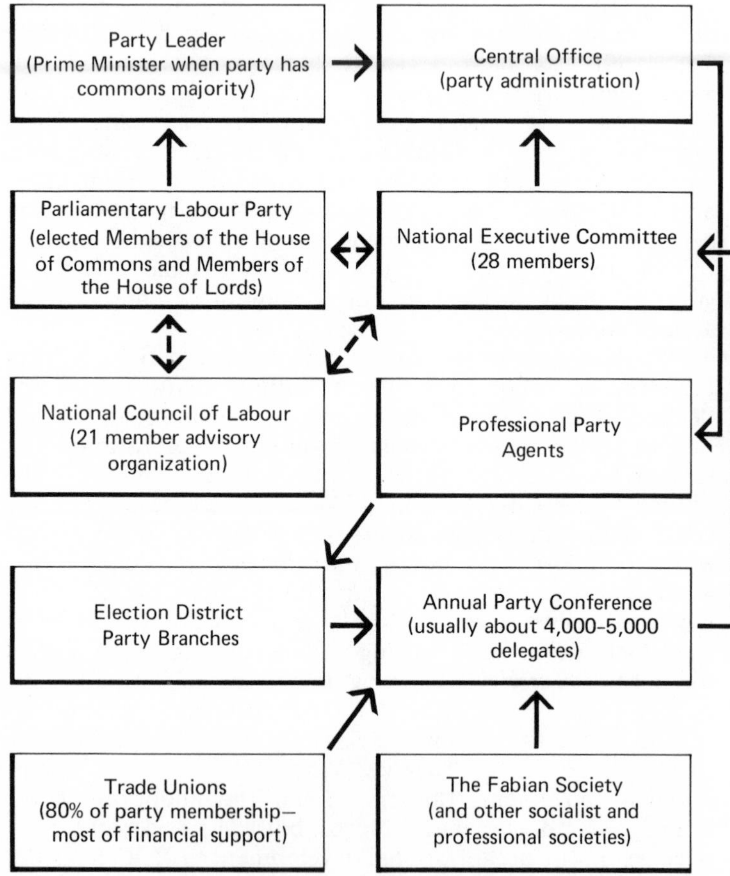

Note: Trade unions as such, but not all members of a union can belong to the Labour party. Any union member who chooses not to have a deduction made from his union dues for Labour party support has the well-established legal right to do so.

Figure 3
Organization of the British Labour Party

tionally many Labour party candidates are directly sponsored by a particular local union. (See Figure 3.)

Also included in the group membership category are a number of socialist organizations of which the most famous is the Fabian Society, the Labour party's long-time brain trust. Established in 1883 as a discussion and propaganda group for socialist intellectuals for the purpose of "reconstructing society in accordance with the highest moral possibilities," its membership has numbered some of the most distinguished British intellectuals of the twentieth century, including George Bernard Shaw, H. G. Wells, and Bertrand Russell.

Among the *affiliated groups* is the British Cooperative party, which formally transformed itself in 1918 from an interest group to a political party by deciding to contest elections. However, it has always supported the Labour party as the most practical alternative, and its own spokesmen are elected to Parliament as Labour-Coop representatives. Those individual members of the Labour party who have joined the party on a personal rather than a group basis are organized into the *constituency parties,* which are present in a majority of the 630 election districts into which Great Britain is divided.

From the affiliated groups and the constituency parties, delegates are elected to an annual conference which, in theory at least, lays down the policy guidelines for the party for the following year. Each Labour delegate has a voting card for every 1,000 members of his organization whose dues are current. This explains why, although only a few thousand delegates may be present, press reports of Labour party conferences speak of motions having been carried by half a million votes or so. In terms of voting strength at the annual conference, it is estimated that the six largest trade unions can approve or defeat any resolution. According to Labour policy, the party leader is supposed to appear before the conference to give an account of his management of party affairs and accept the reactions of the delegates.

One of the traditional differences between the Labour and Conservative parties is supposed to be that the Labour leader is truly held accountable, whereas his Conservative counterpart exercises an autocratic control over his party. The truth of the matter seems to be that the status of Labour and Conservative leaders has grown more and more alike. In both parties, the leader, whether currently prime minister or not, and the members of the party's parliamentary delegation, have the dominant voice in the determination of party policy.

On a somewhat complicated basis intended to give representation to all the diverse elements in the party, the annual conference elects the National Executive Committee which supervises party activity and governs policy in between annual conferences. Under the NEC is the Central Office, which comprises the career bureaucracy of the party organization. The Central Office (Transport House) is responsible for keeping the party in a constant state of readiness for the next general elections by providing speakers, carrying on research, conducting public relations, and training professional party agents responsible for the efficient functioning of the constituency parties.

Working closely with the NEC is both the parliamentary Labour party, composed of the elected members of Parliament and the National Council of Labour, composed of senior members from the most important trade unions who serve as advisors on general policy and, in terms of the votes and finances they control, are in a powerful position to cast a deciding voice.

Organization of the Conservative Party

Unlike Labour, which first developed its organization as a mass party before it ever held governmental authority, the Conservative party represents the successful modification of an elitist party of notables into a modern mass party. But the Conservative party gives more deference to its leader than does Labour, and its branches are not as active. (See Figure 4.)

The National Union of Conservative and Unionist Associations is a federation of constituency associations. The central council of the NUCUA organizes the annual conference which elects the National Executive Committee which, as in the case of the Labour party, supervises the activities of the party's central office. The Conservative party's central office has essentially the same responsibilities as its Labour counterpart, above all the training and supervision of the full-time agents and organizers who keep party activity going in 500 or more of the 630 election districts.

The successful transformation of a traditionalist party such as the British Conservatives into a branch party seems to make a strong case for Duverger's proposition of the inevitability of the mass-membership party. But before evaluating this, let us look at American developments.

Organization of the American Cadre Party

As we have noted, there was intense organized political activity in America some years before independence. This did not diminish in the first years of the union when Hamilton's Federalists and Jefferson's Democratic-Republicans were struggling for power. But with the collapse of the Federalist party in the early nineteenth century, the control of national politics fell into the hands of the con-

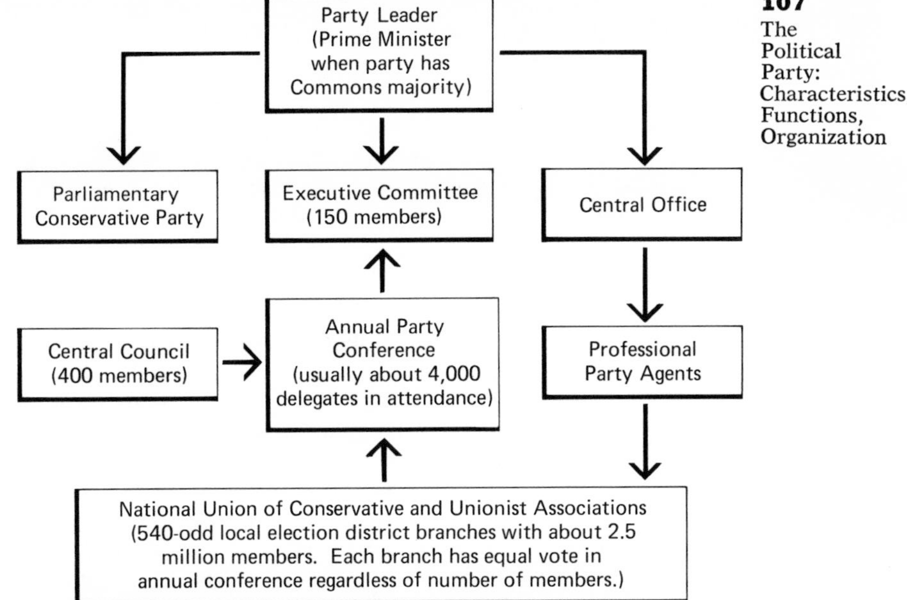

Note: Theoretically the Central Council is the governing body of the National Union, but it is actually mainly a ceremonial organization.

Figure 4
Organization of the British Conservative Party

gressional caucus composed of the Democratic-Republican members of House and Senate. It was they who for almost twenty years decided party policy and picked the next candidate for president. His election, in a manner reminiscent of certain parties in the world today, was assured the moment he became the official choice.

The emergence of "the second American party system," the broad organizational outlines of which are still with us, was brought about by the refusal of the caucus to elect General Andrew Jackson, the popular-vote choice, as president in 1824.[12] Instead, in one of the two times the House of Representatives has so functioned, John Quincy Adams, the caucus choice, was elected.

The eventual result was the birth of Jacksonian Democracy with its emphasis on the role of the common man, the president as the only spokesman for all the people, and, most important for the construction of a new type of political organization, with the winners taking control of all jobs and patronage. This so-called spoils system became the

[12]For a further discussion, see Richard P. McCormick, "Political Development and the Second Party System," in *The American Party Systems,* ed. William Nisbet Chambers and Walter Dean Burnham (New York: Oxford University Press, 1967), pp. 90–116.

basis for political organization for the next century and more. Jackson himself put the case bluntly:

> In a country where offices are created solely for the benefit of the people, no man has any more intrinsic right to official station than another. Offices were not established to give support to particular men at the public expense. No individual wrong is, therefore, done by removal, since neither appointment to nor continuance in office is a matter of right. . . . It is the people, and they alone, who have a right to complain when a bad officer is substituted for a good one.[13]

No one was more responsible for laying the foundations for the strength of the presidency in the twentieth century than Jackson. From beginning to end, he regarded himself as above all the leader of his party, and he systematically constructed a widespread organizational structure based on the concrete rewards of patronage. Its most significant new institutional device was the acceptance of the convention, composed of delegates chosen by local party groups, instead of the caucus as the means for nominating candidates from president down to local office. In theory, the effect was to take control of party affairs out of the hands of legislators and give it to the common man. In actuality, it was Ranney's leaders and workers who thus gained control of party activity.

It is curious that in the twentieth century European scholars have viewed the party system of the United States as lacking in organization compared with branch systems. The layers of conventions and party committees, extending from top to bottom, have really created a highly complex organizational structure. As McCormick points out, "Because candidates had to be nominated at so very many different levels of government, elections were held so frequently, and the party system embraced the entire range of offices, the organizations that had evolved in most states by the 1840's were marvels of ingenuity and intricacy and required enromous manpower to staff them." It is worth remembering that in Great Britain at this time party organization was still in a rudimentary stage, and in other European countries it was nonexistent.

At the end of the nineteenth century, two foreign observers paid high tribute to the sophisticated development of American political organization. Wrote Lord Bryce in his classic *American Commonwealth:*

> Government by popular vote, both local and national, is older in America than in continental Europe. It is far more complete than even in England. It deals with larger masses of men. Its methods have engaged a greater share of attention, and enlisted more inventive skills in their service, than anywhere else in the

[13]Frank Otto Gatell and John M. McFaul, eds., *Jacksonian America, 1815–1840* (Englewood Cliffs, N.J.: Prentice-Hall, 1970), p. 122.

world. They have therefore become more elaborate and, so far as mere mechanism goes, more perfect than elsewhere.

The greatest discovery ever made in the art of war was when men began to perceive that organization and discipline count for more than numbers. . . . The Americans made a similar discovery in politics between 1820 and 1840. . . . Both parties flung themselves into the task, and the result has been an extremely complicated system of party machinery, firm yet flexible, delicate yet quickly set up and capable of working well in the roughest communities.[14]

Echoing Bryce, a Russian scholar, Moisei Ostrogorski, published in 1902 the first comprehensive description of the workings of the American party, *Democracy and the Organization of Political Parties.* Although long neglected, Ostrogorski's "study of social and political psychology" still offers rewarding perceptions of the nature of the American party system.

In broad basic outlines, American party organizational structure has changed little since Bryce and Ostrogorski wrote. It still continues as a cadre system composed, to use Ranney's apt comparison, of " 'chiefs' of varying degrees of importance" and "relatively few 'Indians.' " In theory American party organization consists of a neat pyramid of committees extending from the county to the national level. At the peak are the national committees, but their roles are far different from the national executive committees of the British Labour or Conservative parties. Composed of state party chairmen and two committe members for each state, elected by the presidential convention, the national committees do little more than decide where the next convention will be held and how its program will be ordered.

The national committee chooses the party's chairman but he is an anemic imitation of his British counterpart. Routinely the job goes either to a supporter of the party's last successful presidential candidate or, as was the case with the Republicans in 1965, to an appointee of the group which has taken over the party machinery from the supporters of the last unsuccessful presidential candidate. In either case, it is usually a thankless task lacking in both power and prestige. Senators and congressmen have their own national and state campaign committees, while the fifty state committees of the party are grimly concerned with their own local election schedules and have little interest in national party fortunes a remote four years hence. Within state parties, county and city committees often behave in the same fashion.

The influences which have weakened American party ties, including the impact of technological strides in communications, will be discussed in later chapters. Here we men-

[14]Lord Bryce, *American Commonwealth* (New York: Macmillan, 1917), 2:76.

tion only one change in the basis of party organizational activity in the last fifty years or so. This is the disappearance of that spoils system on which Andrew Jackson built the new type of party organization. For the political reformers of the early twentieth century, the "boss" was a figure of evil, representing all the aspects of corruption and lack of principle that were wrong with political activity. Now, even in city governments, civil service systems have largely eliminated the possibilities for political appointment as a reward for faithful party service. An even more important factor has been the emergence of the welfare state which, since the era of social politics in the 1930s, has performed the functions that gave the old-time boss his political power. In *The Last Hurrah,* a best-selling novel and successful movie of the mid-1950s, one of the characters explains why the political boss was so successful prior to the era of social politics and what led to his decline and fall:

> Well, of course, the old boss was strong simply because he held all the cards. If anybody wanted anything—job, favors, cash—he could only go to the boss, the local leader. What Roosevelt did was to take the handouts out of local hands. A few little things like Social Security, Unemployment Insurance, and the like—that's what shifted the gears, sport. No need now to depend on the boss for everything; the Federal government was getting into the act. Otherwise known as a social revolution. So you can see what that would do in the long run. The old-timers would still string along with the boss. . . . But what about the kids coming along?
>
> To begin with, they were one step further away from the old country; he didn't have the old emotional appeal for them . . . finally, most of them never had the slightest contact with him because it wasn't necessary. . . . It was a new era, sport.[15]

As of 1972 it seems hardly necessary to point out that "the kids" referred to in this quote are now grandparents and that the sentimental ties of common old-country origins mean little. Today, when one needs help it is routine to go to the nearest federal agency for assistance.

Some Contrasts Between American Cadre and British Branch Parties

Aside from the obvious factor of membership and nonmembership, there are several other points of contrast between the organizational structures of American and British parties, or, in a broader sense, between cadre and branch parties. Some that we can mention are:

1. Centralization Versus Dispersion. Aside from the four-year contest for the presidency, there is no other nationally unifying contest in the American political sys-

[15]Edwin O'Connor, *The Last Hurrah* (Boston: Little, Brown, 1956), pp. 374–375.

tem. Instead, the multitude of offices which the federal system provides on state and local levels encourages, indeed almost forces, dispersion. In contrast, in British politics the only important prize is control of the House of Commons and thus of the central administration. Of necessity political efforts must be focused on this central objective. This, in turn, leads directly into our second important difference between British and American parties.

2. Party Discipline. The American senator or representative depends very little on his national party headquarters and a very great deal on local support. It is from this source that his major financial and political support comes. When there is disagreement or conflict between the opinion leaders in his election area and the national administration, there is little question as to whom he must side with for political survival. Time and again American political experience has shown that so long as a congressman is supported by his own constituency, he can defy the most powerful of presidents with impunity. But once out of touch with the home folks, his future becomes a dubious bet.

The British situation is quite different. Within a few years after the advent of mass democracy in 1867, it became clear that political success depended on the appeal of the party's program and leader and the effectiveness of the national organization. Lacking any sources of local patronage and support, only an independently wealthy parliamentarian could even dare risk trying to conduct an independent campaign. It very quickly became established practice that if a Member of Parliament expected party financial and organization help in his election campaign, he must expect to follow the leaders of his party and vote as expected. Since candidates lack the possibility for local support which American national legislators have, British experience of defying party leadership has been exactly the reverse of American. Invariably those who have fought their party leadership have gone down to defeat in the next election.

3. Intermittent versus Consistent Activity. American elections, as multitudinous as they are, are neatly structured in terms of two-, four-, and six-year terms. There is a reliable timetable for preparation and campaigning which never varies. It is almost universally true that American party activity disappears in the periods between elections, aside from the speeches and statements of career politicians. Indeed, a curious quality of American politics, often commented on by foreign observers, is that for even the small percentage actively involved when politics is in season (estimated at probably 3 percent to 5 percent of eligible voters) it has seemed a sort of game; for those who bother to follow its developments—and about one-third of all potential voters do not even go to this trouble—it is simply a spectator sport. It is a curious irony that in a time when foot-

ball, baseball, and even table tennis have become commercialized, politics is perhaps the only amateur sport left on the American scene!

In the British political system, on the other hand, party activity of necessity goes on all year round, right down to the grass-roots level, for there is always the possibility that the leadership of the governing party may decide to call the next general election at any moment, giving only a brief six weeks before judgment day. Naturally, this necessitates a constant readiness on the part of the party organization to leap into action, and it is for this reason that, in contrast to the almost total hibernation of the typical American party local organization between elections, a British constituency party carries on, under the guidance of the professional party agent, a constant program of education and recruitment. It reaches its peak activity in the periods shortly before general elections of course, but, at some level, it is constant.

4. Membership versus Cadre Organization. One of the favorite proposals of those seeking to reform the American party system is to turn American parties into dues-paying organizations. By so doing, the argument runs, candidates will be freed from having to depend on selfish interests and will acquire a degree of independence permitting them to act as statesmen rather than politicians. While there have been scattered efforts to create dues-paying organizations, success has been meagre. The one outstanding success in national presidential elections seems to be the exception that proves the rule. Fired by the uniquely crusading zeal of the Goldwater campaign, the Republican party received some 650,000 contributions of less than a $100 each. But this exception aside, the typical American campaign contribution seems to be a substantial donation to an individual candidate, thus enhancing his independence from central party control.

In any case, the British experience does not seem to indicate that mass-membership parties offer a solution to the problem of financial indebtedness to a few big contributors, for neither the Conservatives nor Labor could survive financially if they had to depend on the dues paid by individual members. Without the large contributions given to the central party organizations by trade unions and business interests, further enhancing the centralized discipline element, clearly both Labor and Conservative parties would be on a meagre financial diet.

There is, then, little to be gained financially from transforming a cadre party into a mass-membership party. Nor does such a transformation represent a modernization of party structure, as Duverger believed. Writing in 1950, he commented critically on the "archaic" structure of American parties, as compared to the branch type which he regarded as the organizational wave of the future. At that time his "contagion from the left" thesis seemed to be borne out by developments in a number of Western European countries. But in perspective, his thesis seems more and more dubious. Even in Western Europe mass-membership parties have not appeared in new areas. In France, which Duverger used as his prime example, the socialist party and others based on mass membership, have declined, and right-wing parties have maintained their cadre-style organization. In Great Britain, over-all membership totals have also declined since 1950.

In part this failure of European parties to convert to a mass-membership basis may be due to the weakening force of the "contagion from the left." In the twenty years both the numbers and the intensity of European leftist parties have steadily declined. From this, an authority on European party development concludes:

> If then, a strong socialist working-class political movement is essential for the development of mass-membership party organization, by contagion or otherwise, the future of the latter is indeed in doubt.
>
> Then there is the fact that, in a broader social perspective, the middle class and the middle-class style appears to be growing at the expense of working-class preponderance. This is important, for it has been argued that mass membership in political groups is more congenial to the working class, with its acceptance of the need for collective action, than to the more individualist middle class. If this is so, the possibilities for highly developed membership organization would recede with the spread of the middle-class way of life.[16]

In short, it is not impossible, as the *embourgeoisement* (middle-classing) of Western Europe continues in the late twentieth century, that the "archaic" cadre system of party organization instead of mass-membership parties may be the organizational wave of the future.

FACTORS IN THE EMERGENCE OF NON-WESTERN PARTIES

The development of parties in the Anglo-American political system and probably in most of the countries of Western Europe is reasonably, though not fully, explained by Weber's and Duverger's theories of the challenge and response relationship between the development of representative institutions, the expansion of the franchise, and the appearance of modern parties. But of the 105 polities mentioned at the beginning of this chapter as having some type of party expression, approximately 42 have appeared on the

[16]Leon D. Epstein, *Political Parties in Western Democracies* (New York: Praeger, 1967), p. 128.

world scene since Duverger wrote in 1950. Neither Weber's nor Duverger's versions of challenge and response do much to explain why and how parties have appeared in the newly independent nations of Asia and Africa, for all of these countries either currently have some type of party expression or have experimented with it since independence and found it wanting.

Why and how did party expression appear in the first place? In very few cases was it encouraged by the colonial regimes. Even when, as in India, representative bodies and limited suffrage were developed, the nationalist movements as a matter of principle often refused to function within this framework until just before independence was achieved. Under the worst of circumstances, as in Indonesia and Algeria, the nationalist movements had to fight their way to power through armed revolt. Further, in China and in parts of Latin America, political parties have been organized under the most difficult conditions in the absence of the encouraging evolutionary factors of either developing representative institutions or an enlarging electorate.

There are, suggest La Palombara and Weiner, two explanations for the emergence of political parties other than those culture-bound explanations of Weber and Duverger. They are: (1) "the historical crises or tasks which systems have encountered at the moment in time when parties developed" and (2) the relationship of parties "to the broader processes of modernization."

The authors go on to suggest that the three most important crises a country can encounter are crises of "legitimacy, integration, and participation." In varying degree they may all occur simultaneously, thus creating an overload for the political system involved. When an existing authority structure fails to cope with political crises, then parties, or more likely an aspiring movement regime, may emerge with the intent of both establishing a new political order and opening up new channels for participation in it. Crises of integration may literally mean how to integrate different geographical areas within a new polity. As in the case of the emergence of the Muslim League in British India near the end of the colonial period, the objective may well be an opposition position to that of yet another "party" with an entirely different philosophy on not only integration but also legitimacy and participation.

On the subject of the relationship between the emergence of some type of political party expression and the drive for modernization in the new nations, La Palombara and Weiner claim that "while the presence of one of the historical crises may be a catalyst for the organization of parties, it seems clear that parties will not in fact materialize unless a measure of modernization has already occurred."

Included in their tentative prerequisites for "a measure of modernization" are such factors as:

1. The development of a degree of both political and occupational autonomy which in terms of "spatial and social mobility" will encourage new perceptions of authority
2. The development of a certain level of communication permitting physical contact and the easy exchange of ideas among different sections—i.e., the relationship between the growth of the Indian Nationalist Congress and the development of railroads
3. The emergence of a secular education system, the growth of urbanism, the change from a subsistence to a monetary economy and the intervention of an activist state
4. A cultural background encouraging cooperation and participation in "voluntary or quasi-voluntary organizations"
5. Finally, the acceptance of the modern Western secular philosophy that the world is here to be molded by man, rather than man regarding himself as a helpless piece of driftwood on the great river of time

CONCLUSION

Perhaps the most fascinating aspect of the study of political parties is that from Weber and Duverger to La Palombara and Weiner, there continues to be endless speculation but still no one is quite sure precisely how or why. It is possible to compile a typology of how Western-type parties originated, or the tentative prerequisites for "a measure of modernization" may be listed, but still there is uncertainty. Here is a challenging area of research for the scholars of the late twentieth century The same is true of the efforts to schematize party systems to which we turn in our next chapter.

THE MOVEMENT-REGIME PARTY AND OTHER PARTY SYSTEMS

In Chapter 4 we suggested that the forms of party expression elsewhere than in the Anglo-American world and Western Europe cannot be explained by the typologies of either Weber or Duverger. Historical crises and problems of modernization have obviously occurred in Western European development also, but seldom with the telescoped impact that has been the case in the emerging nations of Asia and Africa.

For this reason, it is not surprising that party expression has not followed, for the most part, the Anglo-American or Western European models. The coupling of the crises of legitimacy, integration, and participation, and the drive for instant modernization, have demanded the creation of a new type of party. The remolding of the social and political order is the major objective of such a party. Participation in election activities is only one of its tactics in the drive to conquer state power by any means. Power once conquered, the party guards it jealously and usually suppresses all opposition.

This new type of party is uniquely a product of the chaotic, revolutionary political upheavals of our century. When its expression is communist or fascist, we will call the party an *order* party. When its expression is monopolistic and nationalist and dedicated to a program of social revolution, we shall refer to it as a *solidarity* party[1].

Just how widespread order and solidarity parties are today is indicated by the fact that of the 105 polities in the world having some type of political party expression, approximately 35 are in either the order or solidarity categories. Of the 22 or so solidarity party regimes, all but 3 are located in Africa.

It has long been standard to refer to communist and fascist parties and the

[1]The term *solidarity party* is taken from David Apter, *The Politics of Modernization* (Chicago: University of Chicago Press, 1965). See in particular Chapter 6, "The Political Party as a Modernizing Instrument," pp. 179-222.

regimes they create as totalitarian. This nomenclature, however, is inadequate because it does not distinguish between communist and fascist parties. And further, comments Professor Robert C. Tucker, "it also fails to direct attention to significant resemblances between *both* these phenomena and a further class of phenomena belonging to the same genus: Single-party systems of the nationalist species." He continues:

> We see the need for a comparative-political framework within which communist, fascist and nationalistic single-party regimes may be analyzed in terms of their significant similarities as well as their significant differences, or as three species of a single political genus.
>
> The definition of the political genus presents obvious difficulties. Ideally this definition should fix upon (1) that which is common to all phenomena of the class and specific to no one of the three postulated sub-classes, and (2) that which differentiates this whole class of phenomena from others that may be more or less closely related to it. As a rough attempt I would propose the following formula: *the revolutionary mass-movement regime under single-party auspices.* For brevity I shall refer to it as the "movement-regime."[2]

CHARACTERISTICS OF MOVEMENT-REGIME PARTIES

The characteristics shared by both varieties of movement-regime parties are as follows:

1. The obligations of membership are far more demanding than in either a cadre or even a branch party. In the case of the order party, there is, of course, literally no other obligation but that of service to the party. For most of the solidarity parties the requirements are far less stringent, but party meetings and attendance at "spontaneous" demonstrations of one sort or another are a constant and time-consuming requirement.

2. The party is formed in the course of revolutionary struggle. In the case of the solidarity parties the struggle is directed against the colonial regime with its alien rule. For the order parties, the "pattern is one of revolutionary struggle against an indigenous order that is treated *as though* it were foreign."

3. The movement-regime party has a detailed program for social and economic change. The program, usually derived from Marxist, Marxist-Leninist, or utopian socialist sources, serves both as an aid in party recruitment and a blueprint for the future ideal society.

4. When the movement-regime party is not yet in power, whether it is organized on an elitist or mass-membership

[2]Robert C. Tucker, "Towards a Comparative Politics of Movement-Regimes," *The American Political Science Review* 55, No. 2 (June 1961): 283.

basis, it seeks to organize and control, directly or indirectly, a mass movement for revolutionary change.

5. It regards itself as the organized vanguard of the only true revolutionary movement. Once in power, it jealously guards its monopoly of governmental authority by rigid control of the communications media and the banning of all opposition activity.

6. Whatever the particular organizational structure of the movement-regime party, its leadership in its early years is almost always highly concentrated in a small inner circle, usually dominated by a charismatic leader who is universally accepted as the living symbol both of the party and the movement for national regeneration.

7. In spite of its monopolistic control and elitist outlook, the movement-regime party appeals to mass, popular support as the basis for its legitimization as a regime. Under the guidance and leadership of the party, large masses of people who, as in Czarist Russia, had no previous sense of civic involvement, are given a sense of participation in the building of the new order. As an additional means of symbolic identification, the party at regular intervals goes through the ritual of offering its candidates for a triumphant and impressive 98.8 percent vote of approval at the polls with 99.2 percent of all eligible voters participating.

For anyone accustomed to the competitive party situation of a typical Western political system, such statistics seem absurd. But the fact should not be overlooked that there may well be an overwhelming approval of the policies of the movement-regime party, particularly in its first years of power. For consider the circumstances which brought it to power.

WHY MOVEMENT-REGIME PARTIES COME TO POWER

What type of society fosters the emergence of a movement regime? For a social system to become the more-or-less passive object of intensive political control and social regulation, a rather special set of circumstances must be present. It is difficult, for example, to imagine a movement regime emerging in our own society or in Great Britain or Australia or the Scandinavian nations. What are the circumstances that make a movement regime possible?

Typically, a movement regime emerges as a result of a four-phase pattern of social development which has run the gamut from *conflict* through *disintegration* culminating in *revolution* and succeeded by an effort at *reintegration.* We can illustrate this pattern by a sketch of the way in which the world's first movement regime emerged in Russia in 1917.

Most historians seem to agree that conflict became increasingly dominant in the imperial Russian political system from the time of the country's defeat by the Western powers in the Crimean War of the mid-1850s. From that point on, the revolutionary movement could not be subdued, and Russian society became increasingly ideologically divided and emotionally strained.

With the even more disastrous debacle of the Russo-Japanese war, culminating in the revolution of 1905, the imperial political system entered into disintegration. Its supports fell away at a disastrous rate, and it could produce little or nothing in the way of outputs to satisfy such demands as were still being made upon it. Whether it could have survived without the shattering impact of World War I seems questionable as best.

It is, however, irrelevant whether three ruinous years of world war hastened the inevitable or created the inevitable. The fact remains that in 1917 imperial Russia moved from the phase of disintegration to revolution at a time when, by one of history's more ironic accidents, the world's first order party led by the political genius of its creator, Nicolai Lenin, was waiting on the scene to pick up the pieces and initiate the *reintegration* of Russian society.

Since then, with local variations, the scenario for the takeover of power by an order or solidarity party and the creation of a new regime has essentially followed the Russian prototype. There is always a prolonged preliminary phase of conflict, whether it be purely internal or the struggle between a nationalist movement and a colonial ruler. Conflict is followed by a period of disintegration when everything seems to come apart at the seams. This is when the movement-regime party comes to the fore and makes its bid for power, though not always successfully. For many of the solidarity parties in colonial countries, this is often little more than a formal matter, since as the nationalist movement in the country the party's eventual acquisition of power has long been both unchallenged and inevitable.

Then, following its takeover, usually dominated by a "father of his country" figure, the solidarity party seeks to institutionalize the new order so that even when the leader and his revolutionary generation have passed on the party's vision for the future of the new nation as embodied in its ideological program will continue to survive and develop. Hence interference with this program is not only intolerable but treasonable. For the salvation of the nation, the party feels justified in using any coercive measure to suppress whatever opposition threatens its dominance.

The leaders of the solidarity party must be constantly at their task of building the new order. The organizational and ideological goals of the Afro-Asian solidarity parties are to achieve a Leninist efficiency in organization and a fanaticism in ideological devotion. Although, with few exceptions, they fall short of these goals, the solidarity parties do, like the order parties, monopolize the political stage. Of all the different kinds of parties, the movement-regime party is the best example of the political party as an independent variable, which is the original and dynamic source of actions that shape the nature of the whole society. In diagrammatic form, we can show it like this:

Obviously there is feedback from both government (the intervening variable) and society that affects the actions of the party. But the party remains the dominant factor in the equation.

So much then for the common characteristics of both types of movement-regime parties and the forces that bring them to power. But now for a closer look at the similarities and differences between the order and solidarity variations. You will recall that both communist and fascist parties fall into the order-party category. We will use as our example the Communist party, which claims a world enrollment of some 45 million members.

THE COMMUNIST VERSION OF THE ORDER PARTY

For some readers the term *order* may have a familiar sound. In religious terminology, an order is composed of those dedicated men or women, monks or nuns, who have given up all worldly ambition and possessions and taken solemn vows to serve their church with total dedication for the rest of their lives as far as they can foresee. Their numbers are always limited, and they have always been carefully chosen and rigorously tested before final acceptance into their particular order. It is because Lenin, the brilliant creator of the theory and organization of twentieth-century communism, applied the same criteria to his concept of membership in this party which was to be the blueprint for the totalitarian parties of the world that political sociologists have borrowed this religious term in an effort to describe it.

As early as 1902, in his famous statement on party organization that shaped so much of the history of the twentieth century, Lenin insisted that "no revolutionary movement can endure without a stable organization of leaders that maintains continuity . . . [and] that such an organization must consist chiefly of people professionally engaged in revolutionary activity."[3]

Using this new type of professional revolutionary party as his instrument, Lenin, against heavy odds, was able to seize power amid the chaos of Russia's political and social disorder of 1917. The result was that the Leninist concept of party organization became an absolute requirement for any party wishing to be counted as communist. Since the establishment of the Third International in 1919—although Stalin abolished it in 1943—the communist parties of the world have been organized as order parties.

There has developed, however, an important difference in the membership policies of order parties in and out of power. Where order parties control the government, as in the Soviet Union, admission to the ranks of the party is highly restricted, since in itself party membership means admission to the ruling elite with its extensive special privileges. Even now, when the Communist party of the Soviet Union is at its peak strength, membership is estimated at only approximately 14 million individuals out of a population of about 242 million. In noncommunist countries, where the party is still striving for power, the situation is quite otherwise. The Italian Communist party, for example, as of 1970 had a membership of a little over 1.5 million, and prior to its destruction in 1965 the Indonesian Communist party claimed 3 million members.

But more important for our purposes is to see how an order party guides and controls its society when it holds the reins of power. With more than a century of unbroken power behind it, the Communist party of the Soviet Union is our best example.

THE COMMUNIST PARTY OF THE SOVIET UNION

As with all other communist parties, decision-making in the Soviet party is based on the Leninist concept of *democratic centralism.* As defined in the Rules adopted by the Twenty-second Party Congress in 1961, democratic centralism means:

1. Election of all leading party bodies, from the lowest to the highest
2. Periodic reports of party bodies to their party organizations and to higher bodies
3. Strict party discipline and subordination of the minority to the majority

[3]Lenin, *What Is To Be Done?* in *Selected Works* (Moscow: Foreign Languages Publishing House, 1952), 1:336.

4. That the decisions of higher bodies are binding upon lower bodies

But from the beginning, the guiding rule for the conduct of Communist party affairs has been in terms of centralism and control from above rather than any element of democratic control. During Lenin's lifetime, his role as the creator of the party effectively stifled any challenge to his dictates. Except for the brief period in the early 1920s before he was able to consolidate his power, Stalin's control of the party administrative machinery for a quarter-century set the mold for the conduct of party affairs in terms of rigid control from the top.

The theory of democratic centralism is illustrated by Figure 5. It presents a picture of all the guiding bodies of the party from bottom to top, elected by the rank-and-file members and accountable to them. Note that even in terms of this theoretical structure, democracy exists only within the party itself. In characteristic order-party fashion, the right, indeed the duty, of the party to conduct itself as a jealously restricted ruling elite over the masses is taken for granted.

In Figure 6 we see the reality of the power flow within the party. A small group of twenty or so make up the mem-

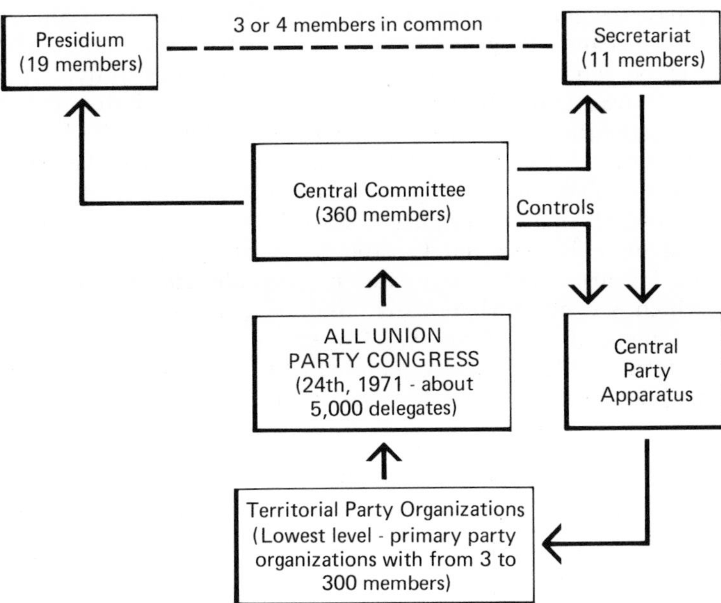

Note: All minor bodies have been omitted.

Figure 5
Simplified Theoretical Organization of the Communist Party of the Soviet Union

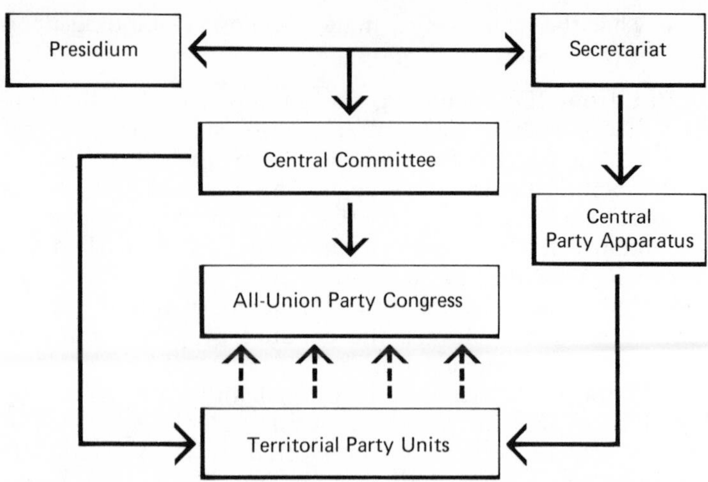

Figure 6
Actual Organization of the Communist Party of the Soviet Union

bership of the Presidium and the Secretariat, with the inner core of this group holding positions in both. These are the men who not only run the affairs of the Communist party of the Soviet Union but determine policy for the conduct of governmental affairs. Those who hold either party or governmental position beneath this level do so only because they are tested and trusted lieutenants who can be relied on to carry out their duties faithfully.

It was Lenin himself who provided the administrative basis for this total control of party affairs by the elite leadership. At the Eighth Party Congress in 1919, when the party was involved in a desperate struggle for survival, Lenin pushed through a resolution stating that "outright military discipline is essential for the party at the present time." Two years later Lenin was responsible for a resolution which sternly forbade any kind of "factionalism" in the interests of "Party unity." The effect of this was to make it treasonable for party members to form an opposition to policies laid down by the leadership.

Party Organizational Structure

In theory, a party congress, until the revision of the rules in 1961, was supposed to be held at least every third year. The congress is "the supreme organ of the CPSU," and at the congress the 5,000 or so delegates review policy and administration since the last congress and lay down guidelines for the future. Additionally, the congress selects the Central Committee, composed of prominent regional leaders, which directs the work of the party between the meetings of the congress. An indication of how centralized and arbitrary party control became after Stalin consolidated his power is indicated by the time lapses that took place between congresses. The Sixteenth Party Congress took place in 1930, the next in 1934, the next in 1939, and the Nineteenth Party Congress, the last before his death in 1953, not until 1952.

The Central Committee, elected by the congress, is composed of approximately 330 members. It can be called the "Who's Who" of the party, for the members are chosen because they are outstanding not only as party officials, but in their careers in government, the armed services, industrial management, trade-union leadership, and such activities as diplomacy, journalism, and other intellectual activities. However, the very basis on which these individuals have won their positions on the Central Committee makes it difficult for them to devote much time to its ostensible purpose of running the party's and the nation's affairs.

As a result, the Central Committee elects the Presidium, formerly known as the Politburo, and the Secretariat from among its own members. The twenty-odd members of the Presidium and the nine members of the Secretariat, with three or four individuals holding membership in both bodies, represents the summit of power in the party. The Presidium is often referred to as "the cabinet" of the party, but it has far more power than the cabinet of any democratic state, for it decides the broad policy lines which determine not only the economic and social future of 242 million people but also the Soviet Union's foreign policies, with all of its awesome implications for the rest of the world. The members of the Secretariat head the various party departments which not only supervise party affairs but keep a close watch over the various governmental ministries to insure strict loyalty to party directives and efficient performance of duties.

The Secretariat constitutes the very heart of the control system exercised by the order party. In itself it is a microcosmic state with sections continuously engaged in supervising and checking all other aspects of party and government activity. The decision-making employees of the Secretariat, estimated to number between 2,000 and 4,000, constitute the cream of the civil servants who have made party work a lifetime career. It is impossible to diagram the organization of the Secretariat, since a number of its departments have always been secret. However, it is vaguely known that its major divisions deal with the affairs of the Soviet party, the foreign communist parties, and the operation of the ministries. In addition to the Secretariat, there are two lesser bodies, elected respectievly by the party congress and the Central Committee. The first of these, the central auditing commission, combines the functions of management consultants and public accountants in a private business in the United States. The party control committee is a combination FBI and prosecuting attorney concerned with the private and official conduct of party members.

The Web of Party Control

The party-sponsored Pioneers and Little Octobrists play an important role in the political socialization of all Soviet youth. Membership in the Komsomols, an organization for older youth (15 to 26 years) is more selective, although it is far more inclusive than the party. From the best of the older Komsomol members are selected most of the new candidate members for the party itself. In a movement regime such as that of the Soviet Union, membership in the party makes the difference between being in the ranks of those who run things and being just an ordinary citizen. To conclude our survey of the control web of the Soviet order party, we can note that from the beginning of the Soviet state, the trade unions have been firmly under party control and constitute yet another strand in the web of party control.

In some Eastern European post-World War II communist regimes, although it seems superfluous, another device has been used to insure the widest possible contact with and control of the masses. This is the creation of a so-called Fatherland Front (Bulgaria) or National Front (Czechoslovakia and the German Democratic Republic) which associates from two to four other parties on a common election slate with the ruling communist party. Thus, in East Germany, those who still have scruples about voting for the communist Socialist Unity Party can salve their consciences by voting for the Christian-Democratic Union and still avoid taking an opposition stand against the regime. Interestingly, Communist China has utilized the same device for mobilizing maximum support for the regime's legitimacy.

THE SOLIDARITY VERSION OF MOVEMENT-REGIME PARTIES

The solidarity or nationalist movement regimes are represented by more parties and a greater variety of structure and ideologies than the order movement regimes, although they represent smaller population totals. But in their approach to the problems of membership all differ from the Leninist tradition. The typical solidarity party of a contemporary Asian or African newly independent nation is simply the old nationalist movement transformed. Under the later phases of both British and French colonial rule the nationalist movements were allowed virtually complete freedom of action. This allowed them to carry out their goals of mobilizing the greatest possible mass support in order to impress the colonial authorities with the power of the nationalist movement and the desirability of granting independence at the earliest possible moment.

The result has been that, while an elitist approach to membership has always, in theory at least, been basic to the communist order type of movement-regime party, a wide-open mass approach which tried to enlist virtually every man, woman, and child in the new nation under the banner of unity and social progress has been characteristic of the solidarity parties.

It is true that some of the African movement-regime parties, such as that of the Islamic Republic of Mauritania, have not followed the typical solidarity pattern of mass participation. But their elitist approach has been in traditional terms rather than Leninist, and they have sought to base their strength on the influence of such local notables as landowners or tribal chieftains. Far more typical of African solidarity regimes is the Democratic party of Guinea (Parti Démocratique de Guinée) which its founder and leader President Sékou Touré describes as "a mass party created to defend the interests of the people and to speed the movement for the emancipation of Africa."

The Guinean Democratic Party as a Solidarity Regime

Although in its emphasis on its role as a mass party, the Democratic party differs very obviously from the elitist approach of the communist order party, the similarities between the two are many. Until 1958, when Guinea opted for independence from France, the party was a section of the African Democratic Rally, the coalition of nationalist movements in French Black Africa. From the time that Touré became its secretary-general in 1952, the Democratic party became the only political movement in Guinea and Touré its unchallenged leader. With independence the party officially became Guinea's only vehicle for political action in contrast to some of the other African movement-regime party states such as Senegal where, legally at least, opposition parties have a theoretical right to exist.

More than most African solidarity parties, Guinea's is closely modeled on the Leninist pattern of organization. Democratic centralism, the official administrative principle, makes possible the functioning of a highly disciplined and closely knit party structure. As in the case of the CPSU, the theoretical and actual flows of power are in direct contrast with each other. In theory, power and decisions flow

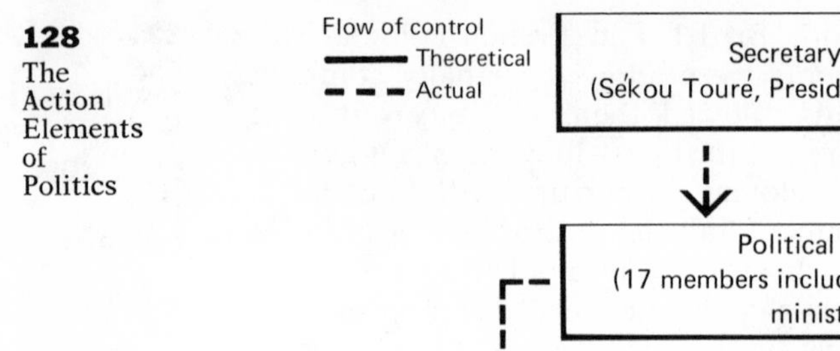

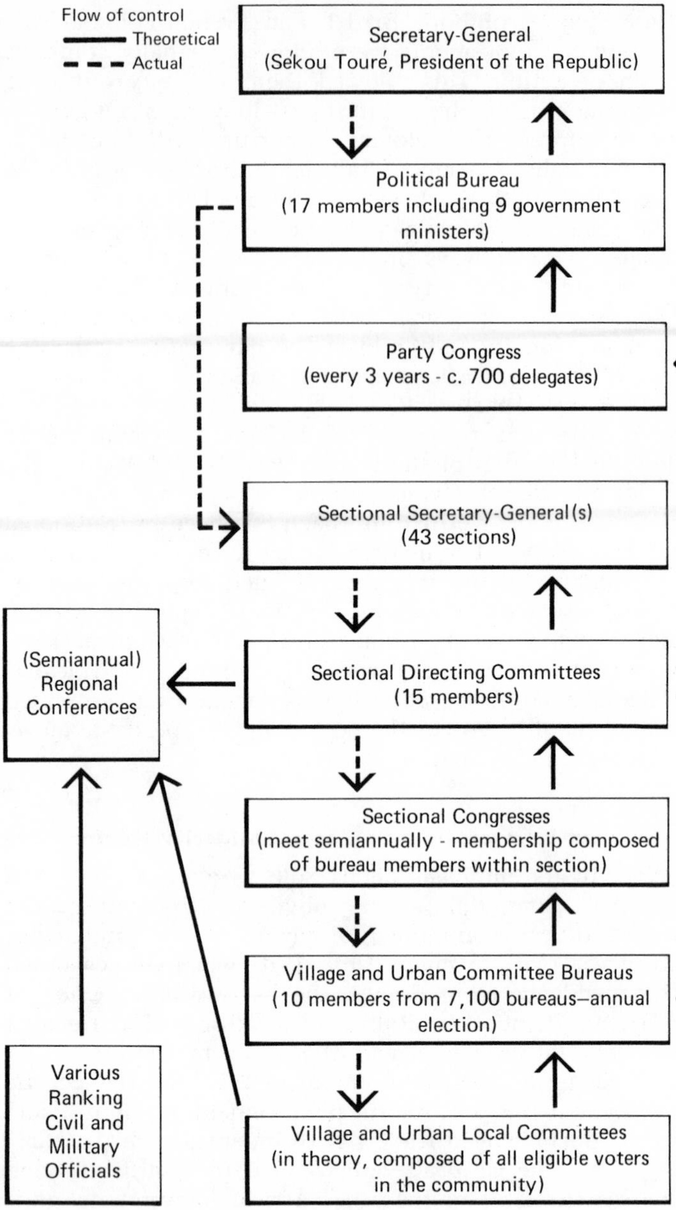

(Touré – "The Parti Démocratique de Guinée is a mass party created to defend the interests of the people and to speed the movement for the emancipation of Africa.")

Figure 7
Organizational Structure of the Parti Démocratique de Guinée

up from the 7,100 village and local urban committees through the twice-annual regional-section congresses to the supreme political bureau of the party headed by Touré as secretary-general. In actuality, as the broken arrows on the organizational chart of the party indicate (Figure 7), the 17-member political bureau, as in the case of the Presidium of the CPSU, determines party policy, which is then handed down the line through the full-time party functionaries in the 15 directing committees, and the 43 sections to the members of the village and local urban executive bureaus.

The party also controls a youth movement and a nationwide network of women's groups which funnel into the party's activities. Since 1961 the African Democratic Youth Rally (Jeunesse du Rassemblement Démocratique African) has been directed by a cabinet-level youth ministry. As an example of the thoroughgoing effort to achieve order-party efficiency in organization, the youth group is divided into two sections. One of these organizes all types of youth sports activities in the service of the state, and the other supervises cultural and scholastic affairs and is an exact copy, even to the name, of the Soviet Pioneers.

Far more than most other solidarity parties, the Democratic party of Guinea possesses an ideology to guide its actions. Whatever else may be said about it, the sources are not limited. The Guinean credo contains elements of Marxism-Leninism and of European populism, with particular emphasis on Rousseau's concepts of the general will, and also relies heavily on traditional African concepts of communalism and decision-making through consensus. We will have occasion to refer to this ideology when we are discussing alternative guidelines to both Western-type constitutional democracy and Marxism-Leninism for a time of troubles.

Few other solidarity parties, with the exception of the former Sudanese Union (Union Soudanaise) before it was ousted from power by a military coup in 1968, approximate the totalitarian organization and ideological outlook of the Guinean party. Rather more typical of the solidarity parties is the Democratic party of the Ivory Coast (Parti Démocratique de la Côte d'Ivoire). The Ivory Coast, along with Senegal, has always been regarded as one of the most highly developed territories of French West Africa. In contrast to the democratic centralism of Touré's order party, its Democratic party is organized on the nineteenth-century branch basis. Nor does it attempt the total involvement in its activities of all its citizens as is the case in Guinea. And although the party's leader, Ivory Coast president Félix Houphouet-Boigny, has long been one of the most effective and most highly regarded African statesmen, the party has sponsored a rather amorphous and low-key political philosophy rather than a full-blown ideology.

REGIMES OF REASSURANCE

Movement-regime parties of either type usually come to power because of some combination of historical crisis and pressure for modernization. For this reason they must present themselves to the masses as, above all, regimes of reassurance led by divinely inspired or at least kindly and highly expert figures. And whether in power for a few months or fifty-odd years, the controlling movement-regime party must convey a public image of calm certainty and unanimity among its leaders.

As we suggested in Chapter 3, wherever there is governmental authority to be exercised, there will be at least several groups within, if not without, the official structure contesting for a preponderant influence over its distribution. Within the top decision-making levels of the solidarity parties and in a number of communist order parties, particularly those like the Soviet which no longer have a semi-deified leader, there is very probably a high degree of give-and-take in the decision-making process. But given the fundamental necessity for a movement-party regime to project a symbolic reassurance, it is likely to be a long time before we have any firm data on these matters.

OTHER PARTY SYSTEMS

We have not included movement regimes in a typology of party systems simply because one of anything is no system. This is contrary to hallowed tradition in political science, for it is almost routine to include in any such text as this discussions of the characteristics of one-party, two-party, and multi-party systems. But, as Professor Eckstein pertinently observes:

> The fundamental difficulty with the established numerical typology involves its application to concrete cases: the typology cannot sensibly be taken to mean literally what it says, and it is difficult to use it in a non-literal sense. Take, to begin with, the concept of a *one-party system*. Strictly speaking, there can be no such thing. If party systems involve interactions among party units in the process of electoral competition, then the idea of a one-party system is logically absurd, for one cannot have a competition or an interaction with only one actor. It follows that if the concept is to be used, there must be specific conditions under which the existence of all parties but one should be ignored for purposes of generalization, even in genuinely competitive systems, or under which a single party without competitors is nevertheless considered to be genuinely engaged in electroal competition. This in fact is the procedure in most writings on one-party systems. Duverger, for example, includes in this category . . . the American South as well as Nazi Germany, Fascist Italy, Portugal under Salazar, and Turkey from 1923 to 1950. . . . Coleman has listed as one-party systems

in Africa (as of 1959) northern and eastern Nigeria, Ghana, Somalia, and the Federation of Rhodesia and Nyasaland, despite the fact that in each case more than one party actually contested elections and managed to win representation. Blankstein similarly regards Mexico as a one-party system. . . .

These writings raise the essential problem of finding sensible but unconventional criteria for including and excluding parties in a party system.[4]

We shall now attempt to find "sensible but unconventional criteria for including and excluding parties in a party system." In doing so, we will not question that traditional categories of two-party and multi-party systems have sufficient interacting units to meet the definition of a system, but we will ask if such designations really explain anything, or if they only further obscure the whole concept of party systems.

The Pointlessness of the Numbers Game

La Palombara and Weiner base their classification of parties on the dichotomy between competitive and noncompetitive systems. Of the former classification, they comment:

> It will be observed that we have included in this first major category all of the two-party and multi-party systems. We take this step primarily on the assumption that the traditional distinction between two-party and multi-party patterns has not led to sufficiently meaningful insights. It is more than a little perplexing, for example, to be reminded that we have multi-party systems that "work," such as those in Scandinavia, and others that do not "work," such as the parties under the Third and Fourth Republics of France. We also have two-party configurations that have remained essentially unchanged for a century (as in the United States) and other so-called two-party systems that have seen the near demise of one major party and the rise of another (the British case).[5]

A competitive system as defined by these authors is one in which the party or coalition of parties in power must struggle to stay there under competitive conditions, since there exists another party or coalition for which it is both legally and actually possible to take over power by achieving majority support in the next regularly scheduled election. In short, a competitive system is any system functioning, in terms of an Anglo-American political-culture frame of reference, within a "normal" constitutional democratic framework.

[4]Harry Eckstein, "Party Systems" in "Parties, Political," *International Encyclopedia of the Social Sciences* (New York: Macmillan, 1968), 11:439–440.

[5]Joseph La Palombara and Myron Weiner, *Political Parties and Political Development* (Princeton, N.J.: Princeton University Press, 1966), p. 33.

Within this broad competitive grouping, La Palombara and Weiner suggest four subcategories based on either a time factor and called *turnover* or *hegemonic* systems, or on the characteristics of the parties making up the political system, a category expressed on a continuum ranging from *ideological* to *pragmatic*. An example of a turnover party system would be the British system since World War II, where at irregular time intervals the power balance has shifted from Conservative to Labour and back again. A hegemonic system describes the situation in the United States between 1932 and 1952, where one party held power continuously for twenty years.

La Palombara and Weiner's ideological-to-pragmatic continuum corresponds to what another set of analysts have described as the distinction between "missionary" and "brokerage" parties. Clearly, a communist or a fascist party would fit into the ideological or missionary category, although this can be a matter of degree. Since the mid-1960s, for example, the Italian Communist party has increasingly become about as much of a pragmatic or brokerage party as is possible without abandoning its basic ideology entirely. On the other hand, the Indian Congress party, which long ago seemed to have evolved into an office-hungry brokerage party, under the dynamic leadership of Mrs. Gandhi fought and triumphantly won the 1971 election on a rejuvenated ideological-missionary program of national reform. The two major British and American parties, on the other hand, except for transitory episodes such as the Goldwater candidacy in 1964, for the past twenty years have consistently been in the pragmatic-brokerage category and seem likely to continue. And the mere fact that in the late 1960s it was possible for West Germany's two major parties, the Christian Democrats and the Social Democrats, to participate in a coalition is concrete evidence that here, too, pragmatic-brokerage politics dominates.

The varying combinations of these linked pairs of alternatives offer possibilities for strikingly different types of political systems. A turnover-ideological party system, for example, is likely to produce not only turmoil but impotence as the differing party combinations vie to undo each other's policies as they gain and lose office. And a hegemonic-ideological system might well develop into one characterized by the suppression of the opposition, armed revolt by the opposition from sheer frustrated desperation, or the disintegration of the opposition as its leaders flee abroad to avoid arrest or, less dramatically, decide that their situation is hopeless and withdraw from political activity. In contrast, a turnover-pragmatic party system might jog placidly along from election to election with no one, except the party militants, intensely concerned over who wins or loses.

WHAT DETERMINES PARTY SYSTEMS?

What determines whether a party system is one-party or two-party or hegemonic or turnover or in another category or combination of categories? There are, suggests Professor Eckstein, three important determinants of party systems:

> One is the general political system or certain of its substructures: party systems might be treated mainly as responsive to larger or other aspects of politics. The second is social structure and culture: party systems might be treated primarily as structures that politically crystallize socio-cultural forces. The third is their own histories: party systems with a past might be conditioned largely by that past, that is, might be self-propelling along predictable paths once set in motion, or even self-maintaining, regardless of external forces.[6]

In connection with the influence exerted by the general political system, the factor most often cited as determining the type of existing party system is the type of electoral system. The most often cited example of this is the alleged cause-and-effect relationship between the Anglo-American plurality election system and the existence of the two-party system. In capsule form, the argument runs that under the plurality system whichever party gets the most votes wins all the elective offices involved. But the number two party can always hope that at the next election the situation will be reversed. Thus it has every incentive to stay in the political arena and redouble its efforts. But for the number three, let alone a possible number four or number five, the situation is hopeless. They have no choice of ever winning unless one of the two major parties disintegrates, and historical precedents for this are rare. Since 1800 it has happened only twice in American political history—the disintegration of the Federalists early in the century and the Whigs in the 1850s—and only once in British experience—with the withering away of the Liberals in the early twentieth century.

The Indian Party System

How then can we explain the Indian party system? Since independence in 1947 India has conducted all five of its elections for the national parliament under the Anglo-American plurality system. Although it has never won a majority of the popular vote, the Congress party's share of legislative seats has varied from a low of 55 percent in the 1967 general election to a high of 72.4 percent in the 1952 election. In March of 1971, the Congress party won 67.6 percent of the legislative representation, a total of 350 out

[6]Eckstein, "Party Systems," p. 447.

of 515 seats.[7] The next strongest party, the Maoist Communist party, won only 25 seats.

In view both of the electoral system and the unbroken hegemonic dominance of the Congress party for a quarter-century now, it would be logical to find only one opposition party and a bedraggled and dispirited one at that. Instead, as has been the case in every other election since India's independence, seven other national parties and a number of regional parties have disputed the election with the dominant Congress party.[8] This discrepancy between the results produced in the Anglo-American political systems and the Indian using precisely the same electoral system suggests that while the electoral system may be a conditioning factor, it is hardly a dominant one.

Of more importance than the mechanics of the electoral system, it would seem, is the role of social and cultural influences in shaping the form of party systems. Myron Weiner has sought to explain why, in view of the already long-lasting hegemony of the Congress party, so many splinter parties exist in India. Among the reasons he suggests are these:

1. The complete lack of consensus among the opposition parties on either tactics or ultimate goals stemming from long-existing "physical and social barriers to communication—illiteracy, traditional caste and religious allegiances, language barriers, etc.—and a general lack of experience with democratic parliamentary institutions."[9]

[7]There are 518 seats in the House of the People, the elective second chamber of the Indian Parliament. At the time of writing, no figures were available on the results of three of the election districts. Hence the three seat discrepancy.

[8]In 1971, however, there was more reason for optimism than in almost any other election. In 1970 approximately 20 percent of the Congress parliamentary representation had broken off from the regular party to form the Opposition Congress, bitterly opposed to Mrs. Gandhi's program of radical political and social reform. It was widely predicted that the 1971 election would see the final disintegration of the old Congress party. Instead Mrs. Gandhi's Ruling Congress representation was increased from 228 seats to 350 seats while the Opposition Congress lost 49 of its 65 seats. Of the 16 seats it retained, 11 were in the state of Gujerat, thus reducing it to the status of a provincial opposition party. For that matter, of the 25 seats won by the Maoist Communist party, 20 were in West Bengal. Among the other six "national parties," only the pro-Moscow Communist party drew its modest 23 seat representation from as many as 8 different states of the 19 which comprise the Indian federal union. The term "national party" is used to describe the 7 opposition parties which run candidates on a nationwide basis. There are a number of parties which have strength in but one ethnic or geographical area and make no effort to conduct campaigns elsewhere. A total of 66 such regional and independent candidates were elected to the House of the People in the March, 1971, election.

[9]Myron Weiner, *Party Politics in India* (Princeton, N.J.: Princeton University Press, 1957), p. 264. The other points listed are all taken from pp. 263–264.

2. An apparent widespread "unwillingness or an inability to make calculations which would improve their electoral prospects."

3. A lack of that competitive power drive and desire to succeed which, until recently at least, has been so conspicuous a factor in Western culture since the Renaissance.

4. A disinterest in electoral activity as a road to power and a concern with maintaining purity of doctrine.

5. For the rank and file of many parties, their particular political group is a closed psychological and emotional security system which provides them with a known and reassuring outlook on the "outside" with which they have little incentive or desire to establish contact. This, coupled with a low power drive, gives little incentive to making mergers or contracting compromise alliances.

6. The lack of significantly strong and independent interest groups in the Indian political system removes a potent influence for compromise and consolidation which is present in the Anglo-American political culture. Since there is no need to court the support of such groups, "parties and especially the rank and file of parties are inclined to make decisions on the basis of internal rather than external considerations."

Obviously in the Indian case, social and cultural factors are highly influential, but they are not exclusively so. Where there are party systems with a past new social and cultural divisions may not even be able to find expression and will seek outlets other than the established party system. So, once again we are faced with the fact that there are no simple answers or explanations, for the third factor of "their own histories" seems to influence party systems also. As Eckstein puts it, "their development is largely inherent in their original shape," making it difficult, if not impossible, for new social and cultural influences to penetrate sufficiently to bring about any major changes.

Party systems then are formed by a number of complex causes and, once the mold is set, are surprisingly resistent to change. Like all institutions they tend to go on functioning in established and familiar patterns. In part, of course, this is due to the human element involved. Those who are profiting from the way in which the system is organized have no incentive for change; indeed they have every reason to oppose it. Those on the outside, barring unique developments, do not have the strength to force it. It is against this background of systemic persistence that we would like to suggest a three-part typology for the classification of systems which are not movement-regime party systems. The three categories are *smother-party* systems, *alternating-majority* systems, and *fragmented-party* systems. With these three categories we have tried to avoid playing the numbers game and instead use terms that convey some feeling of what the system is like and how its system of action functions.

SMOTHER-PARTY SYSTEMS

Smother-party systems are similar to movement regimes, but they can be classified as genuine systems, since there is interaction of two or more units. In the case of India, on the national level there are seven other units involved. In the case of Mexico, the other outstanding example of what we mean by a smother-party system, there are three other units in the party system.

We could classify both India and Mexico as having multiparty systems; why then use the odd term smother-party systems to describe them? To smother is to stifle or to suffocate, and this is just what the dominant party in a smother system does, whether deliberately or not. Unlike the restrictions under a movement regime, however, in a smother system the other parties may have full freedom of political activity, as in India and Mexico. On the other hand, as in the case of Liberia where the True Whig party has held power continuously since 1878, a mixed combination of official and unofficial harassments and inducements may make it impossible for any other organized party activity to develop.

The criterion for the inclusion of any party system in the smother category, then, is that there is one party which, although it does not formally prohibit opposition, completely dominates the political scene and has been in undisputed control of national policy for a period of years without any likelihood of change. The Mexican Party of Revolutionary Institutions, for example, ever since it was first organized in 1928, has made the nomination of its presidential candidate equivalent to his election and has consistently controlled the legislature by majorities of 80 percent or more. It is on this basis that one authority on Latin American politics classifies the Party of Revolutionary Institutions as constituting a one-party system of the "*dominant non-dictatorial*" type.[10] In the 1967 congressional election, for example, it elected 189 of the 210 members with 84.4 percent of the vote. Of the three other parties represented in the legislative branch, the next largest, the National Action Party, elected 20 deputies with 13.8 percent of the vote. So thoroughly does the Party of Revolutionary Institutions blanket the nation in terms of its affiliated and subsidiary organizations that in a nonelection year its membership is quoted as comprising 3.5 million members, as

[10]George I. Blankstein, "The Politics of Latin America," in *The Politics of the Developing Areas*, ed. Gabriel A. Almond and James S. Coleman (Princeton, N.J.: Princeton University Press, 1960), p. 480.

compared with a total of less than a half million for the other three parties combined.

Until its surprising victory in the 1971 general elections, the Indian Congress party was an example of how a "single-party dominant" system disintegrates into multi-partyism. In the decade of the 1960s, the legislative strength of Congress consistently declined and, after the party split of 1970, the prophets seemed proven correct.

But once again the persistence of habit seems to have been demonstrated. It may well be that at the next election, four years or so hence, the Congress party will disintegrate. But after the 1971 experience, there will be few who would dare to predict it. We could cite other examples from Asian, African, and Latin American sources. For that matter, within the United States party system, the "Solid South" in the period from the election of Rutherford B. Hayes in 1876 to the election of Eisenhower in 1952 constituted a smother-party system within the broader national system.

Very briefly, let us try to summarize how and why in such countries as Mexico and India such a system occurs. In several respects the smother party's origins are similar to those of a movement-regime party. The Indian Congress party is the oldest example of this. Organized in 1885 to struggle for self-government for India, the Congress party switched its goal to national independence in the early twentieth century. Under the leadership of Gandhi and Nehru, it became a national mass movement which achieved its goal of independence in 1947.

Although Mexico was never formally in the colonial status of India, for decades prior to the national revolution of 1910, as in the similar case of China, it was the victim of foreign exploitation through the medium of a corrupt and tyrannical native regime. For both India and Mexico the result was the development of mass movements for independence from foreign control through a mass-based nationalist movement led by various inspiring figures.

But here the resemblance to movement-regime parties ends. In neither India nor Mexico was any order party available to furnish a model for organization. Further, the political culture from which each of these movements developed, whether filtered through British or Latin interpretations, was based on the democratic liberal credo of the French Revolution. The idea of a suppression of opposition groups, as is the case in the movement regimes, was not part of either movement's philosophy. In neither case has there ever been any serious incentive to take such a step. It is yet to be tested whether or not this liberal tradition would survive the shock, if it ever had to, of surrendering power. The temptation could be strong to regard the victorious opposition as a threat to the welfare of the nation.

In the early days of power, the continuing presence of the leaders who achieved national independence plus the factor of the gratitude felt toward the party as an organization sufficed to make both Congress party and the Mexican revolutionary movement able to dominate their respective political systems even to the extent, in Mexico, of surviving the challenge of serious armed revolt in the late 1920s.

Again, both parties since formally assuming governmental power have built up such extensive networks both of party and affiliated group organization that on the basis of patronage and patron-client relationship the continuance in power of the party is a very practical bread-and-butter concern for a large section of the most active members of the political community. Finally we can note again Eckstein's point that "party systems may simply become incorporated into the habit background of society."

Though with far less means of compulsion, and much less wish to use them, the smother parties, like the movement regimes, are dedicated to the modernization of their respective societies. It would be fruitless to attempt an assessment of the different degrees of persuasion and compulsion used by these differing categories. But given the open structure of the smother parties and the fact that they are regularly faced with a potentially meaningful electoral challenge, it seems logical to assume that there is both a greater degree of persuasion involved and greater interaction with society in general.

On this basis, although the smother party is the dominant variable in the party-government-society relationship, it is more open to feedback from the other two units and more willing to lead rather than to drive. For these reasons, we can diagram the variable role of the smother party like this:

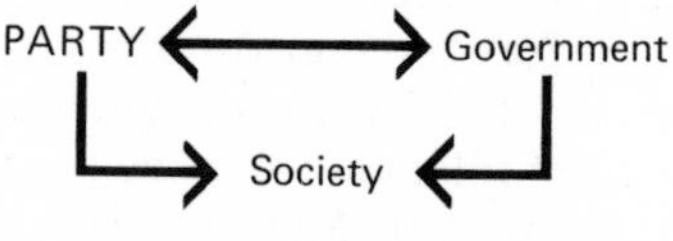

Note, that in contrast to our diagram of the dominant variable role of movement-regime parties, all of the arrows here are solid lines with strong and continuous interaction among all of the elements involved.

ALTERNATING-MAJORITY SYSTEMS

The type of party system which for Americans comes closest to being "normal" is represented by what we call the alternating-majority category. This system has nothing in common with the movement parties, but it shares with the smother parties, before they begin to decay, certain aspects of organizational structure and the fact that no one party has a legal monopoly on political action. Included in the alternating-majority category are those party systems which accept as a routine fact of political life that, with the next general election, which *must* occur within a prescribed time period, it is quite possible that the present ruling party will lose its control of the governmental machinery and will then peaceably and routinely surrender power to the successful opposition and itself assume that role with the hope of reversing it at the next election. Even in a situation such as that of the Republican Party of the United States, which lost five presidential elections in a row from 1932 through 1952, there is always the optimistic expectation that "next time things are going to be different." Above all, there is no question in the minds of either winners or losers that inevitably there will be a "next time."

This may seem an unnecessary statement of the obvious, but unfortunately it is not. Until very recently in world history, it was generally accepted that being on the losing side in any political struggle meant being stripped of honors and property and at best becoming a hunted exile if one were lucky enough to escape execution as a traitor to the state. It would be pleasant at this point to draw a flattering contrast between those dark and backward times and the enlightened outlook of the modern age. But regrettably for many of the world's political systems today, it is still highly dangerous, frequently fatal, to have lost out in the power struggle. In the movement-regime political systems, both communist and solidarity, the odds are against there being any "next time" in which to try to reverse the existing political power situation.

Indeed, so rare still is this phenomenon of accepted political opposition that a distinguished political scientist a few years ago thought it worthwhile to edit a volume of essays by various experts dealing with the topic. In his preface to *Political Oppositions in Western Democracies*, Professor Dahl comments:

> Somewhere in the world, at this moment, a political group is probably engaged in the antique art of imprisoning, maiming, torturing, and killing its opponents. Somewhere, as you read these words, a government and its opponents are no doubt trying to coerce one another by violent means. For without much question the most commonplace way for a government to deal with its opponents is to employ violence. . . .
>
> Legal party opposition, in fact, is a recent unplanned invention that has been confined for the most part to a handful of countries in Western Europe and the English-speaking world . . . of the 113 members of the United Nations in 1964, only about 30 had political systems in which full legal opposition

among organized political parties had existed throughout the preceding decade.[11]

As of 1972, the majority of the political systems where legal opposition exists are found in Western Europe and among the English-speaking countries. But due to the emergence of various new nations, the total number is now around 40 instead of the 30 mentioned by Dahl, and all are in either the alternating-majority category or the fragmented-party system group.

FRAGMENTED-PARTY SYSTEMS

The smother-party category can be classified as a system, because there is regularly recurring interaction among a definable set of units, but the alternating-majority and fragmented-party categories constitute party systems not only in name but also in the actual roles they play. In both of these two-party systems there is genuine interaction among the units involved, both in theory and in practice; the electoral process involves a genuine contest; and as a result of this, significant changes are quite likely to occur both in important officeholders and in the policies they apply.

The alternating-majority and fragmented-party systems also have in common the fact that they represent a different type of variable from any that we have diagrammed so far. Obviously in neither of these systems is any party ever in a position to dominate either society or government as in the case of the movement-regime parties. Nor, for that matter, except for brief periods such as occurred in the famous Hundred Days of Franklin Roosevelt's New Deal, is either the alternating-majority or the fragmented-party system likely to play as a dominant a role in shaping the development of either society or government as a smother party. In both systems the parties involved succeed or fail in direct relation to their abilities to understand the demands which society in general is making upon the political system and then to offer appealing formulas for translating these demands into governmental action. Given this intervening variable role then, we can diagram the part played by both these party systems like this:

This diagram in itself tells us some important facts about the nature of parties in both these systems. Would-be move-

[11]Robert A. Dahl, ed., *Political Oppositions in Western Democracies* (New Haven, Conn.: Yale University Press, 1968).

ment-regime parties, for example the communist variety, are present in virtually every alternating-majority or fragmented-party system. In most instances, however, except during periods of unique social and political upheaval, they receive only a negligible percentage of the popular vote and have only a few seats in the popularly elected chamber of the legislative branch. Significantly the only two-party systems where communist parties regularly get 20 percent or more of the vote are the fragmented-party systems of France and Italy where a state of potential, threatening, or actual political and social crisis has long been characteristic.

To succeed in terms of the political culture of their particular societies, then, parties in both the alternating-majority and fragmented systems must have the following characteristics: (1) Since success depends on electoral support, a party must try to be as inclusive as possible rather than exclusive; (2) for this reason its electoral program must possess broad appeal and offend the least possible number of voters; and (3) to accomplish both these objectives, a party can make no stringent demands on its members or potential supporters nor present radical programs which offend traditional social and political norms. It must offer policy alternatives which are innovative enough to offer new solutions to old problems but not so radical that they threaten or alarm any important groups in society. In the fragmented systems, parties obviously tend to appeal to a more limited public for support than in the more pragmatic alternating majority systems. However, under the competitive competition of elections, no party, no matter what it calls itself, is going to refuse any support it can muster or try to brand all nonparty members as undesirables.

The frame of reference within which parties must operate in the alternating-majority or fragmented systems, though less so in the latter case than in the former, indicates a good deal about the political culture of those systems. Although the political systems of Italy and France are characterized by chronic crisis, they are the exceptions to the over-all pattern. In most cases, neither the preemptive consensus of the solidarity regimes nor the coerced consensus of the communist regime is typical. Rather, the political cultures which produce the alternating-majority and fragmented-party systems are characterized by various types of cleavages. The cleavages most frequently mentioned as dividing Western societies are race, religion, language-culture, social-economic class, and section or region. The effect of these cleavages is often intensified by the impact of two other less tangible but significant cleavages: political ideology and a feeling of subcultural separateness, such as has long been perceived as characteristic of the American South. The degree to which these cleavages reinforce each other in a divisive sense or group themselves into several broad patterns, centering around one or two major cleavages to which the rest are supplemental, is an important influence in determining the type of party system which develops.

In connection with any category of cleavages it is crucial how deep and how broad they are. There is a point beyond which they cannot go without shattering the political system and producing armed struggle or actual civil war. In American political history, for example, the North-South regional, subcultural, and ideological cleavages, in the period between John Brown's raid on Harper's Ferry in 1859 and the firing on Fort Sumter in 1861, became so deep and so intense that the political party system disintegrated under the load involved.

We have then this paradoxical situation: For competitive party systems to exist there have to be varying degrees of cleavage. However, if the party system is to function at all, the intensity of cleavages must never get beyond a certain point. The American Civil War, the collapse of the French Fourth Republic under army pressure in 1958, and the military seizures of power in Asia, Africa, and Latin America are obvious examples of party systems no longer able to function successfully in processing the demands of its society for governmental action. It seems probable that an important element in the ability of the party system to cope with the demands made upon it is not necessarily associated with the volume or intensity of the demands. It is possible that a combination of adaptability, organizational strength, and the experience born of long practice are at least equally important. There is, of course, a paradox here. Often, precisely those party systems which are most lacking in these qualities are confronted with the maximum challenges and hence, in short order, burst under the pressures involved.

While it might seem almost axiomatic that virtually all such situations would be likely to develop from fragmented-party systems, such is not the case. True enough, in the developing countries the evidence seems to indicate that those among them with fragmented, i.e., multiparty, systems have had, next to those countries with no parties at all, the highest number of either successful or attempted military coups.[12] But in contrast to this is the fact, mentioned earlier, that on any list of the world's most stable democracies, a number of long-time fragmented-party systems rank high. Examples of these would be the Scandinavian countries, the Netherlands, Switzerland, and Israel. Here, perhaps, is where adaptability, organizational strength,

[12]See the article by Samuel P. Huntington, "Political Development and Political Decay," *World Politics* 17 (April 1965): 386–430.

experience, and the accustomed "set" of the party system play important roles. Above all, what has made it possible for these factors to develop over a period of time has been the character of the political culture that has produced these stable fragmented-party systems. Even France, traditionally regarded as the most volatile of all the fragmented party systems, had enough set in its party and political system to come through the crisis of de Gaulle's sudden resignation in April, 1969, with a degree of calm and self-discipline which disproved the expectations of political chaos predicted as inevitable when de Gaulle passed from the scene.

Indeed in such a country as France where political and social cleavages are wide and deep and existed long before the appearance of the modern party system, it would seem that the more parties the better. A large number of parties has the effect of dispersing and weakening the political and social antagonisms which, if they polarized in an either/or dichotomy, might well explode into outright violence, if not civil war. Under the circumstances of such aggravated social tension, a fragmented system can act as a lightning rod to dissipate potential destructive energy. Further, with the need for coalitions to gain a parliamentary majority, it can offer a sense of participation to a much larger number of groups than would be possible if there were only two huge either/or aggregations of political power to choose from.

There is another aspect to fragmented-party systems: They are not nearly so fragmented as might seem from the number of parties that contest elections, as Table 3 makes clear.

It is interesting to note that in only Finland, the Netherlands, and Switzerland with six, ten, and eight parties respectively involved in the electoral struggle, does the percentage of the total vote received by the two most important parties go down to 50 percent or lower. In eight other cases, it is 60 percent or more of the total vote cast. Even more significant is the fact that when the roles of the three largest parties in any of these fragmented systems are surveyed, in no case do they receive less than 68 percent of the total vote, and in eight cases they account for 75 percent or more. This points to the obvious conclusion that even in the fragmented-party system it is far more a matter of polarization than fragmentation. However, in the next chapter we shall consider the role played by electoral systems in fostering this fragmentation.

But in spite of the predominance of two, or, at the most, three parties, the fragmented-party system, while it shares the highly competitive character of the alternating majority parties, must be described as being shifting rather than rotating. In the American or British examples of the

Table 3
The Cohesion of Fragmented Party Systems 1967–1970

Country	Average number parties contesting election	Average % vote of two largest parties	Average % vote of three largest parties
Belgium	5	60	87
Ceylon	6	72	81
Denmark	9	54	73
Finland	6	49	70
France	7	60	78
Iceland	4	66	84
Israel	8	61 (legislative seats)	71
Italy	8	66	81
Luxembourg	4	68	84
Netherlands	10	50	61
Sudan	6	70 (legislative seats)	86
Switzerland	8	50	75
Venezuela	8	53	68

NOTE: Although the percentages for Israel and the Sudan are in terms of the number of seats held in the legislative branch, under proportional representation there would be little variance between these percentages and those received in the popular vote.

alternating-majority systems, it is usually clear within a few hours after the polls close who the next president or prime minister will be. The same can be said even where a significant third party exists, as in the case of the Australian Country party, when it is closely associated with one of the two major parties, election in and election out, in victory or defeat.

Quite different, however, is the situation with the fragmented-party system even when, as in the case of Belgium, there are only three important parties usually controlling 85 percent or more of the total vote. Under the operating conditions of the fragmented-party system, there are no automatic alliances, and it is always a matter of long and hard bargaining before it is possible to form that majority essential for the control of the legislative branch under the parliamentary system. Nor is it necessarily a matter of the third party deciding which of the two major parties it is going to support. In Belgium, the present majority was formed after a particularly severe political crisis in 1968 by a coalition of the Catholic and Socialist parties which between them had accounted for approximately 60 percent of the total vote cast. Perhaps the most extreme example of the shifting coalition created by a fragmented-party system is afforded by Belgium's neighbor, the Netherlands, where the two largest of the eight or ten parties which regularly compete in elections usually command only approximately 50 percent of the votes cast. Under even these extreme conditions, however, although it is never clear which of the minor parties may be included in the next government coalition, it is axiomatic that either the Catholic or Labor party will be its main element.

CONCLUSION

In this chapter we have tried to survey some of the possibilities for various types of party expression and the reasons for their appearance. Obviously this is but the barest outline of a highly complex and extensive subject. As important as the subject of party systems is to an understanding of the functioning of any political system, little is still understood and much more remains to be done in achieving some degree of meaningful understanding. As Professor Eckstein puts it:

> Few problems of comparative politics, then, are more crucial than those of discovering what kinds of party systems optimize satisfaction of the various ends that they may have to serve and how, and to what extent the development of such systems may be promoted. Before these problems can be coped with, however, the whole universe of party systems must be better charted, and the forces that bear upon them, and which they in turn exert, must be better understood.[13]

[13]Eckstein, "Party Systems," pp. 452–453.

ELECTORAL SYSTEMS: HOW VOTERS BEHAVE

At the beginning of Chapter 4 it was suggested that the chief function of a political party is to get control of government by placing its leaders in public office through some sort of electoral process. In this chapter we are concerned with looking at the various electoral processes which can be used for this purpose. But this is not merely an excursion into the area of mathematical analysis. In theory, electoral systems function as a means of organizing the expression of preferences by voters as to which set of leaders they prefer. But, as is often the case, electoral systems long ago came to be recognized as not merely means or techniques or convenient mechanisms but important causal factors in their own right. As we shall note later in this chapter, the structure of electoral systems has an important bearing on the way in which party systems develop and function. As the title of a brief but important book on the subject has recently expressed it, there are indeed "political consequences of election laws."

HOW VOTES ARE COUNTED

A Dutch authority on election organization has commented that "the choice of an electoral system and of its constituent parts is determined by a large number of factors of a sociological and psychological nature, which differ from country to country."[1] He then points out that the chief function an electoral system serves is to produce a representative body which will not merely be so in theory but will in reality be "truly representative." Clearly the degree of accurate representation which any electoral system is able to produce varies directly with the homogeneity of the society concerned. To put it another way, if you are electing the municipal council of a small isolated mountain village where everyone has the

[1]G. Van den Bergh, *Unity in Diversity* (London: B. T. Batsford Ltd. [ca. 1955]), p. 44.

same ethnic origins and economic, social, and religious interests, then any electoral system will suffice. It would be virtually impossible not to elect councilors who represent the feelings of the voters and are closely attuned to their outlook.

The election of the legislative body to represent the interests of a large and complex country is, however, quite a different matter, for that body will have to represent the most diverse sort of economic, social, religious, ethnic, geographical and even linguistic, differences. Under these conditions, the choice of the proper electoral system becomes a matter for intensive study.

THE PLURALITY SYSTEM

The electoral system most prevalent in the English-speaking countries of the world has remained unchanged for centuries and can be traced to the system used, particularly in Great Britain, to select representatives for the Commons when medieval kings called together assemblies of the realm. In the medieval period of Western Europe, the king was in a far different position from that of Louis XIV or the other absolutist rulers of the eighteenth century. A medieval king was often little more than first among equals and often not even that.

In order to keep power the king had to be able to gauge the mood of his people. Hence from time to time, both for this purpose and to raise money, medieval kings called periodic gatherings of the *estates of the realm.* In medieval terms, estates really meant social classes with the representation of the first and second estates, those of the clergy and the nobility, in theory being composed of everyone in those particular status groups. In English practice, however, the third estate, that of the Commons, was composed not only of representatives of the newly developing merchant class but also of the lowest and most numerous rank of the nobility, the knights who made up the country gentry. The inclusion of the knights with the town merchants and the laws of inheritance that encouraged intermixture between the two social classes were among those several lucky accidents which so greatly facilitated the development of Great Britain as the source for modern constitutional democracy.[2] As far back as 1265, for example, when Parliament was called together, the leading royal local officials, the sheriffs, were instructed to send as repre-

[2]Another fortunate accident was the English rule of primogeniture (right of the first-born to inherit). Only the oldest son could inherit his father's title and estate; other sons became commoners, happy to marry the daughter of a rich merchant who, for his part, welcomed an alliance with the gentry.

sentatives of the Commons two burgesses from every burg and two knights from every shire.

Here, in contrast to the widespread medieval practice of status or class representation, is the basis for the long-established concept of representation in terms of geography rather than of social groups. Apparently the medieval English sheriff called together as many knights of the shire or merchants of the town as were able to attend and let them, by a show of hands, choose two of their number as parliamentary representatives. Election required only getting more votes than anyone else. It was from this origin that the Anglo-American plurality system of election developed over the centuries.

For reasons peculiar to its political and social development, it was only in England during the seventeenth and eighteenth centuries that the concept of a representative assembly became firmly established. But the very existence of such a body as the House of Commons necessitated some sort of electoral procedure. For this purpose the old medieval pattern served very well. Small local districts continued as the geographical basis for representation. The electorate was highly restricted (approximately 5 percent of the adult males before 1832) and homogeneous, drawn as it was from a limited socioeconomic group. Thus it was by the accident of history that the Anglo-American plurality system or, as some foreign observers like to term it, the *first-past-the-post* system, came into existence.

Spread of the Plurality System

In many ways the plurality or simple majority system is a peculiar one that shouldn't work as well as it does. As Van den Bergh comments with some irritation:

> It is a strange experience—for us—when someone with 30 votes is elected chairman, while his two opponents get 25 and 20 votes, respectively. But an Englishman, generally speaking, does not see anything uncommon in this. The first-past-the-post system has struck root there. Does this expression perhaps denote that the system is bound up with the sporting spirit so inherent in this great nation? For a horse which is the first to pass the winning post it is, indeed, a matter of indifference whether it has left one or many horses behind it. . . . Thus the average Englishman considers the chairman with his thirty votes a smart fellow; he has left two opponents behind him, the one at a distance of five, the other at a distance of ten votes!
>
> This English system could not possibly be transplanted to other countries. It has come to stay there—it could never thrive elsewhere.[3]

Nevertheless, "this English system" has thrived elsewhere. Such widely separated and socially different coun-

[3]Van den Bergh, *Unity in Diversity,* p. 48.

tries as the United States, India, Canada, New Zealand, and South Africa all use it. Admittedly the reason has little to do with logic or any particular virtues of the first-past-the-post system. It is rather that all of these countries, as one-time British colonies, became familiar with the system during the colonial period and simply continued to use it.

It is not surprising that the United States, Canada, New Zealand, and South Africa settled in large part by people of English stock, who for so long dominated political life, should have continued to use the English system simply because they were accustomed to it. What is surprising is that India, with no similar cultural ties and a multiparty system which includes at least eight parties represented in the federal House of the People and several dozen more in the various states should have continued to do so. It is a good illustration of how tradition and the familiar ease of the accustomed way of doing things so often outweighs the logical advantages that change would bring. In things political as well as personal, emotion often outweighs logic as the determining factor.

Deficiencies of the Plurality System

The deficiencies of the simple-majority or plurality system are quite obvious. As long as only two parties are involved, it doesn't matter what type of electoral system is used. In the usual organizational pattern of electing one representative from a district, either Party A or Party B will get the most votes and represent a majority opinion. When more than two parties are contesting the election, however, the shortcomings of the plurality system become immediately apparent. The most recent and dramatic example of this was in the United States presidential election of 1968 when the popular vote for Richard Nixon was only 43.5 percent of the approximately 73 million votes cast. Two other times in the last hundred years American presidents have received a minority of the popular vote: Woodrow Wilson in 1912 with not quite 42 percent of the vote and Abraham Lincoln in 1860 with only 40 percent. The most important objection to the plurality electoral system, however, is the way in which it destroys the prospects of the number 3 party, not to mention any others.

The British Liberal party knows this all too well. After its disintegration as one of the two important parties early in the twentieth century when its left wing joined the newly emerging Labour party and the Business Liberals officially became Conservatives, the Liberal party continued to hang on. But particularly since World War II, the party's hopes for any sort of comeback have been consistently frustrated by the workings of the plurality system. Even when the Liberals have been able to attract a substantial number of new voters disenchanted with both Conservatives and Labour, it has meant little in terms of any gains in party representation in the House of Commons, the place where it would count the most. To their frustration, in election after election the Liberals have had the meaningless satisfaction of seeing their candidates place second instead of third. Under the plurality system the winning candidate is just as successful whether he has received 90 percent of the vote cast or, in a three-way race, 34 percent, so the Liberal party has continued to survive but never to prosper.

One of the most dramatic examples of the way in which the plurality system penalizes a third party is the unhappy fate of the Liberals in the British general elections of 1955 and 1959. In the 1955 election, the Liberal party received a modest 2.7 percent of the vote and elected six members to the House of Commons. Four years later a greatly increased Liberal vote gave the Liberal party almost 6 percent of the vote cast, more than a 100 percent increase over the support of four years previously. But translated into the realities of the cold gray dawn of the morning after, the Liberals discovered to their frustration that they had still won only six seats in the House of Commons. The only achievement of the newly won support was the empty one of having displaced either the Labour or Conservative candidate as the number two man in election district after election district.

The comparative results in a typical election district are shown in Table 4. The Liberal party in this election district doubled its vote but in terms of practical results it achieved only the empty satisfaction of displacing the Labour party as number two in the district. The grim reality faced by the British Liberals and any other third party under the plurality system is that, barring a highly unlikely political revolution, it can occasionally become number two on the political totem pole but never number one. Other than in times of extreme dissatisfaction by the voters with one of the two major parties, a third party will continue to eke out a drab existence supported by a probably diminishing band of faithful followers who support it as a matter of dedicated principle, not practical politics.

In Indian elections, the way in which the plurality system inflates the triumph of the number one party, even though it has won by a small percentage over its competi-

Table 4
Comparative British Election Results

	1955 Election	1959 Election
Conservative candidate	10,512	9,311
Labour candidate	7,802	5,309
Liberal candidate	3,614	7,228

Table 5
Popular Vote of Congress Party in India

	1952	1957	1962	1967	1971
Percent of seats won	72.4	70.5	73.2	55.0	67.6
Percent of popular vote	45.0	47.8	44.7	40.8	43.6

tors, is very clear indeed. In the national elections which India has held since achieving its independence in 1948, the percentage of the popular vote received by the Congress party and the percentage of the seats that this won for the party in *Lok Sabha* (the popularly elected lower chamber) were as shown in Table 5.

Because the Congress candidates have so consistently received more votes than any other single party, the 12 to 15 other parties which have contested every general election have consistently experienced the same frustrating experience as the British Liberal party. But as long as the Congress party continues to maintain a majority in the legislature, any change in India's British-type plurality electoral system seems unlikely.

Impact of the Plurality System

There are some rather obvious conclusions that can be drawn from the impact the mechanical workings of the plurality system have on the nature of the party and on the political system as a whole. But before we turn to a survey of the positive effects of the plurality system, an important and widely held proposition should be considered first. And that is that the plurality system almost automatically creates a two-party electoral system. Most of the time, this is true, but, under certain special conditions, this "sociological law" does not apply.

Rae made an extensive investigation of the truth of this proposition in terms of Canadian elections and found that of the 107 cases he examined, 89.7 percent did show a direct relationship between the plurality election system and a two-party pattern as the norm. He found, however, that in some areas of Canada, notably Quebec Province with its totally different French-Canadian cultures, the candidates of Canada's two major parties, the Progressive Conservatives and Liberals, were often defeated by the candidates of locally popular minor parties such as Social Credit and various French separatist parties. He comments, "The Canadian exceptions have a fairly obvious explanation: the intense hostility between overlapping regional, cultural, and linguistic groups produced a strong base of support for locally strong minority parties."[4]

[4]Douglas W. Rae, *The Political Consequences of Electoral Laws* (New Haven, Conn.: Yale University Press, 1967), p. 94.

As a result of his research, Rae found it necessary to modify the basic proposition about the relationship between the plurality system and two parties to read, "Plurality formulae are always associated with two-party competition except where strong local minority parties exist." This amended proposition goes far to explain why in India there is the seemingly contradictory combination of the Anglo-American plurality system and a large number of parties, particularly in provincial elections.

One of the most obvious positive effects of the plurality system is the way in which it so richly rewards the number 1 party. To win, it needs only vote more than any other party, even if the total number of votes cast runs into the thousands. But the corollary of this agreeable political consequence is that next time around it will be equally easy to lose by one vote. In similar fashion, the leaders of the number 2 party, even if as badly defeated as were the Republicans in 1936 and 1964, can take much comfort from the fact that next time around all that is needed for a comeback is one more vote than the opposition. While leaders of third or fourth parties may grasp hopefully at this encouraging straw, the more realistic among them will realize that it is very unlikely, barring an unprecedented political upheaval, that this offers them any reason for optimism about the next election.

ABSOLUTE-MAJORITY SYSTEM

The frequently distorted and unfair results produced by the simple-majority or plurality system has led to the creation of *absolute-majority* systems of voting, still based on a one-member district but designed to insure that the successful candidate represents a majority of the voters rather than merely a plurality. One way of accomplishing this is the two-election or run off system used in France under the Fourth Republic (1946-1958) and widely used in American party nominating primaries. The system operates in two simple stages. In the first election, any number of candidates may run for office. Then, some two or four weeks later, there is a run off between the two who received the most votes in the first election. This system results in a majority choice for representation and gives a continued reason for existence to a number of political groups.

The two-round system makes it logical to rally behind whichever of the two top vote winners in the first round is closest to one's own particular party program. It is part of the rules of the game that next time around, if your party or group comes out number one or number two, the favor will be returned. Thus, the absolute-majority system permits both diversity in electoral competition and the choice of a representative who can claim to speak for a majority of the voters in his district. But the shortcoming of the two-round or any other variation of the absolute-majority system is obvious.[5] While it permits diversity of competition, it still does not offer even a sizable minority an opportunity to have its own representation. It offers only the not very satisfactory choice of the lesser evil. For this reason some variation of proportional representation (PR), first invented by the Englishman Thomas Hare in the mid-nineteenth century, is a much more widely used alternative.

PROPORTIONAL-REPRESENTATION SYSTEM

Although its detailed workings are often highly complicated, the purpose of the proportional-representation system is exactly what the name implies: to insure, with as much mathematical precision as possible, that all significant currents of political opinion are guaranteed a voice in the legislative body. As you realize, the need for this varies from one political culture to another. In some cases, it is an absolute necessity for the sheer survival of the political system concerned. In others it is mildly desirable. In still other cases, proportional representation is a needlessly complicated and even undesirable electoral system.[6] We shall discuss the reasons for these varying situations, but first let us look at the mechanical operation of one of the most widely used PR systems, that of *the highest average*, often referred to as the *D'Hondt system* after the Belgian mathematician who devised it.

[5]The other variation on the absolute-majority system, in current use in Australian national elections, is the *preferential ballot* system. Voters mark a one, two, three preference among the candidates. If no candidate has enough number one preferences to win, the lowest man is eliminated and his second and third preferences distributed among the other candidates. This procedure is repeated until one candidate has accumulated enough of second and third preference choices to give him an absolute majority when added to his own first choice votes.

[6]From 1937 through the election of 1945, New York City used a system of proportional representation. The initial result was to reduce Democratic dominance of the city council from 92 percent to 54 percent. In subsequent elections held under PR, however, the Democratic percentage of seats on the council varied from a low of 61 percent to a high of 67 percent. While several small minority groups did obtain representation during this period, the basic role of the Democrats as the mother party of New York City was not changed and the sole benefit to the other parties was that they had a new setting in which to continue being impotent. For the composition of the city council, before, during, and after PR, see Wallace S. Sayre and Herbert Kaufman, *Governing New York City: Politics in the Metropolis* (New York: Norton, 1965), pp. 618–619. Clearly under such conditions as this, PR is more an expensive nuisance than a useful device.

Before we describe the workings of the system, there are several important differences that should be noted between the plurality, the absolute-majority, and any type of proportional-representation system. Most important is the difference in the number of legislative members elected from a single district under the other two systems and PR. Under PR, at least two candidates must be chosen from a single district since there are obvious physical and ideological difficulties in apportioning a single representative among various parties. While the election of from three to five candidates from a single district seems to be the usual case, in theory in both the Netherlands and in Israel the whole country constitutes a single election district for the selection of the entire membership of the popularly elected legislative branch, the Second Chamber.

Another important and distinctive characteristic of PR requires comment: its focus on party rather than on personality. In the single-member electoral district, regardless of what system is used, the result is often determined by the personal impression made by the candidate on the voters. However, when each party is offering three or five or more candidates, as is the case in the usual PR district, the party label and what the voter thinks it stands for rather than personality is usually the deciding factor. But in categorizing systems, as Max Weber pointed out long ago, there are in reality no "ideal" types. Undoubtedly many voters in single-member districts blindly support any candidate of the party to which they feel allegiance, and in multiple-member districts there are those who feel strong personal rather than party attachments.

Usually, however, the *list system* of PR does encourage voting in terms of party. Under the appropriate party emblem and official name, the election ballot for each party lists in one-two-three order candidates for as many seats as are to be filled from that district. In theory each party conducts its campaign with the expectation that it will win every seat. In actuality this seldom happens and only in a very unusual district. Indeed if this were not so, there would be no need to use PR at all. Under normal conditions even the most important parties do not expect to elect other than the number 1 or 2 candidate on their lists when there are five or six seats to be filled. Under these circumstances, each party will list its leading figures as top choices both to insure that they, at least, are elected and also to offer a good way to combine both personal and party appeal. Most PR systems require a straight vote for the party label. Some, however, permit the voter to cast his vote for the party by placing his *X* opposite the name of his favorite candidate on the list. This, in theory could mean that a number 5 man would be elected instead of the name heading the list. But, since the reason for the number

1 man having that position is his personal standing in the party and among voters, such an upset is highly unlikely. Usually the candidates in other than the top positions on the list are either junior party leaders who are campaigning for the sake of experience or dedicated party members who have let their names be put on the list simply to fill it out.

We mentioned above that lists are identified by party emblems and names. But there is another method of identification which is unique to the multiple choices offered under PR. This comes from the custom of giving each party list a number which determines its location on the election ballot. Sometimes the numbering is done by lot. More often, however, the rank of the party in voting preference after the last election determines its number. If nothing else, the system makes for convenience in campaign advertising. Anyone who has been in a Western European country during an election campaign will remember seeing numerous election posters bearing nothing but the particular party's familiar symbol and the slogan, "Vote List 1" (or 2 as the case may be).

The D'Hondt System

The actual workings of the proportional-representation system can best be understood by seeing how the seats would be distributed among the various parties in a single election district. For our purposes we will assume that this is a large district with ten seats at stake. In sequence, these would be the steps under the D'Hondt system in determining the distribution of the seats.

Counting the Votes for Each Party List. Let us assume that in this large election district seven parties each offered a list. For simplicity's sake we will designate them alphabetically and round off the vote received by each of the party lists as follows:

1. List A	15,800
2. List B	14,200
3. List C	13,700
4. List D	9,600
5. List E	6,500
6. List F	3,200
7. List G	1,800
	64,800

As would be expected, the parties which in their vote totals in the previous election earned the number 1, 2, and 3 positions have become parties A, B, and C. One of the characteristics of parties under PR is that, barring political revolutions, their relative positions change very little from one election to another, unlike the frequent and violent oscillations possible under majority-type systems. It is, of course, precisely because the divisions of political opinion are so constant, both as to concepts and degrees of support, that a PR electoral system was necessary in the first place.

Determining the Election Quotient. At this point the distribution of legislative seats under a PR system begins to take the appearance of a vote auction, and an exclusive one at that. Unless a minimum price is met, one is not even permitted to bid. The minimum price, in terms of votes, which must be paid for a legislative seat is determined by a set formula. This involves dividing the total vote received by all parties by the number of seats to be allocated. In our example this means that no party has any hope of getting even a single seat unless it is able to *pay* a minimum price of 6,480 votes. The immediate result of this is to eliminate parties F and G right away, while parties A through E have each won at least one seat. In the case of party E this is it. But only five of the ten seats have been distributed. So the next step is to determine how to distribute the remaining five seats among parties A, B, C, and D.

The Principle of the Highest Average. It is at this state in the distribution of seats that the auction comparison becomes obvious. For the remaining seats are given to whichever party can afford to pay most votes for them. Each party's total vote is divided by one more seat than it has already won. The result then looks like this:

1. List A	7,900
2. List B	7,100
3. List C	6,850
4. List D	4,800

Seats 6, 7, 8, and 9 are distributed in order to parties A through D. The repetition of this process, with each party's total this time divided by three, results in the tenth and last seat going to party A which yet again is able to pay more votes for it than any of the other parties. The final result is that Party A has won three seats, Parties B, C, and D have won two seats each, and Party E has won one seat.

While it would never happen under a plurality system that ten individuals would be elected from the same district, if it did the rather ridiculous result would be that Party A would win all ten seats. Under an absolute-majority system, Parties A and B, as the two leading parties, would be the only ones eligible to compete in the second-round run off election. As was the case in France under the Fourth Republic, in the interim between the first and second elections, these parties would try to outbid each other for the support of the other parties which received almost 50 percent of the total vote cast. For the other parties, under these conditions, there are two alternatives. If a party feels intensely that its program is the only possible "gospel of salvation" for the nation, then it might well decide that it would be a betrayal of principle to make any kind of political deal with one of the two major parties and simply withdraw from the political arena at this point. This policy was frequently followed by the Communist party in France under the Fourth Republic. Or, and this is far more often the case, swallowing their ideological pride, the other parties would make the choice of the lesser evil between A and B and support whichever of them comes relatively closest to their particular program. Also inevitably involved in this, of course, is the question of which of the two major parties is prepared to offer the most meaningful inducements in terms of a share of influence in various appointments and the determination of policy.

Role of Proportional Representation

Before we turn from this survey of electoral systems, several observations should be made. Among English-speaking peoples there is a widely held belief that proportional representation is a bad thing. Always mentioned as the triumphant proof of this is the chaotic state of the French political system under the Third and Fourth Republics (1873-1940 and 1946-1958). Yet of the world's 21 most stable constitutional democracies, 16 conduct their elections under some type of proportional-representation system. Electoral systems do reflect the nature of their particular systems, and they even intensify certain already existing characteristics. But no electoral system is primarily responsible for good or bad, stable or unstable government.

We mentioned earlier that for some political systems a form of proportional representation is necessary if the system is to maintain itself, let alone achieve its goals in an orderly way. In Chapter 5 it was suggested that under certain socioeconomic and cultural conditions, a fragmented-party system may well offer the best guarantee of political stability. At the risk of repeating some points already made, let us think about the connection between PR and fragmented-party systems. The fragmented-party systems came into existence because, long before the era of mass democracy and political parties, wide and deep cleavages existed in various societies. In these societies disparate groups accepted some sort of coexistence, however strained and uneasy, perhaps based on fear of chaos and civil war or perhaps out of the sheer inability to extirpate the other groups because of the even balance of forces. Coexistence may even derive from the fact that, over a long period of time, a grudging if distant tolerance towards other groups as being well-meaning, if mistaken, has come about. The scrupulously maintained but coolly correct cabinet alliances between Catholics and Protestants in the Netherlands are an example of this. In any case, each group needs its own individual means of political expression in party terms, for these parties are in existence because they are minorities which already have a feeling of apartness.

If the electoral system is of such a nature that it is obviously hopeless for these groups to expect ever to play any role in determining policy or to have any voices to speak for them in legislative bodies, alienation will rapidly become embittered frustration, and any sense of having a stake in the system will soon be lost. It is under these conditions that PR, which gives some meaning and purpose to a fragmented system, serves a constructive role in promoting political stability and in furnishing an important source of support for the maintenance of the political system.

In contrast, PR serves little practical purpose in the Anglo-American political culture, where there is a minimum of ideological division and conflict over policy issues is essentially the question of how much, how soon. Under these conditions it is logical for voters to group themselves under either the "do it now and as much as possible" party banner or that of the "wait a while and do it gradually" opposition. As the fate of American third parties has demonstrated, efforts to create any kind of an ideological movement are frustrated by the basic character of the political culture and by how voters behave.

HOW VOTERS BEHAVE

If asked to sum up how voters behave in a single word, most veteran politicians would probably reply, "Inexplicably." Ever since election results became an important aspect of the political system's functioning, what the electorate is going to do has been a cause for deep concern on the part of candidates and of intense interest to political scientists. But until 1916 this was a matter of guesswork, based on political experience. In 1916 the *Literary Digest,* a popular national weekly, conducted the first presidential straw poll by mailing out ballots to its subscribers during the election campaign and asking them to indicate their choice for president. In 1916, and in every election through 1932, the *Digest* predicted the results of the presidential election well in advance and established itself as the leading news magazine of the 1920s.

In 1936, the *Digest* followed its well-tested procedures on a greater scale than ever before, mailing out 20 million preference ballots and getting an impressive 7 million replies. In late October the magazine predicted that the Republican candidate Alf Landon would defeat Franklin

Roosevelt with 59 percent of the total vote and 370 electoral votes. In the election, Landon received only 41 percent of the popular vote and carried only Maine and Vermont for a total of 8 electoral votes out of a possible 531![7]

However, in that same presidential election, a new type of public-opinion polling pioneered by Dr. George Gallup, who the year before had established the American Institute of Public Opinion, predicted the election outcome within a few percentage points of the actual results. These contrasting results dramatically demonstrated the difference between the old and the new polling techniques. The tried-and-true method, at least until 1936, and the one used by the *Digest* had been to mail ballots out to subscribers and to an extensive list of names drawn from city telephone directories and property-tax rolls. In the elections from 1916 through 1932 this had been an accurate enough procedure. None of these elections had seen the voters sharply divide on the basis of social or economic differences. Further, throughout the 1920s there was a normal Republican predominance which drew strong support from all sections of the population and, with the exception of the Democratic Solid South, from all parts of the country. In 1932 there was even greater unanimity of opinion in opposition to Herbert Hoover, who had been elected president in 1928 just in time to be held responsible for the Great Depression, which set in the following year.

Why the *Digest* Poll Failed in 1936

But between 1932 and 1936 a great divide had been crossed in American politics. With Franklin Roosevelt's launching of the New Deal in 1933, the United States was pushed into the modern era of the active state and social politics. One of the most important results of this was that voting preference rapidly became a matter of social and economic pressures and loyalties. This was the direct cause of the *Digest*'s humiliating fiasco. In 1936 only relatively well-to-do people could afford to subscribe to magazines, have their own telephones, or own their homes. The vast majority of Americans in 1936 were not in the groups to which the *Digest* in all good faith sent out its straw ballots. Further, in Franklin Roosevelt they had come to see a great leader who was trying to help the "little guy." In 1936 the ele-

[7]Prior to 1936, while Maine was still voting for its presidential electors in September, two months ahead of the rest of the nation, there was a never very accurate slogan, "As Maine goes, so goes the nation." After the Landon debacle of 1936, some political wit revised it to read, "As goes Maine, so goes Vermont!" Shortly thereafter the Maine legislature changed the time of choosing presidential electors to coincide with the rest of the nation.

ments of social status and economic interest became the important determinants of American political thinking.[8]

PURPOSE OF VOTING SURVEYS

Today, it is customary to make elaborate surveys of the characteristics of the typical voter for a particular candidate. Table 6 gives a profile of the voting patterns in the 1968 elections.

To take only the distribution of the ethnic- or occupational-group vote, it is clear that the voting patterns estab-

Table 6
Voting Patterns by City, Size, and Income

	Nixon	Humphrey	Wallace
Residence			
Cities over 500,000	34	59	7
Cities 50,000 to 500,000	40	51	9
Cities less than 50,000	45	46	8
Suburbs	51	40	9
Rural and small town	48	37	16
Income			
High income (above $10,000)	54	39	6
Middle income ($5,000 to $10,000)	43	47	10
Low income (below $5,000)	40	49	11
Ethnic or Occupational Group			
Negro ghetto	15	79	6
Blue collar	43	47	10
Farm white	48	32	20
Other whites	51	42	7
Region			
New England	36	59	4
Mid-Atlantic	43	49	7
Midwest	46	45	9
Great Plains	48	44	8
Rocky Mountains	53	39	8
Southwest	52	40	8
Pacific Coast	45	47	7
Border States	42	33	25
Deep South	21	25	52

SOURCE: *The National Observer*, November 11, 1968. Compiled and furnished by the Columbia Broadcasting System and the Congressional Quarterly, Inc.

[8]But compared to the distinctive political loyalties of different social classes in even so moderate a country as Norway, both American parties are still surprisingly broad in their appeals. In the 1960 presidential election, two researchers concluded that "The Democratic Party draws 30 per cent of its adherents from the white-collar occupations, 46 per cent from the blue collar. The Republicans come 36 per cent from the white-collar occupations and 39 per cent from the blue-collar." Angus Campbell and Henry Valen, "Party Identification in Norway and the United States," *Public Opinion Quarterly* 25 (1961): 514–515.

lished in 1936 have changed but little. The blue-collar and Negro-ghetto voters are overwhelmingly Democratic while farm white and other whites, by which presumably is meant much the same group as the nonmanual group of the 1936 survey, is predominantly Republican in its sympathies. Again, in the income category, the high-income group continues predominantly Republican.

Voting-profile surveys are now routine in most of the constitutional democracies where it is possible to carry them on. In Great Britain, for example, over a 20-year period, the Labour Party drew 57 percent to 68 percent of its support from voters in the manual occupation category. During the same period, almost the reverse was true for the Conservatives who drew from 53 percent to 73 percent of their strength from nonmanual sources.

The sophistication of modern survey techniques makes it possible to sketch a rather detailed picture of what sort of people are most likely, or unlikely, to participate in elections. One survey summarizes it:

> Thus we see that in 1960 (and the findings are much the same for other years) high electoral turnout was associated with the following interrelated cluster of attributes: college education, professional, managerial or white-collar occupation, metropolitan residence. Low turnout was related to factors such as grade-school education, unskilled occupation, and the especially deprived status in which a large proportion of American Negroes find themselves.[9]

In August, 1968, approximately two months before the presidential election, the Gallup Poll conducted a survey to determine the number of unregistered eligible voters. As of mid-August a surprising total of some 29 million Americans of voting age were still not registered, or 41 percent of the approximately 73 million votes actually cast in that year's election.

The breakdown of these nonregistered voters by sex, party, and age groups is shown below:

Men	25%
Women	26%
Republicans	16%
Democrats	24%
Independents	33%
21–29 years	49%
30–49 "	24%
50 and over	16%

The low percentage of nonregistered Republicans very probably could be attributed to the smell of victory in the air, while the high percentage of nonregistered Democrats, and even higher percentage of Independents, quite possibly indicated an alienation from political participation in the

[9]Fred I. Greenstein, *The American Party System and the American People* (Englewood Cliffs, N.J.: Prentice-Hall, 1965), p. 20.

period just after the traumatic shock of the events at the 1968 Democratic convention. Even more significant in terms of alienation (or apathy) is the very high percentage of eligible nonregistered voters in the 21-29 age group. The potential power of younger voters in terms of sheer numbers is indicated by the fact that in 1968, even before the 1970 census, the median age was estimated at 27.7 years, with 125 million under the age of 30 out of a population of 201 million individuals. In connection with low turnout in voting, it is interesting to note that one of the earliest studies made of voting behavior, shortly after World War I, was concerned with nonvoting. This study, based on an empirical survey of certain Chicago wards, cited such factors as physical difficulties (illness, absence, need to nurse dependent family member); legal and administrative obstacles, including "fear of disclosure of age" which presumably was most characteristic of the just enfranchised feminine section of the population; disbelief in women's voting ("objections of husband"); disgust with politics including "disbelief in all political action"; and finally "general indifference and inertia." While it is doubtful that in 1972 any husband would (dare?) object to his wife's voting, political alienation and "general indifference and inertia" remain as hardy perennials.

POLITICAL INVOLVEMENT

In his book *Political Life,* Robert E. Lane distinguishes six categories of political involvement. In degree of intensity and percentage of voters involved, they are: 1. Organization activists (1 percent); 2. Organization contributors (5 percent); 3. Opinion leaders (25 percent); 4. Voters (35 percent); 5. Nonvoters (30 percent); 6. Apoliticals (4 percent). The first two categories correspond to Duverger's first two types of involvement in strictly party activity. These are the groups of the militants and supporters. Like Lane, Duverger regards militants (organization activists) as the individuals who make it possible for a party to operate. Whatever their motives, the individuals in this category feel very strongly about the welfare of their party and are working for its interests both between and during election campaigns. It was Lenin's hope when he outlined his famous concept of the order party in *What Is To Be Done?* (1902) to create a whole party composed of such individuals. But even in communist parties today certainly no more than a small percentage of the membership is in this category.[10] Rather

[10]Most logically it would be the approximately 10 percent of the total membership of the CPSU who are full-time party functionaries. In a party not holding power, where the level of revolutionary dedication would presumably be higher the percentage would be greater.

more realistically, Duverger notes that in those parties which have membership lists, the great majority of members fall into the supporter group. Both Lane and Duverger mean the same by the voter category: citizens whose political involvement begins and ends on election day. In his nonvoter category, Lane apparently includes those citizens who vote once in a great while when some unique issue stirs them out of their normal apathy and who glance at the political headlines in their newspapers as they look for the sports section.

Lane's category of opinion leaders includes those who constantly discuss and comment on political affairs to family and friends and thus influence *their* feelings and reactions. In Almond and Verba's classic study of political attitudes and democracy in five nations, percentage distributions were compiled on the frequency with which political and governmental activities are followed. The distribution of the results for the five nations involved is shown in Table 7.

Several interesting hypotheses could be drawn from this table about voting behavior in these five countries. Let us, first of all, see what line 1 seems to suggest. In connection with the percentages for the U.S., U.K., and Germany, can the conclusion be drawn that political activity in these three countries tends to be strongly issues-oriented while in Italy and Mexico, since there are so few regular followers of political and governmental developments, it is largely personality-oriented? Here is an interesting proposition for further research. Further, what does it mean that the U.S. and the U.K., the world's two oldest democracies, have a lower percentage of individuals in the "Regularly" category than does Germany, where democracy has always led a somewhat precarious existence?

In Table 8, Almond and Verba show the relationship in these same five countries between education and interest

Table 7
Frequency with which Political and Governmental Activities Are Followed

Percentage who report they follow accounts of political and governmental affairs	U.S.	U.K.	Germany	Italy	Mexico
Regularly	27	23	34	11	15
From time to time	53	45	38	26	40
Never	19	32	25	62	44
Other and don't know	1	1	3	1	1

SOURCE: Gabriel A. Almond and Sidney Verba, *The Civic Culture* (Princeton, N.J.: Princeton University Press, 1963), p. 89. Copyright © 1963, Princeton University Press. Final percentages for each column and the total number of interviewees for each country have been omitted.

Table 8
Relationship Between Education and Interest in Political Affairs

Nation	Total percentage	Primary or less	Some secondary	Some university
U.S.	80	67	84	96
G.B.	68	60	77	92
Germany	72	69	89	100
Italy	36	24	58	87
Mexico	55	51	76	92

SOURCE: Almond and Verba, *The Civic Culture,* p. 96. Total number of interviewees for each country has been eliminated.

in political affairs in terms of following politics regularly or from time to time.

Once again the relationship between education, political interest, and political participation is obvious. It is clear that a cluster of factors is involved. Even in Italy, where the degree of alienation from political affairs is so much more pronounced than in the other four countries, the top educational and social level has an impressively high percentage of interest in political affairs. It is interesting to note that Germany, which across the chart is higher at each of the three levels than any other country, does not offer much confirmation of that widely and long-held theory of the relationship between an informed citizenry and a strong democracy.

DETERMINANTS OF VOTING BEHAVIOR

Party allegiance, issue appeal, and candidate magnetism are powerful determinants of voting behavior. When all three coincide, there is no question of how the voter will behave. But far more often the voter is confronted with a series of cross-pressures which collide with each other. In 1960, for example, studies show that many a dedicated Southern Democrat who was also a devout Baptist found it emotionally difficult if not impossible to vote for the party's presidential candidate, John F. Kennedy, the first Roman Catholic to run for the presidency since the unsuccessful effort of Al Smith in 1928. Similarly, in 1964 large numbers of normally Republican voters deserted their party because they distrusted the domestic and foreign policies which Barry Goldwater proposed to follow. And, of course, the triumphs of Eisenhower both in 1952 and 1956 had nothing to do with party allegiance or issue appeal. Rather they were due to the magnetic attraction he exerted.[11]

[11]Eisenhower's appeal, particularly in the 1956 election, makes dubious a number of the conclusions drawn from the election results. There is general agreement that Eisenhower could have been elected on either of the two major party tickets and probably would have won running as an independent. Therefore conclusions drawn from

More often than not the results of these conflicting cross-pressures are purely negative. If the voter is unhappy with both candidates and issues, his family and friends are divided on their own stands, and information about issues and personalities is conflicting and confusing, there is a strong incentive simply to go fishing on election day or simply stay home and not vote. If, added to all of the above nonincentives, the polls have predicted a landslide victory for one of the candidates or it rains or snows on election day, the odds become lopsided indeed. Those who in any degree are confused, bewildered, frustrated, or uncertain will seize on one or all of these reasons for not voting. Only the professional party workers and the most strongly militant supporters can be counted on to appear under these discouraging conditions.

In contrast, the more concurrent pressures there are working together, the more likely it is that the voter will cast his ballot on election day. If, besides the fact that the party he usually supports is offering an appealing candidate who has the "right" stand on the issues the voter is concerned about, all of his family and friends feel the same way, and, finally, the election is forecast as being excitingly close, it is highly likely, fair weather or foul, that he will go to the polls.

There are, of course, a number of other factors which condition political participation besides those we've just mentioned. In a classic sociological analysis of the elements of modern democracy, Lipset notes that there are very similar social characteristics connected with voting and nonvoting for a number of the Western democracies. Whether in the United States, West Germany, or Scandinavia, an individual is far more likely to participate in elections if he has better than average education and income, is in a business or profession, is over 35, is married, is a member of various organizations, and has lived in his community for some time.[12] Nor was the consistent use of the masculine pronoun in the previous sentence accidental. For "he" is far more likely to be interested in political affairs than "she." Also, in the United States, electoral participation is more likely if the man is white than if he is Negro or a member of another group such as Puerto Rican or Mexican-American.[13]

---

either or both of these elections about shifts between the two parties are of dubious value. Probably the most normal election of recent years on which valid conclusions for electoral behavior can be based is 1968, since 1960 was distorted by the Catholic issue and 1964 by the Goldwater crusade.

[12]Seymour Martin Lipset, *Political Man: The Social Bases of Politics* (Garden City, N.Y.: Doubleday, 1960).

[13]There seems to be some indication that since the Voting Rights Act of 1965 the lower-class Negro has come to feel less impotent and

One point of contrast which Lipset notes is that there is a higher turnout among workers in Western Europe and a lower turnout among American workers. This seeming inconsistency in itself is an indication of the different patterns of development of Western European and American political culture. In Western Europe the labor movement has a much longer tradition of militant political, rather than purely economic, action and from its beginnings has always been strongly under the influence of Marxist and socialist groups imbued with a concept of class consciousness and keenly attuned to the need for political participation.

The reasons why the more active participants in political affairs have the characteristics that Lipset notes are obvious. In terms of both the printed word and personal contact, the individuals in this group have access to a number of sources of information about political affairs and a feeling, in contrast to both the ignorance and feelings of impotence of lower socioeconomic groups, that they can do something about political affairs since they are aware of how the levers of political power can be pulled.

Role of Childhood Socialization

How do people in general acquire an awareness of political affairs? Apparently at a very early age. In the early 1960s two political scientists discovered that political socialization begins at the kindergarten level and even perhaps as early as age 3 when such questions as "Who pays the policeman?" and "Why can't we park here?" are asked. Along with the policeman, the president is an early recognized authority figure. And, "as early as the second grade," the researchers found, "large numbers are nevertheless able to assert a party identification."[14] Even at this early age there appears an acceptance of the fact that others are entitled to have a different partisan commitment and that everyone must accept the results of the election campaign.

Another such study (see Table 9) indicates the significant roles played both by parents' political orientations and changes in economic status in determining the party allegiance of voters. There was, the study noted, "a substantial stability of political preference from one generation to the next." However, there is a noticeable shift from both Democratic categories to (presumably) Republican support.

This rather close correlation between students and par-

---

less alienated while his white counterpart, as a result of the attention given to Negro and other minority groups, has come to feel more so.

[14]David Easton and Robert D. Hess in *Political Opinion and Electoral Behavior*, ed. Edward C. Dreyer and Walter A. Rosenbaum (Belmont, Calif.: Wadsworth, 1966), p. 155.

Table 9
Political Identification by Generation

Political Identification	Percentage of parents	Percentage of students
Republican	42.4	40.6
Independent Republican	20.0	29.8
Independent	2.3	5.1
Independent Democrat	13.1	9.7
Democrat	21.1	14.8

SOURCE: Richard W. Dodge and Eugene S. Uyeki, "Political Affiliation and Imagery Across Two Related Generations," in *Political Opinion and Electoral Behavior,* ed. Edward C. Dreyer and Walter A. Rosenbaum (Belmont, Calif.: Wadsworth, 1966), p. 169.

ents in voting preferences is an indication of the way in which we Americans acquire not only our political values but party affiliations. A survey of the results of approximately a hundred such studies on the relationship between parents and students and political attitudes reports a clear correlation. Apparently, party identification plays a much more important role in the United States than in other Western countries. In contrast to the great majority of Americans who had some recollection about their parents' political affiliations, only 25 percent of Frenchmen could do so, with a rather higher percentage for Norwegians and Swedes. In France, and to a lesser degree in the two Scandinavian countries, there is apparently much less family discussion of political matters and a lower degree of party identification. Obviously this directly influences the extent to which party affiliation is passed on from one generation to another. Why this is the case in the European countries surveyed would clearly make an interesting subject for field research.

Socioeconomic Influences

There is another factor influential on voting behavior which we have not yet mentioned. That is the influence of the family's socioeconomic status on party choice. Here again, not very surprisingly, there is a rather direct relationship between education, economic level, and the degree of political information and involvement. It is virtually axiomatic in American political behavior research that the higher the socioeconomic status (SES level) the more likely it is that the individual will vote Republican instead of Democratic. In the United States since 1936, except for the two unique Eisenhower elections, manual workers have consistently voted more strongly Democratic than Republican. Surveying the voting pattern of American elections from 1936 through 1960, one analyst said, "It may be concluded . . . that there has been no substantial shift in the class basis

Table 10
Relationship Between Social Origin, Consumption Patterns, and Voting Behavior Among Men in Sweden

	Manual from manual homes		Non-manual from manual homes		Non-manual from non-manual homes	
	w/o car	w/car	w/o car	w/car	w/o car	w/car
Non-Socialist	15%	14%	38%	74%	79%	83%
Socialist	85	86	62	26	21	17

SOURCE: Seymour Martin Lipset, *Political Man: The Social Bases of Politics,* Table X, p. 256. Copyright © 1960, Seymour Martin Lipset. Reprinted by permission of Doubleday and Company, Inc.

of American politics since the 1930's, despite the prosperity since World War II, and despite the shifts to the right in the Eisenhower era."[15]

Table 10 illustrates the importance of the SES level in a typical Western European democracy. The percentages would seem to indicate that when occupational (social) level remains consistent, improvement in economic status affects voting loyalties very little. The highly skilled workman whose father was also a worker, even though he is earning a much better wage than many a white-collar worker, in Sweden and probably elsewhere in Western Europe, thinks of himself as a worker. In the same fashion the ill-paid clerical son of a business or professional father feels no economic identification with workers in the same income category but instead votes his feelings of superior social status.

The most interesting statistics in Table 10, however, are those in the center column, for they seem to offer support for theories on the effect of upward social mobility on political preference. Apparently those individuals who are from a working-class background but who "have it made" sufficiently to buy a car (no small status symbol by European working-class standards!) have shifted their political loyalties to conform with their newly acquired bourgeois status.

The American equivalent in this theory of economic determinism is, of course, the widely held proposition that when a working-class Democrat reaches executive status and moves his family out of the city to a suburban setting, he begins voting Republican. Whatever may be true of Sweden in this connection, there is apparently more myth than fact in the theorizing about American upward social mobility. In an illuminating analysis of suburban voting patterns and their sources of recruitment, David Wallace

[15]Robert R. Alford, "The Role of Social Class in American Voting Behavior," in *Political Parties and Political Behavior,* ed. William J. Crotty, Donald M. Freeman, and Douglas S. Gatlin (Boston: Allyn & Bacon, 1966), p. 387.

concluded that, for various reasons, "the sources of suburban growth have been more Republican than Democratic."[16] Initially Republican, the suburbs have stayed that way by recruiting upwardly mobile Republicans from countryside and small town as well as from the city. Rather than simple geographical determinism, family tradition coupled with the SES level apparently explains to a considerable degree why the suburbs are Republican and the big cities Democratic.

NEW POLITICAL TRENDS IN THE 1970S

But in the 1970s a new trend in voting preferences has emerged which makes dubious the customary generalizations about the political preferences of cities, suburbs, or any other areas. This new trend is the apparently rapidly intensifying disintegration of party loyalties. A Harris Poll, taken in May, 1971, disclosed that independent voters comprised 23 percent of the total, an increase of 6 percent since the election of 1968. The number who consider themselves Democrats has dropped 5 percentage points to a total of 47 percent of potential 1972 presidential voters and the Republican party can now count on only 30 percent of the electorate.

This dramatic rise in the number of independent voters is an indication of that growing sense of alienation we mentioned in Chapter 1 as a characteristic of advanced industrial societies. Although the reasons have not been analyzed in depth, very probably the traumatic impact of the war in Indo-China has greatly intensified this growth of antiestablishment feeling and dissatisfaction with the policies and philosophies of the established political parties. The feeling of disaffiliation, coupled with the unpredictable factor of the extension of voting rights to 18-year-olds as a result of Supreme Court approval in 1970 of congressional legislation authorizing this and the Twenty-sixth Amendment, seems likely to produce a state of flux and upheaval in political loyalties in the 1970s not seen since the Depression years of the 1930s. But this time neither Democrats nor Republicans are likely to profit.

The impact in 1972 and thereafter of the new voting group of approximately 11 million 18- to 20-year-olds has been extensively discussed. There has been much disagreement on its results. Before 1970 only Georgia and Kentucky permitted 18-year-olds to vote while Hawaii and Alaska extended voting rights to those over 19. In these states only a third of these young voters participated in the 1968 election. Projecting from this base, Richard M. Scammon,

[16]See David Wallace, "Suburbia—Predestined Republicanism?" in Dreyer and Rosenbaum, *Political Opinion and Electoral Behavior*, pp. 102–111.

director of the Elections Research Center of Washington, D.C., concluded that had 18-year-olds been able to vote in all 50 states in 1968, their participation would not have changed the results in a single state.[17]

Another variant on this "business as usual" expectation is the proposition, comforting to both parties, that youthful voters will split their allegiances in virtually the same proportions as the rest of the electorate. A corollary to this, particularly comforting to Democratic politicians, is that because youth is always more liberally inclined, the majority of these new voters will support Democratic candidates.

But in a thoughtful article, entitled "Young Voter Survey: A Potential for Calamity," written in early 1971, national columnist Kevin F. Phillips suggested that there were quite different possibilities in the new voting group. First of all, he noted, an unprecedented rate of mobility and the emergence of a youth subculture makes young people "less inclined to follow their parents' politics than at any other time during recent U.S. history."

Then, within the 18- to 20-year-old group, there apparently exists a high degree of polarization on socioeconomic grounds. Notes Phillips:

> Straw ballots and political rallies on fashionable campuses demonstrate a prevalence of chic radicalism and left-wing Democratic (or Socialist or SDS) sympathy. Very few representatives of this cash-coddled youthful elite agree with the conservative economic politics of their parents. Theirs is a new socially-determined outlook—the so-called "counter-culture" of drugs, sex, "peace," and anarchy.
>
> At the same time, the children of the white working class are also freer from economic worry than their parents ever dreamed of being. And so young policemen, truck drivers, steel workers, supermarket clerks, and gas station attendants do not share their parents' depression-based concern with economic liberalism and Democratic fidelity. Instead, they lean toward a kind of hippie-stomping, anti-intellectual social conservatism in the George Wallace vein.

After noting that the new voters in the affluent areas of traditionally Republican territory will add to Democratic strength while Republican gains seem likely in the South, Phillips concludes:

> The most striking thing about the "youth vote" is its potential, direct and indirect, for polarization. Among 18–21 year-old voters, some 35–40 per cent support either leftist or rightist (Wallace) radicals. Among persons over 40, say, the national "radical" percentage is something like 6–10 per cent. . . .
>
> The tension and rebellion of youth politics—and youth con-

[17]Cited by Kevin F. Phillips, "18-Year-Old Vote—A Liberal Impact on the U.S.," *St. Petersburg Times,* January 2, 1971, p. 15-A.

frontation—may further radicalize the adult electorate. What all this will lead to is, of course, conjectural.

In the opinion of this analyst, there is a little-appreciated potential for calamity—a possibility of cultural hostility that could do severe damage to our system.

The validity of the "business as usual" theory or of Phillips' somewhat apocalyptic expectations are very much subject to the trend of basic political and social influences in the early 1970s. Such factors as the rate of unemployment, the problems of inflation, the level of racial tension, the quiet or turmoil of the campuses and the state of the war in Indo-China will all be the dominant variables that shape the role played by the new youth vote in 1972 and for the rest of the decade. These variables will, of course, affect the voting patterns of all age groups, but youthful voters will no doubt react to them more intensely than any other group.

THE ROLE OF PUBLIC-OPINION POLLS

In the Western democracies the prediction of voting behavior has reached a high degree of accuracy. It has become almost routine, in the United States at least, for parties or candidates to commission a public-opinion survey organization to learn what issues and what types of candidates are likely to be most appealing to the voters. Both candidate and party can begin a campaign knowing what groups are most and least likely to support them and where the maximum effort needs to be made. Throughout the campaign further surveys can indicate what issues are catching on and which have little appeal.

Nor has the prediction of the final outcome of elections become any less accurate. The failure of the polls in the 1948 election was one of human error not of the techniques involved. The election of Dewey, the Republican candidate, over the seemingly highly unpopular Democrat Truman seemed so obvious that the pollsters ceased sampling several weeks before the election. It was during those last weeks, however, that an illogical but powerful wave of sympathy for President Truman as "a little guy with guts" who was going down fighting swept the voters and produced the most astounding upset in American politics, to the mutual embarrassment of both Dewey and the pollsters.

But the lesson was well learned. In the 1968 election, one of the closest in American history, a leading pollster was still polling only 24 hours before election day. Both the two leading polls, Gallup and Harris, declined to call the winner, with Gallup showing Nixon with 42 percent of the vote to Humphrey's 40 percent, while Harris, who had polled until the day before election, gave Humphrey 43 percent to Nixon's 40 percent. Since both candidates received just over 43 percent of the total vote cast, the polls were well within their expected 3 percent to 4 percent margin of error. Except in such an unusually close election as that of 1968, complicated as it was by the rather rare factor of a strong third party, the margin of victory is usually sufficient to make possible a firm and accurate prediction of the results on the basis of the final preelection polls.[18]

It is at this point that those suspicious of polls raise objections to the whole concept. Wouldn't it, they ask, be possible to "fix" a poll and thus create a bandwagon psychology among those voters who have remained undecided up to the very end but who would like to be on the winning side? The answer is rather simple. Important elections, congressional or gubernatorial or presidential, come only once every two or four years. No polling organization can stay in business doing only election polls. What enables them to meet their payrolls and satisfy their stockholders are the fees received year in and year out for conducting market surveys of the potential sales for a new "super cleanser" or a new type of sports car. These market surveys are costly to the firms that commission them, and their accuracy determines whether or not millions or tens of millions of dollars would be wisely or foolishly invested in the development of a new product. Before any business firm accepts the results of a market survey at face value and invests heavily in a new product, it has to have faith in the accuracy of the results. Here is where the crucial importance of political polling comes in for any survey research firm. If it can point with pride to the fact that it predicted the results of an important election with almost pinpoint accuracy, then there is empiric evidence as to the excellent quality of its services. Election forecasting provides the acid test for the prestige and business survival of any polling firm. No established pollster would be naive enough to risk destroying his future credibility and losing millions of dollars worth of future business by taking a bribe to fix a poll.

For that matter, the evidence seems to indicate that it would be both ruinous and futile for even the most desperate of losing political candidates to try to bribe a pollster. In the first place, when, as it inevitably would, first the rumor and then the story of the transaction began to circulate, the politician would find himself regarded as a political leper not only by the voters but by his own party leaders. This aside, there is always the possibility that the same underdog sympathy which led to Truman's victory

[18]If we define a strong third party as one which has received electoral votes and/or a million or more popular votes, such parties have been present only in the elections of 1912, 1924, 1948, and 1968.

would operate for the other candidate. Finally, while a few last-minute wavering voters might be swayed, it seems clear that, whatever else might bring about a last-minute change, a pollster's prediction of victory for the other side is not among these factors. Throughout the campaign in 1964, for example, all polls consistently predicted a landslide victory for President Johnson. The evidence does not seem to indicate that voters who began the campaign supporting Goldwater shifted because of the polls' forecasts. Again, there is apparently an optimistic and unquenchable belief that *this* time the polls will be wrong and that if campaign efforts are redoubled the tide can be turned at the last minute.

There is no question but that techniques for the survey of actual and potential behavior have reached a high degree of accuracy. As an aid to understanding and analyzing the political process, this can be welcomed. But it is already clear that polls have had a highly undesirable effect in the structuring both of political campaigns and of candidates. It takes a brave, perhaps foolhardy, candidate to follow his convictions and take a strong stand against a proposal which a survey has just indicated 72.3 percent of the potential voters enthusiastically favor. As far as candidates are concerned, there is an even stronger pressure on a party which wants to win to present a candidate with good "image" appeal. His dedication as a public servant, his knowledge of the issues, and his ability to offer solutions may weigh but little against a survey indicating that voters are automatically prejudiced against a short, stout bald man who mumbles, wears bifocals, and has a heavy beard growth. One of the most telling psychological points made against Richard Nixon in his narrowly lost 1960 presidential campaign was a cartoon of a beady-eyed, heavily "five-o'clock shadowed" Nixon standing in front of a used-car lot with the damning caption, "Would you buy a used car from this man?" "Packaging" political candidates to appeal to what the surveys indicate are the voters' preferences or prejudices has become standard practice. As in the equally competitive brand-name market, the contents of the package are frequently often glossed over or ignored.

The British 1970 Polling Debacle

By the end of the 1960s the omniscience of political polls had become virtual gospel. The failure to predict the Truman-Dewey election of 1948 was regarded as a dated example of the mistakes possible only in a remote and naive period in the development of polling science. Rather, as typical of the awesome accuracy of modern polling techniques, the remarkable correctness of the major polls in forecasting the Nixon-Humphrey presidential race were complacently cited.

Particularly in the Anglo-American world, where polling had been most developed, professional politicians had become devout, even fanatical, converts to the new religion. Former British Prime Minister Harold Wilson, for example, tells how in the course of a lengthy and wide-ranging survey of world affairs with President Johnson, he thought he understood the president to say, "Have you seen what the Poles are saying?" Wilson continues:

> I rapidly tried, but failed, to recall some weighty pronouncement by Mr. Gomulko or Mr. Rapacki. But the president pulled a folded sheet of notepaper from his pocket and read the details of the latest public opinion poll. As I recall them, some 70% were stated to be "opposed" to the president's policies, but the detailed figures went on to show that 43% or so felt he should pull out of the war and 44% that he should escalate the fighting. The poll obviously had worried him, most of all because the almost equal division of his critics left him stranded in the center, without any clear guidance about the direction the American public, at that moment in time, wanted him to take.[19]

So great indeed was President Johnson's faith in the infallibility of the polls that three years after the 1965 meeting with Wilson, the picture given by the polls of his steadily sagging political popularity is credited as the major reason for his dramatic decision not to run for re-election.

But because of opposite polling results, Mr. Wilson himself was no less credulous a victim of their presumed infallibility. Under the British parliamentary system, a government may hold office for as long as five years before having to submit itself to the voters. But, any time within that five-year period the prime minister as leader of the governing party may ask the Queen to dissolve Parliament so that new elections may be held. Obviously it is to the advantage of the party in power to pick a time within the five-year period when its political fortunes are at their peak. Until the advent of public-opinion sampling, this was largely a matter of a lucky guess or a brilliantly intuitive feeling on the part of the prime minister and the other leaders of the majority party.

Elected in 1966, Prime Minister Wilson as leader of the majority Labour party kept a wary and worried eye on the public-opinion polls in 1969. Throughout that year the polls showed that the Labour party would lose any general election, probably by such landslide proportions as 20 percent. In 1970, however, a dramatic and apparently highly

[19]"Opinion Polls: Their Role in Government," *Britannica Book of the Year 1971* (Chicago: Encyclopaedia Britannica, 1971), p. 45.

encouraging change took place when poll after poll indicated (or seemed to indicate) that the British voter was now well satisfied with the results of Labour party policies and was now ready to grant the party another maximum five-year lease of office.

Logically enough, Mr. Wilson decided in May, 1970, that the time was ripe. Parliament was formally dissolved by the Queen, and in mid-June candidates for the new Parliament "stood" for election. Not until election day on June 18, 1970, was there any reason to doubt the political astuteness of Wilson's judgment. Four out of five polls commissioned by the leading London papers predicted either an easy or a substantial Labour victory. The day before the election *The Times,* oldest and most prestigious of British papers, ran the headline, "Labour Leading by 8.7 PC."

The exact results of the British general election were 46.6 percent for the Conservatives and 43.4 percent for Labour. Translated into seats in the House of Commons, where a majority is necessary for any party to take over power, the number of Labour seats dropped from 364 to 287 while the Conservatives went from 253 seats to 330, a gain of 77 seats instead of the widely predicted losses.

Writing shortly after the British elections, an American political journalist summarized the meaning of the results:

> For the poll takers it was *technically* the greatest disaster since the Literary Digest predicted that Alf Landon's victory margin over Franklin Roosevelt would be a landslide 19 per cent. It was *dramatically* the greatest poll-taking disaster since Harry Truman upset Tom Dewey, the poll-takers' narrow choice."[20]

This analyst listed among the lessons to be learned from England: "First, poll takers can, and do, make serious errors. . . . Second, people who should know better still don't know the limitations of polls. . . . Some Labor voters may have stayed home on Election Day, convinced by the polls that a landslide for their party was in the making. . . . Taking polls seriously is bad business."

Reflecting on the significance of polls for the professional politician from the dubious vantage point of hard-earned second thought, ex-prime minister but still leader of the British Labour Party, Harold Wilson cautioned:

> Accord to the polls interest but not idolatry. . . . Regard them as an honest attempt to record the state of public opinion, at one moment in time, on one issue of political importance; or, less reliably, as an assessment not of opinion but of that indefinable phenomenon, the public mood on the broad political situation—a factor in, not a determinant of, policy. . . .
> Treat them, then, with respect, as you would give to any

[20]James M. Perry, "The Scandalous Performance of Polls in Britain's Election," *The National Observer,* June 29, 1970, p. 11.

honest and expert professional assessment of facts that you have to take into account. And then recognize that you were elected, as legislator, as an executive, to exercise a judgment—not on what is expedient, or electorally rewarding, but a judgment on what is right.[21]

In the future Mr. Wilson will no doubt take his own hard-won advice. But it seems likely that other aspiring politicians and those dedicated to the discovery of an infallible method of political horoscope-casting will ignore it. For objective and serious students of political affairs, however, the lessons of the American election of 1948 and the British equivalent of 1970 should never be forgotten. It seems worthwhile to repeat the point made in Chapter 2 to illustrate the importance of the imponderable and unpredictable which is always present, even if often fatally overlooked, in any political equation. Without question, *"The root is man."*

CONCLUSION

The examples we have been using make clear that studies of potential and actual voting behavior are phenomena of the more highly developed and mature political systems. There is a rather direct relationship between the communications process and the style of political life. The result is that much of the theorizing about the nature of political life in non-Western countries is just that. For example, there have been few, if any, studies made of the family role in political socialization in non-Western societies. Dawson and Prewitt suggest that: "In fact, the relationships in non-Western, more traditional societies may well be even greater. As a rule family ties are stronger in traditional cultures, and there are not as many other agents of socialization."[22]

This proposition probably represents an educated guess, but it is not subject to empirical verification. As far as voting behavior is concerned, it would be highly probable that in an African country, voters would vote for a candidate from their own tribe even though the opposition candidate might be far more qualified. Presumably, in India voters, particularly in rural districts, would support a fellow caste member. Or would they? The greatest challenge confronting the development of studies of voting behavior in the years ahead will be less the refinement of analysis techniques in the Western countries than devising ways to extend those techniques to the new nations of Asia and

[21]"Opinion Polls: Servant or Master," *Britannica*, p. 48.

[22]Richard E. Dawson and Kenneth Prewitt, *Political Socialization* (Boston: Little, Brown, 1969), p. 111.

Africa which are still trying to operate some type of regime dependent on periodic appeals to mass electorates. This emphasizes a point often overlooked: The development of more refined techniques both for analyzing the behavior of the electorate and for counting their votes more equitably takes for granted that ultimate power does lie in the masses of the people—in short, that some type of democratic political system exists. It is appropriate to examine now what we mean when we refer to a country having a democratic type of political system.

7

DEMOCRACY: CONCEPTS, DEVELOPMENT, CHARACTERISTICS

7

For most of its long history, *democracy* has been little more than a disparaging word in the vocabulary of political theorists. Not until well into the nineteenth century did it begin to become respectable, and it was not until after World War I that it became the unchallengeable "good think" term it is today.

By mid-century a UNESCO committee, surveying the replies to an international questionnaire on democracy, could conclude that

> In spite of the violence of conflict concerning basic social and political ideas and concerning means of international co-operation, there are abundant indications of fundamental agreement. The agreements in statements of purpose and in aspiration appear in a controversial context of contradictory interpretations of the intentions that motivate the statement of facts that seem to belie them. The agreements are themselves involved in the ideological conflict. *Yet the unanimity which appears in the statement of aims is an impressive fact. For the first time in the history of the world, no doctrines are advanced as antidemocratic.* The accusation of antidemocratic action or attitude is frequently directed against others, but practical politicians and political theorists agree in stressing the democratic elements in the institutions they defend and the theories they advocate. *This acceptance of democracy as the highest form of political or social organization is the sign of a basic agreement in the ultimate aims of modern social and political institutions—an agreement that the participation of the people and the interests of the people are essential elements in good government and in the social relations which make good government possible.*[1]

But the very universality of this acceptance of democracy as a normative and institutional concept in itself creates unprecedented problems in understanding and evaluating what the term really means. For who can tell which is the *real*

[1]Richard McKeon, ed., *Democracy in a World of Tensions* (Chicago: University of Chicago Press, 1951), pp. 522–523. (Italics added.)

product and which is "brand X" when asked to choose between Western democracy and peoples' democracy, between bourgeois democracy and proletarian democracy? Further, can we accept as legitimate such variations as "property democracy" or "guided" or "participatory" or "elitist" or any of the other of the endless list of variations that are enthusiastically proclaimed by their originators as the one and only true version?

If we are to come to any conclusions at all, we must try to see what fundamentals are involved in democracy. What has been the meaning of the term in the past? Is it consistent with what we mean now? Also, when we talk about democracy are we dealing with a normative ideal (one which establishes a standard), or a goal, a possible philosophy of government, or an actual institutional arrangement for processing the demands fed into a political system? In the latter connection, should we be discussing this in the singular or the plural? And why is it that only in the last hundred years or so has democracy, after long centuries in the "demimonde" of political theory, achieved such universal respect and prestige? It is to an examination of these questions that the rest of this chapter is devoted.

WHAT DEMOCRACY MEANS

As a concept, democracy can best be understood as having not just one but three interrelated meanings. First and most important, it is a way of making decisions. Second, it is a set of principles by which those decisions are made. Third, it offers a set of normative values. This simply means that the whole purpose of the decision-making process in a democracy and the values by which that democracy is guided are to make a presently idealized set of ethical norms and political values the routinely accepted frame of reference within which public affairs are conducted. Let us examine each of these three interrelated meanings in some detail.

As is so often the case, the ancient Greeks had a term which, translated literally, admirably summarizes the basis on which democracy makes its decisions. The Greek term *demos kratos* means simply *people power.* Probably not very long after this term was in common use, Pericles, leader of Athens when it was the model democracy among the Greek cities, could say, "We are called a democracy because the government is in the hands of the many not the few." This definition of democracy has remained remarkably consistent throughout history. Over two thousand years later, the great French political theorist, de Montesquieu, who so strongly influenced the thinking of the American founding fathers, wrote in words very similar to those of Pericles, "When the body of the people is possessed of the supreme power, it is called a democracy." And, of course, best known to Americans, is Abraham Lincoln's famous description of democracy as "government of the people, by the people, and for the people."

But in spite of the seeming consistency of the words which have been used throughout history to describe democracy, the term has had a very different content at various times and places. Nothing would seem to be simpler, for example, than to say that democracy means "people power." But immediately two vital questions demand an answer. The first of these is: What does *people* mean? The other is: How is this power to be organized and exercised? The history of democracy for more than two thousand years has been little more than the story of the various efforts to give satisfactory answers to these two questions.

People, for instance, has never, from the time of Pericles to the most recent U.S. election, meant *all* the people. Its meaning has varied considerably in both qualitative and quantitative terms. First of all, whatever the means used, government has been by the citizens of the polity in question, not by all of those who happen to live within a particular set of geographical boundaries. In Pericles' Athens, it is estimated that the "many" to whom Pericles referred as controlling the government consisted of 43,000 citizens out of a total population of 315,000. If the fact that a bare 14 percent of Athenians had the right of participation in the affairs of state seems like an example of ancient backwardness, let it not be forgotten that it is estimated that only one of 15 Americans, or less than 7 percent of the total population, was able to meet the property requirements of 1788 for voting for representatives to the various state constitutional conventions. And in the 1830s, in Great Britain and France, the two major sources of the modern democratic ideal, slightly over 4 percent of Englishmen and less than 1 percent of Frenchmen possessed voting rights.

In the United States it has been only since the passage of the Voting Rights Act of 1965 that tens of thousands of blacks have been able to vote in the Southern states, more than a century after the passage of the Fifteenth Amendment which provided that "the right of citizens of the United States to vote shall not be denied or abridged by the United States or by any State on account of race, color, or previous condition of servitude." Aside from this special factor of racial discrimination, residence requirements and other factors still disenfranchise millions of voters in presidential elections. And it was not until early 1971 that Switzerland, long regarded as one of the world's model democracies, gave women the right to vote! Nevertheless, it is true that in the late twentieth century, the term *people* is a closer synonym for the adult population than ever before.

HOW DEMOCRACY DEVELOPED

Democracy's long history is the story of how people instead of property became its frame of reference. It is also the story of how the term for a particular type of governmental institution in ancient Greece has come to express a philosophical approach to the control and regulation of governmental power regardless of the particular institutional format in which it is organized. From the fifth century B.C. until the establishment of the American republic, *democracy* meant a government which functioned on the basis of direct and constant participation by the mass of its citizens. Before we consider how democracy came to have a normative instead of a specific institutional meaning, let us look at the long, slow transition from property to people democracy.

Athenian Democracy as the Classic Model

Citizenship in Athens was not so much a matter of property ownership as it was an affair of biological status. A citizen was a male past the age of 21 *born of two free* (nonslave) *Athenian parents.* Basic to the existence of Athenian democracy was the property relationship of slavery. But for that fortunate 14 percent with the rights of citizenship, the governmental structure offered an opportunity for truly meaningful participatory democracy such as its late twentieth-century proponents can only wistfully regard as a utopian goal.

The basic governing body of the Athenian democracy was the Assembly (*ekklesia*) which every citizen was eligible to attend. In this connection, we are again forced to note the influence, albeit negative, of technology. For in the fifth century B.C., even within the limited boundaries of the little city-state of Athens, slightly smaller than Rhode Island, communications were so poor that only those citizens living in Athens itself or nearby were able to attend the four meetings a month of the Assembly. As a result, the average attendance seems to have been from 2,000 to 3,000, except on occasions of unique interest. Only at the first meeting of every month could new legislation be proposed, and then only after it had been reviewed by the Council of Five Hundred which, while it could not reject any proposals, had the option of reporting them to the Assembly with or without recommendation. Debate was continued as long as anyone, in order of age, desired, and each speaker was allowed the same amount of time. The final and irrevocable decision of the Assembly was made by a show of hands unless an individual was directly affected, in which case it was taken by secret ballot with white and black stones used for affirmative and negative votes.[2]

When the Assembly was not in session, Athenian affairs were administered by the Council of Five Hundred. Its membership of fifty citizens from each of the ten tribes of Athens was chosen annually by lot. Since no one was eligible for reelection until all other eligible citizens had served, this meant that many citizens had the experience of actually running the affairs of the city. In his famous *Politics,* Aristotle considers it to be an important "principle of liberty . . . for all to rule and be ruled in turn."

To make it possible for even the poorest citizen to perform this duty, the members of the Council received a daily wage and, not surprisingly, the trend was always toward increased pay. From the first, the Council organized its administration by lot. Each month one of the ten committees into which the Council was divided was selected to serve as the steering committee for the month with a different daily chairman, again chosen by lot.[3]

It would be difficult to devise a more popularly controlled and equitable system than that of Athenian democracy—keeping in mind the severely limited group of participants. Majority rule, one man–one vote, equal justice before the law—all these were present. Such influence as was wielded even by the great Pericles, who gave his name to Athen's golden age, was based on annual election as one of the city's ten military commanders and his ability to argue his proposals successfully before the Assembly. It was only on this basis that Pericles maintained his power as Athens' leader for almost thirty years until his death in 428 B.C.

The remarkable degree of fulfillment which Athenian participatory democracy gave its citizens is described by an American political philosopher in these terms:

> Modern states are relatively so large, so remote, so impersonal, that they cannot fill the place in modern life that the

[2]This system of voting with the different colored stones made it possible for what must have been an almost 100 percent illiterate electorate to cast a "secret" ballot. It is an interesting foreshadowing of the way in which similar voting was made possible for equally illiterate electorates in such countries as India or Indonesia by the use of ballots with different symbols, such as a banyan tree or a bullock, for the various parties contesting the election. By the use of symbol voting, India has been able to conduct successful parliamentary elections involving tens of millions of voters, even though its official illiteracy rate is put at 76 percent.

[3]The major reference source used for this brief survey of the organization of Athenian democracy was Will Durant, *The Story of Civilization, Part II: The Life of Greece* (New York: Simon & Schuster, 1939), pp. 254–257.

city filled in the life of a Greek. The Athenian's interests were less divided, fell less sharply into compartments unconnected with each other and they were all centered in the city. . . . For the Greeks, therefore, the city was a life in common; its constitution, as Aristotle said, was a "mode of life" rather than a legal structure; and consequently the fundamental thought in all Greek political theory was the harmony of the common life. . . .

The pervasiveness of this common life and the value which the Athenians set upon it is apparent upon the face of their institutions . . . government was a democracy, "for the administration is in the hands of the many and not of the few." In modern politics such an expression is likely to be taken not quite literally, unless it be understood of the rather colorless right to cast a ballot. Certainly the holding of office counts for little in the calculations of modern democrats, other than those few for whom politics is a career. For the Athenian it might be a normal incident in the life of almost any citizen. On the strength of figures given by Aristotle in his *Constitution of Athens it has been estimated that in any year as many as one citizen in six might have some share in the civil government.* . . . And if he held no office, he might still take part, regularly ten times each year, in the discussion of political questions at the general assembly of the citizens. The discussion, formal or informal, of public matters was one of the main delights and interests of his life.[4]

Here indeed is participatory democracy in action!

The Liabilities of Athenian Democracy

For all its proper historic claim to being a model for the operation of a democracy, there are certain liabilities in the Athenian example. The most obvious of these, the fact that 86 percent of the total population was uninvolved in the decision-making process in even the most formal manner, we have already stressed. But there is another important liability which makes the Athenian version of democracy, in terms of a literal application, unworkable in a modern industrial state. It would seem that the degree of successful functioning of Athenian democracy was in inverse proportion to the level of technological development of communications. To say that only 14 percent of a total population of 315,000 persons was entitled to participate in the governmental process sounds like a very modest statement indeed. But when one remembers that every one of the 44,000 citizens involved had the right to be physically present and have his vote counted, it is something else again.

Although it must have been time-consuming, it was physically possible to conduct the affairs of government in terms

[4]George H. Sabine, *A History of Political Thought*, rev. ed. (New York: Holt, Rinehart & Winston, 1953), pp. 13–14. (Italics added.)

of a town meeting of several thousand persons. Even with all the assistance which modern technology can offer today, including amplifying systems and voting machines, it would obviously be impossible to get any results from a mass meeting of some 40,000 citizens. Athenian direct democracy was made possible only by the transportation system based on either walking or riding in an ox cart. Unlike contemporary civic leaders it seems unlikely that any Athenian friend of democracy ever felt any inclination to "get out the vote." The success of any such campaign would have been the worst thing possible for the continued viability of the Athenian system. Not surprisingly the only examples of such direct democracy still to be found in the modern world are, aside from private associations, the New England town meetings and the assemblies in some of the sparsely populated rural cantons of Switzerland.

The other obvious deficiency in the Athenian system is one that continues to plague modern democracies: the high cost of political office. Only a wealthy state such as Athens could afford to pay its citizens adequately for holding office. There seems to be evidence that the high cost of operating a democracy was probably one of the justified arguments against the system. In our modern age it has become increasingly and unfortunately the case that no man can run for office, let alone hold it, unless he has access to considerable independent means.

The Roman Contribution

As in the case of Athens, Roman citizenship was originally based on the status requirement of being a male over the age of fifteen who had been born or adopted into one of the three original tribes into which the Roman people were divided.[5] But early in its history, Rome introduced a property requirement which weighed the voting powers of the various "centuries" into which citizens were divided on the basis of their property holdings. On this basis the Roman electorate was divided into six classes of citizens with the different classes voting in the order of their financial rank. Although each century had but one vote, the limited membership of the centuries at the top of the financial pyramid could determine by a bare majority how the vote of their century was to be cast and thus outweigh the vote of a century in the lowest financial category which might have many thousands of citizens enrolled in it; in true Roman fashion, however, political power was equated with responsibility. Both in terms of liability for military service and for the major share of taxes, those in the lower

[5]Will Durant, *The Story of Civilization, Part III: Caesar and Christ* (New York: Simon & Schuster, 1944), pp. 25–26.

property group had little burden except in times of unusual need.

From a very early time, Roman law guaranteed for all citizens certain basic rights such as immunity from legal torture and the right of appeal from the decision of any official to the Assembly during the republican period and then to the emperor on the basis of a personal appearance in Rome. In the imperial period, although it had already come to mean little as far as participation in government was concerned, Roman citizenship became a prized possession, the rights of which were spelled out by successive generations of jurists. It should not be forgotten that at the height of the persecution of the early Christians, the Apostle Paul was able to save himself from torture by the simple statement, "Civus Romanum sum" (I am a Roman citizen) and by using his right to appeal to the emperor for judgment on his case. In the latter period of the empire, Roman citizenship was made virtually universal in order to extend the tax base for raising revenue. If nothing else, this established the concept of the universal application of citizenship.

The Greco-Roman requirements for citizenship have shaped the definition of the term ever since. To be a citizen of any country, one must either be born in it or naturalized into it (the Roman tribal "adoption"), and until very recent times property qualifications, in the Roman manner, determined eligibility to participate in the selection of rulers.

In those few polities in the Middle Ages where there was any concept at all of citizen participation in the affairs of government, particularly in the Italian city states, these twin concepts of birth and wealth continued to provide the frame of reference for the operation of quasi-democratic political systems.

THE STRUGGLE FOR POPULAR DEMOCRACY

Although it continued to bear the "mobocracy" stigma which Aristotle had placed on it, popular democracy continued as a persistent underground influence in the shaping of political thought. For long periods it exerted no influence, only to erupt now and again in the Middle Ages in savage peasant revolts. Although church officials consistently supported the idea of autocratic authority as embodied in the concept of the divine right of kings, Christian doctrine furnished powerful support to the belief in the brotherhood of man and the spiritual equality of all men. As the old churches in the rural areas of southern Germany still bear witness, medieval peasant artists obviously took sly delight in depicting bishop and great lord standing side by side with serf and peasant before the judgment seat of

God, or the peasant raised to heaven while the once-mighty lord withers in the fires of hell.

People Versus Property in England

It was not until the end of the English civil war in the mid-seventeenth century that the first modern reasoned statement of the case for people power was made. The circumstances were dramatic in the extreme. In the late medieval period, England had become not only the world's first nation-state but also the first country in which the rising middle class played an important economic and political role. Although it took almost a decade of civil war in the 1640s, the English middle class, composed of the town merchants and a substantial section of the country gentry, prevented Charles I from establishing the French type of absolute monarchy which was being widely used throughout Europe as the model for a modern state.[6]

The opposition to Charles I's absolutist bid was composed of a number of groups which had little in common other than their opposition to the king, for although they were virtually all members of various Protestant groups their religious and political philosophies differed sharply. The wealthy, who comprised the leadership of the parliamentary forces, saw their economic and political power as an obvious indication of the high favor in which they were held by God. It seemed obvious to them that those not so favored simply did not deserve to participate in political matters and should be happy to be governed by their spiritual, economic, and political betters. Not surprisingly, the rank and file did not see the matter in these terms. From their own intense study of the Scriptures, they reasoned that if all men were spiritually equal, then they were certainly also politically equal.

The conflicting viewpoints found clear expression in the famous Putney debates. The civil war had concluded in the beheading of the king. The major problem was how to reorganize the English political system. Encamped at Putney, the members of the victorious parliamentary army endlessly discussed this urgent problem in a series of remarkable public debates on the proposed Instrument of the People put forward by the Agitators, the elected representatives of the army rank and file, as the basis on which the English governmental structure could be reorganized. The details of this early effort to create a modern constitutional document need not concern us here. What is pertinent is that the Putney debates produced the first clear modern

[6]For a good, brief review of this development, see Max Beloff, *The Age of Absolutism, 1660-1815* (New York: Harper & Row, 1962).

statements of the cases for people power and for property democracy.

One of the leading spokesmen for the Agitators stated the case for people power in words that still ring eloquently across the centuries:

> For really, I think, that the poorest he that is, in England hath a life to live, as the greatest he; and therefore, truly, Sir, I think it's clear that every man that is to live under a government ought first by his own consent to put himself under that government; and I do think that the poorest man in England is not at all bound in a strict sense to that government that he hath not had a voice to put himself under . . . insomuch that I should doubt whether he was an Englishman . . . that should doubt of these things.[7]

The case for property democracy was put bluntly by Commissary-General Ireton, leading spokesman for the Grandees, the well-to-do officers in the parliamentary army. Appealing to the traditional property qualifications, he argued:

> No person hath a right to an interest or share in the disposing of the affairs of the kingdom, and in determining or choosing those that shall determine what laws we shall be ruled by here—no person hath a right to this that hath not a permanent fixed interest in this kingdom and those persons together are properly the represented of this kingdom and consequently are also to make up the representatives of this kingdom, who taken together do comprehend whatsoever is of real or permanent interest in the kingdom.[8]

Ireton's supporters, including the great Puritan military leader Oliver Cromwell, soon to become Lord Protector of England, so effectively organized their political and economic power that property democracy carried the day. It was not until the electoral reform bill of 1884 that manhood suffrage was introduced into England, although with qualifications that were not removed until after World War I.

The Continued Dominance of Property Democracy

For two centuries after the Putney debates the popular concept of democracy continued to be a highly controversial proposition in the programs of radical reform movements. One reason for this was the widespread influence of the property concept of democracy set forth forty years after the Putney debates by John Locke (1632-1704), probably the single most influential political thinker the English-speaking peoples have ever produced. Not only did

[7]Quoted in H. N. Brailsford, *The Levellers and the English Revolution*, ed. Christopher Hill (Stanford, Calif.: Stanford University Press, 1961), p. 274.

[8]*Ibid.*, pp. 275–276.

Locke's concept of the organization of political society dominate English thought for almost two centuries, it also substantially influenced the French eighteenth-century philosophers who prepared the way for the revolution of 1789, and the American founding fathers, above all Thomas Jefferson. One has only to read the Declaration of Independence to see how its ideas and at times almost its precise language are influenced by Locke.

John Locke was like one of those men who in the late twentieth century hold endowed chairs at Ivy League schools, from the campuses of which they are usually absent by virtue of continuous demands to serve as special advisors to presidents or secretaries of state. As a physician in early life, John Locke became associated with the Ashley family, one of the great aristocratic commercial families that ruled England for the two centuries between the civil war and the Labour Party's electoral victory of 1945. But his obvious gift for expressing political ideas led to his appointment to various important administrative posts under the patronage of his powerful friends. It was these political connections that in 1690 led John Locke to write one of the most important pamphlets in the history of Anglo-American political thought. Usually referred to as the *Second Treatise*, its official title was *An Essay Concerning the True Original, Extent and End of Civil Government.*

By driving James II into exile as a result of the Glorious Revolution of 1688, the English had once again seemingly confirmed the judgment of their European neighbors that they were a volatile and erratic people addicted to constant political upheaval and turmoil.[9] Anxious to counteract this impression, the English establishment asked Locke to prove the case to the contrary. Starting from this utilitarian inspiration, Locke went on to construct his classic justification of property democracy, which even today commands respect for its brilliance.

Employing the political vocabulary of his time, Locke began with the proposition of the existence in the remote past prior to any political or social organization of a *state of nature*. For the seventeenth-century political philosopher Thomas Hobbes, who wrote *Leviathan*, his justification of authoritarian rule, a generation before Locke, the state of nature was one where there existed:

> no place for industry, because the fruit thereof is uncertain; and consequently no culture of the earth, no navigation, nor use of the commodities that may be imported by sea; no commodious building; no instruments of moving and removing such things as require much force; no knowledge of the face of the earth; no account of time; no arts; no letters; no society; and

[9]There is no more dramatic reversal in the roles played by any particular peoples than the exchange of roles between the British and the French from the seventeenth to the twentieth centuries.

which is worst of all, continual fear, and danger of violent death; and the life of man, solitary, poor, nasty, brutish and short.[10]

Locke saw it quite otherwise. His state of nature was the Garden of Eden without the serpent. Hobbes saw the creation of governmental authority as the result of society's overwhelming need for law and order at any cost to individual liberty. Locke saw man agreeing to a social contract and then delegating limited powers to government, operating on the basis of majority rule. As to why this was done, Locke believed "The great and chief end therefore, of men's uniting into commonwealths, and putting themselves under governments, is the preservation of their property: to which in the state of nature there are many things wanting."[11]

To this theme of government existing above all for "the preservation of their property" Locke returns again and again. From it comes his famous right of revolution to which the American founding fathers appealed. He argued that "whenever the legislators endeavor to take away and destroy the property of the people or to reduce them to slavery under arbitrary power, they put themselves in a state of war with the people, who are therefore resolved from any farther obedience. . . ."[12] Implicit in Locke's theory was the proposition that only those who owned property, who had a stake in society, were entitled to participate in the affairs of government.

THE NEW MYTH OF PEOPLE POWER

While it persisted as a stubborn underground current in democratic thought, the concept of people power did not find a spokesman of the caliber of Locke until near the end of the eighteenth century. As an individual this was an odd bird indeed. Jean-Jacques Rousseau (1712-1778), Swiss by birth, the first hippie by temperament and inclination, was the herald of the new age of mass democracy. Using the same intellectual framework as Locke, Rousseau published his *Social Contract* in 1762 and created an immediate sensation in the intellectual world of Europe. At first glance this was odd because for some decades the intellectual elite had prided itself on having arrived at the Age of Reason when men's thoughts and actions were governed by dis-

[10]*Leviathan,* Part I, Chapter XIII, *Great Books,* pp. 84–86.

[11]John Locke, *Second Treatise,* Chapter IX, par. 124 in *Social Contract,* introduction by Sir Ernest Barker (New York: Oxford University Press, 1952), p. 105.

[12]*Ibid,* p. 184. Typically this was also the justification for the Glorious Revolution. The argument was that James II had violated his contract with the English people rather than the reverse.

passionate logic and cold calculation. But the truth of the matter was that secretly people had become increasingly bored with logic and rationality and were longing for a chance to feel emotion rather than to intellectualize theory. This afforded Rousseau with his new interpretation of the social contract. For him, the social contract was no calculating business arrangement to protect the interests of property. Rather, it was a passionate dedication to create a society to which total loyalty could be given. What Rousseau envisaged was the emergence of a new living personality with a life and, above all, a will of its own. This latter proposition Rousseau stated in his famous concept of the *general will.* Every participant in society was to surrender himself totally to the general will, although Rousseau argued, that "Each, giving himself to all, gives himself to nobody." In short, since everyone is carrying out the same act of submission to community authority, everyone equally gains authority. However, as various commentators have pointed out, there is a considerable difference between surrendering control over one's life to 999 people and to acquiring a one-thousandth part control over them.

Rousseau described the result of this collective transfer of power:

> As soon as the act of association becomes a reality, it substitutes for the person of each of the contracting parties a moral and collective body made up of as many members as the constituting assembly has votes, which body receives from this very act of constitution its unity, its dispersed *self,* and its will. The public person thus formed by the union of individuals was known in the old days as a *City,* but now as the *Republic* or *Body Politic.*[13]

By some mysterious process of political chemistry which Rousseau never makes clear, a general will is created which "remains constant, unalterable and pure," and which "is always right and ever tends to the public advantage." Although Rousseau never used the term *direct democracy,* he makes it clear that regular mass participation in the management of the Body Politic is essential to the functioning of the general will. In his own words, "If, then, the general will is to be truly expressed, it is essential that there be no subsidiary groups within the State, and that each citizen voice his own opinion, and nothing but his own opinion."

In contrast to Locke, Rousseau did not regard property ownership as a prerequisite to participation in community affairs. For that matter, "the State, by reason of the Social Contract which, within it, is the basis of all Rights, is the master of its members' goods. . . ." But in spite of the unchallengeable power which the Body Politic had over the

[13]Rousseau, *Social Contract,* p. 257.

lives of the members of the political community, Rousseau saw no need for it to be achieved by total consensus. In his usual vague fashion, he stated, "For the Will to be general, it is not always necessary that it be unanimous, though it is necessary that every vote cast should be counted."

Elsewhere, however, sounds a different and more sinister note. Apparently as a deeply felt conviction, he voiced the disturbing suggestion that "whoever shall refuse to obey the general will must be constrained by the whole body of his fellow citizens to do so; which is no more than to say that it may be necessary to compel a man to be free. . . ." If it be accepted that the general will can *never* err, that it *always* seeks only "the general good of all," then the proposition would not be unreasonable. But immediately the question arises, who is to interpret the general will and decide how it is to be applied? From Rousseau's time until now this has been one of the major problems of that populistic democracy to which he gave modern form and meaning.

There is a striking similarity between this doctrine of Rousseau's and the philosophy preached by Herbert Marcuse, who in the late 1960s became the intellectual mentor of the New Left. Though his thinking is based on Marx and Freud rather than Rousseau, Marcuse also feels "that it may be necessary to compel a man to be free . . ." Again in Rousseau's elitist vein, Marcuse's basic premise is that he knows best the direction in which men should be forced to be free. In Marcuse's case the political left has not only the right but the moral duty to suppress opposition to its policies.

What this means in practice is graphically illustrated by an anecdote published in 1968. Noted the author:

> When, last fall, a Dow Chemical recruiter was put under siege at Harvard, a leader of the demonstration was asked why a recruiter from Dow, the U.S. Marines, or the CIA should not be extended the same privileges as those offered the Peace Corps or the Communist Party. His indignant answer—"Because some things are just *too* evil"—was implicitly a restatement of the theme of Dr. Marcuse's essay, "Repressive Tolerance."[14]

In contrast to the antidemocratic authoritarianism of both Rousseau and Marcuse, there has been a new and significant development in recent years in the never-ending quest to make democracy more meaningful in both form and content. In large part this seems to stem from that sense of alienation and rootlessness mentioned earlier as a social problem of the advanced technological societies.

[14]Bruce Cook, "Student Rebels Hawk the Views of the Mild Dr. Marcuse," *The National Observer*, July 8, 1968, p. 18.

PARTICIPATORY DEMOCRACY AND POLITICAL ALIENATION

It is now more than two centuries since Rousseau regretfully concluded that "no true democracy has ever existed nor ever will." But as an ideal, the yearning to make true democracy operational has become an important objective of practical politics in the late twentieth century. It is no exaggeration to say that the drive to achieve true democracy has gathered strength in direct proportion to the degree of frustration and alienation felt in the face of the bafflingly complex and dishearteningly impersonal political and social institutions of our society.

This old desire for a sense of meaningful participation in the decision-making process has entered on the contemporary political scene as the drive for *participatory democracy*. As defined by the Students for a Democratic Society (SDS), which first publicized the term, this means that:

> political life would be based in several root principles:
> that decision-making of basic social consequences be carried on by public groupings;
> that politics be seen positively, as the art of collectively creating an acceptable pattern of social relations;
> that politics has the function of bringing people out of isolation and into community, thus being a necessary, though not sufficient, means of finding meaning in personal life;
> that the political order should serve to clarify problems in a way instrumental to their solution; it should provide outlets for the expression of personal grievance and aspiration; opposing views should be organized so as to illuminate choices and facilitate the attainment of goals; channels should be commonly available to relate men to knowledge and to power so that private problems—from bad recreation facilities to personal alienation—are formulated as general issues.[15]

It is easy to dismiss the concept of participatory democracy as naive and utopian. But it is impossible to ignore the fact that there is a very great need to bring "people out of isolation and into community." It is a serious indictment of the shortcomings of American democracy as an institutional system that in the tense and closely fought 1968 presidential election 40 percent of eligible voters did not participate. As we noted earlier, various legal disabilities account for a part of this noninvolvement. But it is generally accepted that millions of citizens simply did not care, felt no sense of involvement or community. Clearly life-and-death matters of national policy cannot be decided by

[15]"Port Huron Statement of 1962," one of the founding documents of the Students for a Democratic Society, in *American Radical Thought*, ed. Henry J. Silverman (Lexington, Mass.: Heath, 1970), p. 362.

debates in the style of Athenian assembly. But is it beyond the bounds of possibility to decentralize our political system sufficiently to permit full involvement for the average citizen at local levels on important issues? If this is not achieved, some way, some how, then it is reasonable to anticipate growing alienation and apathy. Neither singly nor in conjunction do these two factors augur anything but ill for the future of a democratic system alleging as one of its tripartite aspects, "government *by* the people." Long ago it was written that "where there is no vision, the people perish." The somber warning of the growing popularity of participatory democracy can be interpreted to mean that *where there is no participation, democracy perishes.*

In 1970 a unique effort was launched to make participatory democracy real. This was the organization by John W. Gardner, former Secretary of Health, Education and Welfare, of Common Cause as "A national citizens' lobby . . . in the public interest at all levels of government, but especially the federal level." Designed primarily to give men and women over thirty an opportunity to influence policy-making, Common Cause has established itself as the voice of those concerned but frustrated citizens disenchanted with their unions, with their trade and professional associations, and with both political parties. To date it represents the most realistic and concrete effort to try to create an interest group for the average citizen which will give him that much too long and dangerously lost sense of participation in the governmental process.

This upsurge of interest in participatory democracy by both students and adults demonstrates again how the interpretation of democracy as a system of government has changed over the centuries. This, of course, is not particularly surprising. As various thinkers make new contributions, continuing change in institutional expression will occur. What is more surprising, however, is that from ancient Greece until now there has been so little alteration in the perception of the guidelines which democracy should use in its decision-making process and the normative values which it should try to realize.

DEMOCRACY'S GUIDELINES FOR DECISION-MAKING

There is no better illustration of the remarkable consistency in the essentials of the democratic credo over the past two thousand years than once again to return to Aristotle and consider his concept of the points common to all democracies:

the election of officers by all out of all;
that all should rule over each, and each in his turn over all;

that the appointment to all offices, or to all but those which require experience and skill, should be made by lot;
that no property qualification should be required for offices, or only a very low one;
that a man should not hold the same office twice, or not often, . . . that the tenure of all offices, or of as many as possible, should be brief;
that all men should sit in judgment, or that judges selected out of all should judge, in all matters, or in most and in the greatest and most important, . . .
that the assembly should be supreme over all causes, or, at any rate, over the most important, and the magistrates over none or only over a very few.
The next characteristic of democracy is payment for services; assembly, law-courts, magistrates, everybody receives pay, . . .
Another note is that no magistracy is perpetual, . . . the holders should be elected by lot and no longer by vote.[16]

Except for the addition of a demand for general education, American democrats from Samuel Adams to Andrew Jackson advocated a program for popular government which differed little from Aristotle's prescriptions. In the late eighteenth and early nineteenth centuries they, too, were urging limited terms of office with maximum rotation, legislative control over all aspects of government, full manhood suffrage with no property qualifications, the smallest possible bureaucracy, and pay for public service. Even more ironically, while the American democrats mostly achieved these aims by Jackson's election in 1828, it was not until 1867 that their British counterparts in the home of modern constitutional democracy were able to begin to enact such a program.

THE MODERN CONCEPT OF A CONSTITUTIONAL DEMOCRACY

In any list of the contemporary guidelines for the operation of a democratic political system, there is scant change from the points raised by Aristotle. There would be little disagreement, for instance, that the framework for the operation of a constitutional democracy should include the following five points:

1. *Mass participation* in the selection of policy-makers
2. Participation conditioned by:
    a. *Alternative choices* between two or more competitive groups of would-be policy-makers
    b. Complete *equality of voting rights*
    c. Maximum *uniformity of representation*
3. Complete *freedom of activity* for legitimate political groups and of choice for individual voters

[16] *Politics,* Book VI, 2, *Great Books,* Vol. 9, pp. 520–521.

4. Determination of policy decisions by the elected representatives through *majority vote* after lengthy discussion
5. *Accountability* of elected officials by the voters through regular elections at frequent intervals.

Mass Participation

In the late twentieth century we live in the era of the participatory state. Ever since Rousseau's revolutionary statement in the late eighteenth century that the political community existed only because all are involved in it, mass participation, or the appearance of it, has been regarded as one of the hallmarks of any modern state. At the height of their power, the most autocratic rulers of modern times have felt it necessary to demonstrate that there was mass support for their regimes. In 1805, for example, when Napoleon Bonaparte, already the supreme military dictator of France, decided to declare himself emperor of the French, he did not simply parade the army and announce the decision, as he might have done a century earlier. Instead, Napoleon felt it necessary to prove the legitimacy of his new regime by organizing a demonstration of overwhelming mass support. In the twentieth century both of the world's first totalitarian states, Nazi Germany and the Soviet Union, justified their legitimacy by similarly manipulated demonstrations of mass support.

The Conditions for Mass Participation

In contrast to the manipulated participatory state, constitutional democracies can be termed *autonomous* participatory states, because they are characterized by the other four conditions just listed as requisite for a constitutional democracy. Particularly important in this connection is the way in which mass participation in the selection of policymakers is organized. Without a choice among one or more alternatives, there is no freedom, no autonomy involved. It is worth noting that because of the sheer geographic size and number of citizens involved in the modern national political system, participation by the citizens resolves itself simply into the opportunity to decide which set of policymakers (political elites) will govern them during the next term of office. But aside from the need to have alternative choice available, there is no accurate expression of people power unless all adult citizens can vote and have their votes count equally. This may seem obvious, but historically the achievement both of equal voting rights and uniformity of representation involved a long and difficult struggle.

For even in the model constitutional democracies, the achievement of "one man, one vote" has been a rather recent development. In Great Britain for example, until after World War II, voters with university educations and voters residing in one voting district and having a business address in another were entitled to two votes. In the United States, until the redistricting of state legislatures in the late 1960s, one representative in a state legislature might have been elected by two thousand or three thousand voters while another, also with one vote, spoke for perhaps two or three times as many.

Freedom of Activity

It is important to keep in mind that the third point, "complete freedom of activity for legitimate political groups and of choice for individual voters," frequently means less than it implies, even with the best of intentions on the part of everyone concerned. Let us define a legitimate political group as one which is willing to abide by normal rules and regulations before it comes to power and accepts the fact that if it does come to power it will in time have to resubmit itself to the judgment of the voters and be prepared to surrender political power peacefully if it is the loser in free elections.

Even with this broad definition, complete freedom of activity is likely to be lacking. To have the abstract right to freedom of activity is well and good. But the exercise of it by any political group is very much limited by the group's ability to finance the facilities needed to reach the voters. The freedom of activity which any party can exercise and, therefore, the amount of informed choice which any voter can make are very much conditioned by the high cost of communications. This is one of the problems faced by new or small parties that have no adequate financial base from which to operate.

Majority Vote

No believer in a democratic system disagrees with the proposition that decision should be by majority vote. But there is always disagreement on what is or should be meant by *majority*. Does it mean unlimited or limited majority? Both answers pose a dilemma which seems to challenge essential points of democratic belief. If we accept the proposition that majority rule has no limits on it and that whatever 50 percent plus one of the eligible voters decide on must then be executed, what happens to minority rights? Indeed, what happens to democracy itself if 50 percent plus one of the eligible voters opt in favor of its abolition?

Instead of the potentially capricious tyranny of a system of unlimited majority, it has often and long been argued that a system with some type of limited majority rule is preferable. The basic concept of this approach is not so much "The people, yes" without any further equivocation as "The people, yes—but." Actually this has been the dominant interpretation of how democratic government should be carried out during most of American history.

The founding fathers favored a republican rather than democratic form of government because for them, as for Aristotle, democracy meant direct democracy and smacked of mob rule by the most undependable and ill-informed elements of society. In Number 14 of the famous *Federalist* papers, James Madison defined the difference between a republic and a democracy: "The true distinction between these forms . . . is, that in a democracy the people meet and exercise the government in person; in a republic, they assemble and administer it by their representatives and agents."

It is commonplace to refer to the United States as having a democratic form of government. In spirit and philosophy, it does. But in technical institutional terms, this is a republic, not a democracy. American political history from 1789 to the present is mostly the story of how an elitist republican form of government based on a small number of property-owning voters evolved into a twentieth-century mass democracy.

Accountability of Elected Officials

Point 5 is perhaps the core item in the whole concept of democratic government. From the time of Pericles to de Gaulle's withdrawal from public life after the French people failed to endorse his policies, the accountability of public officials and the right of the citizens to accept or reject them has been basic to the democratic process. This marks the difference between a democratic governmental system and any other.

Throughout American political history there has always been a concern, indeed almost an obsession, with the possibility of the tyranny of the majority. This concern produced what is often referred to as one of the few original American contributions to political thought: John C. Calhoun's concept of the concurrent majority. Calhoun, the leading spokesman for the minority interest of the South in the mid-nineteenth century, proposed his doctrine in an effort to insure that, whatever the odds against them, "the different interests, orders, classes, or portions into which the community may be divided can be protected, and all conflict and struggle between them prevented—by rendering it impossible to put or to keep it [the government] in action without the concurrent consent of all." Long before Bentley startled conventional political science with his group theory of politics in 1908, Calhoun took for granted that political life consisted in the interaction of groups whether of the geographical or interest type. No action should be taken by any numerical majority unless the particular group or groups most affected by it also gave concurrent agreement. To use Calhoun's own explanation:

> By giving to each interest, or portion, the power of self-protection, all strife and struggle between them for ascendancy is prevented . . . the individual and social feelings are made to unite in one common devotion to country. Each sees and feels that it can best promote its own prosperity by conciliating the good will and promoting the prosperity of the others.

To those who argued that this was expecting too much of human nature, Calhoun replied, "When something *must* be done—and when it can be done only by the united consent of all—the necessity of the case will force to a compromise . . ." He then pointed out that "to form a juster estimate of the full force of this impulse to compromise, there must be added that in governments of the concurrent majority each portion, in order to advance its own peculiar interests, would have to conciliate all others by showing a disposition to advance theirs."[17]

Although never formally enacted as an operating principle of American government, Calhoun's concept of the concurrent majority has nevertheless exerted potent influence. Very few legislative measures have ever cleared the halls of Congress on the basis of the majority ruthlessly ramming them through over the objections of a protesting minority. Rather, in considerably less elegant language than Calhoun used, it has been a case of "scratch my back this time and I'll scratch yours next time" or, in a biblical phrase made famous by President Johnson in his happier years as a legislative leader, "Come, let us reason together!"

THE ROLE OF ELITES IN A DEMOCRACY

Calhoun's concept of the concurrent majority was based on his practical experience as a long-time member of the legislative branch in both House and Senate (1810-1816 and 1832-1850, respectively). It was from this background that he wrote his remarkably perceptive account of the actual workings of the decision-making process at the highest levels of governmental power. It is worth remembering that between his periods of House and Senate service Calhoun held office as secretary of war and vice-president.

As an outstanding spokesman for his particular regional interest group, he found himself in constant contact with

[17]John C. Calhoun, *A Disquisition on Government*, ed. C. Gordon Post (New York: Liberal Arts Press, 1953), pp. 20–21, 37–38, 50, and 52.

men of similar status from other areas. There were times when they had certain areas of interest which were vital to their concerns—and political futures. There were also times when for Calhoun and his interest group the reverse was true. The realistic and reasonable solution was to give priority to whichever group interest was paramount at the moment with the expectation that as fellow members of the club they would do likewise when the occasion arose.

As a recent and "uncommon introduction to American politics" puts it:

> Since pluralism contends that different groups of leaders make decisions in *different* issue areas, why should we assume that these leaders compete with each other? It seems more likely that each group of leaders would consent to allow other groups of leaders to govern their own spheres of influence without interference. Accomodation, rather than competition, may be the prevailing style of elite interaction.[18]

The "irony of democracy," the authors, Professors Dye and Zeigler, suggest, lies in the fact that "democracy is government 'by the people,' but the responsibility for the survival of democracy rests on the shoulders of elites. In both contemporary terms and historically there is much evidence to support their contention that elites, the tiny group at the top of the power pyramid which makes the final decisions for a society, make possible the survival of government "by the people." We have spoken of ancient Athens as the model for classic democracy. Yet it is significant that its period of greatness is known as the Periclean age and that after Pericles' death in 428 B.C., Athens' decline came very rapidly.

It is no exaggeration to say that history is little more than the record of the roles played by succeeding elites. As the Italian sociologist Mosca summarizes this proposition:

> In all societies—from societies that are very underdeveloped and have largely attained the dawnings of civilization, down to the most advanced and powerful societies—two classes of people appear—a class that rules and a class that is ruled. The first class, always the less numerous, performs all of the political functions, monopolizes power, and enjoys the advantages that power brings, whereas the second, the more numerous class, is directed and controlled by the first, in a manner that is now more or less legal, now more or less arbitrary and violent.
>
> In practical life we all recognize the existence of this ruling class. . . . We all know that, in our own country, whichever it may be, the management of public affairs is in the hands of a minority of influential persons, to which management, willingly or unwillingly, the majority defer. We know that the same thing

[18]Thomas R. Dye and L. Harmon Zeigler, *The Irony of Democracy* (Belmont, Calif.: Wadsworth, 1971), p. 16.

goes on in neighboring countries, and in fact we should be hard put to it to conceive of a real world otherwise organized.[19]

Mosca's reference was to Italy, but Dye and Zeigler find widespread agreement among social scientists that all types of important decisions affecting the definitive allocation of values in American society, whether social, economic, or political, are made by very small groups of decision-makers. It is possible for these elites to make decisions because they "share in a *consensus* about fundamental norms underlying the social system."

It is this basic acceptance of the rules of the game which makes possible the successful functioning of Calhoun's concurrent majorities. In these competitive but nonhostile elite groups, there are disagreements over policies and interest, but no elite group questions the fundamental values of a society which has treated it so well. This explains why it is the elites not the masses who are most deeply committed to what are considered to be the core values of democratic society.

In this connection, it has been said:

> A widespread public commitment to the fundamental norms underlying the democratic process was regarded by classical democratic theorists as essential to the survival of democracy . . . [but] today social scientists tend to reject this position. They do so not only because of their limited confidence in the commitment of non-elites to freedom, but also because of the growing awareness that non-elites are, in large part, politically activated by elites. The empirical finding that mass behavior is generally in response to the attitudes, proposals and modes of action of political elites gives added support to the position that responsibility for maintaining "the rules of the game" rests not on the shoulders of the people but on those of the elites.[20]

Empiric research bears out this conclusion. In broad generalities there is widespread acceptance of the freedoms of speech, press, protection against self-incrimination, and the like guaranteed in the Bill of Rights. But their specific application is something else again. Table 11 offers concrete evidence that, ironically, it is elites rather than masses who have the greatest commitment to the traditional values of democratic society.

Dye and Zeigler observe:

> This portrait of the elite and the masses indicates that survival of a democratic system does not depend upon a consensus that penetrates to every level of society. It is apparently not necessary that most people commit themselves to a democracy; all that is necessary is that they fail to commit themselves

[19]Gaetano Mosca, *The Ruling Class,* trans. Hannah D. Kahn, ed. Arthur Livingston (New York: McGraw-Hill, 1939), p. 50.

[20]Peter Bachrach, *The Theory of Democratic Elitism* (Boston: Little, Brown, 1967), pp. 47–48.

Table 11

Political Influentials vs. the Electorate: Response to Items Expressing Support for Specific Applications of Free Speech and Procedural Rights

Items	Political Influentials (N = 3020)	General Electorate (N = 1484)
	% Agree	
Freedom does not give anyone the right to teach foreign ideas in our schools.	45.5	56.7
A man oughtn't to be allowed to speak if he doesn't know what he's talking about.	17.3	36.7
A book that contains wrong political views cannot be a good book and does not deserive to be published.	17.9	50.3
When the country is in great danger we may have to force people to testify against themselves even if it violates their rights.	28.5	36.3
No matter what crime a person is accused of, he should never be convicted unless he has been given the right to face and question his accusers.	90.1	88.1
If a person is convicted of a crime by illegal evidence, he should be set free and the evidence thrown out of court.	79.6	66.1
If someone is suspected of treason or other serious crimes, he shouldn't be entitled to be let out on bail.	33.3	68.9
Any person who hides behind the laws when he is questioned about his activities doesn't deserve much consideration.	55.9	75.7
In dealing with dangerous enemies like the Communists, we can't afford to depend on the courts, the laws and their slow and unreliable methods.	7.4	25.5

SOURCE: Herbert McCloskey, "Consensus and Ideology in American Politics," *The American Political Science Review*, 58 (June, 1964), 367.

actively to an anti-democratic system. . . . However, it is important to keep in mind that although the masses may have anti-democratic attitudes, they are also inclined to avoid political activity. And those with the most dangerous attitudes are the least involved in politics. . . . The apathy of the masses acts to counterbalance the radically conservative and potentially irrational nature of their values.[21]

It is only in times of severe social and political crisis, such as occurred in Germany in the early 1930s, that the masses are stirred into action by leaders of the counter-elite attempting to use them as instruments for their own power goals.

[21]This and the two following quotations are from Dye and Zeigler, *Irony of Democracy*, pp. 137–139, 200, and 339.

The survival of the American and other democratic systems seems to rest on four rather shaky pillars. They are:

1. That the elite not feel its control fundamentally threatened
2. That the elite be sufficiently isolated from the masses to continue to feel commitment to the strengthening of democratic values
3. That no traumatic political or social upheavals occur to galvanize the masses into abnormal involvement in the political system
4. That the elite be sufficiently open to permit able individuals from the masses to be assimilated into it.

The reasons for the first of these points stems from Lenin's observation that no ruling class ever gives up power peacefully. Or, as Dye and Zeigler put it:

> While elites are *relatively* more committed to democratic values than masses, elites may abandon these values in crisis periods. When war or revolution threatens to tear down the existing order, the established elites may move towards the "garrison state." Dissent will no longer be tolerated, the news media will be censored, free speech will be curtailed, potential counter-elites will be jailed, and police and security forces will be strengthened. Usually these steps will be taken in the name of national security or "law and order." The established democratic elites will take these steps in the belief that they are necessary to preserve liberal democratic values. The irony is, of course, that the elites make society less democratic in order to preserve democracy.

In theory democracy is based on the proposition that the more individuals involved in the decision-making process, the better. Not so, argues Professor William Kornhauser in his *Politics of Mass Society*. Actually this is a danger signal. "Mass politics occurs when large numbers of people engage in political activity outside of the procedures and rules instituted by the society to govern political action. Mass politics in democratic society therefore is anti-democratic, since it contravenes the constitutional order."[22]

When *not* under pressure, the elites will neither resort to the garrison state nor feel themselves pressed sufficiently by the politically active masses to arouse themselves to defend democratic values. For this reason some political scientists argue that apathy constitutes a support for the functioning of a democratic political system. The proposition seems debatable.

The fourth and last of the pillars for the maintenance of a democratic system can be put in colloquial terms. Where the most able and determinedly upward mobile elements of the masses have the prospects of getting a piece

[22]William Kornhauser, *Politics of Mass Society* (New York: Free Press, 1959), p. 227.

of the action, there is no incentive for them to resort to revolutionary tactics to destroy the existing system. By accepting the predominant elite values, they, too, can make their way upward within the system to positions of economic and political power. This, of course, has been the story of minority groups in American society.

Although in *The Irony of Democracy* Dye and Zeigler generalize only about the prospects of American democracy, their conclusions have significance for democratic systems in general. They conclude:

> The future of American democracy depends on the wisdom, responsibility, and resourcefulness of the nation's elite. . . . It is the irony of democracy that the responsibility for the survival of liberal democratic values depends upon elites, not masses. . . .
>
> Democratic systems are particularly vulnerable to anti-democratic movements, since democracies invite mass participation. But it is also possible that democracy will collapse as a result of elite overreaction to the threats of these counterelites.
>
> Democracy cannot be taken for granted. . . . we have observed that both the procedures of the democratic process and the values of liberal society are not widely shared by the masses of Americans and are occasionally abandoned by America's elites. We have little cause for complacency about the survival of democracy.

ECONOMIC DEVELOPMENT AND DEMOCRACY

Among the myths of democracy equally important to the necessity of an alert and educated mass citizenry is the presumed relationship between the emergence and survival of a democratic system and a high level of socioeconomic development. The belief in this relationship goes back very far. Surveying the Greek world of the fourth century B.C., Aristotle observed that extremes of wealth and poverty led to political turmoil bound to end either in mob rule or dictatorship. He concluded:

> Thus it is manifest that the best political community is formed by citizens of the middle class. . . . Great then is the good fortune of a state in which the citizens have a moderate and sufficient property; for where some possess much, and the others nothing, there may arise an extreme democracy or a pure oligarchy, or a tyranny may grow out of either extreme, . . . democracies are safer and more permanent than oligarchies, because they have a middle class which is more numerous and has a greater share in the government; for when there is no middle class and the poor greatly exceed in number, troubles arise, and the state soon comes to an end.[23]

Some twenty-three centuries after Aristotle, political sociologist Seymour Martin Lipset, among others, reached

[23] *Politics*, IV, 2, *Great Books*, Vol. 9, p. 82.

the tentative conclusion, based on extensive empiric research, that there existed "possible connections" between the emergence of a democratic system and such conditions as an open class system, economic wealth, equalitarian values, a capitalist economy, literacy, and high participation in voluntary organizations.[24] In the contemporary world there would seem to be, at first glance, considerable evidence to support this allegedly close relationship between a high level of socioeconomic development and the emergence of a democratic system. One researcher who tested Lipset's hypotheses rigorously found, for example, a close correlation between a high level of political development and such factors as high levels of development in communication, urbanization, and education, with an inverse relation to the proportion of the work force engaged in agriculture. Obvious examples of countries which seem to validate these correlations are the English-speaking nations, the Scandinavian countries, the Low Countries, West Germany, Israel, and Japan.

Some of the more extreme proponents of the cause-and-effect relationships between high socioeconomic development and democracy have gone on to draw highly optimistic conclusions for the future development of democracy. They reason that as the nations of the world industrialize and thus are able to raise their standards of living, more democratic tendencies in their political development are bound to follow.

Although it would be comforting to look forward to the time when economic development will bring political liberalization, the evidence does not seem to support such a hope. First of all, it is becoming grimly obvious that a number of the countries of the world which need economic development the most have the least prospect of achieving it. Indeed, given their mounting population pressures, many of these countries may not even be able to maintain their present precarious positions. Most of these countries achieved their independence from colonial rule under the leadership of political groups dedicated to the achievement of programs of popular democracy and economic development that were utopian in nature. The failure of these initial independence leaders to achieve the impossible has served to discredit the very idea of democracy itself and to encourage, usually in modernist-minded military oligarchies, a resort to authoritarian and semitotalitarian government. However, such is the influence of the concept of people power in the twentieth century that virtually all such regimes feel it necessary to assert that their seizure of power is temporary and for the sole purpose of making

[24]Seymour Martin Lipset, "Some Social Requisites of Democracy: Economic Development and Political Legitimacy," *The American Political Science Review* 53 (March 1959): 69–105.

possible the reestablishment of a more perfect democratic system. In Burma in 1962 and in Ghana in 1969 such military regimes actually did hand back power to civilian leaders chosen in properly conducted elections.

In short, industrialization does not automatically give rise to a democratic political system. As the Czechoslovakian tragedy of 1968 unhappily demonstrated, the Soviet Union's gigantic strides in industrial development have little effect on its rigid political system. The Russian people and those of East European satellite countries undoubtedly are much better fed and clothed now than 15 years ago. But in terms of political development they are still in the unhappy position of a leashed animal with 20 feet of rope to pull on instead of 15! The order party is still holding very firmly to the end of the leash and can jerk it at any time.

There is another aspect of the relationship between democracy and industrial development which needs consideration. The nineteenth-century conditions which produced the simultaneous expansion of modern industrialism and mass democracy may have been, and probably were, a unique product of a particular time and place unlikely to be repeated. Given the lack in all of the new states of an economically powerful and politically influential middle class such as existed in Western Europe and the United States in the nineteenth century, the only way for industrial development to occur is by governmental action. As de Schweinitz puts it:

> Because of the industrialization of the western world, political leaders in underdeveloped economies have a picture of social welfare from which they can reasonably argue individuals will receive great benefit. But if individual conduct in these countries now will not lead autonomously to the achievement of this welfare position, then they might have to be taken in hand and led forward *in their own interests*.[25]

It is not argued that this makes the development of constitutional democracy impossible but only far more difficult and far more a matter of deliberate choice on the part of the leaders of these new nations than of logical social development. De Schweinitz gives a description of the role this leadership must play. "Not only do they have to take the initiative in accelerating economic growth, but in forming the political community as well. . . . To paraphrase Winston Churchill, never before has the history of democracy depended so much on the actions of so few."

Realistically speaking, this does not offer a particularly hopeful prospect for the emergence of new democratic

[25]This and the following quotation are from Karl de Schweinitz, Jr., *Industrialization and Democracy* (New York: Free Press, 1964), pp. 257 and 279. This book presents a thoughtful and well-argued statement of this proposition. (Italics added.)

regimes. We have already noted that the sheer force of long-established custom and routine can be a powerful factor in political development. Once the pattern has been established for an antidemocratic or nondemocratic operation of new political systems, even if it proves only relatively successful, it is very hard to change. As the Soviet example shows, there is no automatic process of evolutionary political development that can be counted on to bring change about. The prospects seem to be that democracy, as understood in Western terms, is likely to experience few, if any, new triumphs in the years ahead and in fact may well suffer setbacks in such new nations as India or Ceylon, where for more than twenty years constitutional democracy has functioned successfully.

The fact that, in spite of comparatively low levels of socioeconomic development, democracy has been possible in India and Ceylon is an indication of the role played by other factors in the creation and operation of a democratic political system. Once again, the importance of sheer habit, of continuing to follow the patterns of a well-established routine, comes to the fore. In both India and Ceylon, as elsewhere in the Empire, the British had created an opportunity for natives to experience the operation of democratic political systems. Over thirty years ago, a distinguished political scientist suggested, with but slight empirical evidence to substantiate his position, that habitual behavior patterns rather than stated agreement on a democratic credo constitute one of the major supports for a democratic system.[26]

A certain minimum level of socioeconomic development is necessary to create the "threshold" conditions for the development of constitutional democracy. Below this rather vague minimum level the sheer struggle for survival, both on a national and personal basis, is likely to be so difficult as to allow no leeway for the relatively relaxed and noncoercive atmosphere of a democratic system.

Pluralism and Cleavages

As we have noted, for a democratic system to function it must be possible for various groups to play a part in the political system. In short, there must be *pluralism* to permit the widest possible expression of opinions and programs. But like all other concepts, pluralism has a bad side as well as a good, for if pluralism operates within a framework of deep and bitter *cleavages* among the groups involved, it may make impossible the operation of a politi-

[26]Carl J. Friedrich in 1940. See his *Man and his Government* (New York: McGraw-Hill, 1963). In particular, Chapter 4 on "The Function of Ideas and Ideologies in Politics" and Chapter 6 on "Religion and Ritual."

cal system based on majority rule and the acceptance of even a minimum consensus. France, of course, is the best, or worst, example of a nation which has had a great deal going for it in socioeconomic terms, but which as a result of the various unhealed political wounds inflicted on the French body politic ever since the revolution of 1789 has had all its attempts at operating democratic political systems frustrated by the depth of the cleavages among various hostile groups.

CONCLUSION

Democracy has behind it a long history with many differing interpretations in a variety of social and cultural contexts. A half-century ago, James Bryce, one of the most perceptive political scientists of his time, anticipated the victory of democratic political systems on a world scale. Today, with good reason, we are less sure of democracy's future. Far more characteristic of democracy in the late twentieth century is its limited practice in contrast to the widespread lip service given its ideals.

Following a brief expansion of democratic political systems in the 1950s and the early 1960s as the last colonial territories became independent, its area of meaningful influence contracted. Indeed it seems very likely that it may not be able to survive in some Asian and African countries where it now ekes out a somewhat precarious existence.

There is no direct cause-and-effect relationship between socioeconomic development and the successful functioning of a democratic political system; but for a democratic system to come into existence at all, a certain threshold level of socioeconomic development must be achieved and, even more importantly, maintained. Many observers of world affairs warn that democracy may well be restricted in its extent by the demanding, perhaps historically unique, convergence of circumstances which produced it in the political systems of the Atlantic Community. But it is equally clear, as we noted at the beginning of this chapter, that as a normative idea its influence has never been greater in the world. In the next two chapters we will discuss the current alternative guidelines to democracy: communism and nationalism. These philosophies claim to represent a more realistic effort to achieve the basic goals of the democratic dream within the context of their social and cultural conditions than the simple transplanting of the institutions of Western-type democracy could accomplish.

THE ALTERNATIVE OF COMMUNISM

As we have noted, in name at least democracy has won the day in the twentieth century. No political movement anywhere in the world is on record as opposed to its concepts, and world leaders as widely differing as Mao, Nixon, Castro, and Meir pay tribute to its goals.

But obviously there is a considerable variation among the interpretations of democracy to be found in Washington and Paris, Moscow and Peking, Cairo and Djakarta. To regard them all as variations on the same theme would be to abandon all attempt at arriving at any meaningful classification. For Western democracy, communism of any variety, and the new nationalisms are notable for their points of difference rather than of similarity. Indeed, it is customary to regard Western democracy, with its pluralistic outlook, and world communism, with its monolithic interpretation of man's past history and inevitable future, as the two great poles of conflict in the modern world, with the new nationalisms of the developing nations lying somewhere between these dichotomous world outlooks.

In this chapter we will outline the major traits of communism, and in Chapter 9 we will discuss the governmental philosophies of the new nations insofar as it is possible to generalize about such a variety of viewpoints. For that matter, for almost a decade it has been unrealistic to generalize about communism. Moscow and Peking, Belgrade and Havana all interpret differently the grand design for mankind's future originated by Karl Marx and revised for the twentieth century by Nicolai Lenin. In our discussion of the development of Marxist-Leninist thought, we shall distinguish the major differences among the several currents of contemporary polycentric communism.[1] But since all of these currents

[1]The state of disarray of world communism since the early 1960s, known as *polycentric* communism, bears no resemblance to the accepted pluralistic interpretations of democracy. For what the original Sino-Soviet split and the

accept as their "sacred scriptures" the propositions concerning man's history and inevitable future development originated by Marx and reinterpreted by Lenin, it is to a survey of these basic concepts that we first turn.

THE THEORY OF MARXIAN MARXISM

The emergence of Marxism as an important current in world thought and as a guide to political action was a unique phenomenon. Within two generations after the death of its founder in 1883, it had become the guiding philosophy by which a third of the human race was ruled and the inspiration of a world-wide political movement numbering its adherents in the millions. Directly or indirectly, in terms of challenge and response, it was also shaping the calculations and policies of the leaders of the noncommunist countries of the world. This fact is all the more extraordinary because within twenty years of its founder's death, Marxism seemed to be destined to become just another political movement, although an important one, rather than the source of a formula for the creation of "the kingdom of freedom" for the human race.

Karl Marx (1818–1883) and his collaborator Frederick Engels (1820–1895) spent their long lifetimes from the time of their initial association in 1845 working out the details of their brilliant and sweeping vision of how society had developed and must develop. We have Engels's word for it that, by the time their lifetime collaboration began, both had arrived independently at essentially the same conclusions. That these were hostile to the existing order of affairs was not surprising. The period of the 1830s and 1840s was a time of unique political and social upheaval in the history of Western Europe. The Industrial Revolution was causing the patterns of society to change with unprecedented speed and thoroughness and, as in all such periods of wrenching change, a host of seemingly insoluble problems threatened social and economic chaos. Added to the impact of the Industrial Revolution was the far-reaching attack on the political status quo inspired by the democratic concepts of the French Revolution: liberty, equality, fraternity.

One of the most important influences of the Industrial Revolution was the transformation in the long-established rhythms of economic activity. For centuries the economic life of even the most advanced countries had been geared to the minor ups and downs of agricultural existence. Barring bumper crops or the disaster of drought, there was

---

subsequent emergence of other interpretations of communism is all about is simply the struggle to determine which of these is to prevail as *the* one and only true interpretation of the teachings of Marx and Lenin.

little deviation from the long-established level of existence. Production was primarily for the purposes of immediate consumption with, at best, a meager surplus for trade or barter purposes. The Industrial Revolution transformed this placid pattern of life for Western Europe. The high level of technological development it represented made possible the factory production of large amounts of manufactured goods for purposes of sale. Indeed, for those involved in the process, the goods had to be sold if they were to eat, since no family was any longer in a position to provide all its own food sources. By the time Marx and Engels formulated their philosophy, this frenzied drive to sell the mounting flood of products from the expanding factory system had led to a crisis of overproduction and economic depression. In graphic form the difference in the rhythms of the economic life of traditional agricultural and modern industrial societies might be illustrated like this:

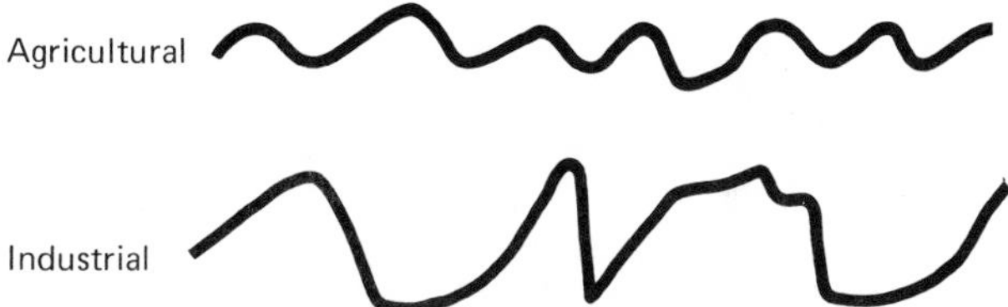

Translated into social (i.e., human) terms, this means that traditional agricultural societies, except at rare intervals, have but little economic impetus to social unrest and upheaval, whereas in modern industrial society there are always very strong pressures in this direction.

In their *Communist Manifesto* (1848), Marx and Engels described it this way:

> Modern bourgeois society with its relations of production, of exchange, and of property, a society that has conjured up such gigantic means of production and of exchange, is like the sorcerer who is no longer able to control the powers of the nether world whom he has called up by his spells. . . . It is enough to mention the commercial crises that by their periodic return put on its trial, each time more threateningly, the existence of the entire bourgeois society. . . . In these crises there breaks out an epidemic that in all earlier epochs would have seemed an absurdity—the epidemic of overproduction. . . . And how does the bourgeoisie get over these crises? On the one hand, by enforced destruction of a mass of productive forces; on the other, by the conquest of new markets, and by the more thorough exploitation of the old ones. That is to say, by paving the way for more extensive and more destructive crises, and, by diminishing the means whereby crises are prevented.[2]

[2]*Marx and Engels: Basic Writings on Politics and Philosophy,* ed. Lewis S. Feuer (Garden City, N.Y.: Doubleday, 1959), pp. 12–13.

To many thoughtful observers besides Marx and Engels it seemed as though this new industrial system had a built-in self-destruct mechanism. The prospect seemed not unlikely that, like a great engine which tears itself to pieces because of its gears pulling against each other, the industrial system would one day enter into a gigantic crisis of overproduction and business collapse that could end only in a chaotic revolutionary destruction of the entire social and political framework of the capitalist system.

But the results of the new state of affairs, as Marx and Engels saw it, were not only economic. There were social implications of equal, if not greater, importance. The emergence of the new capitalist society had been possible because to serve its needs it had brought two new social classes into existence. These Marx and Engels termed the *bourgeoisie* (middle class) and the *proletariat* (industrial workers).[3] By bourgeoisie was meant that small group of individuals, more commonly referred to as the capitalists, who had the capital to build the mills, factories, and other parts of the *infrastructure* of the new industrial system.[4] In the *Manifesto* the origin of the bourgeois class is described as follows: "From the serfs of the Middle Ages sprang the chartered burghers of the earliest towns. From these burgesses the first elements of the bourgeoisie were developed."

In creating the new economic system ". . . not only has the bourgeoisie," Marx and Engels maintained, "forged the weapons that bring death to itself; it has also called into existence the men who are to wield those weapons—the modern working class—the proletarians." They continue:

> In proportion as the bourgeoisie, i.e., capital is developed, in the same proportion is the proletariat, the modern working class, developed—a class of laborers, who live only so long as they find work, and who find work only so long as their labor increases capital. These laborers, who must sell themselves piecemeal, are a commodity, like every other article of commerce, and are consequently exposed to all the vicissitudes of competition, to all the fluctuations of the market.[5]

Marx eloquently summarizes what he foresaw as the inevitable end of this process:

> As soon as this process of transformation has sufficiently decomposed the old society from top to bottom, as soon as the labourers are turned into proletarians, their means of labour into capital, as soon as the capitalist mode of production stands

[3]Actually, these terms were not originated by Marx or Engels but it was they who popularized them and gave them their current meaning.

[4]The term *infrastructure,* originally military in usage, means the physical supporting framework which makes the operation of any system possible.

[5]*Marx and Engels,* p. 14.

on its own feet, then the further socialisation of labour . . . takes a new form. That which is now expropriated is no longer the labourer working for himself, but the capitalist exploiting many labourers. This expropriation is accomplished by the action of the immanent laws of capitalistic production itself, by the centralisation of capital. One capitalist always kills many.[6]

The central focus of Marx's 40 years of research, writing, and not very effective efforts at revolutionary activity were devoted to trying to prove the truth of his vision of the inevitable fate to which the capitalist system was predestined. Marx is correctly regarded as the major influence in the development of the modern socialist and communist movements. But one of the curious ironies of the endless research and thousands of pages of writing that he did is that almost all of it is devoted to explaining and analyzing the capitalist system. In the approximately 3600 pages of his best-known work, *Das Kapital,* there is almost no mention of even the broad outlines, let alone the details, of that socialist-communist social order towards which Marx argued economic and social development was so inevitably moving. Rather he sought to prove his case by a detailed analysis of the dynamics of capitalist development which made this certain.

The outstanding characteristic of capitalism, said Marx, was that it represented the highest form of commodity production which any economic system had ever been able to attain. By *commodity* is meant an article that is produced for the specific purpose of trading for another article or, more importantly, in order to sell for a profit. Such an organization of economic activity is possible only when technology has reached such a level of productivity that there is a considerable surplus beyond what is needed for immediate use. Further this implies that a small number of individuals are able, as a result of scientific development, to produce enough food to feed everybody.

Commodity production is not, except in its very early stages, an isolated or small-scale affair. A large amount of capital is needed to furnish the machinery for production, and a large group of people must be brought together to operate the machines. It is this fact, incidentally, that produced the urbanism, the concentration of population into great industrial centers, that is characteristic of a highly developed technological society. This concentration makes possible that social production, i.e., the cooperation of a number of individuals in the productive process, which Marx quite correctly saw as an intensifying development of modern industrial society.

[6]K. Marx, *Capital: A Critique of Political Economy,* trans. Samuel Moore and Edward Aveling, ed. Frederick Engels (New York: The Modern Library, 1936), pp. 836–837.

Marx drew several important conclusions from this dominance of commodity production. Above all there was the fact that under capitalism every relationship became a commodity relationship, something to be bought and sold. In his own scathing words, "The bourgeoisie, wherever it has got the upper hand, has put an end to all feudal, patriarchal, idyllic relations. It . . . has left remaining no other nexus between man and man than naked half-interest, than callous 'cash payment.'" This meant that "for exploitation, veiled by religious and political illusions, it has substituted naked, shameless, direct, brutal exploitation."

Nowhere was this more true than in the commodity called labor power, the exploitation of which makes possible the very existence of the capitalist system. For the survival of capitalism depends on the production of profit, and only labor power can produce it. In Marx's terms, this is the reason: All other commodities used in the production of new items for the market simply transfer their original value, increment by increment, to the new product. If this were all that happened in the production process profit would be impossible; for all items, the occasional outright swindle aside, are bought and sold at their actual value. Alone among all commodities, labor power has the unique characteristic of producing more value during the time of its use than it cost to buy it initially.

Labor power like all other commodities was able to command its fair value in the market, which means the cost of replacing it with another unit which could perform the same functions. Thus, the going price for labor power at any time was controlled by what it cost a worker to maintain his family for twenty-four hours. Marx, like other economists of his time, always assumed that this level would fluctuate only slightly above or below the minimum daily income necessary for sheer survival. Nor did Marx see that workers had much choice but to accept such wages. Given the social framework of his time there was much justification for this conclusion.

The prevailing philosophy of the new industrial age was a laissez faire liberalism which stemmed from the impetus provided by the French Revolution to end all hampering restrictions. The new business classes interpreted this to mean complete freedom of action for every man to make his own way and a total lack of government regulation of business activities. But when it came to wage negotiations the principle was applied unevenly. On the one hand, efforts at labor-union organization were hampered by restrictive laws. On the other, the worker needed work to feed his family. The result was to give the factory owner a "take-it-or-leave-it" position as far as wage rates were concerned. Even more important to Marx's analysis was the freedom with which the capitalist could determine the amount of labor power his wages purchased. For here, as Marx saw it, lay the whole secret of capitalist profit.

It could be assumed, he reasoned, that by working for five hours the worker could repay to the capitalist the expense of hiring him, i.e., the cost of replacing the commodity of labor power. But, said Marx, the capitalist makes use of his superior economic and political position and instead requires the worker to put in 16 hours, the last 11 of which he is involuntarily giving to the capitalist. It is from this alleged free time that the capitalist gets his profit margin or, in Marxist terms, the surplus value which enables him to stay in business.

Marxian Argument. If the capitalist could maintain this situation indefinitely, all would be well with him. But he cannot. Driven by the inexorable pressure of trying to increase his profits, the capitalist installs the most modern machinery, both to increase production and to cut labor costs, in an effort to get a bigger share of the available market. But, since every capitalist producer tries to sell more goods than anyone else, a crisis of overproduction is bound to occur. The result is a period of unemployment and misery for large numbers of the proletariat and the bankruptcy of the minor capitalists who themselves are forced into the ranks of the proletariat. Meanwhile economic power is concentrated more and more in the hands of a few. As Marx laconically summarized this development, "One capitalist kills many."

The other result of this drive for improved mechanization of production is even more damaging to the prospects for survival of the whole capitalist system. Capitalism, remember, must have profits to continue. The sole source of these profits is from the unpaid labor time which the worker is forced to hand over in order to work at all. Therefore, only that part of the capitalist's total investment which he uses to hire workers produces any profit for him. When shortsightedly he shifts his major concentration of capital from wages to machinery, automatically and inexorably his rate of profit drops. No matter what desperate measures he may try, nothing can change this.

But try he will. Obsessed as he is with the idea of more production and lower costs, it immediately occurs to the capitalist that if only he could lower wages, extend the working day, and, if possible, also intensify the pace of work, this would solve his dilemma. Thus begins the application, says Marx, of the "law of increasing misery." When the first turn of the screw produces no results, the capitalist can only conclude that he has not applied the remedies rigorously enough. So he continues the process with increasing desperation as the boom-bust cycle intensifies and the over-all crisis of the whole capitalist system becomes worse and worse. Marx describes the inevitable outcome eloquently:

> Along with the constantly diminishing number of the magnates of capital, who usurp and monopolize all advantages of this process of transformation, grows the mass of misery, oppression, slavery, degradation, exploitation; but with this too grows the revolt of the working class, a class always increasing in numbers and disciplined, united, organized by the very mechanism of the process of capitalist production itself. The monopoly of capital becomes a fetter upon the mode of production which has sprung up and flourished along with, and under it. Centralization of the means of production and socialization of labor at last reach a point where they become incompatible with their capitalist integument. This integument is burst asunder. The knell of capitalist private property sounds. The expropriators are expropriated.[7]

Marx's description of the exploitation of industrial labor in the first decades of the Industrial Revolution has very little, if any, exaggeration in it. Indeed Marx based one of his most famous (and heart-rending) chapters in the first volume of *Das Kapital* almost entirely on British government reports. Drawing on these sources, in Chapter 10, "The Working Day," Marx cites example after example of the brutal treatment which the defenseless industrial working class suffered at the hands of the capitalist factory owners. With the expectation that inevitably the situation must worsen, Marx concluded that the proletariat would have no choice but violent overthrow of the existing system. Curiously, it seems to have escaped Marx's attention that the mere fact that British government commissions were concerned enough to investigate the situation was a possible indication of the desire to correct it.

CRITICISM OF MARXIAN MARXISM

As forceful as Marx's presentation was, it had two major faults. The first was that it was incorrect in theory. The second was that it did not work in practice. The economists of Marx's time were much concerned with attempting to work out a theory of value and unconcerned with a theory of prices, which modern economists regard as the only indication of value. But Marx went one giant step further than did any other of the nineteenth-century economists by dogmatically asserting that the only source of value came from this allegedly unpaid labor time. This, of course, quite ignores the contribution to the creation of value made by raw materials, the capital which provides the facilities for

[7]Marx, *Capital*, pp. 836–837.

labor to work, and the managerial skill which coordinates the productive process.

A number of practical objections can be made to Marx's economic propositions, but two should suffice to illustrate its incorrectness. The first is Marx's much too narrow definition of a commodity. To have value, he says, a commodity must be the product of labor power. But this is obviously untrue. In 1969 the state of Alaska, for example, received almost a billion dollars for the sale of merely the rights to prospect for oil. Nor is it unusual for millions of dollars to change hands for the purchase of wheat and other grain crops still unharvested or diamonds as yet unmined.

Marx's picture of how revolutions occur is also contradicted by the record of history. None of history's great revolutions developed under conditions of constantly increasing misery; rather they occur when the social classes involved have experienced a degree of economic improvement which, however, still falls short of their expectations.[8] To go from deprivation to utter misery produces only apathy and resignation. To experience some degree of improvement but not enough stimulates revolutionary unrest.

Additionally, reality has refuted Marx's economic predictions. The lot of the proletariat has not become one of increasing misery, nor has the middle class disappeared in the advanced capitalist countries. Rather, as the productive capacity of the new industrial system has steadily increased over the past century, there has been a steady rise in living standards, and technology has created a new middle class undreamed of by Marx. Ironically, in the most advanced capitalist countries, above all the United States, an important section of Marx's proletariat has become so middle class, and so fearful of losing this hard-won status, that it is the most belligerently antileftist element in society. Witness the American "hard hats"!

Far from driving the rate of profit steadily down, the increasing mechanization of industry, even during Marx's lifetime, simply made greater production and profits possible. Perhaps the crowning irony is that precisely those countries in which, according to the Marxist theory of history, the inevitable revolutionary transition to socialism should have first occurred are the most stable of all capitalist countries and the most unlikely prospects for revolutionary upheaval. In contrast the communist countries of the world, such as Russia, China, Yugoslavia, or Cuba, would have been regarded by Marx as among the last prospects for revolution because of the low level of their economic development.

[8]For a detailed and interesting comparative study of the nature of revolutions, see Crane Brinton, *The Anatomy of Revolution,* rev. ed. (New York: Vintage Books, 1965).

Marxist Economics as a Theory of Social Exploitation

The fact of the matter is, of course, that Marx was very little concerned with economic theory as such and intensely interested in developing a theory of social exploitation which would provide moral justification for revolutionary activity and, in accord with his theory of history, prove the inevitability of capitalism's doom and the certainty of the triumph of the socialist order. Perhaps the most interesting point of all about Marxian economic theory is one which Marx himself so took for granted that he didn't think it necessary to put it into words, although many of his disciples have produced virtual sermons on the subject. This is the implicit assumption that profit is immoral if not downright sinful. Marx saw no need to offer any proof of this; it went without saying in his day. To Marx, profit was possible only because of the brutal exploitation of the worker by the capitalist, who performs no useful function and is simply an undesirable parasite.

"Production for use not for profit" has a nice moral ring to it. But history demonstrates only one alternative to some variation on the profit motive: compulsion, based on the willingness to use force ruthlessly and without limit, as Stalin did in the 1930s when, with a contemptuous disregard for human life, he made backward agricultural Russia into a great industrial power. In all the most industrially developed communist countries today, the Soviet Union, Yugoslavia, and the Soviet satellites, some variation of the profit motive has been developed as an incentive to increased production. It is naive to think that this means these countries are, to use the Chinese phrase, "taking the capitalist road," but it is an important indication that in advanced technological societies organizations and individuals need to be induced to produce rather than forced to either by fear and/or appeals to the worker to regard his work as "an emanation of himself, reflecting his contribution to the common life, the fulfillment of his social duty."[9]

Marx's Theory of History

Marx's "laws" on the dynamics of capitalist development towards inevitable doom were designed to coordinate with his theory of history known as *historical materialism.* This in itself was only part of the impressive Marxist philosophical system of *dialectical materialism,* which was designed to provide an explanation for all types of natural and social development. The range of subject matter included in dialectical materialism is best illustrated by the

[9]Che Guevara, *Socialism and Man* (New York: Merit Publishers, 1968), p. 13.

material in *Fundamentals of Marxism-Leninism,* the text used in Soviet universities for the required ideology course which all students must successfully complete to receive their degrees. With dogmatic certainty the "party line" is laid down on everything from the most abstract philosophical problems to the correct tactics and strategy of the struggle of the international working class movement.

The action framework for dialectical materialism was taken by Marx from the philosophical system of the great nineteenth-century German philosopher Hegel, whose devoted pupils both Marx and Engels had been. Hegel in his turn had revived an almost-forgotten Greek approach for developing ideas in the course of philosophical discussion known as the dialectical method. Its basic techniques are simple enough. Discussion begins with a basic proposition (*thesis*) in opposition to which it is possible to marshal a number of objections which constitute a counter proposition (*anti thesis*). Then, by a process of clash and conflict what is best and most enduring in each of the two propositions is combined in a *synthesis.* But since perfection is an ultimate goal which can never be achieved, the synthesis almost immediately becomes a new thesis which generates its own anti thesis and the whole process is infinitely repeated, but, and this was important to Marx's goals, always in an upward direction and always with the new synthesis representing an improvement over the previous level of clash and conflict.

Both the ancient Greek philosophers and Hegel applied the dialectical method only to the development of ideas. But to Marx, who considered material factors as the important ones in man's history, this was incorrect. Marx felt that his joining of the dialectical method with a materialistic basis paved the way for the first scientific interpretation of history. In his own famous words applying this dialectical analysis to human affiairs, "The history of all hitherto existing societies is the history of class struggles." With supreme self-confidence he divided all human history into four phases with a fifth and final stage as the inevitable end. The first four stages were the primitive communal, slave, feudal, and capitalist. The fifth would be the socialist/communist stage. Basic to Marx's analysis is the acceptance of technological development as the motive force for change and progress. Stalin, one of Marx's most famous twentieth-century disciples, explains that social change begins, "in the first place, with changes and development of the instruments of production."[10]

[10]J. V. Stalin, *Dialetical and Historical Materialism* (New York: International Publishers, 1940), p. 31. A number of students of Marxism reject this interpretation of technology as the major influence, but

In every society technology is organized in terms of a particular type of property relations, i.e., slave, feudal, or capitalist. Stalin divides the material forces of production into three elements: workers, materials, and instruments of production (MFP). The way in which these are organized is determined by the social relations of production (SRP) "or—what is but a legal expression for the same thing—with the property relations within which they had been at work before,"[11] as Marx expressed it. The MPF conditions the SRP to yield the mode of production (MP), i.e., the type of economic system that results: slave, feudal, or capitalist. In a simple diagram it can be expressed like this, with *f* representing "conditions":

$$W + M + T^{N} \longrightarrow MFP^{N} \, f \, SRP \longrightarrow MP^{N}$$

The type of economic system (MP) a society has, Marx goes on, is the foundation for the society's superstructure, by which he means all of its "legal, political, religious, aesthetic or philosophical" characteristics. We can express the relationship between economic system and society in this fashion. MP $\longrightarrow$ S. Using the expressions we employed when we were talking about party systems, MP is always an independent ruling variable and S always a dependent controlled variable.

Basic to Marx's theory of historical materialism is his second law, "the reality of change":

> At a certain stage of their development the material forces of production in society come into conflict with the existing relations of production, or—what is but a legal expression for the same thing—with the property relations within which they had been at work before. From forms of development of the forces of production these relations turn into their fetters. Then comes the period of social revolution.[12]

The inevitable result of this period of social revolution is a more satisfactory readjustment of the relationship between the MFP^{N} and the SRP, which is completely reorganized in a different set of property relations designed to provide a more efficient framework for the functioning of the MFP. But once more the reality of change continues its inexorable development, and in due course MFP^{N} finds itself again frustrated by the existing SRP and there is repeated the period of social revolution. The Marxian view of how society has developed looks like this:

---

it seems to be implicit in Marx's own thought and quite explicit in Stalin's interpretation, which is still regarded as authoritative in communist circles.

[11] *Marx and Engels,* p. 44.

[12] "The Communist Manifesto," in *Marx and Engels,* p. 8.

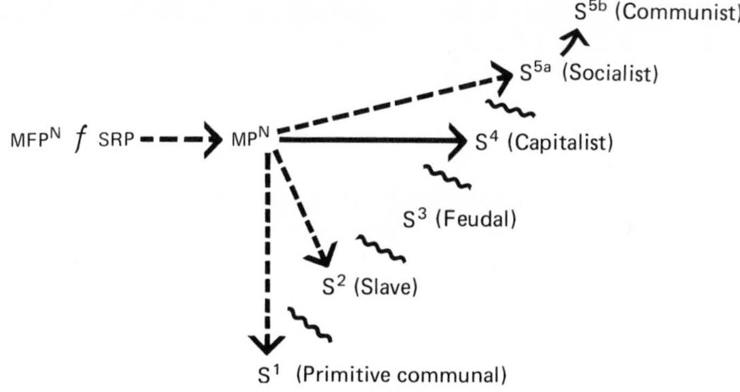

The jagged lines up to Society 5a represent the revolutionary breakthroughs necessary for the transition to a new type of society, which is to say, in Marxist terms, to a new type of property relationship. You will note that this jagged symbol is missing between societies 5a and 5b. This is because the last antagonistic class or property relationship occurs in Society 4, capitalist society, which has the distinctive features of having simplified class antagonisms. "Society as a whole is more and more splitting up into two great hostile camps, into two great classes directly facing each other: bourgeoisie and proletariat."

Therefore when the proletariat is finally driven to violent revolutionary overthrow of capitalism, for the first time since man's social development began there will be permanent harmonious adjustment between the MFP^N and the SRP, which will permit unprecedented expansion of productive facilities without any further antagonistic conflict or frustrations. As technology expands to its ultimate possibility for development, the most important changes in all of human history will take place both economically and politically.

Under socialism, Marx reasoned, although production will be for use not for profit, there will still be inequality of rewards. "From each according to his ability, to each according to his merits" was the slogan with which Marx summarized this phase. But as technology soars to undreamed of heights of productive abundance, almost unconsciously the human race will move from socialist society to the last and final pinnacle of human achievement—communist society, where the basis of economic distribution will be "from each according to his ability, to each according to his needs," and where in political terms, as Engels once expressed it, "the government of men will give way to the administration of things."

This phrase of Engels's summarizes one of the most important elements of Marxian theory, the concept of "the withering away of the state." The role of the state, or rather of government, for this is what Marx was really talking about, plays a very important role in Marxist theory. At the dawn of history, in the primitive communal phase, there was no government. This was because there were no classes, and above all there were no ruling elite and oppressed mass. Mankind, as yet uncorrupted by private property, shared everything in common. Indeed, given the low level of technological development, communal ownership and equal sharing of the fruits of cooperative labor was the key to survival. But the pressures of technological development forced the emergence of a more efficient organization of the three elements of workers, materials, and tools, which constitute the material forces of production. This led to the appearance of the slave system of production which, because it was economically more efficient, was therefore, in Marxist terms, a higher stage of historical development than the primitive communal.

The slave system was not only a progressive economic change; it was also responsible for the initiation of political society. From that distant time to the present, all government, said Marx, has but served as the political instrument of the economically dominant class to insure its continued rule. "The executive of the modern state is but a committee for managing the common affairs of the whole bourgeoisie."

Nor will this class nature of government change in the period just after the overthrow of capitalism. During this socialist period of economic development, political control will be exercised by the dictatorship of the proletariat, which will be just as much a class rule as the just-overthrown dictatorship. But there is one important difference. All previous government represented the rule of the minority economic elite over the mass. For the first time in history the dictatorship of the proletariat, Marx argued, would constitute the rule of the vast majority in society over the small minority of the former capitalist class and their followers. Diagrammatically the difference would look like this:

All Previous Class Dictatorships
(slave, feudal, capitalist)

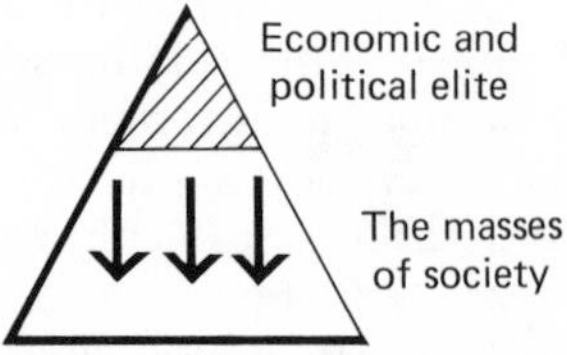

Dictatorship of the
Proletariat

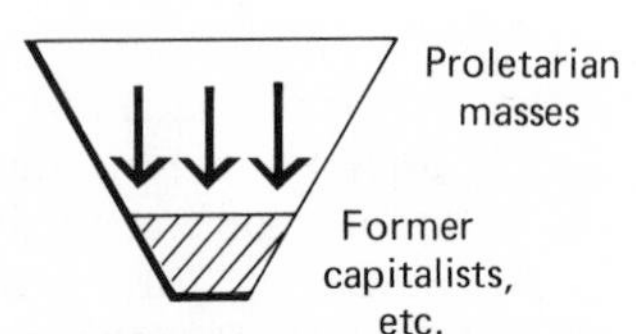

Therefore, ran the Marxist argument, the so-called dictatorship of the proletariat actually would be the most democratic governmental system, with the greatest number of individuals participating in it, ever known.

But even this greatly relaxed class dictatorship represented but a transitional stage to the complete disappearance of all government under communist society. This withering away of the state will occur because of the fundamental change which the experience of living under socialist and then communist society will bring about in human nature. Lenin, who developed Engels's writings on the role of government, summarized the how and why of the process:

> Only Communism makes the state absolutely unnecessary, for there is *nobody* to be suppressed—"nobody" in the sense of a *class,* in the sense of a systematic struggle against a definite section of the population. We are not utopians, and do not in the least deny the possibility and inevitability of excesses on the part of *individual* persons, or the need to suppress such *excesses.* But, in the first place, no special machine, no special apparatus of suppression is needed for this; this will be done by the armed people itself, as simply and as readily as any crowd of civilized people, even in modern society, interferes to put a stop to a scuffle or to prevent a woman from being assaulted. And, secondly, we know that the fundamental social cause of excesses, which consist in the violation of the rules of social intercourse, is the exploitation of the masses, their want and their poverty. With the removal of this chief cause, excesses will inevitably begin to "*wither* away." We do not know how quickly and in what succession, but we know that they will wither away. With their withering away, the state will also *wither away.*[13]

And in *Fundamentals of Marxism-Leninism,* a section called "Future Prospects of Communism" puts the case even more strongly:

> It is with the victory of communism that the real history of humanity in the loftiest meaning of this term begins. . . . The victory of communism enables people not only to produce in abundance everything necessary for their life, but also to free society from all manifestations of inhumanity; wars, ruthless struggle within society and injustice, ignorance, crime and vice. Violence and self-interest, hypocrisy and egoism, perfidy and vain-glory, will vanish for ever from the relations between people and between nations.
>
> This is how Communists conceive the triumph of the genuine, real humanism which will prevail in the future Communist society.[14]

Such statements make it easy to understand why Marxism has exerted an emotional appeal over so long a period. It is impossible to quarrel with the professed idealistic

[13]N. Lenin, *Selected Works* (Moscow: Foreign Languages Publishing House, 1952), vol. 2, pp. 293–294.

[14]*Fundamentals of Marxism-Leninism* (Moscow: Foreign Languages Publishing House, 1963), p. 715.

goals. But they also help to explain why it has never been possible to destroy Marxism's appeal by logical argument anymore than it is possible to discredit the democratic ideal by "proving" that government by the people has been a largely unrealized dream throughout the human experience.

The fact remains that the basic goals of both Marxism and democracy are probably more meaningful now than when originally stated. Both assert the dignity and worth of man as a unique individual and his need to have a harmonious and integrated relationship with his environment. The misapplications in practice still do not change the appeal of the basic vision. Above all this is true in a technological society.

In the non-Western world, Marxism still has attraction as a formula for industrialization and the achievement of a modern society. In the industrialized West it is quite otherwise. Marx's continuingly potent appeal has little to do with economic theory or historical analysis. Rather, it is the message of what has been called "the young Marx," as a prophet of that feeling of alienation increasingly produced by the growing impersonality of a complex technetronic society. At the very beginning of modern industrialism, Marx put his finger on the frustrations and sense of depersonalization produced increasingly by a computer society in the late twentieth century.

In the *Economic and Philosophical Manuscripts of 1844,* Marx pointed out that the modern factory system has reduced the worker simply to an extension of the machine without any feeling of creativity or worthwhile personal involvement. He wrote:

> Till now we have been considering the estrangement, the alienation of the worker only in one of its aspects, i.e., the worker's *relationship to the products of his labour.* But the estrangement is manifested not only in the result but in the *act of production*—within the *producing activity* itself. How would the worker come to face the product of his activity as a stranger, were it not that in the very act of production he was estranging himself from himself? . . .
>
> What, then, constitutes the alienation of labour? . . . the fact that labour is *external* to the worker, i.e., it does not belong to his essential being: that in his work, therefore, he does not affirm himself but denies himself, does not feel content but unhappy, does not develop freely his physical and mental energy but mortifies his body and ruins his mind. The worker therefore only feels himself outside his work, and in his work feels outside himself. . . . His labour is therefore not voluntary but coerced; it is *forced labour.* It is therefore not the satisfaction of a need; it is merely a *means* to satisfy needs external to it. Its alien character emerges clearly in the fact that as soon as no physical or other compulsion exists, labour is shunned like the plague. . . . Lastly, the external character of labour for

the worker appears in the fact that it is not his own, but someone else's. . . . It belongs to another; it is the loss of his self.[15]

It is never possible to do justice to the fundamental message of any complex philosophy in a single sentence. But, perhaps we can try to express the continuing appeal of Marxism in the Western world by saying that Marxism seeks to make man and the best of his humanistic values the masters rather than the slaves of technological development. In essence, Marx said, quantity of production is meaningless unless paired with an improved social quality of living.

CRITICAL THOUGHTS ON HISTORICAL MATERIALISM

Any theory of history has the great advantage of past knowledge of chronological and social development. But even in this usually safe area, historical materialism makes some dubiously sweeping statements as to how history has developed when it dogmatically asserts:

> The conclusion that the history of mankind constitutes a succession of socio-economic formations is based on scientifically verified knowledge of the past. Mankind as a whole has passed through four formations—primitive-communal, slave, feudal, and capitalist—and is now living in the epoch of transition to the next formation, the communist formation, the first phase of which is called socialism.[16]

This statement has no basis in fact. Indeed, nowhere in its 700 pages does *Fundamentals* offer any proof for this "scientifically verified" knowledge of the past. It would be far more accurate, in fact, to say that mankind as a whole has *not* passed through four formations. First, there is no indication that the so-called primitive communal phase ever existed. Second, feudalism as a social and economic system developed in relatively few societies. Third, slavery and feudalism existed side by side in virtually all ancient societies. With equal justification the Roman Empire could be designated as a feudal society based in part on its concept of serfdom, and feudal Europe could be characterized as a slave society.

The importance of material factors, in Marx's words "the cold cash nexus," in our lives is something of which we are all painfully aware. But that it is always the dominant factor or that political power inevitably follows economic power is not true. This aspect of Marxist thought is akin to the nineteenth-century liberal concept of a highly rational

[15]Karl Marx, *Economic and Philosophical Manuscript of 1844* (Moscow: Foreign Languages Publishing House, 1961), pp. 72–73. (Italics in original.)

[16]*Fundamentals of Marxist-Leninism,* pp. 125–126.

"economic man" who always acts on the basis of cold logic after carefully weighing the financial potentialities of his actions. As the history of our own bloody century demonstrates, men base their actions on reasons that have nothing to do with economics, and frequently to their own disadvantage. Often in history, as in the Middle Ages, political power is based on military strength and economic influence plays a very minor role.

Another illustration of the way in which Marxism is a product of the mood of its times is its naive optimism about the perfectability of human nature. To nineteenth-century thinkers, the political freedoms which the French Revolution had promised and the exciting possibilities of technological development seemed to offer a possibility of horizons unlimited in man's social and material development. Along with this was a deeply cherished conviction that, freed from the social and economic injustices of the past, and aided by the civilizing influence of universal education, human nature itself could be radically remolded to make man into a thoroughly rational and highly civilized creature who would see the folly of "wars, ruthless struggle within society and injustice, ignorance, crime, and vice" and do away with them.

Again, one needs only to look at the grim record of our own century to see that none of the liberal expectations of a hundred years ago has been borne out. There has been little relationship between increased economic well-being and the moral development of man. Indeed one of the ironies of even Soviet society is that more than half a century after the Revolution, crime and vice, not to mention alcoholism, continue as social problems. Moreover one of the most serious threats to world peace lies in the active hostility between Russia and China, the two great communist powers of the world.

Criticism of the Dialectic

Let us close our critique of Marxism with a final comment on the theoretical structure of the famous dialectical process which combines both an intellectual and an emotional appeal. Within the dialectical framework all the elements move with such precision and march so inevitably upward and onward that there is a strong impulse to accept it at face value. But dialectical development does not hold up under scrutiny.

In the first place its assumption that all important development takes place through clash and conflict is patently false. Obviously *some* development does do so. But equally obviously, both in nature and the affairs of men there is a steady and relatively harmonious evolutionary process at work also. Here is a good example of how

Marxism, and many other grand designs, seize on one single factor to the neglect of other equally important ones.

A major problem for Marxism in this connection has been how to keep its theory of economic causation intact and yet defend it against the charge of oversimplification. Near the end of his life, Engels tried to explain it to a troubled inquirer in this fashion:

> According to the materialist conception of history, the *ultimately* determining element in history is the production and reproduction of real life. . . . Hence if somebody twists this into saying that the economic element is the *only* determining one, he transforms that proposition into a meaningless, abstract, senseless phrase.[17]

But Marx, in the classic statement of historical materialism, said that "the mode of production in material life *determines* the general character of the social, political, and spiritual processes of life."[18] The question is, does it determine now, or does it determine "ultimately"? And how ultimate is "ultimately"? This calls for an act of faith, for there is no scientific proof of anything.

The same criticism can be made of the attractive optimism of the dialectic. Neither in practice nor in theory do clash and conflict always result in either a more advanced social development or an improved understanding of the problem at issue. Unfortunately, more often than not clash and conflict lead to decline or disintegration, and intellectual discussion to stalemate or compromise.

The last criticism we will make of the dialectic is that it can be used to prove or disprove almost anything. It can be stopped or started at any point, depending on which factor is designated as thesis or antithesis or synthesis. Here again, while highly convenient, this is not within the realm of scientific method.

How History Falsified Marx

As a theoretical system Marxism found itself facing increasing difficulties in the last third of the nineteenth century. The ancient Greeks would probably have seen it as a colossal joke by the gods. For consider the sequence of events. In 1867, after long and agonizing years of research, Marx finally published the first of the four volumes of his masterwork, *Das Kapital*. In it he employed the dialectical method to "prove" that the following developments were inevitably on the urgent agenda of history:

1. More frequent and more intense economic crises which were bound to tear the capitalist system apart
2. A constant increase in the ranks of the unemployed

[17]*Marx and Engels*, pp. 397–398.
[18]*Ibid.*, "Preface to the Critique of Political Economy," p. 43.

("the industrial reserve army") and a steady worsening in the social and economic life of the proletariat ("law of increasing misery")

3. The disappearance of the middle class (bourgeoisie) as more and more of its members were pushed down into the ranks of the revolutionary proletariat and the number of capitalists became fewer and fewer with each economic crisis ("one capitalist kills many")
4. An increasing resort to naked force and political oppression on the part of the remaining capitalists in a desperate effort to keep their economic and political power

Almost from the very time that *Das Kapital* appeared, all of these predictions began to go wrong. To be sure there continued to be periods of economic prosperity and depression but, remarkably, each period of depression was followed by a long-lasting period when prosperity and general well-being reached unprecedented heights. Nor did any industrial reserve army of the unemployed become a permanent aspect of the social scene. Although there were periods of widespread unemployment, there were also times when labor was at a premium. Furthermore, the economic lot of the proletariat, which for that matter was becoming less and less proletarian and more and more bourgeois, improved steadily. As one authoritative source describes it:

> Between 1873 and 1895 thhere was a steady fall of prices, estimated at 45 per cent, while average money wages over all trades rose by 5 per cent, thus constituting a rise of real wages of 35 to 40 per cent. From 1896 onwards the price trend was reversed; but up to 1900 wages kept pace with it, and it was calculated in that year that they were 15 to 16 percent higher than in 1873, and that their purchasing power was 42 to 43 per cent higher. It followed therefore that the employed worker had only to avoid wage reductions to enjoy a steady rise in his standard of living.[19]

The same development has continued into the present with the added factor that today the increasingly managed economies of the modern industrial state seem to make the likelihood of catastrophic depression a rather remote possibility.

In much the same fashion as Engels's "ultimately determining" explanation of 1890, in 1963 *Fundamentals of Marxism-Leninism* still tried to make a case for Marx's law of increasing misery in this fashion: "Marx had in mind *not* a *continuous* process but a *tendency* of capitalism, which is realized *unevenly* in different countries and periods owing

[19]R. N. Carew-Hunt, *The Theory and Practice of Communism*, (Baltimore: Penguin Books, 1965), p. 150.

to *deviations* and *irregularities*, and which is *counteracted* by *other* forces." [Italics added.] Here is another excellent example of a nonexplanation. Possibly it is correct, but of that no proof is offered; and what the italicized terms really mean is never explained.

In political terms precisely the same period went even further to falsify the grim Marxian expectation of an increasingly oppressive and restrictive dictatorship of the bourgeoisie. Instead mass democracy became the dominant force in country after country of Western Europe at a rate and on a scale quite unexpected by even the most optimistic of liberal reformers. Between 1867 and 1900, in country after country either universal male suffrage was established or became an irresistible development. As one historian summarizes the developments of this period:

> Behind the whole checkered story, in spite of the many divergences and restrictions, there can be discerned a great tide of movement. Democracy was advancing everywhere in Europe, and by 1914 it was lapping the frontiers of Asia. The symbol was the right of the individual citizen to vote—a right increasingly buttressed from the 1880's onward by secrecy of the ballot.[20]

Economically, socially, politically, the forecasts of Marxian Marxism had compiled a dismal record of shortsightedness and error by the end of the century. It is not surprising that it occurred to more than one acute thinker that, however much a genius Marx may have been, he was a product of a particular time and a particular social environment and that substantial rethinking of his basic premises was not only desirable but necessary.

THE EMERGENCE OF REVISIONIST MARXISM

The result was the emergence in the early twentieth century of revisionist Marxism, which, since communism became a separate and distinct movement with the founding of the Third International in 1919, has developed into democratic socialism. The most influential source of socialist ideas in the English-speaking world, the famous Fabian Society, has little actually to do with Marxism. Founded in 1883 by a group of non-Marxist socialist intellectuals, the society was dedicated to the propagation of evolutionary socialism and the basic liberal goal of assuring the greatest happiness for the greatest number by state intervention. Indicating its policy of gradualism, the society took its name from a Roman general whose principal tactic was to exhaust the enemy by forcing them to chase him endlessly. After vainly attempting to infiltrate the Conservative

[20]David Thomson, *Europe Since Napoleon* (London: Longmans, Green, 1957), p. 325.

and Liberal parties, the Fabian Society was instrumental in the emergence of the British Labour party in 1906. It has since served as the brain trust of the Labour party.

But of more significance in the emergence of revisionist Marxism is socialism, which found spokesmen in both the French and German Socialist parties. Perhaps the most influential of these was Eduard Bernstein of the German Social Democrats who, in 1899, published *Evolutionary Socialism,* which became the intellectual foundation for the development of modern social democracy. Bernstein's basic proposition was summarized in his famous statement, "What is generally called the goal of socialism is nothing to me, the movement everything." It was not that Bernstein and those who shared his views were hostile to socialism's ideals, but rather that they saw their achievement as a matter of gradual development not a sudden apocalyptic explosion of revolutionary violence. Rather than dream of a remote and dubious future, Bernstein urged the socialists to concentrate on making life more enjoyable and improving living conditions here and now. The conclusions which led Bernstein to this viewpoint were never better summarized than in a few brief phrases found scribbled on an envelope among his private papers after his death. He wrote. "Peasants do not sink; middle class does not disappear; crises do not grow ever larger; misery and serfdom do not increase. There *is* increase in insecurity, dependence, social distance, social character of production, functional superfluity of property owners."[21]

In short, Bernstein largely passed over the economics of Marxism and emphasized its psychological and philosophical appeals, thus unconsciously anticipating Marxism's appeal to many today. As he noted of his own pragmatic approach, "Marxism is an insight, not a recipe." This, in essence, has been the approach of the socialist and social democratic parties of the twentieth century.

LENIN AND THE CREATION OF MODERN COMMUNISM

Without Nicolai Lenin, who almost single-handedly created modern communism, Marxism in our time would have a very different status both as a philosophical system and as a political creed. Many students of political philosophy are fascinated by the intricacies of the Marxist dialectic, but as a political force only tags and tatters of Marx's original propositions are found today in the platforms of the various labor and social democratic parties of the world. Today's socialist parties are short on theory and long on social and economic benefits within the existing frame-

[21]Peter Gay, *The Dilemma of Democratic Socialism* (New York: Collier Books, 1962), p. 250.

work of the capitalist system. In this there is much of Bernstein and little of Marx.

The system's present and continued existence is taken for granted. In large part, of course, this is because the capitalist system today is very different from the one Marx knew. Ironically, it is one of Marx's most enduring legacies that his scathing criticisms of the many obvious wrongs of early industrialism inspired precisely those reforms which have led to the participatory capitalism of the late twentieth century.

The early nineteenth-century capitalist system of economic prosperity and depression; wealth and poverty; callous, profit-mad businessmen and the unorganized and economically powerless proletariat has slowly evolved into the welfare-state capitalism of the late twentieth century. Callous profit-mad businessmen there still are, but significantly the biggest corporations have found that participatory capitalism in terms of profit-sharing, pension plans, and other fringe benefits have a tendency to raise both worker morale and capitalist profits. There are still oppressed workers also, but their causes are usually well and widely publicized. Nor is there much resemblance between the dispirited and poverty-stricken proletariat of the early industrial revolution and the highly organized and economically affluent trade unions of the twentieth century, who conduct their national activities from their self-owned, imposing, modernistic office buildings.

As parties, the socialists and social democrats have long been an important but routine part of the scene, particularly in Western Europe. Their role is that of one of several parties in fragmented party systems dedicated to social and economic reform. In this respect they differ so little from other such parties which owe their orientation to religious rather than ideological inspiration that in West Germany, for example, from 1966 until the election of 1969 the Social Democrats found little difficulty in cooperating in a coalition government with the largely Catholic-based Christian Democrats.

This social democratic approach is quite alien to the world view of communism or, to give it its official name, Marxism-Leninism. For what Lenin did was to take nineteenth-century Marxism and remold it into twentieth-century communism in the pattern of his own personality and the unique Russian political heritage.

COMMUNISM'S RUSSIAN CULTURAL HERITAGE

Prior to 1900 Russia was involved in European affairs, but always as a strange and rather odd outsider, never as a member of the family sharing the same cultural heritage and historical experiences. And indeed the accidents of history and geography had given Russia a very different experience. Early in the Middle Ages it had taken its political structure from the Asian-type despotism of the long-enduring Eastern Roman Empire with its capital at Byzantium (now Istanbul). Then, during the period of Western Europe's Renaissance and Reformation, Russia suffered, alone among European peoples, under 240 years (1240-1480) of rule by Asian barbarians. It had never shaken off this very different political, cultural, and, for that matter, religious heritage.

At the end of the nineteenth century when democracy and constitutionalism were long-established among Western countries and spreading widely elsewhere, Russia still had no constitution, no parliament, no elections, no political parties, and above all, no Western-type guarantees of constitutional liberties. Its population was still at least 85 percent semiliterate peasants who, until 1861, had been bought and sold like horses and cattle when agricultural estates changed hands. For almost a century the Czars, the autocrats of all the Russias, had viewed any attempts at reform as tantamount to revolution and dealt with reformers as dangerous individuals who should be either hanged, imprisoned, or subject to that unique Russian institution, exile to Siberia.

Not surprisingly what revolutionary activity Russia had had was composed of dedicated small groups of intellectuals desperately aware of their country's backwardness and groping for any answers that would offer a way out. With typical German condescension, Marx jeered at the Russian revolutionaries for always running after new ideas, and Engels once commented to a friend:

> If you have followed the Russian emigration literature of the last decade, you will yourself know how, for instance, passages from Marx's writings and correspondence have been interpreted in the most contradictory ways, exactly as if they had been texts from the classics or from the New Testament, by various sections of Russian emigrants.[22]

But for Lenin, even more than for the usual Russian revolutionary, Marx's writings represented nothing less than a divine revelation. As a true believer, Lenin regarded the revisionist movement with the same instinctive hostility which a fundamentalist Christian feels towards any efforts to demythologize the "old-time religion." To Lenin it was inconceivable that Marx and Engels could have been wrong in their analysis of the inevitable fate of capitalism. If all the evidence that Bernstein and other revisionists took at face value seemed to contradict this faith, then the evidence

[22] "Letter to Hourwich, May 27, 1893," in *Marx and Engels*, p. 442.

was wrong or had not been correctly analyzed. Lenin set himself the task of proving Marx right. The result was the publication in 1916 of *Imperialism: the Highest Stage of Capitalism,* one of the most influential books of the twentieth century.[23]

It is true, Lenin admitted, that in Western Europe the patterns of social and economic development seemingly contradicted Marx's predictions. At least for a section of the working class there were improved living conditions, and, even though at best it was a fraud, the bourgeoisie did give lip service to democratic principles, and the working man now had the doubtful privilege of voting in elections. But none of this, Lenin asserted, contradicted Marx; indeed it only made more inevitable the ultimate day of reckoning for capitalism and the fulfillment of Marx's prophecies. To understand what really was happening, he said, it was necessary to survey world political and economic developments in the last third of the nineteenth century.

"The characteristic feature of the period under review," wrote Lenin, "is the final partitioning of the globe . . . in the sense that the colonial policy of the capitalist countries has *completed* the seizure of the unoccupied territory on our planet. For the first time the world is completely divided up, so that in the future only redivision is possible." Lenin explained how and why this had come about as follows: The sole source of profit (Marx's "surplus value") comes from the percentage of capital which is paid out for wages. Therefore, as industry becomes increasingly mechanized, the rate of profit must inevitably fall. If capitalism had been forced to work out its destiny solely in terms of Western Europe, Marx's expectations of its early collapse would have been borne out, for by the last third of the nineteenth century the greatest part of capital investment was being used to buy and maintain machinery rather than to pay workers. If this process had continued, the fall in the profit rate would have been unavoidable.

At the same time Marx's prophecy about "one capitalist kills many" had been proven correct. Not only was there an increasing monopoly of ownership but also, Lenin noted, there had taken place the merger of bank and industrial capital into a new category to which an earlier Marxist economist had given the name *finance capital.*

Thwarted by the falling European profit rate, the finance capitalist began to export capital instead of goods in search of areas where the cheapness of labor and the low level of technological development made investment still profitable. From these areas they were able to draw superprofits as

[23]There are many editions of this communist classic. Perhaps one of the most easily available is the 139-page paperback edition published by International Publishers, New York, 1939. All quotations are from this edition.

the result of even more brutal exploitation than had been the case in Europe earlier in the century. To protect their investments and their superprofits, the European capitalists used the superior military power of their governments to conquer those underdeveloped areas of Asia and Africa where their capital was invested. As proof of how this took place, Lenin pointed to the fact that in 1876 only 11 percent of African territory was under European rule, while by 1900 this had increased to over 90 percent. The seeming prosperity of Western Europe, as well as the improved living conditions of its workers, was based directly on this merciless exploitation of brown-, black-, and yellow-skinned peoples as a result of superior military might.

Capitalism, Lenin maintained, could not keep itself going forever on this basis, because by launching on a policy of imperialism it had merely expanded all its contradictions and conflicts on a global scale and, as Marx had foreseen, they would continue to work themselves out no less inevitably. Not only did all the old problems remain, but several important and highly destructive new ones had been added. For one thing, to the old conflict of bourgeois and proletarian classes there had now been added an international conflict between bouregois and proletarian nations, between the imperial masters and their colonial slaves. Also, as capitalism developed economically in the colonial areas, new proletariats were created as new allies for the workers of Europe.

Imperialism, Lenin was convinced, was the highest and last stage of capitalism, and one final cataclysmic development guaranteed that this was so: the result produced by the "law of uneven economic and political development." This law can be summarized as follows: In contrast to the even economic development which characterizes the early period of capitalism, during the imperialist era there is great unevenness. This occurs because some countries that once were ahead become tired and let down or are so strongly tied to the investment they have in obsolete industrial plants that they cannot afford to take advantage of the newest technological developments. In contrast, late starters in the race for industrial development can take advantage of the newest scientific inventions and thus construct more effective and modern industrial complexes, giving them a competitive advantage in the world market. In the same way, Lenin argued, uneven *political* development would take place in the era of imperialism, although no general prediction could be made as to which country or group of countries was most ripe for revolution.

Another result of this uneven development was that it prepared the way for the weakest link in the global chain of world capitalism to snap under revolutionary pressures. Inevitably, Lenin argued, the imperialist countries would wage a constant round of world wars to redivide the colonial empires, for it is only from the superprofits of the exploited peoples that capitalism is able to survive and enjoy its hectic prosperity. Therefore as the new additions to the ranks of the great capitalist powers reached maturity, they would be forced to try to take away the empires of the old capitalist nations in order to guarantee their own survival. Under these conditions, constant wars between the capitalist countries would be inevitable, and each war would not only weaken the countries involved but offer new opportunities for revolution to their dissatisfied peoples. Thus Lenin swept on to the climactic conclusion that Marx and Engels had been absolutely right, the doom of capitalism was never more inevitable than at the time when its strength and success seemed so obvious. We live, he concluded, in the epoch of imperialism, which "is the eve of the socialist revolution."

It is not hard to see why the theory of imperialism has had such long-lasting and widespread influence. It quickly became the mainstay of the communist movement with its reassuring message that Marx had been right in every detail and that victory had never been more certain. The final minutes of the final hour of capitalism's existence were ticking off to their inescapable doom.

The fact that this final collapse has not yet happened seems to trouble communist theorists very little. The era of imperialism still exists, they say, but since World War II it has entered a new and final stage known as the period of state monopoly capitalism, which is supposed to produce a further merger of financial and political power in terms of a fusion between private business and government. The fact that many of the most prosperous nations in the world today have either lost their colonies, as in the case of Japan and Great Britain, or have never had any, as in the case of Sweden and West Germany, is explained away by the ingenious theory of neo-imperialism, which asserts that through financial and economic rather than political control the same old game of exploitation is continued.[24]

Like all the rest of Marxist theory the theory of imperialism is a mixture of facts carefully selected to prove theoretical propositions, illogical conclusions, and faulty predictions. Although it is true that a great period of Western empire building did take place in the last third of the nineteenth century, it took place for a variety of reasons, not purely for economic advantage. More often than not the reasons were very uneconomic indeed. Bismarck, the German chancellor, for instance, discouraged Germany but encouraged France to build an African empire after

[24]A good statement of this proposition is the book by the former Ghanaian dictator, Kwame Nkrumah, *Neo-Colonialism, the Last Stage of Imperialism* (New York: International Publishers, 1966).

France's humiliating defeat by Germany in the Franco-Prussian war in order to take the minds of the French people off possible revenge. Frequently, as in the case of the French conquest of Algeria in the 1830s or Mussolini's war on Ethiopia a century later, governments have launched programs of imperialism to distract their people from their domestic troubles. Finally, it is worth noting that at the peak of its imperial power shortly before World War I, Great Britain had 83 percent of its foreign investments outside the colonial areas of the British empire.[25] And in the 1970s the proportion of American investment in the highly developed areas of the world, such as Canada or Western Europe, outweighs many times over the amounts invested in the so-called neo-colonial underdeveloped areas[26]

The fact remains, however, that the theory of imperialism, regardless of its truth or falsity, relevance or irrelevance, has been the theoretical backbone of modern communism and widely accepted throughout the non-Western world as a correct analysis of the state of affairs. In varying degrees, regardless of their feeling of friendliness or hostility towards Soviet Russia, most leaders of non-Western nations for almost two generations have thought and acted in terms of the theory of imperialism.

The reason is not hard to find. The theory has an appealing logic and a seeming straightforwardness that puts complicated events in simple black-and-white order. There is another reason why it has been so eagerly accepted in the Afro-Asian world. The colonial experience was an ugly and debasing one. Since the achievement of independence, Asian and African peoples have become painfully aware of their political immaturity and economic backwardness. It is reassuring to be told that no personal responsibility or guilt need be felt for this, but rather that it represents the evil influence of the colonial period of Western imperialist domination. As we shall discuss in the next chapter, the proposition that imperialism equals colonialism equals capitalism has become an important article of faith in the ideologies of the non-Western nations.

[25]For that matter, 75 percent of British foreign investments in 1910 were in the United States, Canada, Australia, and South Africa, none of which by any stretch of the imagination was either backward or colonial. And today, for both political and economic reasons, the major foreign investments of any country exporting capital are to be found in areas that are on the upswing, not in primitive and unsettled phases of development.

[26]In 1968, for example, 70 percent of the $64.7 billion of direct investments abroad were in such areas as Western Europe, Great Britain, Canada, Australia, and Japan. Only 30 percent ($18.6 billion) was invested in *all* of the low-income countries. S. M. Miller, Roy Bennett, Cyril Alapitt, "Does the U.S. Economy Require Imperialism?" *Social Policy*, September-October, 1970, as excerpted in *Current*, January, 1971, p. 46.

THE EMERGENCE OF CONTEMPORARY POLYCENTRIC COMMUNISM

It was never Lenin's intention or anticipation that revolution would occur only in Russia. He expected the Russian revolution to be the fuse that would ignite successful proletarian revolutions in all the advanced capitalist countries of Western Europe. Lenin thought of the Communist International as a single world revolutionary party run by an international directorship of the leading successful revolutionary parties.[27] But the failure of revolutionary uprisings everywhere but in Russia itself made the International from the start a Russian-controlled and financed organization.

By the time of the Fifth Party Congress in 1924, the International had become an official instrument of Soviet foreign policy. Added to this, from 1928 until his death in 1953 Stalin imposed his own absolute personal control on the communist parties of the world. There was little objection to this in the face of the awesome fact that only the Soviet party had been able to bring off a successful revolution. But aside from this prestige factor, there was also the practical reality that only the Soviet party was able to give financial aid to the financially desperate revolutionary movements of the 1920s and 1930s. Ideologically, for dedicated revolutionaries there was no question but that the survival of the Soviet state offered the one prospect for success elsewhere in the world.[28]

The *monolithic period* in world communism began to disintegrate following Stalin's death. To be sure, in 1948 Yugoslavia had started on its own independent path. But this was no free choice on the part of the Yugoslavs. Stalin, like a medieval pope excommunicating heretics, expelled the Yugoslav communists from the world movement for their failure to accept the servant role towards the Soviet Union that he believed was proper. But unlike the other communist parties of Eastern Europe, the Yugoslav party had not been put in power by the Red Army after its routing of the German occupation force in 1945. Instead the Yugoslavs took pride in the fact that they had carried on a grim and brave four-year struggle against the German occupiers and rewon their own independence before the Red

[27]But given Lenin's own highly dictatorial nature and the feelings of superiority over the Russians which the German communists felt, it seems likely that nationalism might well have split the world communist movement in the early twenties and that polycentric commuinsm could have emerged forty years earlier!

[28]For a scholarly discussion of the reasons for the development and disintegration of monolithic communism, see Pio Uliassi and Eric Willenz, "Origins and Limits of Communist Pluralism," in *The New Communisms*, ed. Dan N. Jacobs (New York: Harper & Row, 1969), pp. 74–102.

Army ever reached their country. Added to this confidence in their own abilities was a long tradition of proud patriotism and fierce nationalism tempered by centuries of struggle against the efforts of big powers to conquer their little country. In 1948, however, Yugoslavia's expulsion from the world communist movement seemed to offer further proof of the strength of monolithic communism. Actually it was the first swell of that tidal wave of nationalism which was to rend world communism asunder in the years ahead.

Increasingly since 1948 Yugoslavia has furnished a pattern for the development of a pragmatically oriented communist society concerned only with its own affairs and eager to try any economic measures which will increase industrial development. In line with this, Yugoslav factories are operated by councils of their workers on a strict profit-and-loss basis. Since the early 1950s the party has been known as the League of Communists and, although there is no question that it holds ultimate authority, independent candidates can compete against its members in elections. For a communist-ruled state, this represents a surprising degree of political independence. Freedom to criticize the administration and even Marxist principles is not severely circumscribed in Yugoslavia.

Khrushchev Revises Lenin

At the opposite extreme from Yugoslavia, of course, is communist China, the self-proclaimed defender of pure Leninism against revisionism and those right-wing deviationists who are "taking the capitalist road." According to the Chinese, their split with the Russians, which brought *bipolar* communism into existence, dates from 1956. However it first surfaced publicly in 1960 when the Chinese began to attack "Khrushchevism" as a betrayal of Lenin's teachings.

Many expert observers date the Sino-Soviet split from the late 1950s when, according to the Chinese, the Russians lacked the courage to use their achievements in thermonuclear development to further world revolution. Khrushchev's denunciation of Stalinism and his restatement of communist ideology at the Twentieth Party Congress in 1956 was, they assert, simply a pretext seized on by the Chinese as a justification for their long-standing resentment of Russian misleadership of the international communist movement, which, in the late 1920s, had so misguided the Chinese party that it was almost destroyed by an ill-timed and badly organized effort to seize power. The Chinese had felt it necessary to defer to Stalin, but for his successors Mao Tse-tung and other Chinese leaders felt only contempt. Moreover, the long-standing Chinese sense of cultural superiority to the rest of the world made it galling to them to accept a second-place role. Another factor in the break was that, like the Yugoslavs, the Chinese had finally made their own successful revolution in 1949 in their own particular fashion with very little guidance or material help from the Russians.

The fact remains that Khrushchev in 1956 had put forward a number of propositions calculated to shock devout true believers. Among these were (1) peaceful coexistence, (2) the noninevitability of war, (3) the possibility of the peaceful takeover of power, and three years later (4) the possibility that there were various paths to socialism. At the same time, in a long oration to a closed meeting of the party congress, Khrushchev blamed Stalin personally for the bloody purges and slave-labor camps of the 1930s, which, to quote a British historian, had turned Russia "into one vast madhouse." Khrushchev's portrayal of Stalin as a paranoid madman, the Chinese pointed out with some justification, was not calculated to improve the image of the world communist movement.

In the first of his revisionist propositions, Khrushchev disclaimed any desire on the part of the Soviet Union to "export revolution." Instead, he said, let the communist and the capitalist worlds compete on the basis of a peaceful coexistence, and let the world's peoples judge for themselves which system had the most to offer and choose accordingly. On the surface nothing could seem fairer than this. But as Khrushchev and many other communist spokesmen have pointed out, peaceful coexistence by no means implies a live-and-let-live policy and may the best man win. It takes for granted the use of any and all means to achieve victory, short of thermonuclear war. One commentator has compared the concept of peaceful coexistence to the role played by a boxer who keeps jabbing his opponent while carefully avoiding a final showdown, until he feels his opponent is sufficiently worn down to make the chances of victory almost certain.

Khrushchev's second proposal, the noninevitability of war, was a much more radical departure from Lenin's theory of imperialism. The balance of world power had so changed since Lenin's time, Khrushchev argued, that even though capitalism was deeper into its final imperialist phase than ever before, this still did not make world war inevitable. There now existed a number of socialist countries besides the Soviet Union, plus the new nations of Asia and Africa, all of whom formed a "mighty camp of peace" which would make even the most reckless capitalist think twice before launching war. Also, newly aroused masses in the capitalist countries were fully aware of the impossible horrors of modern thermonuclear war. Not only world opinion but revolution at home would threaten the capitalist rulers who would dare let war loose on the world.

Khrushchev's third point and the fourth point (made later, in 1959) were obvious efforts to appease the Yugoslavs and the new nations of Asia and Africa with their vaguely Marxist-oriented nationalisms. His purpose was to avoid Stalin's mistake of insisting that everything must follow the Russian blueprint and to lay a basis for common sympathy and collaboration. For much the same reasons that war was no longer inevitable, Khrushchev argued that revolutionary change no longer need be violent. Overwhelmed by the obvious, the capitalist countries might well decide to give up peacefully in the hope of getting better treatment after the revolution.

Khrushchev's revisions were greeted enthusiastically by Western European communist parties which, like their socialist predecessors of two generations earlier, now found it both convenient and comfortable to work within the existing social and political frameworks of their respective countries. In particular this was true for the Italian party with its huge membership, strong representation in the legislature, and important trade-union influence.[29] The Italian communist leaders seized on Khrushchev's propositions and developed them into a theory of the right of every party to independent nationalist development. To this theory the Italian party's secretary-general Palmiro Togliatti gave the name *polycentric communism*. By the end of the 1960s the move towards nationalist communism had gone so far that the Italian Communist party publically condemned the Soviet Union for invading Czechoslovakia in 1968 when that satellite tried to develop its own variety of reformist communism. In the 1960s all the communist parties became increasingly independent and nationalistic. They no longer regard themselves as primarily *communist* parties but rather Dutch or Swedish or British parties, each with its particular national problems.

Within the zone of communist-governed states, this trend towards nationalism has made inroads, even though the Czechoslovakian experience has demonstrated its dangers. Rumania, for example, until the mid-1960s was regarded as among the most docile of all the Soviet client states. In the Soviet blueprint for the economic organization of the communist states, Rumania was slated to remain indefinitely an abundant producer of agricultural products and crude oil for Soviet use, while all of its manufactured goods were to be supplied by the Soviet Union. In the mid-1960s, while remaining strict party-line communists as far as domestic policies were concerned, the Rumanian leaders rejected this role and turned to Western sources for aid in industrial development.

[29]With its membership consistently listed at over 1.5 million individuals, the Italian party for some years has been the largest of the world's nonruling communist parties.

The Nature of Maoism

The most flamboyant of all the interpretations of Marxism-Leninism in recent years has been the Chinese version, usually referred to as *Maoism* because of the way in which Mao Tse-tung has put his individual stamp on its doctrines. As early as 1946, Chinese communist spokesmen were claiming that Mao's interpretation and application of Lenin's doctrine represented a unique and creative adaptation of Leninism to Asian conditions.

In summarizing the major characteristics of Maoism, we can best begin by saying that Maoism is far more a guide to practice than an effort to create philosophical theory. After 1927, when the Chinese communists were almost crushed, survival, not abstract theorizing, was an immediate problem which had to be met. For more than 20 years (1927-1949) Mao's leadership was dedicated to the problems of maintaining and expanding the revolutionary movement. Because of China's backward economic development, the Chinese communists had to base themselves on a revolution of the peasants rather than, in proper Marxist fashion, the proletariat. Again, constant struggle, constant risk-taking, constant maneuvering was the key to success. Finally, the Chinese communists developed a whole new concept of guerrilla warfare as the key to victory. This was based on a brilliant mixture of political and military tactics calculated to wear down enemy resistance over a long period of time and to move in stages from hit-and-run actions in the remote countryside to bigger and bigger battles culminating in the revolutionary takeovers of the cities, rather than beginning in the cities as Marx had anticipated would be the case and as was the pattern of the Russian revolution in 1917.

Making a virtue of necessity, Maoism lays much emphasis on sheer manpower and, ironically for a Marxist-Leninist ideology, on such an intangible item as revolutionary spirit. In contrast to the sober public awareness which Soviet leaders have shown of the catastrophe of thermonuclear war, a typical Chinese statement in the early 1960s ran like this: "The facts in the past ten years have powerfully proved that man, and not materials, is the decisive factor in a war, that wars cannot destroy people, and that the awakened people will, through wars, win victory as well as progress. This is the universal truth of Marxism-Leninism."[30] And Mao himself has proclaimed that "the people and the people alone are the motive force in the making of world history."

The Chinese have consistently talked, although frequently not acted on, a much more revolutionary line than

[30]General Li Chi-min quoted in *Chinese Communist World Outlook* (Washington, D.C.: State Department Bureau of Intelligence and Research, 1962), p. 96.

have the Russians. It is interesting that they have attracted relatively little support. In 1968 it was estimated that the world communist movement numbered approximately 44 million members, with 21 million of them generally supporting the Soviet position and 17,160,000 the Chinese. The remaining numbers were divided among parties which were either neutral or independent. But a truer picture of the real division in the world communist movement comes when it is realized that Soviet support is divided among some 65 parties around the world, while 17 million of the 17,160,000 pro-Chinese supporters are, or were, in the Chinese party itself.

Technology has been another influential factor in the development of the split in the world communist movement, for Khrushchevism and even more Togliattiism represent efforts to adapt Marxism to fit the needs of highly developed and sophisticated technological societies. Characteristic of both of them is the lack of any special sense of urgency. Essentially, revolutionary success, on either an international or a national scale, is considered desirable but by no means essential. In the meantime, life is not at all bad and is gradually getting better. To put it in proper scholarly terms, we can say that both Khrushchevism and Togliattiism represent the emergence of middle-class communism. To put it more colloquially, both these developments represent the emergence of the communism of the full stomach, the paid vacation, the extensive social-security benefits, and, in the case of the Western European versions, the motorbike. The basic drives behind Maoism are quite different: the desperate urgency of the communism of the empty rice bowl, the exploding population, the unachieved goals of overdue industrialization, and a sense of the pressures of time. In China there is neither a basis for nor a feeling of complacency, but rather particularly in the case of Mao himself, an almost hysterical compulsion to achieve immediate success. Maoism has staked its success on such desperate experiments as the effort at instant industralization, the unsuccessful Great Leap Forward of the late 1950s, and the Great Proletarian Revolution of the mid-1960s in an effort to maintain an unflagging revolutionary drive operating at a fever pitch of dedication and demanding the ultimate physical and emotional commitment for an indefinite period. In this, as in other respects, it is its style and its manner of operation that constitute its outstanding characteristics.

CONCLUSION

As an organized political system, it is possible that Marxism-Leninism may have a limited future, or, like democracy, a future which will see its basic propositions greatly modified. But whatever the fate of Marxism-Leninism, it is safe to predict that Marxian Marxism will continue to have something to say. Above all it will continue to have something to say to those sensitive and perceptive seekers among the educated young everywhere who are disillusioned and disturbed by the developments of a sophisticated technetronic society.

Marx's humanism, his concern with the right of man to be a full and complete individual even in an industrial society, his indignation over the problems of alienation and depersonalization, all these will have more, rather than less, meaning in the late twentieth century. Applied with proper scepticism and an alert awareness of present realities, there could well be much benefit in recalling Bernstein's perceptive comment that "Marxism is an insight, not a recipe."

THE NATIONALISMS: OLD AND NEW

It seems normal and natural today to be living in a world of nation-states. The goal of the various peoples of the world is for each to have its own sovereign state, and this goal is rapidly being achieved. In 1946, 51 states founded the United Nations; in 1971 the flags of 131 sovereign nations fly in the United Nations plaza, and there are 15 more nonmember states in the world political community.

The emotional drive which has led to the creation of the greatest number of independent states in modern history is known as *nationalism*. Nationalism can be defined as a sense of supreme and prideful loyalty to the interests and goals of a particular nation-state. The expression of this feeling is patriotism, which can be defined as "devoted love, support, and defense of one's own country."

Just as the ancient Greek who did not belong to a particular city was a "natural outcast," today the man without a country is considered pitiable. The existence of nations and the feelings of nationalism seem so obvious that it is difficult for us to realize that it was not always so. For many centuries Western man was obsessed by the dream of loyalty to one supreme political or religious authority. But for modern man the more natural focus for his loyalty is his country.

The most important priority of the new nations which have emerged since World War II from the former colonial areas of Asia and Africa is to achieve precisely this same sort of loyalty from their diverse and frequenty hostile social and ethnic groups, for they know that if they are to endure, their old regional, tribal, and ethnic loyalties must be submerged in a new nationalism. For most of them the growth of nationalism is the key to continued existence.

This is one of the many paradoxes of nationalism. In the Western world after 1945 there was widespread revulsion against the whole concept of nationalism as being chiefly responsible for the tragedies of the two world wars. For some years this revulsion gave strong impetus to efforts to find new international and supranational focuses for men's loyalties. But simultaneously with this temporary ebbing of nationalism among the old nations of the West, for the new emerging nations the successful development of nationalism, became a credo for survival.

Western nationalism had evolved slowly over centuries, but the new nations and would-be nations had to weave equally as complex a set of factors in a fraction of the time needed for Western nationalism to grow and mature. This has constituted a challenge in nation-building calculated to test the abilities of the most talented and dedicated of leaders. Since the pattern for the development of the new nationalisms comes from Western sources, it seems appropriate that, before turning to our survey of the Asian-African variants, we first sketch how and why nationalism emerged in Western Europe.

EMERGENCE OF THE CREDO OF WESTERN NATIONALISM, 1600–1850

In a later chapter, we shall discuss how the growth of the dynastic state in the sixteenth century was made possible in large part by the important role played by the middle class, itself but newly arrived on the scene of history. But this is only one aspect of the contribution of this remarkable social group to the making of the modern age. If in the sixteenth century their technical skills made possible the development of the dynastic state, in the seventeenth and eighteenth centuries their religious and intellectual concerns, the concurrent breakdown of medieval universalism and the religious-political concepts of Puritanism, then the influence of the French Revolution and the industrial revolution gave birth to nationalism.

Breakdown of Medieval Universalism

From the time of the early Roman Empire until the sixteenth century, men thought first in terms of a universal political authority and then in terms of a universal religious authority. Largely unsuccessful efforts were made for hundreds of years after the collapse of Rome in the fifth century to re-establish the vanished political unity of Western Europe. Charlemagne, greatest of medieval rulers, tried to revive the old unity by founding a Holy Roman Empire that claimed to be the successor of the old Roman Empire. Although it lasted until 1804, except for brief periods early in its existence, Charlemagne's empire was never able to assert any universal authority. With considerably more success over a longer period of time the popes of Rome were able to assert their claim to be the supreme head of all Christendom.

By the sixteenth century both of these ecumenical concepts of authority had come to have little influence over men's minds. In part this was due to the breakdown of communications during the Middle Ages. Rome's far-flung political control was possible only because of the excellent road system which made it a matter of days at the most to transmit imperial edicts to the farthest corners of the empire. The medieval communications collapse made it impossible to exert effective political control except within a limited geographical area. The memory of the peace and prosperity of the old empire served for many centuries to keep alive the hope of re-establishing universal political authority, but by the sixteenth century it had become obvious that this would never be accomplished. In the church, a long series of scandals and mismanagement had undermined the authority of the popes to such an extent as to bring about the Protestant Reformation—the emergence of a number of religious groups outside the Roman Church, each with its own particular theology. Since none of these was more important to the development of modern nationalism than Puritanism, it is to a brief survey of the theological-political concepts of Puritanism that we now turn.

The Religious-Political Concepts of the Puritans

If any one social group can be regarded as the creators of modern nationalism, it is the English Puritans of the seventeenth century. Socially they represented the first wave of that remarkable English middle class which has transformed the history of not only its own country but the world. Its membership extended from upper social and economic levels as represented by its leader, Oliver Cromwell, down into the ranks of those tradesmen and artisans who comprised the American pilgrim community. But all sections of the Puritan movement held certain theological views which furnished the basis for some of the most fundamental concepts of modern nationalism and even of modern capitalism.

The Puritans revived certain concepts of the ancient Hebrews to justify their efforts to purify the state church. The most important of these were the belief in themselves as a *chosen people,* the existence of a *covenant* between the chosen people and God, and a *special mission* in world history to be carried out by the chosen people. Associated with these concepts was a belief in "liberty of conscience, and liberty of the subject—two as glorious things to be contended for, as any God hath given us," as Cromwell expressed it to Parliament in 1654 when, after the abolition of the monarchy, he had become Lord Protector of England.

From Christianity to Marxism, very few new concepts have had an important impact until their proponents had access to political power. Certainly this is true of the Puritans' theological beliefs, which became the political philosophy of the English state as a result of the victory of the Puritan armies over King Charles I in the civil war of the 1640s. For over a decade, from 1649 to 1660, the justification for authority in England was not divine right, as elsewhere in Europe, but rather the proposition that the English were a chosen people, operating under a special contract from God to accomplish his purpose on earth. As important as the Puritans' influence on English development was, their transformation of Hebraic tradition into political reality and their emphasis on those "truths" which the founders of the American nation were to call "self-evident" were their greatest contribution. But not until the French Revolution had done its work can modern Western nationalism really be said to have arrived.

Influence of the French Revolution

Once again it is necessary to pay tribute to that strange genius, Rousseau. For just as his unique interpretation of the social contract provided the emotional and moral basis for modern democracy, his concept of a body politic with a will and personality of its own made possible the emergence of modern patriotism. In contrast to the rights of the individual and the limited nature of the state which Locke had stressed, Rousseau's idea of political community emphasized the fullest possible involvement of the citizen.

In the French Revolution these ideas found their fulfillment, and the emergence of modern nationalism was signalized by the erection in towns and cities of patriotic altars bearing the inscription, "The citizen is born, lives, and dies for the fatherland." Most of the characteristics of modern nationalism emerged from the intellectual and social upheaval of the French Revolution. Important among these was the concept of the "nation in arms," replacing the traditional reliance on mercenary soldiers. Implicit in this new approach was that every man had an involvement and a stake in his own country and its welfare. Above all, the French revolutionary armies transformed the special-mission concept of English Puritanism into a *mission sacrée* ("sacred mission") to give other peoples of the world the glorious benefits, by conquest if need be, of French culture and French civilization. Such standard symbols of modern nationalism as a national flag, patriotic national holidays, and national anthems were initiated by the French revolutionaries.

The governments of the medieval and dynastic states

had cared little about the languages and local loyalties of their subjects as long as political allegiance remained firm. The French revolutionary regime was the first to demonstrate that such tolerance was unacceptable to the credo of modern nationalism. Not only in France itself but in its conquered territories, the French language and the acceptance of French culture became an official requirement. A universal elementary school system was organized, not merely to end ignorance and illiteracy but in large part to provide a means for the early socialization of youth and to teach patriotism and the virtues of things French. In France and later elsewhere, this emergence of a semieducated general public led to the rise of a national journalism appealing largely by its use of the new patriotic symbols.

The success of French arms not only smashed the old European state system but spread the new and revolutionary concepts of nationalism far and wide. Not surprisingly, however, it was not an appreciation of French nationalism which stirred the various peoples of Europe but rather a sudden fascinated awareness of their own unique nature and a desire to have it officially recognized by the rest of the world.

In part this increasingly widespread drive for national independence was responsible for the romantic revival of the early nineteenth century with its emphasis on searching out half-forgotten history, legends, and even folk music. As a result of the romantic revival, people, particularly those of Eastern Europe, rediscovered almost forgotten senses of national tradition, and intellectuals, often with much success, struggled to create modern written languages from archaic peasant dialects.

Long after the French Revolution officially ended, the nineteenth century continued to experience a mounting tidal wave of nationalism as people after people struggled to become masters of their own destinies. The low point of the nationalist struggle was probably the defeat of the revolutions of 1848; its peak was the creation for the first time in centuries of a unified Italy and a unified Germany in the second half of the century.

Technological Role of the Industrial Revolution

We have noted how the breakdown of the Roman communications system made it impossible for centuries to achieve any sort of political unity except within limited areas. Even in such a geographically isolated land area as the British Isles, Wales and Scotland were able to maintain their independence for hundreds of years, while Ireland struggled with some success to assert its own nationalism.

The greatest technological contribution of the Industrial Revolution to nationalism was the invention of the railroad and the high-speed printing press. The new railroad networks provided, for the first time in history, a speedy and efficient means for conveying both people and ideas from one end to the other of even such vast countries as the United States, Russia, and India. In India, ironically, one of the major contributions to the development of the Indian nationalist movement in the late nineteenth century was the extensive railroad-building program of the colonial administration, which allowed Indians from all over the subcontinent to meet and exchange ideas.

The printing press made possible the dissemination of ideas quickly at insignificant cost, and the telegraph, invented in 1837, made possible an unparalleled degree of contact and communication. Without these technological developments, it is unlikely that the United States, for example, could have grown to become a continental nation. American nationalism owes more than most to the technological developments of the industrial revolution.

CHARACTERISTICS OF WESTERN NATIONALISM

From this survey of the forces which formed Western nationalism we are now in a position to draw some conclusions about its raw materials, its evolutionary development, its variety of sources, and its political and cultural orientation.

Abundant Raw Materials for Nationalism

Once effective administration and improved communications had developed, the emergence of nationalism was a foregone conclusion. For many years in such areas as France and Spain, and even in Germany and Italy, there had been a growing sense of common destiny and shared historical experience. Membership in the same linguistic and cultural family provided a common basis for all Italians, not merely Florentines, to pay tribute to Dante and for all Germans, not only the subjects of a minor grand duchy, to appreciate Goethe. For centuries an abundance of raw materials for the development of the different nationalist faiths was stockpiling in historical, geographical, cultural, ethnic, and, frequently, religious terms.

The Long Evolutionary Development

We have said that the emergence of the various Western nationalisms was an almost inevitable result of the dynamic forces pushing for unity. Yet the fact remains that in two of the areas where these forces were strongest, it was not until relatively late, 1860 and 1871 respectively, that united

Italian and German nations emerged on the world political scene. And recall the long time required for the emergence of a united American nationalism, which many take for granted as having appeared no later than July 4, 1776. Yet in 1861, several million of his fellow countrymen were one with General Robert E. Lee when he rejected command of the Union army with the statement, "I am a Virginian first and an American second." And the Dominion of Canada, more than a century after federation, is still plagued by the threat of possible secession by the French-speaking Catholic Province of Quebec. For that matter, in the country which produced the first of modern nationalisms, Great Britain, there is a Scottish nationalist movement strong enough to have elected a Member of Parliament in the late 1960s, and more than eight centuries after the English conquest, a Welsh nationalist movement is also aiming at autonomy.

These examples are cited to emphasize the important point that, while in its initial phases of development nationalism functions as a powerful *integrating* force, it seems to have a tendency to evolve later into an equally dynamic *disintegrative* force. It is a catalyst which cannot be stopped in mid-course. Two countries as far removed in geography, cultural background, and dates of independence as the United States and Nigeria have both been made painfully aware of that fact through bloody civil wars. This disintegrative tendency of nationalism has, not surprisingly, been particularly noticeable in those countries where one among a number of minority groups has taken the lead in achieving independence from alien rule. For example, even in the late twentieth century, Belgium continues to be torn by the conflict between the French-speaking Walloons who have largely dominated Belgian life since independence in 1830 and the once-passive and less advanced Dutch-speaking Flemish. And in Eastern Europe, both the Macedonians and the Ukranians, divided among several countries, have constituted submerged nationalisms for over a century. The problem of submerged would-be nationalisms is even more acute and dangerous for a number of the new nations of Asia and Africa.

Formed from Variety of Sources

With the possible exception of British nationalism, all others have drawn on a wide variety of international sources for their inspiration and growth. We have noted the predominant influence of British and French ideas; but if we were to discuss this topic in detail, it would be necessary to pay tribute also to Machiavelli's influence in the emergence of Italian nationalism and to Luther's in German development.

Here again, however, is one of the paradoxes of nationalism. It aims at particularism, at making a sharply defined distinction between a particular people and the rest of the world. Yet for its ideas it draws on a variety of international sources. Further, the very existence of any nationalism is possible only because there is an international "community of nations." At one and the same time any nationalism can be parochial only because it is inspired by cosmopolitan sources. A Marxist commentator, viewing this dialectically, would conclude that the next step has to be a higher fusion of these two elements, perhaps on a world scale.

Political and Cultural Orientation

Western nationalism was but little concerned with economic matters. Its predominant concerns and the articles of its credos were oriented toward political and cultural issues. The questions of what boundaries the new states should have, what peoples should be included within them, what language or languages should be official, what materials should be taught to instill patriotic loyalty—all these have been the types of problems with which the Western nationalist movements were concerned.

In part at least, this is typical of the outlook of the nineteenth century when nationalism had its birth and development in Western Europe. Economic affairs were quite outside the area of concern of the dominant liberal philosophy. The fiction prevailed that economic and political matters functioned in different spheres. The philosophy of laissez faire provided the guidelines, or the lack of them, for the manner in which economic affairs were carried on.

Typical of nineteenth-century politics is the slogan of the French Revolution, "liberty, equality, fraternity," with its, for modern minds, curious indifference to or unawareness of the obvious relationship between these objectives and economics. The same unawareness has characterized the programs of Western nationalist movements. This is not only one of the greatest differences between the programs of Western and non-Western nationalist movements, but is a significant indication of the differing frames of reference in which they have developed. It can almost be said that respectively they represent a pre- and a post-Marxist outlook on the world and the interrelationship of its problems.

CHARACTERISTICS OF NON-WESTERN NATIONALISM

For non-Western nationalism, colonialism fills the same role that the devil did for medieval Christianity. Yet without the colonial period, it is doubtful if most of the new nations of Asia and Africa would exist today. The most important result of the period of European world domination which began in the last half of the nineteenth century was the jarring and often forcible destruction of the old traditional societies and the laying of at least the foundations for the construction of a modern, legal-rational economic and political order.

For their own purposes, the Western colonial rulers frequently found it convenient to create a Western-educated middle class. The ranks of this Western-oriented group were increased by the sons and daughters of the old aristocracy who, as an aspect of their rank and privilege, were given Western educations by their families. The members of this new predominantly intellectual middle class were acutely aware of the economic and social backwardness of their homelands. To them, social and economic modernization represented the only possible path to salvation, but it was very clear that even the most benevolent of colonial rulers had no reason to carry out any such sweeping reform programs. Only an independent government, acting for the people of the former colony, would have the incentive to do so. Thus, prompted above all by the intensely felt need to modernize, the native nationalist movements were born.

Beginning in India in the 1880s with the organization of the Indian National Congress, non-Western nationalism has gone on to sweep the former colonial areas of Asia and Africa. In the late 1960s, it increasingly replaced the traditional Latin American regime with a modern type of nationalist movement regime, usually led by a revolutionary council composed of young, often foreign-educated army officers. Essentially, modern Latin American nationalism is in a different category, however, since it represents the regeneration of already long-established but degenerated nationalist movements.

Although the variety of non-Western nationalist movements almost defies generalization, we can try to point up the essential difference between Asian-African nationalism and Western nationalism under the same four points which we used to survey the latter's characteristics.

Few Raw Materials for Nationalism

In prospect the emergence of most of the non-Western nationalist movements seemed almost impossible, for the areas in question lacked unity or a common destiny. Even India, one of the oldest and most sophisticated of societies, had never known unity until the establishment of effective British power in the latter half of the nineteenth century. Nor, until Dutch rule in the same century created the Netherlands Indies, had the thousands of islands of the Indonesian archipelago ever been united under one rule. When Pakistan achieved independence in 1947 as the world's sixth most populous nation, young people born in 1930, the year that the Pakistani nationalist movement had its beginnings, were only finishing their secondary education.

The development of the various African nationalist movements is even more extraordinary than the development of those in Asia. In Asia, at least, the colonial rulers had taken over whole territories or areas which had cultural and political ties extending far back into history. The establishment of the colonial empires in Africa occurred under quite different circumstances. The Berlin Colonial Conference of 1884–1885 almost literally drew lines across the map of Africa to insure its equitable division among the great powers. There was little regard for the fact that this method frequently divided tribes among two or three different colonial rulers or equally arbitrarily put bitter enemies under the same administration. Even more diverse were the cultural levels and the social orientations of the various peoples thus so summarily united.

In the African colonies as in Asia, though much later, a Western-educated, intellectual group emerged. Depending on the colonial possession involved, its members learned English, French, or Portuguese as their language. Language and an awareness of Western political and social concepts were frequently all they had in common.

As a result, when it came to organizing a nationalist movement, there was neither a mass base nor any long-shared set of common social and cultural traditions to draw on. The sole link that united the disparate elements of the native intellectuals and such ties as they had with the masses was the purely negative one of eliminating colonial rule.

Non-Western Nationalism Invented, Not Evolved

It took a period of several centuries for Westerners to grow accustomed to think of themselves as Englishmen, Frenchmen, Italians, or Germans, but for the non-Westerner there was no such time span involved. Africa's largest nation, Nigeria, was first organized in 1914 as an administrative merging of various British possessions on the African west coast. Here, and in other colonial areas, virtually the only point of common agreement among regional and ethnic groups so accidentally joined together was their desire to end colonial rule. As the troubled history of too many of the new nations illustrates, independence began rather than completed the task of achieving a sense of national identification.

For many new nations one of the most difficult problems has been the lack of a common language, whereas in the development of Western nationalism a common language was frequently one of the strongest forces pushing for cultural unity. Ironically, frequently the only solution to the problem of finding a "national" language that would make communication possible, at least among the educated elite, has been to continue using the former colonial language in which Western education was received. Even India, more than twenty years after independence, has not found it possible to do away with English. The new African states continue to use English or French. One of Pakistan's constant problems has been the quite different languages (and alphabets) used by its western and eastern sections. Indonesia, which tore itself away from Dutch rule under conditions that made distasteful the continued use of the colonial language, through intensive effort has achieved the remarkable feat of literally inventing an Indonesian language from the old widespread commercial patois of *pasar Meleyu* ("market Malay").

But even more important than the problem of language has been the need to provide an outlook or an ideology that could offer a unifying credo for loyalty to the new and strange concept of being first a Nigerian or an Indonesian and only secondly a Hausa or a Yoruba or an Ibo or a Javanese or a Sudanese or a Madurese. Trained in the pragmatic British tradition, the Nigerian regime in the years after independence was gained in 1960 largely neglected this "ideological" aspect of nation-buildng, to its tragic loss in the civil war of the late 1960s. But one of the most interesting aspects of non-Western nationalism is the fact that other new regimes took this problem very seriously indeed and, to a considerable degree, were able to create a new nationalist credo to replace the old regional or tribal loyalties.

The Many Sources of Non-Western Nationalism

We have mentioned the variety of sources on which Western nationalisms have drawn for their credos. But these, of course, all shared in common Western inspirations and origins. In contrast, nothing is more striking than the cosmopolitan sources from which the credos of many of the non-Western nationalist movements are constructed. In their mingling of Asian, European, and American concepts and their often arbitrary mixtures of traditional philosophies and modern ideologies, they illustrate an uneasy fusion of cultural sources and inspirations. Perhaps the most extreme example of any is furnished by the official state philosophy of the Indonesian nationalist movement, stated in the last weeks of the Japanese occupation in June, 1945, by Sukarno, Indonesia's nationalist leader and first president. In a long speech to the preparatory independence commission, Sukarno outlined a five-point program, known as the *Pantjasila* from the ancient Sanskrit term for five principles. But this borrowing from the ancient Hindu cultural background of Indonesia was only the beginning of the wide range of Asian and Western sources on which Sukarno drew for his statement of an Indonesian nationalist credo. Dutch, French, German, Japanese, and Arabic quotations from the Koran were scattered throughout the rest of the speech. Both European philosophers and Sun Yat Sen, the leader of Chinese nationalism, were cited to support Sukarno's propositions. As an example of this widely ranging appeal to sources, Sukarno asked:

> What is our *Weltanschauung* upon which to build the state of Indonesia Merdeka? Is it national-socialism? Is it historical-materialism? Is it San Min Chu I, as enunciated by Dr. Sun Yat Sen?
>
> . . . we want to establish a state "all for all," neither for a single individual, nor for one group—whether it be a group of the aristocracy or a group of the wealthy—but "all for all."[1]

The five principles which he stated were:

> A. Nationalism
> Indonesia is our country. Indonesia as a whole, neither Java alone, nor Sumatra alone, nor Borneo alone, nor Celebes alone, nor Ambon alone, nor the Moluccas alone, but the whole archipelago ordained by God Almighty to be a single unity between two continents and two oceans—that is our country.
>
> B. Internationalism
> Internationalism cannot flourish if it is not rooted in the soil of nationalism. Nationalism cannot flourish if it does not grow in the flower garden of internationalism.
>
> C. Democracy
> That principle is the principle of . . . unanimity, the principle of . . . representation, the principle of . . . deliberation among representatives.

Sukarno's definition of democracy points up one of the most important differences between the philosophies of Western and non-Western nationalism. There was, he insisted an important difference between "liberal democracy," which he identified as a Western corruption unsuitable to the Indonesian spirit, and "guided democracy," which best expressed in modern terms the classic Indonesian approach to the solution of problems by talking them out until complete unanimity had been reached.

Some years after his 1945 *Pantjasila* speech, Sukarno summed up the case for guided democracy thus:

> The state is an instrument to implement the message of the people's suffering. . . . The government is also an instrument.

[1]An easily available source for the partial texts of this and other important statements on Asian nationalism can be found in Robert O. Tilman, ed., *Man, State and Society in Contemporary Southeast Asia,* "Part Three: Politics, Ideology, Identity, and Political Organization" (New York: Praeger, 1969). Unless otherwise indicated, the quotations from Sukarno are taken from pp. 270–276. *Weltanschauung* is the German term for *world view,* and *merdeka,* the Indonesian word for *free.*

. . . Parliament is also an instrument. The President is an instrument; all are instruments to realize what we refer to as Indonesian socialism. . . .

If you realize this, brothers, you will also understand guided democracy, understand that guided democracy is not liberal democracy which is, in fact, not an instrument for achieving a specific goal. Liberal democracy is merely a channel of various sentiments without having a specific collective goal. . . . On the other hand, guided democracy is a democracy which clearly, firmly, and specifically points in one direction, that is, in our case, toward the realization of the message of the people's suffering, or of socialism à la Indonesia or Indonesian socialism.

In differing terms, but with the same intent, other spokesmen for the beliefs of non-Western nationalisms have drawn this same sharp distinction between Western and non-Western interpretations of democracy. Particularly interesting is the association they make between Western democracy and capitalism as an unjust economic system and their own desires to build on traditional concepts of communal cooperation to achieve a political system compatible with the national heritage and to serve as an instrument for the achievement of social justice in vaguely socialist terms. We will discuss this latter point again in our survey of the content of non-Western nationalism. But for the present, let us continue with Sukarno's fourth point, social justice:

D. Social justice

The principle that there shall be no poverty in Indonesia Merdeka. . . . Do we want an independent Indonesia whose capitalists do their unscrupulous will, or where the entire people prosper, where every man has enough to eat, enough to wear, lives in comfort, feels cherished by his Motherland which gives him . . . the basic necessities? . . .

. . . if we are looking for democracy, it must not be Western democracy, but . . . that is politico-economic democracy which is capable of bringing in social prosperity.

If we truly understand, remember, and love the people of Indonesia, let us accept the principle of social justice, that is, not only political equality, but we must create equality in the economic field too . . . two principles: political justice and social justice.

Sukarno's coupling of the concepts of political and social justice is significant as an illustration of a post-Marxist frame of reference. A nineteenth-century nationalist leader would have spoken at length on political justice, but social politics was yet to be born.

E. Belief in God

Let us observe, let us practice religion, both Islam and Christianity, in a civilized way. What is that civilized way? It is with mutual respect for one another. . . .

My heart will rejoice if you agree that the state of Indonesia Merdeka shall be based upon belief in the One Supreme God.

Sukarno's five principles have on different occasions over the years been officially redesignated as the continuing philosophical framework for Indonesian political life.

Political and Social Orientation of Non-Western Nationalism

Few statements of non-Western nationalism have been as detailed and as comprehensive as the Indonesian *Pantjasila.* But in the 25 years since, other nationalist credos have regularly reiterated its various propositions, particularly the emphasis on social and economic justice as a necessary part of the objectives of the new nationalisms. Common to all is an emphasis on the creation of some type of socialist society.

Basic to this aim is the regularly proclaimed intention to create a planned and controlled better life for the masses, whether it be expressed in terms of Sukarno's "socialism à la Indonesia," Nehru's "democratic collectivism," Senghor of Senegal's "African socialism," Nasser's "democratic socialist democracy," or Castro's "antiimperialist and socialist revolution." As we commented earlier, the influence of both Lenin's theory of imperialism and the successful economic development of the Soviet Union from an underdeveloped peasant economy have stirred both the emotions and the hopes of the leaders of the non-Western world. But it is worth noting that, except for Castro, none of the leaders of non-Western nationalism have announced their conversion to Marxism-Leninism, although such leaders as Sékou Touré of Guinea, Nkrumah, the former savior of Ghana, and Sukarno of Indonesia regularly used its vocabulary. The outstanding, if somewhat confusing, example of the merging of communism and non-Western nationalism is personified by Ho Chi Minh (1890–1969), a founder of the Indo-Chinese Communist party in 1930 and the leader of the Vietnamese nationalist struggle since the early 1940s. Whether Ho was primarily a communist or a nationalist is immaterial. The important point is that, like Marshall Tito of Yugoslavia, he achieved a uniquely successful merger of these two dynamic forces.

Other Aspects of Non-Western Nationalism

Three other aspects of non-Western nationalism should be noted:

1. The importance of creating nationalist myths
2. The role of the charismatic leader and the "movement regime"
3. The necessity of an enemy.

IMPORTANCE OF NATIONALIST MYTHS

The *Pantjasila* is an excellent example of the wide variety of sources on which non-Western nationalism has usually drawn. But it is even more significant as a deliberate effort to create the necessary framework of belief, of social myth without which any attempt at creating a new type of social relationship inevitably ends in failure.

The importance of a social myth has never been stated better than in a book written almost a century ago by the French scholar Fustel de Coulanges describing the problems of founding an ancient Greek or Roman city. In words that fit the situation which the new nations face, he wrote:

> We should not lose sight of the excessive difficulty which, in primitive times, opposed the foundation of regular societies. The social tie was not easy to establish between those human beings who were so diverse, so free, so inconstant. To bring them under the rules of a community, to institute commandments and insure obedience, to cause passion to give way to reason, and individual right to public right, there certainly was something necessary, stronger than material force, more respectable than interest, surer than a philosophical theory, more unchangeable than a convention; something that should dwell equally in all hearts, and should be all powerful there.
>
> This power was a belief. Nothing has more power over the soul. A belief is the work of our mind but we are not on that account free to modify it at will. It is our own creation but we do not know it. It is human, and we believe it a god. It is the effect of our power, and is stronger than we are. It is in us; it does not quit us; it speaks to us at every moment. If it tells us to obey, we obey; if it traces duties for us, we submit.[2]

If for "belief" we read "myth," and if we realize that, as modern social psychology has demonstrated, it is not only "the work of our mind" but of the emotional need and desire to believe—to have a faith to inspire and guide us—then de Coulanges's words describe well the role of myth-making in nationalism. One of the major problems which non-Western nationalism has faced has been the need to relate modern twentieth-century nationalism and its concepts and institutions to long-cherished and inspiring myths and legends from the traditional past. With all their borrowing of Leninist phrases and organization, both Touré of Guinea and Nkrumah of Ghana claimed lineal descent for the new states from ancient and medieval empires which still had legendary appeal for the people.

But of all the leaders of non-Western nationalism, none demonstrated greater aptitude for skillfully combining the new and the foreign with the old and the traditional than did Sukarno during the years (1945–1965) in which he headed the new Indonesian state. Sukarno's concept of how

[2]Fustel de Coulanges, *The Ancient City* (Boston: 1874), p. 174.

the legislative branch was to be organized and to function is an excellent illustration of this. Its purpose was to achieve "democracy led by wise guidance in consultation by representatives." As explained to the Indonesian people, this would not be a strange and alien Western governmental form; it would be the Gotong-Royong Parliament.[3]

> Let there be no confused discussions, but direct all your discussions toward the realization of socialism. And, indeed, as is my hope and as also set forth in the draft procedural regulations of the Gotong-Royong Parliament, let there be, as much as possible, no debate which requires the taking of votes. You must know that since long ago, I have disliked the system of "one half of the members plus one is always correct." The vote system is based on the argument that the majority, that is, "one half of the members plus one," is always correct. No, let us stand on our own identity and on the one and only appropriate view for guided democracy—namely let us do without the passage of votes. I ask the leadership of the Gotong-Royong Parliament so that, as much as possible, there will be no taking of votes; that, as much as possible, decisions will be made by means of deliberation.

The installation of the Gotong-Royong Parliament in 1960 was only one of Sukarno's unsuccessful efforts to find new sources for fanning the dying flames of the nationalist movement. Just as Mao Tse-tung was to seek this in his Great Proletarian Cultural Revolution of the late 1960s by a return to the "Yenan way," so Sukarno sought to create a new mystique for a regenerated nationalism by a return to "the spirit of '45," as symbolized by the restoration of its institutional framework.[4]

This creation of myth as an indispensable part of any nationalist movement is not, of course, peculiar to non-Western nationalism. For Americans the events of the Revolutionary War, the drafting of the Constitution, the tales about the boyhoods of Washington and Lincoln, all are examples of this. For that matter, no matter how much else might seem strange to him, an ancient Greek would feel a sense of identification in terms of the familiar founder myth if he suddenly found himself in the "temples" of Lincoln or Jefferson in Washington! We have already

[3]*Gotong-royong* is a traditional Javanese phrase which describes the pattern of mutual self-help, of harmonious cooperation on which village life is based.

[4]The isolated mountain areas of Yenan in northeast China were the place of refuge for Chinese communism during the years of its bitterest struggle, also of the most intense dedication and highest idealism when material hardships were ignored and revolutionary zeal was all. Somewhat desperately Mao sought to recreate this atmosphere as revolutionary enthusiasm flagged in the 1960s. Just as the "Yenan way" was an inspiration for the Chinese revolution, the "spirit of '45" symbolized that period of dedicated and idealistic revolutionary struggle after the Indonesian declaration of independence in August, 1945.

spoken of how the French Revolution systematically created a whole new mythology to make possible the change from the royal dynastic state to the people's nationalist state.

But there is one important difference between the development of the mystique of Western and of non-Western nationalism: the time factor. To survive, the new states must be successful in instant myth-making. At one and the same time they must strive for a place in a technologically united world, with all of its disintegrating impact, and attempt to create within an originally artificially created area a sense of common destiny and purpose where none has ever existed before. Of great importance in accomplishing this have been the roles played by the charismatic leader and the movement regime.

THE CHARISMATIC LEADER AND THE MOVEMENT REGIME AS FACTORS IN NON-WESTERN NATIONALISM

In recent years there have been few more abused words in the vocabulary of social science than *charisma* and *charismatic*. At times it has seemed that any politician above the dull-normal level who won an election by more than a ten-vote majority was classified as a charismatic leader.

As in so many other instances, we are once again in Max Weber's debt for having borrowed the term from its original religious usage to describe a particular type of political authority. This charismatic authority, says Weber, "shall refer to a rule over men, whether predominately external or predominately internal, to which the governed submit because of their belief in the extraordinary quality of the specific *person.*" (In another instance pertinent to our consideration of charismatic leadership, Weber speaks of the allegiance it commands as resting on "a 'recognition' of the *personal mission* of the charismatic master. . . . It is a devotion born of *distress* and *enthusiasm.*"[5])

There have been a number of Western political figures who possessed this "extraordinary quality." But in the developing nations a disproportionately large number of charismatic leaders have characterized the emergence of the nationalist movements. The outstanding characteristic of these leaders is that they have developed and taken power at a time when both social and political authority systems either have collapsed or are in an advanced state of disintegration.

To use Weber's terminology, "the authority of the 'eternal yesterday,' " and the " 'traditional' domination exercised

[5]In H. H. Gerth and C. Wright Mills, trans. and eds., *From Max Weber: Essays in Sociology* (New York: Oxford University Press, 1946) see "The Social Psychology of the World Religions," p. 295 and "The Sociology of Charismatic Authority," p. 249.

by the patriarch and the patrimonial prince of yore" was either destroyed or seriously weakened in Asian and African societies during the colonial period. To be sure, where it was destroyed, the colonial regimes substituted an authority based on the modern concept of legal rationality. According to Weber, this type of authority exists "by virtue of the belief in the validity of legal statute and functional 'competence' based on rationally created *rules*."[6] In colonial regimes this authority was based on arbitrary power exerted from outside the societies involved, and it was usually accepted as a hated necessity. In most cases, the disappearance of the colonial regimes created an authority void. But politics, no less than nature, abhors a vacuum. Hence the emergence of the charismatic leader and the movement-regime party.

Such leaders of non-Western nationalist movements as Sun Yat-sen, Gandhi, Kemal Attaturk, Sukarno, Touré, Nkrumah, and Nasser provided a personal basis for loyalty and inspiration to action that, in the postcolonial period, was often the only factor that prevented a collapse into social chaos. Charismatic leadership has served both as the catalyst which made the nationalist movement possible in the first place and as the bridge which enabled new regimes to pass over the authority void to the solid ground of a viable new political system based on popular acceptance of a self-developed concept of legal rationality. As we said earlier, the solidarity variety of the movement-regime parties has played an important role in this process by providing organizational support for the policies of the charismatic leader. In contrast to order parties, it will be remembered, solidarity parties emphasize *mass* participation in their membership. Their prime purpose is to serve as the nervous system of the nationalist movement, transmitting the policies and concepts of the movement and its leader, if possible, to every man, woman, and child in the nation. Such evidence as we have on the interrelationship and relative importance of the charismatic leader and the movement-regime party would seem to indicate that they are necessary to each other's survival. Without the charismatic leader, the movement-regime party, whether of the solidarity or order variety, cannot initially emerge, let alone prosper. And without the party the leader is hard put to maintain his position. It is impossible to think of Lenin without the order party, which is so much the product of his own personal organizing genius. In contrast it was Hitler's good fortune and the world's ill fortune, that, without any organizing ability of his own, he was able to find the proper individuals to organize the National Socialist German Workers' party which served first as the instru-

[6]Gerth and Mills, *From Max Weber*, "Politics as a Vocation," p. 79.

ment to achieve power and then as the foundation for the Nazi regime. On the other hand, Sukarno, along with Hitler one of the century's great charismatic demagogues, himself indifferent to organization, was never able to find the lieutenants to operate his solidarity party.

In the development of a new nationalist credo, in the essential creation of the in-group feeling, the solidarity party plays an invaluable role in the manufacture of that instant myth mentioned earlier as essential to the creation of any new nation. Obviously this is particularly so when the party has not only a monopoly of the political scene but also of the communications media. The positive elements in the new nationalist myth are obvious enough. The glorification of the leader as representing all that is best and finest in the pantheon of traditional heroes and demigods (sometimes as a literal reincarnation), the emphasis on the brilliant fashion in which leader and party have combined the old glories of whatever may have been the golden age with a progressive and dynamic program for the speediest and most comprehensive modernization—these are some positive elements of the nationalist credo which the solidarity party tirelessly cultivates. But in themselves these elements are not enough. There has to be a feeling of necessity, even urgency, to give point to their acceptance and development, and there is no more powerful influence for internal unity and kindred feeling than the threat of an outside enemy. This has been an essential factor in the development of both the old and the new nationalisms, especially the latter.

THE NECESSITY OF AN ENEMY

The higher the internal tensions in any society and the weaker the social and political bonds that tie it together, the greater the need for a threatening outside enemy who equally menaces all elements of "our" group and therefore makes it necessary to submerge internal differences for common survival. It should not be forgotten that one of the most potent influences that drove the quarreling little "nations" of the original thirteen colonies to unite was the very real fear of foreign aggression. And before World War I, Germany's fear of Russian aggression and British encirclement was a potent force in promoting German nationalism to overcome the old separate regional allegiances.

Extreme examples of the discovery of an enemy are Mussolini's justification for his attack in the mid-1930s on backward Ethiopia as constituting a threat to the Italian colonies on its borders, and Hitler's discovery a few years later of the menace which Czechoslovakia constituted for the German people. Except in periods of stress and uniquely high tension when it is necessary to divert attention from internal problems, the outside enemy plays a muted role in the nationalism of long-established states, but the case is quite otherwise in the nationalist mythologies of the new nations, which must strive to achieve the maximum degree of internal cohesion in the shortest possible time.

India and Pakistan have found each other's existence indispensable in the development of their respective nationalisms. So obsessed was India with the threat of possible Pakistani "aggression" that it suffered needless humiliation in the brief 1959 border war with China because all of its best troops were concentrated on the borders of Pakistan. As he did with so many other aspects of nationalist demagogy, Sukarno made constant and brilliant use of the outside-enemy myth as a means of fostering unity among Indonesia's ill-adjusted and often hostile regions. Until 1962 when the Dutch finally ceded their last foothold in Indonesia, Sukarno used their presence to arouse fears in the Indonesian people of antigovernment plots or invasion from Dutch New Guinea. When this enemy disappeared, a neo-colonialist and neo-imperialist threat was discovered in the Malaysian Federation, which was created from former British colonial territories.

New nations not fortunate enough to have a ready-made and tangible enemy on their borders have used the threat, often quite honestly believed, of neo-colonialism, or neo-imperialism. In Latin America this has expressed itself in mounting hostility to the presence of American business operations and investments. The modernizing military juntas of Peru and Bolivia have confiscated American industrial properties, and other seem ready to follow suit. Given the direct relationship between internal political and social instability and the need for an outside enemy, it seems probable that this will long continue to be a characteristic of non-Western nationalism.

PROSPECTS FOR NATIONALISM IN THE LATE TWENTIETH CENTURY

At the beginning of the twentieth century, there were confident predictions that by the end of the century nationalism would be a subject of interest for historians, not for students of contemporary politics. As the century moves toward its end, however, nationalism has never had greater importance in the world. In the *Communist Manifesto* Marx unwittingly pinpointed the irony of the late twentieth century. Quite correctly he paid tribute to the way in which the modern industrial system with its technological developments has "given a cosmopolitan character to production and consumption in every country," and he went on to praise the bourgeoisie for having developed "intercourse in every direction, and universal interdependence of nations." Technologically the modern world has fulfilled Marx's expectations and, in Marshall McLuhan's phrase, has indeed become a global village.

But Marx believed that "national onesidedness and narrowmindedness become more and more impossible" as a result of this universal interdependence, and here he was wrong. Even though the "village's" farflung inhabitants can now communicate with one another in a matter of minutes, they show little disposition to pool property rights or even form effective neighborhood-improvement associations. Indeed the last third of the century will probably see an even further division among existing nations, unless long-standing nationalist minority problems can be solved. While these seem unlikely to disappear, it also seems unlikely that they will cause the disintegration of the political systems. In other words, the governments of Great Britain and the Soviet Union are not likely to face disintegration as a result of the activities of Scottish or Ukrainian nationalists, and the Macedonian nationalists have scant chance of bringing about the disintegration of Greece, Bulgaria, and Yugoslavia to fulfill the old dream of an independent greater Macedonia.

But in the new states of Asia and Africa the presently submerged minority nationalisms do have a considerable potential for disintegrating the independence-structured political systems. Unlike the European systems, the systems of the new states have the sanction neither of time nor of success to give them strength against strong attack. The desperate search for a satisfactory pattern of administration has not permitted much time for consideration of minority problems. Then too, the need to insist on community of interests has often led to a suppressing of minority unrest rather than allowing it political voice or, as in the case of the Soviet Union, skillfully diverting its energies into safely nonpolitical social and cultural forms of expression.

Burma serves as one of the best (or worst) examples in this connection. Aside from several different varieties of communist rebellion, ever since independence in 1948 the Burmese Union has fought almost continuously against rebellions on the part of the three or four largest of the 16 or so minority groups which constitute the 42 percent non-Burmese portion of the population. All of these mini-wars have dragged on for years. Surprisingly the central government has been able to contain them. But there seems to be evidence that Communist China and other outside sources have given them assistance and are likely to continue to do so. These minority rebellions represent potential time bombs not only for the future of Burma but also in regional and international terms.

Almost since its appearance as a nation in 1947, the disintegration of Pakistan has been constantly predicted. Separated by a thousand miles of India, West and East Pakistan share only a common allegiance to Islam; their languages, ethnic origins, and even their climates are different. East Pakistan is the heir to a far older nationalism than that of Pakistan itself. The old Indian state of Bengal, of which East Pakistan constitutes the eastern part, had already developed a strong sense of Bengali nationalism before the Indian National Congress became of any importance. India itself, with its fourteen constitutionally recognized languages and sharp regional differences, is a potentially explosive mixture of submerged nationalism. Should the corrosive dynamics of nationalism bring about the disintegration of either India or Pakistan, one does not need to be an expert in Asian affairs to appreciate the dangerous turmoil and anarchy that would result, perhaps on a global scale.

During its first quarter-century of independence, much of Indonesia's time and energy has had to be devoted simply to holding the country together. Here too there continues to be the potential for the disintegration of the world's fifth most populous nation located in one of the most delicate geopolitical areas on the globe.

As for the African continent, the Nigerian civil war is still so recent that the explosive potentials of the various ill-submerged tribal nationalisms are all too obvious.

The major problem with the new nationalisms of the late twentieth century is how to allow for their logical development without the creation of new nations reaching the level of the absurd. Increasingly in recent years, it has seemed that the point beyond which it was impossible to create another new nation had been reached. Yet, each time, regardless of economic viability or any logic of area or population, the last limit has been exceeded. In 1968, for example, when the island of Nauru in the Southwest Pacific with its eight square miles and 6,000 people became the world's 141st independent state, the ultimate in national self-determination seemed to have been reached. Yet, for some years now the colonialism committee of the U.N.'s General Assembly has submitted an annual resolution seemingly endorsing full independence for the tiny British possession of Pitcairn Island in the Southwest Pacific with its less than two square miles and 100 people! If this were to be acceptable, then so must the disintegration of Burma, India, Pakistan, Nigeria, and a number of other new multiminority states. Possibly the late twentieth century will see the emergence of several hundred unstable mini-states engaged in endless economic and armed conflict. There is also the terrifying prospect created by the increasing proliferation of atomic weapons in the hands of irresponsible and fanatical governments.

The probability, however, is that the forces of nationalism will create neither a nuclear holocaust nor the anarchic confusion of a world with hundreds of sovereign mini- and microstates. This hopeful assumption is based on several other probabilities and one absolute and unchangeable fact of man's existence in the late twentieth century. The first of these probabilities is that the United States and the Soviet Union for their own self-preservation will continue to widen their efforts to control the spread of nuclear weapons. The second probability is that the sheer pressures of economic and political viability will prevent a catastrophic splintering of existing polyglot nations. The third probability is that with every year of continued existence these new political systems will become more stable and more capable of achieving a meaningful integration into a new and viable nationalism of their various minority elements. It is possible, for example, that Nigeria may emerge psychologically and socially stronger than before as a result of its bitter civil war. With the development of its considerable economic potential, Nigerian nationalism may lead to a truly unified state and serve as a prototype for the development of the other new unified states.

Conjecture aside, the unchangeable fact of the late twentieth century is that technologically we live in a global village. Barring a cataclysmic clash of the two great communist nationalisms, long-range pressures should work toward lessening of the strident but economically and politically unrealistic claims of the new nationalisms. Such a development will take time. It would be highly unrealistic to expect total disappearance of nationalism in the foreseeable future. But it does not seem illogical to expect that after the first exciting experiences of being free and sovereign have given way to sober reality, the various nationalist minorities will form regional federations with common economic and political interests.

IDEOLOGIES AND OUTLOOKS

Ideology, like *charisma,* is among the most overused words in the vocabulary of the social sciences. Nationalism, communism, and democracy are often referred to as ideologies. Just as any political leader slightly above the average is dubbed charismatic, almost any statement of political belief is likely to be characterized as an ideology. But how does an ideology differ from an outlook or a belief system? Clearly, democracy, democratic socialism, and nationalism, with all their varieties of expression and interpretation, do not fit into the same category as, say, communism and fascism.

The political sociologist Edward Shils has made the following distinction between ideologies and outlooks:

> Ideology is one variant form of those comprehensive patterns of cognitive and moral beliefs about man, society and the universe in relation to man and society, which flourish in human societies. Outlooks and creeds, systems and movements of thought, and programs are among the other types of comprehensive patterns which are to be distinguished from ideology.[7]

The term *ideology* originated in the late nineteenth century to describe the study of ideas. In the twentieth century, it has come to describe "the body of doctrine, myth or symbol of a social movement . . . along with the devices for putting it into effect." On this basis, some commentators regard all modern political concepts and philosophies as representing different sorts of ideologies. For example, one well-known political scientist, Frederick M. Watkins, has published an excellent brief survey of modern political thought called *The Age of Ideology—Political Thought 1750 to the Present.* Watkins includes as ideologies liberalism, conservatism, nationalism, socialism, political catholicism, social democracy, communism, fascism, and national socialism. All ideologies, he says, have the following characteristics:

1. They have a "militantly revolutionary character."
2. "Democracy is the form of allegiance on which they all depend."
3. They "normally tend . . . to define their goals in unrealistically optimistic terms."
4. They think "in over-simplified terms of we and they, of friend and enemy."
5. They derive "much of their strength from the extreme optimism of their views regarding human progress."[8]

This typology, however, does not seem to serve as a model for the characteristics of all modern political thought. We can test this by setting up a checklist of these characteristics and seeing how representative examples of modern political thought fit into it. Since both liberalism and conservatism are variations of modern democracy, we use the term *democracy* as more inclusive. Along with democracy, we list democratic socialism, communism, and fascism, which, although we have not discussed it separately, fits into the

[7]Edward Shils, "Ideology," in *International Encyclopedia of the Social Sciences* (New York: Macmillan, 1968), 7:66.

[8]Frederick M. Watkins, *The Age of Ideology—Political Thought, 1750 to the Present* (Englewood Cliffs, N.J.: Prentice-Hall, 1964), pp. 3–8.

Table 12
Characteristics of Ideologies—I

Characteristic	Democ-racy	Social-ism	Commu-nism	Fascism
Militantly revolutionary	no	no	yes	yes
Alleges democratic justification	yes	yes	yes	yes
Overoptimistic Utopian goals	no	no	no/yes	yes
A we-or-they viewpoint	?	?	yes	yes
Strong belief in human perfectibility	no	no	yes	yes

same movement-regime pattern as communism. Our checklist is shown in Table 12.

Can these various political philosophies all be characterized as ideologies? Democracy in the age of the crusading armies of the French Revolution certainly was militantly revolutionary, and democratic socialism in the late nineteenth century, though never really militant, might be considered as approaching this state. But today neither democracy nor democratic socialism can be placed in this category. Nor can either be considered as having either Utopian goals or any belief in human perfectibility. Finally, the varied pluralism of expression and openness to new influences and forces excludes both democracy and socialism from the rigid we-or-they, good-guy–bad-guy outlook that characterizes the various interpretations of communism and fascism.

So whatever they are, democracy and democratic socialism cannot by Watkins's classification be regarded as ideologies. Let us consider the four philosophies once again against a longer checklist of the characteristics of an ideology. This time we come up with the results shown in Table 13.

Once again, it is clear that there is a distinction between democracy and socialism on the one hand and communism and fascism on the other. For one thing, neither democracy nor socialism claims to reveal any unchanging eternal truths: A constant process of readjustment and revision is basic to these outlooks. For another thing, both emphasize their internal differences and their receptivity to worthwhile borrowings from other idea systems. As to the question of in what degree and in what way any man is a democrat or a socialist, this is a matter of personal preference, for no one in these belief systems attempts to draw the line between true believers and heretics or to establish a basis for the proper or improper interpretation of doctrine. Finally, the movement-regime party, with its highly structured and disciplined organization, exists to guard a world view, whereas democratic or socialist political move-

Table 13
Characteristics of Ideologies—II

Characteristic	Democracy	Socialism	Communism	Fascism
Claims universality of doctrine	yes	yes	yes	no
Has explicit statement of doctrine	no	no	yes	yes
Possesses core values	yes	yes	yes	yes
Requires 100% acceptance by adherents	no	no	yes	yes
Requires 100% agreement on *what* is to be accepted	no	no	yes	yes
Finds organizational expression in highly structured and disciplined group	no	no	yes	yes
Claims possession of eternal truth—alleges no revisions ever made	no	no	yes	yes

SOURCE: Frederick M. Watkins, *The Age of Ideology—Political Thought, 1750 to the Present* (Englewood Cliffs, N.J.: Prentice-Hall, 1964), pp. 3–8.

ments are not restricted to any one particular type of organizational expression.

To qualify as an ideology by Watkins's terms, then, a political philosophy must meet a rigid set of standards. Since neither democracy nor democratic socialism does this, how shall we categorize them? For this purpose, we can borrow from Shils the term *outlook*. The dictionary describes an outlook as "the view or prospect from a place." In a view or prospect there is nothing limited or restricted, and this is indeed true of the characteristics of outlooks. The term can be used to describe any political philosophy with the following characteristics:

1. No authoritative body of doctrine
2. Pluralistic in expression
3. Highly pragmatic and open to constant change
4. Low consensus on definitions of terms
5. Relative lack of party-line pressures
6. Variety of organizational forms

Clearly, these characteristics very closely fit both democracy and democratic socialism and do not describe any types of communism or fascism. We can, perhaps, summarize the nature of an outlook by saying that it represents an orientation in a particular direction, but that all those sharing that orientation are free to define it in their own terms. There is no one correct and authoritative definition of either democracy or socialism. Both, throughout their existence, have reached out for new ideas and constantly readjusted their concepts to meet changing conditions. The adherents of both these outlooks would be disturbed rather than gratified if there were to be complete agreement on what was or was not orthodox or proper.

It may seem strange that no effort has been made to put nationalism into either the ideology or the outlook typology. The reason is that nationalism does not lend itself to such treatment. Each particular expression of nationalism has to be treated and analyzed separately. Some nationalisms in movement-regime parties come very close to being ideologies both in their organizational expression and in the explicitness of their party line. Into this category would probably fall most of the new nationalisms of Asia and Africa.

CONCLUSION

Other types of nationalisms have no particular organizational expression nor any tightly defined body of doctrine and therefore would fall into the category of outlooks. We can assume that most of the older nationalisms of the long-existing Western countries would fall into this category. But there is nothing permanent about these classifications even if we were to attempt the somewhat pointless task of trying to put all of the world's nationalist movements in one category or another. As contemporary Latin American developments indicate, a nationalism which has long been in the outlook category may well be seized on by a reforming or revolutionary movement and increasingly be remolded in the pattern of an ideology.

Nationalism's endless ability to fit into virtually any type of doctrinal expression or definition is one highly important reason for its remarkable energy and staying power. As a dynamic force it has been affected very little by whether it was liberal or conservative, reactionary or progressive, democratic or communist. As it has in the past, nationalism in the years to come, depending on its particular formulation, will fit itself well into the category of either an ideology or an outlook.

PART THREE
THE ORGANIZATION ELEMENTS OF POLITICS

SOCIETY, GOVERNMENT, AND THE STATE

So far we have used the terms *society* and *government* very little and the term *state* not at all. Yet traditionally the relationship of government and the state to society has been one of the main concerns of political science. Indeed in the late nineteenth and early twentieth centuries, political science as a discipline was often defined as "the study of the state and its role in society."

In contemporary political science this concern with the state has greatly diminished. In large part the reasons for this is the desire to emphasize the *action* elements in the study of politics. But also important has been the feeling that the state was simply part of the political system and by no means the most important part. Then, too, the highly abstract, at times almost metaphysical, approach taken by many writers on the state has not fitted in at all with an effort to place political science on a solid empirical basis.

But this neglect of the concept of the state has been of dubious benefit in the development of political science. For, as we have emphasized before and will repeat a number of times again, we live in a world of states—146 as of late 1971. Nor is it likely that this situation will change in the foreseeable future. The modern concept of the state is the framework for the organization of the international order. Rather than ignoring its existence or treating it as an unacceptable five-letter word, let us ask how society, government, and the state all fit together. Society and government have existed ever since man first appeared on the scene. Indeed, some anthropologists would argue that, in a sense, both are present among animal species, too. The state, in contrast, goes back only to around 4000 B.C., and its modern form, the nation-state, made its first appearance only about 400 years ago. But before we discuss any aspects of the state and its role in the technetronic age, let us survey this long-enduring relationship between society and government.

THE NATURE OF SOCIETY

"Man is a social animal," wrote the Dutch philosopher Spinoza over 300 years ago. Centuries before that, in his *Politics*, Aristotle had commented, "he who is unable to live in society, or who has no need because he is sufficient for himself, must be either a beast or a god. . . . A social instinct is implanted in all men by nature." How this instinct came about and exactly what constitutes a society have been topics for speculation and debate for many years. But that the basic unit of human association is society was accepted long before Aristotle wrote.

The Social Subsystem

There have been an almost endless number of attempts to define society. Let us use here the definition of society generally accepted by sociologists today. In large part this has been developed by Professor Talcott Parsons, one of the molders of contemporary sociological theory. A basic aspect of his definition is that a "society is a special kind of social system."[1] In turn, he regards the social system as "one of the primary subsystems of the human *action* system, the others being the behavioral organism, the personality of the individual, and the cultural system." Parsons prefers to use the term *action* rather than *behavior* because the important element is not events for their own sake but events in constantly evolving patterned interaction. The basic assumption in our examination of things political is that they involve a systematic pattern of continuing interactions, or, to borrow a phrase from contemporary sociologist Leon H. Mayhew, that "society is ultimately an organized process."

The social system is concerned with ordering the relationships between any continuing group of individuals in order to prevent them from collapsing into conflict and anarchy. The systematic structuring of human relationships is essential to the creation of social order. Without it man is reduced to the state of lonely isolation and fear of his fellowman. Parsons calls the social system "the *integrative* subsystem of action in general."

All too often, however, the social system simply fails to integrate and every so often there is collapse into conflict and anarchy. These undeniable facts have led to a criticism of Parsons for failing to account for both integration *and* conflict in society. As a German sociologist put it, "The problem of conflict is no less complex than that of integration of societies."[2] The same critic pointed out, "Stability

[1]Talcott Parsons, *Societies: Evolutionary and Comparative Perspectives* (Englewood Cliffs, N.J.: Prentice-Hall, 1966), p. 5.

[2]Ralf Dahrendorf, "Toward a Theory of Social Conflict," *Journal of Conflict Resolution* 2 (1958): 171, 174–175.

and change, integration and conflict, function and 'dysfunction,' consensus and constraint are, it would seem, two equally valid aspects of every imaginable society."

The fact that we can define society as "ultimately an organized process" in itself implies that conflict and breakdown can occur. No process ever works perfectly all the time. It is a process both because it has relatively persisting elements in it and also because it is subject to constant change which, at times, may be violent. With this caution in mind, we can go on to survey the other subsystems in Parsons's definition of society.

Other Subsystems

Each of the other three subsystems in the over-all system of action provides a portion of the environment within which the social system functions. The cultural system, for example, performs the task of *pattern maintenance* without which there would be nothing for the social system to integrate. This, of course, is an almost obvious function, since culture is commonly defined as being "the sum total of ways of living built up by a group of human beings and transmitted from one generation to another."

Major changes in cultural systems, as Parsons points out, occur only over a long period of time in terms of rather large groups of individuals. Political change, either violent or nonviolent, can occur in a matter of days or even hours. But changes in long-established ways of living take much longer even when there is organized political pressure to bring them about as rapidly as possible. Regardless of his desire for rapid revolutionary transformation, Karl Marx as an honest scholar found it necessary to admit that after "the period of social revolution," the culture of any society would be only "more or less rapidly transformed." And in the Soviet Union, decades after the revolution of 1917, a standard excuse for the persistence of a social problem such as alcoholism has been to explain it as demonstrating the malignant persistence of the culture patterns of the former capitalist society. Clearly the cultural subsystem of any society performs the function of providing the over-all action system with a strong and stable frame of reference within which it can operate.

As to the remaining subsystems, behavioral organism and the personality of the individual, we can note that they are importantly conditioned by the nature of the symbols through which their particular culture expresses itself. The function of the behavioral organism subsystem in the action system is that of *adaptation*. Here again, as in the case of the cultural subsystem, the adaptation process is not in terms of either a short time period or of individuals as such but rather in terms of the whole species, by which we mean a group of genetically related individuals able to perpetuate itself sexually. Over a very long time period, such a group develops biologically in response to changing environmental circumstances.

The personality, or learned behavior system, is in a different category, from either the behavioral or cultural subsystems. Although certain general features, such as language, are shared with all other individuals from the same background, there is wide possibility for individual variation. It is this which shapes the focus of the whole aspect of *goal attainment* in the over-all action system.

As a type of social system, any society is concerned with these functions. The major characteristic which distinguishes the societal type of system is that it has reached a level of self-sufficiency in relation to its environment which makes it possible for it to continue indefinitely as a going concern. This involves both the sophisticated development of the internal organization of the society and its ability to draw strength and energy from the various environments of the other three subsystems. It is these inputs which give the society the energy to function independently in implementing its norms of conduct for its members and pushing toward its collective goals. As long as a society can retain this ability to adapt to changing circumstances it will survive.

Important to Parsons's concept of society is "the *cybernetic* aspect of control by which systems high in information but low in energy regulate other systems higher in energy but lower in information."[3] As a homely illustration of how cybernetic control functions, Parsons cites the way in which the dial of a washing machine, itself possessing very little energy but much "information" about the washing sequence involved, can control and direct the very considerable expenditure of energy which the motor can put out after it has been told what to do.

In cybernetic terms, the cultural subsystem in any society functions as the washing-machine dial, for it programs the orientations toward all other aspects of the environment and the different elements of the overall action system. In the cybernetic ranking of the different elements of the action system, after the cultural subsystem come in order the social, personality, and organic systems.

The major function performed by the cultural subsystem is to *legitimize* the values, standards, and ways of doing things in a society. What is meant when we say that any value or procedure is legitimized is that the value or procedure is generally accepted as the only right and normal way to think about things or to act. Probably the most important role played by the rituals of legitimization is to

[3]Parsons, *Societies*, p. 9.

sanction the use of power in general, and force in particular, in any society. No government or state has ever been able to last very long without establishing itself on a firm basis of legitimacy. We will discuss this in some detail a little later.

This legitimizing role of the cultural subsystem serves as the major support for the societal community which Parsons defines as "the patterned normative order through which the life of a population is collectively organized." This social community constitutes the very "core of a society." The cultural subsystem provides the values, norms, and rules which sustain it. It also determines who are and who are not members of the society.

But no society has ever existed in which values, norms, and rules have been both universally and consistently respected and self-enforcing. Nor can the generally significant goals of any society be achieved without the mobilization of organized collective action. This is the task of political action. In all societies, government has always been present to perform these functions when needed. In sophisticated and large societies, the political entity called the state has monopolized this funtion. Present in all societies is some degree of political organization. There exists not only a sense of togetherness, of community, on the part of individuals but also the need for accepting some type of authority capable of instituting and maintaining with reasonable effectiveness a set of rules and regulations over the society.

Society Summarized

We can summarize the nature of society in a series of simple propositions:

1. A society is composed of a group of human beings who are participating in a self-sustaining system of action.
2. This action system is capable of lasting far longer than the life span of any of its current individual members, with new members recruited, in part, by sexual reproduction.
3. The total action system of a society is composed of four subsystems: the cultural, the social, the personality, and the behavioral organism.
4. The functions of these four subsystems are: pattern maintenance, integration, goal attainment, and adaptation.
5. In shaping the development of a society, the most important cybernetic role (control of low-information, high-energy systems by those with high information, low energy) is played by the cultural subsystem.

6. The cultural subsystem also legitimizes a society's norms and action patterns particularly in connection with the use of power.
7. This power, backed by force, in terms of government or the state, maintains the society's norms and rules and mobilizes its resources for the achievement of its collective goals.

THE ROLE OF GOVERNMENT

All societies have government. Many societies have had government without the state. But as a society becomes more complex and extensive, the state always develops. Government has been defined as "a group of individuals exercising *legitimate* authority, and protecting and adapting the community by making and carrying out decisions."[4]

Stateless Societies

We can only guess what the social and political organization of early man was like. Anthropologists caution us that it is inaccurate to generalize from the condition of various primitive peoples today. But given a low level of technological development and a dominant hunting economy, a society may well have consisted of little more than a single family or a group of related families. The social bond which determined who were members of the society and who were not was based on the degree of blood relationship. Such political control as existed was held by the oldest and strongest male of the family group or males of the clan group. These individuals made the decisions for the society and determined what was or was not to be done. But this was only one aspect, and probably not the most important one, of the roles they played. There were no full-time specialized political roles played by individuals, and no need to structure them in terms of institutional organization. For there were few emergencies or new problems to be coped with in the social and economic patterns of daily existence. Certain regular events, certain routine experiences repeated themselves over and over again. Through centuries, if not millennia, the members of such societies must have learned as small children how to cope with these situations. The repetitive and standardized roles, in terms of age or sex, which each member of such a society had to perform for personal and group survival were so obvious and so necessary as to need little direction or enforcement.

[4]David E. Apter, "Government," in *International Encyclopedia of the Social Sciences,* 5:215. (Italics added.)

The kinship basis of such stateless societies intensified the close ties among the members. Potent controls were exercised by hallowed custom and religious ritual. In fact, ritual control rather than political control seems to be the prime element in regulating stateless societies.

Political control operates in terms of an organized chain of command where the individuals involved consistently play certain stylized roles. All those involved in the political control process accept the need to support the institutional organization in which the direction of affairs is vested. This acceptance may result from an awareness of the desirable universal goals that can be achieved in this fashion or a realization that those in the authority structure have so much force at their command that it would be disastrous not to obey them.

Ritual control has nothing to do with a rational awareness of authority's right to regulate goals for the common good, nor is it necessarily associated with a chain of command. It achieves its ends by personifying divine force or by evoking divine powers to enforce obedience. Authority in stateless societies is based on a combination of what Max Weber has termed "traditional" and "charismatic" legitimacy.

In large part, regulation occurs because there has always been a certain way of doing things. Violation of these age-old rituals will bring down the wrath of the gods. Anyone who does so endangers the existence of the whole society, which must be ritually and literally purged of his presence. No special institutional organzation is needed to do this since the survival of the whole society is at stake. Spontaneously his family or clan group rallies to provide whatever organized action is necessary.

From time to time unique leaders, touched with divine madness and not content to merely follow tradition, will appear. This is particularly likely when intense stresses threaten the continued existence of the society. Then such a leader, receiving a direct revelation from the gods, will reorient tradition in new patterns and establish new guidelines which will become the tradition of future generations. It is also possible, and it must have happened many times, that such a leader was able to transmit his charismatic authority to his descendants and by this "routinization of charisma" make his family into a permanent set of rulers, thus laying the foundations for the transition from a stateless society to the emergence of a state. But, as we shall note, there are other important steps in this transition from a stateless society.

Before we discuss the growth of the state, certain characteristics common to all stateless societies should be considered. In general terms, stateless societies have these five cumulative and interlocking characteristics:

1. They are *multipolities.*
2. Above the political community level, *ritual superintegration* is achieved in a number of ways.
3. Both integrative and disruptive action within the society are directed and regulated in terms of group *complementary opposition.*
4. An important and comprehensive social framework is provided by *intersecting kinship ties.*
5. "A graded and *distributive legitimacy*" characterizes all levels of action.[5]

Polity is the broad term we have been using to describe "a state or other organized community or body." In a stateless society there is no single dominating political "community or body," and thus many polities are present. The society itself is far more extensive than any of the multipolities within it. The boundaries of any particular polity within a stateless society are defined by how far there is a recognized obligation to settle disputes in terms of the traditions and customs of that particular polity. In this sense a society may comprise dozens or even hundreds of multipolities.

But this political atomization of stateless societies is counterbalanced by the role played by ritual superintegration. By this is meant that, although there is no single source of authority or control in the society or even united action against outside enemies, there do exist various rituals and ceremonies which bring together at times the members of all the multipolities. One anthropologist has described how this takes place in an African stateless society: "These festivals are periods of ritually sanctioned truce, when all conflicts and disputes must be abandoned for the sake of ceremonial cooperation. . . . In this festival cycle the widest Tale community emerges."[6]

Another and more fundamental factor which holds together the disparate multipolities of stateless societies is that of complementary opposition. Within every broadly related kinship group, various subgroups belong to different cult and ritual associations which serve to check and balance each other. These "complementary tendencies towards fission and fusion" serve to create an equilibrium which holds together the over-all society in a state of dynamic tension.

This concept of checks and balances is a familiar phrase for even the beginning student of American government. In one form or another, it is often found in the governmental

[5]This list is taken from Aidan Southall, "Stateless Society," *International Encyclopedia of the Social Sciences,* 15: 158–161.

[6]Meyer Fortes, "The Political System of the Tallensi of the Northern Territories of the Gold Coast," in *African Political Systems,* ed. Meyer Fortes and E. D. Evans-Pritchard (London: Oxford University Press, 1961), p. 257.

organization of a number of states. But for stateless societies, this concept is of crucial importance. As Professor Southall has summarized it:

> It is the self-regulating mechanism whereby, without any titular office or institution that represents or embodies sovereign authority within a bounded society, individuals who interact with one another, directly or indirectly, are ordered and positioned with respect to one another by their own reciprocal activities in dyadic [of, or consisting of, two parts] relations and in joint action.[7]

Although noted as a separate characteristic, it is clear that intersecting kinship is simply a specialized aspect of complementary opposition. Related and far-flung blood ties can perform the same function and membership in differing cult groups in terms of relaxing group tensions and defusing explosive conflict situations. From the earliest times, kinship groups have served as a medium of social control because of the joint responsibility of the group for the conduct and proper performance of its individual members.

The final characteristic of stateless societies, distributive legitimacy, is closely connected with the initial characteristic of multipolities. Rather than that monopoly of authority and power characteristic of the developed state, each of the multipolities of a stateless society within its particular sphere of action has full legitimacy; its ordering of affairs is accepted as being natural and proper by the individuals involved.

Stateless societies have almost disappeared in the modern world. To find examples of them anthropologists are forced to search out such societies as the bushmen of southern Africa, Indian tribes of North and South America, various peoples in the Philippines and New Guinea, and the Eskimo peoples of the Arctic. It is tempting to look at these contemporary stateless societies in negative terms. They lack precisely defined territorial boundaries, an exclusive jurisdiction, legitimate monopoly of the use of force, a self-perpetuating ruling elite, codified laws and regulations for their internal regulation, and the highly developed form of polity that is needed when a society evolves beyond the very simple social and economic action patterns which can function satisfactorily in a condition of statelessness.

But this view overlooks positive aspects of stateless societies that are not without value for even the most advanced of modern polities. Fundamental responsibility for the continuance is not regarded as the sole duty of a small group of leaders while the masses go their indifferent and private ways. Among the adult males at least, it is a wide-

[7]Southall, "Stateless Society," p. 160.

spread responsibility in any stateless society. The observance of rituals, the acceptance of traditional patterns of arbitration, the kinship responsibilities, and the fact that leadership is respected only for so long as it achieves the goals of the society tend to make the maintenance of the fabric of society an almost universal responsibility.

A citizen of one of the great modern industrial states might well feel envious of the members of a stateless society. Today, our characteristic attitude toward the present and future state of society is one of bafflement at the immensity and complexity of its apparently unsolvable problems and of frustrated weariness at the rapidity with which threatening crises endlessly appear.

In contrast, life in a stateless society provides constant and, most importantly, manageable stimuli to its members. The struggle for social survival is very much present but it is comprehensible, and tradition and custom have emphasized the personal responsibility from infancy of each member of society for its continued survival. There exists no group of "they" who live in great palaces or ride in the big, black limousines and who, for better or worse, are responsible for society's preservation and development. There is an encompassing unwritten web of reciprocal obligation which shapes the actions of every member of such a society.

It is doubtful if such an intermixture of the social, political, religious, and economic aspects of a society has existed in terms of state organization since the time of classic Greece when the *politeia* of the city community offered a total and meaningful involvement for its citizens. Let us now survey how the concept of the state first originated and how it has developed from the Greek *polis* to what John K. Galbraith has termed the "new industrial state."

THE GROWTH OF THE STATE

Certain constant factors seem to govern the development from stateless to state-ruled societies. These are: (1) an increasingly developed economy; (2) an increasingly stable social life in settled units of at least village size; (3) an expanding population; and (4) the emergence of a sophisticated social organization. In terms of these characteristics, anthropologists distinguish certain societies which have ceased to be stateless but have not reached the level of becoming states in their own right although they have features of government and social organization which are found in the state.

These societies are of interest since, if left to themselves, they might emerge into full-fledged states. It is also possible that they represent a stage of development through which all states originally passed. Present in these societies are governmental and social elements characteristic of the fully developed state. During the period of the great buffalo hunts on the Western plains in the last century, for example, the Crow Indians had an organization of buffalo police to enforce the rules of the hunt. While the buffalo police existed only during the hunt period, in embryonic form it constituted an organization with that legitimate monopoly of power within a certain defined area which is one of the prime characteristics of the developed state. In the same pattern of vestigial state institutions, there were or are African societies with kings who reign but do not rule, but who nevertheless serve as the symbol of the unity of the society in question.

But between the Crow and the African societies with their statelike institutions and a real state there are important differences. In a real state there is nothing temporary or tentative about the exercise or location of power and authority. A true state has these characteristics:

1. Governmental power is concentrated in a central authority.
2. This central authority has an absolute monopoly of physical force in society.
3. It has the option of delegating its ruling and punitive powers.
4. Authority is strongly rooted in tradition, custom, personal loyalties, religious obligation, and sheer force of habit.
5. The central authority rules over a fixed territory with definite boundaries.
6. Within that territory it establishes and enforces a uniform code of laws and ordered existence for the inhabitants.
7. It accomplishes this through a network of administrators who, usually on a full-time professional basis, enforce the law and carry on official business.

The state represents a secondary growth within a large and complex society, and it very quickly assumes its own independent existence. It is concerned with maintaining internal order and external protection not only for the good of the society in question but also because this advances the interest of the state and proves its indispensability. The more efficient it is in so doing, the more its people will unquestioningly obey it.

When, why, and how did the state first originate? The date of the state's origin obviously cannot be fixed as precisely as could a new nation's declaration of independence. All we can say is that sometime after the slow spreading of the Neolithic revolution between 7000 and 6000 B.C., the state appeared on the scene. In our time, accustomed as we are to think of a revolution as an event which occurs in a matter of days or even hours, it seems absurd to apply the term *revolution* to an event which required a thousand years or so to make a significant impact on the societies which experienced it. Yet, except for the Industrial Revolution of the eighteenth and nineteenth centuries, there has been no more revolutionary event in all of human history than the change during the Neolithic or New Stone Age from hunting and food-gathering to settled agriculture. For the first time it was possible for men to live in one place indefinitely, instead of having to follow migrating game, and to support a sizable population. Initially the population of a Neolithic village may have been at most a few hundred souls. But as increasing agricultural skills brought rising standards of living and longer life expectancy, populations swelled to the point where villages became small cities. At a very early period, regular trade routes developed among these villages and cities. Populations became progressively larger and the pattern of social life increasingly complex. By at least 4000 B.C. the emergence of the state had taken place.

There are two widely held theories as to how this emergence took place, for both of which it is possible to cite historical examples. One theory holds that, as in the case of Egypt and the Middle East, the first states originated by internal development. The other theory is that, as in the case of the first Middle Eastern empire or certain African states, states were formed by conquest. At different times, however, both of these elements of state formation were important factors.

Ancient Egypt is an almost classic example of how the influences of geography and economy made inevitable the emergence of a state. Egyptian economic life, then as now, was dependent on the Nile, and so Egypt's emergence as the world's first large state is not surprising. Long before the emergence of the unified Egyptian state in the 32nd century B.C., Egypt had a sophisticated economic life and sharply defined class divisions. As always seems to be the case, state formation and social unification went hand in hand.

By the beginning of the historical period, a system of irrigated agriculture had produced a class-stratified society divided into peasants, craftsmen, managerial personnel, and so on. There already existed various cities with their surrounding hinterland of dependent villages. Significantly, as in the case of Greek and Roman development many centuries later, the local political divisions by 3000 B.C. had made the transition from the original basis of kinship to a purely administrative one.

Numinous Legitimacy

The account of how a unified Egypt was brought into existence is a story that has been told innumerable times in the last 5000 years. It is extraordinary how often throughout history the charismatic leader has played in the key role in the emergence of new states. In the case of Egypt in the 32nd century B.C., it was the legendary figure of its first god-king, Menes. Some 800 years later in the Middle East, Sargon the Great created the world's first imperial state. We have discussed earlier how in this century such new nations as Ghana and Indonesia came into existence because of the leadership of such personalities as Nkrumah and Sukarno. Such leaders have been able to carry out their tasks because of the religious or semireligious awe they inspired in their followers. The cult of the leader has probably been the most frequently used justification for political action in history.

Once established, with power delegated and routinely administered, authority with these origins very quickly develops into what has been termed a *numinous* legitimacy, by which is meant authority based on spiritual or supernatural grounds. Numinous legitimacy throughout history has been the chief support of the patrimonial state which, until very recent times, has been the dominant state form. Four types of numinous legitimacy may be distinguished. They are: (1) *the concept of a god-king,* found in polities as separated in time and space as Egypt of the Pharoahs three thousand years before Christ, in the Inca Empire of Peru prior to the sixteenth-century Spanish conquest, and modern Japan until the end of World War II; (2) authority based on *the ruler being of godly origin,* again found in such widely separated areas as the ancient Middle East and traditional India and Southeast Asia; (3) *legitimacy conferred by divine vocation,* found in those Western European countries whose kings claimed to rule "by the grace of God"; and (4) *divine inspiration,* found when a challenge to existing legitimacy is based on a claim to a new revelation by Heaven as to what is truly right and just.[8]

This fourth type of numinous legitimacy has seldom produced long-lasting regimes, but it has furnished the basis for a number of the great revolutionary movements of history. The Puritan Revolution in England in the seventeenth century, the Taiping Rebellion in China in the mid-nineteenth century, and, for that matter, the communist revolutionary movement of the twentieth century all represent examples of political action based on an appeal to

[8]I have taken the term *numinous* and the material on numinous legitimacy from "Legitimacy" by Dolf Sternberger in the *International Encyclopedia of the Social Sciences,* 9:244.

divine inspiration, whether in actual spiritual terms or the alleged inevitable workings of the reified forces of historical development.

Civil Legitimacy

Only in the twentieth century has the concept of *civil legitimacy* become the dominant justification for obedience to any state. Civil legitimacy has been defined by Sternberger as existing when a governmental system "is based on agreement between equally autonomous constituents who have combined to cooperate toward some common good." Basic to civil legitimacy is the assumption that government, by the consent of the governed, must be based on a carefully defined statement of the rights and duties of both rulers and ruled. Laws are legitimate because they have been enacted in conformity with certain well-defined procedures. These procedures are based on an interpretation of society which views it in legal-rational terms, not as part of a universal cosmic order. There is assumed to exist a fundamental natural law which is equally applicable to all men, and which can be expressed only in terms of specifically enacted written laws which conform to the concept of a political order based on reason and agreement.

The emergence of civil legitimacy as the customary support for the modern state has been linked with the growth of mass democracy over the past two centuries. The basic propositions go back to the idea of the social contract. But actually only since the French Revolution has any state wanting to be regarded as modern felt it necessary to legitimize itself by submitting the actions of its lawmakers, whether in actual practice or ritual gesture, to popular approval by the mass of its citizens. As we commented earlier, regardless of the ideology or outlook of the state concerned, mass popular approval of the policy-makers is regarded as the *sine qua non* for state legitimization.

The Myth Element

All of this adds up to an important point in the study of politics often overlooked by those who dream of reducing the study of political affairs to a series of mathematical formulas: an important role has always been played by elements which are both unmeasurable and unpredictable. From the initial emergence of a system of city states dominated by temples in the Middle East 5000 years ago to the newest nation of the Afro-Asian world today, it has been routine to claim some sort of divine inspiration or guidance for the political system involved. No state in history has ever existed without the sustaining force of some sort of myth. It has been summarized thus:

> Myth is the all-pervading atmosphere of society, the air it breathes. One great function of myth is to turn valuations into propositions about the nature of things. These propositions range from cosmogonies interpreting the whole universe to statements about what will happen to an individual if he violates the tribal code. The forms and kinds of myth are endless, but at the core of every myth-structure lies the myth of authority.[9]

The role of the myth of authority in the existence of both the traditional and modern states has been of paramount importance. Under the conditions of numinous legitimacy which provided the major support for traditional authority, it was almost self-creating. The founder of a new state was an object of awe and reverence from the start. By his mere assumption of power he became a sanctified person, uniquely singled out and blessed by divine powers. Automatically and immediately, ceremony and ritual developed to set the ruler apart from ordinary men; he was either the incarnation of a god or a direct representative. Every aspect of the ruler's existence was different from that of ordinary men. His clothes, the vehicles he rode in, the magnificent palaces he occupied, all were designed to reinforce his image as the "chosen of God." Except for the restraints of tradition and custom, his power was unlimited, and others exercised authority only through his willingness to delegate it. Very shortly certain ways of doing things became hallowed and sacred and to disregard them would have been to challenge unseen powers. Obedience to the traditional authority, as personified by the ruler, was taught as one with obedience to the will of God or the gods.

From the time of the Pharaohs until pre-World War I Russia, a priestly caste has always played a major role in perpetuating and strengthening this myth of authority. Often the only literate group in society, as was the case during the Middle Ages, this priestly caste was comprised also of the chief administrators. So long as both supreme religious and political power culminated in the person of the supreme ruler, as was the case with the medieval Byzantine emperors, the Russian Czars, and the Incas of Peru, all was well. It was to the mutual interests of all concerned to preserve the myth of authority and do everything to strengthen it.

But the unique development of Western political life after the collapse of the Roman Empire in the fifth century introduced an increasingly disruptive element into the unified support of authority by both military and religious sources. In the unshattered eastern half of the Roman Empire which developed into the medieval Byzantine realm, there continued to be a supreme autocrat in which all civil and religious powers culminated. In the thousand years of

[9] R. M. MacIver, *The Web of Government* (New York: Macmillan, 1947), p. 39.

the Middle Ages, however, the question of where ultimate authority originated was never satisfactorily settled. The Roman popes as heads of an as yet undivided Western Christendom claimed universal authority over all other rulers.

Even before the collapse of the Roman Empire early in the fifth century, St. Augustine of Hippo had stated the case for this claim. In his *City of God,* one of the most influential books in the history of Western political thought, Augustine argued that "there are no more than two kinds of human society, which we may justly call two cities. . . . The one consists of those who wish to live after the flesh, the other of those who wish to live after the Spirit." All history, he contended, has been and will be dominated by the eternal conflict between these two cities, respectively the kingdom of Satan and the kingdom of Christ.

Basing his teachings on the proposition of "render unto Caesar the things that are Caesar's and unto God the things that are God's," Augustine was willing to accept a shared legitimate authority between the religious and the secular powers, if the state was a Christian state dedicated above all else to the furtherance of spiritual interests and to preserving the purity of the faith. At the end of the fifth century, this concept of dual legitimacy was given even more pointed statement by Pope Gelasius I in his doctrine of the two swords when he wrote to the Byzantine emperor, "There are two powers by which this world is chiefly ruled: the sacred authority of the priesthood and the authority of kings." The combination of spiritual and secular authority in one source was condemned as "a wile of the Devil." Instead, each should be supreme within its own jurisdiction and both should work harmoniously together.

It is not surprising that most of Western European political history for the next thousand years is little more than the strife-torn and often bloody efforts to work this formula out. Particularly after Charlemagne attempted in the year 800 to re-create universal political rule in the West by crowning himself the new Holy Roman Emperor, "crowned by God," the conflict never ceased over which side had pre-eminence and from whence came legitimacy.

To the conflict between pope and emperor a new dimension was added in the late Middle Ages when the modern states began to emerge. The growth of modern nationalism was still some centuries away, but by the sixteenth century men were already acutely aware of being subjects of an English or French or Spanish state. Even lip service to the pretense of a political universalism had long ceased, and in the age of the Renaissance and Reformation not even the most devout Catholic king was willing to acknowledge himself subject to papal control in his administration of national affairs.

The strong rulers of Western Europe in the early sixteenth century were interested in establishing for themselves, within their individual domains, a separate legitimacy not dependent on any delegation of power from any allegedly universal authority, whether political or religious. These feelings had long been developing, but it was only in the sixteenth century that the apologists for them made their appearance as a new intellectual, nonpriestly class.

In the preceding centuries, as the foundations were laid for the emergence of the modern capitalist age, the rise of trade and commerce created for the first time in a thousand years an educated elite outside the Church. Trade and commerce needed order and uniform laws for development and an end to the anarchy of feudal disorder. In one of history's most obvious marriages of convenience, the new merchant class provided both the finances and the administrative manpower which enabled the British, French, and Spanish kings to erect those dynastic states, free from even the shadow of control by pope or emperor, from which emerged the modern nation-state. Simultaneously, within the new dynastic states there was created both the administrative apparatus and the intellectual justification first to curb and then to destroy the power of the hitherto semi-independent feudal nobility.

Appropriately it was in France, which was to become the model of the absolutist dynastic state, that a representative of this new class stated the classic brief for the legitimacy of the individual state. In 1576 Jean Bodin, a lawyer by profession employed for most of his life in the royal service, published his famous *Six Books of the Republic,* which ever since has not only provided the justification for legitimacy of the modern state but laid the foundations on which international affairs have been conducted for more than three hundred years.

Like Thomas Hobbes a century later, Bodin (1530–1596) lived during a period of civil war and anarchy.[10] Like Hobbes, Bodin was concerned primarily with the problems of authority and legitimate order. Anarchy was the ultimate tragedy and order the absolute human necessity. In his writing he sought to analyze the conditions necessary for legitimate order. Bodin concluded that the key to legitimate order lay in the unquestioning acceptance of the sovereignty of the state, which he defined as "that absolute and perpetual power vested in a commonwealth which in Latin is termed *majestas.*" It is this characteristic of

[10]The sixteenth century in France was a period of bitter religious civil wars between French Catholics and Protestants (Huguenots), just as the next century in England witnessed the turmoil of civil war and political-religious struggle between Puritans and Cavaliers.

sovereignty which makes the state the most important of all social groupings. Sovereignty is *perpetual* ("the true sovereign remains always seized of his power") and constitutes "supreme power over citizens and subjects, unrestrained by law." This sovereignty is unrestrained because sovereignty itself is the only source of law. However, with that curious mixture of the medieval and the modern characteristic of his time, Bodin was quite sure that the ruler was answerable to God and subject to natural law. Never very much of a restraining force, the complete disappearance of even the fiction of these restraints in a more secular age was to provide the ideological foundation for the emergence of the modern order-party state, with a ruling elite answerable only to its own interpretation of truth. For Bodin the essence of government was its power to command, and the subject's only duty to obey. A humane and ethically motivated exercise of this power was desirable he felt, but basically its possession of sovereignty placed the state beyond any moral judgment on its actions.

The implications of this were to make the state into a completely amoral institution. But it was an even more famous sixteenth-century thinker, Machiavelli (1469–1527), who spelled this out in his famous essay *The Prince*. That Machiavelli has been one of the most maligned and misunderstood figures in the history of political thought is not relevant here. With the cold objectivity of a modern physical scientist examining an organism under the microscope, Machiavelli analyzed the dynamics of political power as they were, not as men idealized them. For four centuries his analysis has been regarded in the same light as though a scientist studying bubonic plague had enthusiastically endorsed it. Far more just and exceedingly rare was the tribute paid Machiavelli by the seventeenth-century essayist Francis Bacon who wrote, "Our thanks are due to Machiavelli and similar writers, who have openly and without dissimulation shown us what men are accustomed to do, not what they ought to do."

Like many a present-day thinker, Machiavelli saw politics as the struggle for power. The only objective of political action, as he saw it, was to maximize the power of the state. As long as the action taken is rational, the state has above all else the primary obligation to survive and prosper. Whatever actions encourage this are desirable; whatever policies hinder this must be discarded. Both before and after Machiavelli, the successful states of history have, of course, followed precisely these policies. But Machiavelli's forthright statement baldly established the proposition that the vital task of any state is to survive and prosper, come what may. The welfare of the state is the only morality. For the universalism of medieval thought, Machiavelli substituted that particularism of the individual nation-state which has continued to dominate all societies ever since he wrote.

TRANSITION FROM THE PATRIMONIAL TO THE MODERN STATE

The transition from the patrimonial to the modern state represents the change from traditional to rational-legal authority as the basis for legitimizing the activities of government. We have spoken earlier of numinous legitimacy furnishing the chief support of the patrimonial state, which for so long a time was the institutional expression of traditional domination. The governmental philosophy of the patrimonial state was simply the philosophy of the patriarch's authority over his extended family writ large. In Weber's words, "Where authority is primarily oriented to tradition but in its exercise makes the claim of full personal powers, it will be called 'patrimonial' authority."

In the same way that the head of a traditional family exacted obedience from his children, daughters-in-law, sons-in-law, and servants simply because it was so ordained by custom and traditional law, the patriarchal ruler regards himself as the "father" of his people and the government administrators as his servants or personal representatives. If this seems a quaint idea, it should be remembered that in Great Britain, long an outstanding example of a state based on legal-rational authority, the official fiction is still maintained that all officials are simply personal representatives of the queen serving at her pleasure. The nineteenth century was well advanced before this principle became merely a legal fiction.

As "probably the most consistent example of patrimonialism," Weber cites ancient Egypt, where "the whole country and its government were constituted as one vast patriarchal household of the pharaoh." In ancient Egypt as in eighteenth-century France and twentieth-century Thailand until the revolution of 1932, the top ranks of officialdom were not only recruited from the king's personal household but were usually princes of the royal blood or other relatives. These examples serve to illustrate the remarkably consistent characteristics of patrimonial rule over a vast sweep of time.

It is interesting that, long before any modern sociological analysis of types of states, Machiavelli recognized that there are two types of state based on traditional authority: patrimonial government and feudal government. In the early pages of *The Prince,* he comments: "Kingdoms known to history have been governed in two ways: either by a prince and his servants who, as ministers by his grace and permission, assist in governing the realm; or by a prince and by barons, who hold their positions not by favor of the ruler but by antiquity of blood."

Weber sees as the essential difference between the patrimonial and the feudal state the respective predominance of bureaucratic officials and charismatic warriors. A patrimonial ruler functions as the father of his people with their good will a necessary aspect for rule. Like the government of the modern welfare state, the patrimonial ruler assumed the duty of insuring the proper functioning of the irrigation system, as in the prototype of patrimonial states, ancient Egypt, and undertaking other such protective measures for the well-being of his people. The feudal overlord, with military power as the basis for his rule, needed only to maintain the loyalties of his fellow warriors. A business-like approach to administration or economic affairs was beneath contempt for the ruling warrior class of feudal society. Also, to their ruin, a comprehension of the power of economic forces was totally lacking.

It was a common antipathy towards feudal values that drew together the centralization-minded rulers of sixteenth-century Europe and the business-minded middle class. The fact that the motivations were different was irrelevant to the working alliance formed between kings and middle class. From this uneasy cooperation emerged the strong patrimonial dynastic states of the seventeenth and eighteenth centuries. From these in turn developed the modern Western state which has become the model for twentieth-century political organization.

During this dynastic state period, the preconditions for the creation of the modern state were set down. In terms of Weber's analysis, these preconditions were:

1. A monopoly of the force needed for social control and the creation of an effective administrative system founded on the existence of a centralized and permanent taxation system
2. A monopoly of legal actions and the legitimate use of force by the central authority
3. The creation and control by the central authority of a "rationally oriented officialdom"

These preconditions result in the creation of the modern state with the following characteristics:

1. A universal legal order subject to legislative control
2. A career bureaucracy carrying on its business in accord with legislatively determined legal-rational principles
3. Final authority over all individuals within the state's limits of territorial control
4. Monopoly of the legitimate use of force

All of these conditions must exist, says Weber, for a

modern state to be present. The emergence of the first such states in Western Europe was no sudden affair. It took place over a period of several centuries while legitimacy gradually ceased to be based on some type of traditional justification and instead "came to be attributed to the body of rules that governed the exercise of authority," or, in other words, to the modern concept of legal-rational authority.

THE ROLE OF BUREAUCRACY IN THE MODERN STATE

Bureaucracy is defined as being "the body of officials or administrators of a government or a government department." But this is a minimal definition indeed for that remarkable institution which furnishes the framework for the modern state. Once again for a comprehensive definition we must turn to Weber. He defines modern bureaucracy as having these characteristics:

1. All officials hold office through proper legal formalities with a continuing and consistent relationship from top to bottom of the authority structure.
2. This relationship "is characterized by defined rights and duties."
3. All this is set forth in printed regulations.
4. Superior-subordinate authority relations are systematically ordered.
5. Appointments and promotions are regulated by contractual agreement.
6. Technical training and/or experience are necessary for employment.
7. There is a fixed scale of salary payments in money.
8. No official has a vested interest in his job in terms of "owning" it or being able to regard it as a family inheritance.
9. The major and full-time occupation of any official is his administrative responsibilities.

During the late feudal period, Western Europe alone developed the conditions necessary for the emergence of modern bureaucracy. There were:

1. The emergence of a money economy
2. "The development of a rationally oriented and dependable officialdom . . . encouraged by the quantitative and qualitative expansion of administrative tasks"
3. The superiority of bureaucratic administration to all other alternative forms of conducting official business

Without the emergence of a money economy, the development of modern bureaucracy is impossible. Government officials must be paid in some fashion. If the central government lacks the means to do so, then inevitably some other system of payment develops. This can include letting officials take a certain share of the taxes they are able to collect. In such cases the tax collector almost always tries to squeeze out a bigger and bigger share and also comes to regard his right to do so as a family privilege to be passed on to future generations.[11]

Another obvious way to compensate officials is to assign one or more estates to them from which they can draw tribute in produce and farm labor. Both methods tend to destroy the authority of the central government and its control over its officials. Only if the central government has an adequate and steady income and control over its use can it hope to operate a modern bureaucracy.

Weber's second condition necessary for the emergence of modern bureaucracy ("the development of a rationally oriented and dependable officialdom") is directly shaped by the dynamics of both power and technology. It was "by the quantitative and qualitative expansion of administrative tasks" that the various strong rulers of the sixteenth and seventeenth centuries were able to establish that centralized control over political and economic life which produced both the dynastic state and the mercantile system.

It was during this period that the foundations of modern bureaucratic development were firmly laid. Sir Ernest Barker, one of the best-known English scholars, commented on the development of public administration, "We may begin the history of modern administration, somewhat arbitrarily and yet with some reason, about the year 1660." Around this date in Europe's three most politically sophisticated states, England, France, and Prussia, modern bureaucratic administration, in varying form, became firmly established. In defining *administration,* Barker came to much the same conclusions as Weber:

> Administration . . . is the sum of persons and bodies who are engaged, under the direction of government, in discharging the ordinary public services which must be rendered daily if the system of law and duties and rights is to be duly "served." Every right and duty implies a corresponding "service"; and the more the State multiplies rights and duties, the more it multiplies the necessary services of its ministering officials.[12]

[11]For a full discussion of Weber's views on bureaucracy, and the source of various quotations, see H. H. Gerth and C. Wright Mills, eds. and trans. *From Max Weber: Essays in Sociology* (New York: Oxford University Press, 1946). The summary of Weber's points is taken from Reinhard Bendix's article on "Bureaucracy" in the *International Encyclopedia of the Social Sciences,* 2:206, and from Reinhard Bendix, *Max Weber: An Intellectual Portrait* (Garden City, N.Y.: Doubleday, 1962).

[12]Sir Ernest Barker, *The Development of Public Services in Western Europe, 1660–1930* (London: Oxford University Press, 1945).

On the relationship between the emergence of the dynastic state and modern bureaucracy, Weber said:

> At the beginning of the modern period, all the prerogatives of the continental states accumulated in the hands of those princes who most relentlessly took the course of administrative bureaucratization. It is obvious that technically the great modern state is absolutely dependent upon a bureaucratic basis. The larger the state, and the more it is or the more it becomes a great power state, the more unconditionally is this the case.[13]

Writing in the early years of the twentieth century, Weber could characterize the United States as bearing "the character of a polity which, at least in the technical sense, is not fully bureaucratized." Excluding state and local officials, the national civilian bureaucracy comprised 239,476 individuals in 1901 to serve a nation of slightly over 76 million persons. By 1970 the population had increased to slightly over 200 million (2.6 times) while the bureaucracy had grown to 2,994,000 individuals, or more than 10 times as many.

Clearly, other factors were at work than the ratio between population and the number of civil servants needed. The most important of these was the emergence of the *positive state.* In the nineteenth century when the prevailing ideal was the *negative state* in accord with the dominant laissez faire philosophy, there was no need for the quantitative or qualitative expansion of administrative activity that would cause a professionally trained career bureaucracy to emerge. It was only after the positive welfare legislation of the 1930s that the United States evolved into a full-fledged modern bureaucratic state.

The relationship between the positive state and the increasing technological complexity of a modern industrial society needs little comment. It is only necessary, for example, to think of the way in which the emergence of the automobile and then the airplane as mediums of mass transportation have created a wide range of demands which can only be handled by governmental action from the positive state. These two developments alone have contributed greatly to the quantitative and qualititative expansion of bureaucracy and to the problems created by the need to regulate modern communications media or the problems created by the space program. In the late twentieth century, as technology creates a whole new host of environmental problems, it is clear that bureaucracy will expand on all levels as the modern state becomes ever more dynamic.

The third of Weber's reasons for the growth of modern bureaucracy is its ability to get things done. As he puts it, "The fully developed bureaucratic mechanism compares with other organizations exactly as does the machine with

[13]Gerth and Mills, *From Max Weber,* p. 211.

the nonmechanical modes of production." Bureaucracy, with its emphasis on the execution of precisely defined administrative tasks by highly trained and objective experts, "offers the attitudes demanded by the external apparatus of modern culture in the most favorable combination." It is a question whether the developments of modern technology have been more responsible for creating twentieth-century bureaucracy, both on the governmental and the private level, or whether bureaucracy has played the dominant role. Whichever came first, they are now completely intertwined in their relationship with each other, as Galbraith points out in his classic study *The New Industrial State.*[14]

THE NEW INDUSTRIAL STATE

It is appropriate to conclude our survey of the modern state with a summary of Galbraith's description of its nature. That the modern state in the twentieth century has become a highly dynamic force in the molding of society we have already noted. But the new industrial state of the contemporary technetronic era is no longer separate and apart from society or the industrial system. Indeed Galbraith maintains that "in notable respects the mature corporation is an arm of the state. And the state, in important matters, is an instrument of the industrial system." While there are overtones here of Marx's famous proposition that the modern state is "but a committee for managing the common affairs of the whole bourgeoisie," Galbraith's thesis is one of constant interaction rather than a simplistic one-way pattern of control.

In the past this pattern of one-way control was the way in which relations between the state and business were viewed. In the late nineteenth and early twentieth centuries, it often seemed that Marx's prophecy was on the verge of fulfillment and the modern state would become simply a pawn for manipulation by all-powerful finance-capitalist interests. The reverse of this was characteristic of the New Deal period of the 1930s when business felt the state to be its enemy and became increasingly fearful of the seemingly constantly expanding powers of control it was exercising.

There were two reasons for this change, Gailbraith says. The first was the emergence of the trade-union movement as an important political force as a result of the impetus given to organization by the Great Depression and the favorable attitude of the Roosevelt administration. "It was easy for business enterprise to imagine that it was about

[14]John Kenneth Galbraith, *The New Industrial State* (New York: The New American Library, 1968). The following quotations are taken from chapters 26 and 27, pp. 304–324.

to pass under the political authority of a state permanently dominated by the unions and the 'intellectuals.' "

The second important development affecting relations between business and the state was the gradual disappearance of the early capitalist family-run business enterprise with which Marx had been familiar. By 1930 almost half (44 percent) of the total number of business firms "and 58 percent by wealth were effectively controlled by their management." This emergence of a managerial elite divorced from ownership has brought to the fore a group of salaried men with no incentive to take daring political risks, since unlike the old capitalists they could reap only a small share of the possible returns. Furthermore, they are accustomed to operating as a group which does not lend itself to political manipulation. As Galbraith comments, ". . . the suborning of a legislature or even the persuasion of an electorate is accomplished, on the whole, by men working as individuals."

During this period, the basis was being laid for a new relationship between the state and business, or, at least, the increasingly important managerial section of it. The acceptance by the state, under the influence of Keynesian economics, of its responsibility to regulate aggregate demand and to maintain a stable economy gave particular advantage to the most highly rationalized and sophisticated section of business, the managerial corporations. In terms of their own planning, for example, the regulation of prices, government subsidizing of research, and assured government purchase of the products produced worked to produce an ever-closer two-way relationship between this new type of active state and the new type of business corporation. Indeed, there has developed an increasingly intensified symbiosis between these two once-hostile groups. In such matters as a stable and growing economy, education, technical and scientific progress, and, above all, national defense, there is a merging of the goals and interests of government and business administrators. As Galbraith summarizes it: "No sharp line separates government from the private firm: the line becomes very indistinct and even imaginary. Each organization is important to the other; members are intermingled in daily work; each organization comes to accept the other's goals; each adapts the goals of the other to its own."

In the area of defense affairs this development has produced that monster known as the military-industrial complex. That it exists seems obvious, but it is not unique to American industrial development. In 1968 the Soviet equivalent of the military-industrial complex possessed sufficient political power to force the acceptance of a high-ranking Soviet officer (Marshal Grechko) as defense minister. The American equivalent of this would be the Pentagon and the defense industries successfully insisting that the chairman of the Joint Chiefs of Staff be made Secretary of Defense.

CONCLUSION

There seems to be a tendency for any modern industrial state, given the volume and the complexity of the problems modern technology creates, to fall under the control of a new type of bureaucracy, undreamed of by Max Weber. The members of this new bureaucracy are interchangeable between private and public office. They all give common allegiance to rational-legal principles of administration and the dominant role played by the technical expert. There is no question that their services and their technical skills are needed in the new industrial state.

But the major problem of state development in the late twentieth century may well be how to keep this new group from effectively gaining control of the important aspects of policy-making. Politically it has no particular party loyalties. Its concern is with the realities of power and how the decisions are made. In quiet and unobtrusive ways, while elected officials come and go, the government-business, business-government members of this new bureaucracy are in a position both to shape technical decisions (on weaponry, for example) and defense and foreign policy decisions (determining what kind of weapons are needed).

The ability to do this, Galbraith concludes, is a far more important power than the obvious exercise of political influence. "It is," he writes, "the difference between the formal grandeur of the legislative hearing and the shirt-sleeved rooms with blackboards and tables heavy with data, drawings and tapes where the important decisions are actually made. The technostructure selects its theater of influence with discrimination and intelligence."

The evolution of the state since the sixteenth century has seen it pass through the dynamic formative period of the dynastic states to the semihibernation of the passive states of the nineteenth-century laissez-faire period to the new active social welfare states of the mid-twentieth century to the emergence of the new industrial state of the late twentieth century. This newest type of state, staffed by the new industrial-government elite, has all the potential of developing into an oligarchy behind a facade of popular control. Perhaps the greatest challenge facing the advanced countries today is not so much how to deal with the vexing and increasing problems created by a seemingly ever more uncontrollable technology, but rather how to maintain democratic control over the state or over its indispensable technical-managerial elite. The answer to this agonizing problem will lead us to know whether the technetronic age will witness the emergence of a new creative concept of popular control of government, or whether we shall see the appearance in the twenty-first century of a new type of managerial-technical oligarchic state.

GOVERNMENTAL STRUCTURES AS DEPENDENT VARIABLES

Up to this point we have emphasized the importance of the action elements in political affairs. Interest groups, political parties, ideologies, and outlooks are all part of this dynamic aspect. But for action to occur at all it must have some sort of structural framework to give it shape and direction.

With few exceptions, almost all the world's 146 polities officially describe themselves as functioning under a *parliamentary* or a *presidential* system. By parliamentary is meant that the executive, in theory, is simply "a committee of the legislative body" always answerable to the legislature for its actions and dependent on majority legislative support for its continuing existence. In contrast, presidential government is a broad, vague term often used to describe any governmental system where the chief executive is elected independently of the legislature and is not dependent on it for either his power or the duration of his office.

The terms *parliamentary* and *presidential* are so universally used to describe modern governments that they are meaningless as a way of defining the basic nature of any governmental system. Great Britain, the Fourth Republic of France, the Soviet Union, and Ethiopia all claim to be organized according to parliamentary principles. But the differences among them indicate how pointless such a description can be. Great Britain has always been regarded as a model of the proper operation of a parliamentary system, while the Fourth Republic (1946–1958), not altogether accurately or fairly, is often cited as the outstanding example of how destructively inefficient and ineffective a parliamentary system can be. As for the Soviet Union and Ethiopia, in very different ways they too illustrate the meaninglessness of a label. In the Soviet Union, the world's first movement-regime order state, power lies with the party, while Ethiopia is one of the few states left where the personal will of "the King of

Kings" is almost always the decisive factor in governmental policy-making.

It is no more meaningful to describe a state as having a presidential government. In common the United States, Algeria, Indonesia, and the Ivory Coast vest executive authority in a single official, the president, with powers and term of office separate from the legislative branch. But with this statement all resemblance ends. There are presidents and presidents. With all his vast powers, the president of the United States has a more limited range of arbitrary individual action available to him than do various Latin American and African heads of state who are also officially designated as presidents.

This is why it seems logical to regard governmental structure as a *dependent variable.* By this is meant that the framework of government is in itself often a minor, if not negligible, factor in determining how well or how badly the system functions. The controlling factors are the other institutions and values of that particular political culture.

The more universally accepted the basic patterns of modern governmental organization, the less helpful they are as descriptive terms. This is one of the major reasons why contemporary political science has tended to play down institutional analysis and instead concentrated on the behavioral elements. The official adoption of parliamentary or presidential government today no longer automatically implies either familiarity with or acceptance of the values of Anglo-American political culture. It is simply that these organizational structures are the proper forms for a modern state to use. The result is that some very strange varieties of political moonshine are poured into the old familiar bottles making their labels quite useless. In 1971 the 146 governments of the world could be divided into approximately 80 regimes which officially list themselves as parliamentary; another 50 use the designation presidential.[1] The remaining governments either ignore the problem of describing their organization or designate their executives as chief of state or president of the republican council or "head of the military council," or some other vague designation.

Before going any further, we need to define our basic terms more exactly. We can begin by restricting our use of the terms *parliamentary* and *presidential* to functioning

[1]Good brief summaries of the types of governmental systems can be found in the *World Almanac* and similar annual publications. See also the yearly *Political Handbook of the World* published by the Council on Foreign Relations. The term "presidential government" was apparently coined by British journalists some time before the Civil War to describe the essential difference between the British and American systems. Its best known use is by the British publicist, Baghot, in his classic study on *The English Constitution* published in 1867 and many times reprinted.

democratic constitutional systems. Realizing, as Max Weber points out, that "pure" types are rarely found in reality, let us say that a functioning constitutional democracy must have a competitive party system which regularly offers the electorate two or more policy and leadership possibilities at every election.

Using this criterion, we can eliminate from the genuine parliamentary and presidential categories all those movement regimes, whether of the order or solidarity variety, which either officially forbid or effectively discourage the emergence of any opposition alternatives to their rule. It is worth noting that the communist order variety of regime, in accord with Soviet precedent, customarily uses the sham parliamentary facade of the assembly version of parliamentary organization. In contrast, the solidarity regimes, characteristically headed by the charismatic leader, usually opt for a sham presidential system as offering more scope for the leader's actions. The creation of a strong president who can rule by decree, without even the need to pretend to consult a lgislative assembly, has obvious appeal both for the leaders of solidarity parties and for military juntas as a cover under which oligarchic power struggles can be fought out with a minimum of publicity. For civilian or military groups lacking the experience in parliamentary manipulation of the disciplined order party, a governmental system with a single executive, whether he is an actual charismatic leader or a convenient figurehead, is an easier system to use. It is not without interest in this connection that virtually all of the African solidarity regimes use the presidential facade.

By eliminating both types of movement-regime party, sham presidential and parliamentary systems, we can reduce the number of effectively functioning parliamentary systems to approximately 37, and of presidential systems to approximately 22. In the latter case, we should note that the American version of the presidential system, while it was the prototype for this form, is now only one variation; the establishment of the Fifth Republic in France in 1958 added a new and important alternative form. In both the currently functioning parliamentary and presidential systems, to lesser degree than in the movement regimes but often significantly, the factors of party systems and charismatic leadership, must be taken into account.

We can begin our survey of the development and essential differences between these two types of governmental structure by noting that the lack of separation of the parliamentary executive from the legislature and the separation of the presidential executive from the legislature points up an important difference between them as to how governmental authority should be derived. Accepting the dictionary definition of authority as "the *right* to control, command or determine," the fact remains that "it is power which confers authority upon a command. But it is sanctioned power, institutionalized power."[2] In the parliamentary system this sanctioned power is regarded as deriving entirely from the legislative branch, and the power relationship can be described as a *fusion of powers.* However, as more descriptive of the way in which this came about, we shall refer to the parliamentary system as based on a system of *monopolized* powers. In contrast the American presidential system is often described as characterized by the *separation of powers.* But the very core of the American system is in its *sharing of powers* rather than in their separation into isolated elements. There are, of course, separate legislative, executive, and judicial articles in the Constitution; but they grant no powers that are complete and separate in themselves. The relationship of the executive, legislative, and judicial branches represents a complicated interdependence of action and organization. As for the fabled total independence of the judiciary from either legislative or executive, recall President Andrew Jackson's alleged comment at a moment of constitutional crisis: "Chief Justice Marshall has made his decision. Now let *him* enforce it." For this reason, it is more appropriate to refer to the American presidential system as based on the concept of the sharing of powers.

Of these two basic power systems, that of monopolized powers as personified by the British parliamentary system has had the longest evolutionary development and is by far the most widely imitated. Even the American presidential system in large part represents an attempt to reproduce the idealized character of eighteenth-century British institutional organization with the substitution of an indirectly elected executive for a hereditary ruler. In terms of longevity and widespread influence, it is appropriate to begin with a survey of the development and characteristics of the parliamentary system based on the monopoly of powers.

THE BRITISH PARLIAMENTARY SYSTEM: A PROTOTYPE FOR MONOPOLIZED AUTHORITY

It is possible to name not only the year but the month and the day in which the American constitution and the proclamation of the French revolutionary assembly first made their appearance in modern history. But it is not possible to pinpoint the date of the emergence of the British parliamentary system. It can be argued that its origins go back to the Anglo-Saxons of the early Middle Ages. Most collections of documents which form the basis of the develop-

[2]Robert Bierstadt, "The Problem of Authority," in *Freedom and Control in Modern Society,* ed. Morris Berger, Theodore Abel, and Charles H. Page (New York: Van Nostrand, 1954), p. 79.

ment of the British institutional system begin, at the very latest, with the Magna Carta of 1215. Because the emergence of the British system has been so gradual, we can best look at the development of the parliamentary system in terms of a series of snapshots at widely separated intervals. Considering only the major elements, a starting point is the year 1300.

Medieval British Government

There is no particular reason for picking the year 1300 except for the fact that the Middle Ages had reached their peak by that time, and the first outlines of the modern parliamentary system had already begun to appear. In diagrammatic form we can represent it like this:

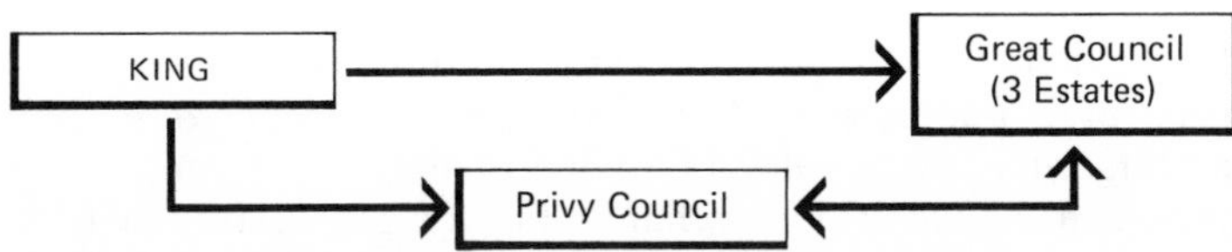

At this time there was no great difference between the British pattern of government and that in any other medieval monarchy of Europe. It was what happened from here on that made the difference and created the remarkable British parliamentary system which became so universal a model.

Under God, and subject only to the dictates of his own conscience, a medieval king held unquestioned supreme authority. But his position was a far different one from that of Louis XIV, the resplendent Sun King of France, who in the early eighteenth century could say with truth, "I *am* the state." Unlike Louis, the medieval king possessed neither an effective tax system to give him financial independence nor a professional bureaucracy to carry out his commands. His position was very much like that of the top man in a human pyramid, imposing but precarious. Frequently one or more of his vassals had access to greater sources of both financial and military power than he.

The result was that even the most powerful of autocratic personalities found it both advisable at regular, but unspecified, intervals to have "deep speech" (in Latin *colloquium,* in French *parlement*) with the Great Council of the realm composed of the three estates into which medieval society was divided. In England, as elsewhere in the medieval world, the two most important of these estates were the military barons (the lords temporal) and the clergy (the lords spiritual). It was in the composition of the third estate, the commons, originally composed of the infrequently summoned representatives of the emerging merchant class of the towns and cities, that English development early in the fourteenth century made a significant and crucial departure from the European pattern.

At one extreme the nobility included wealthy and militarily strong barons often more powerful than the king himself. But its bottom ranks, made up of the knights of the shire, were in a far different situation. The "castle" of a simple baronet was often little more than a not-too-impressive farmhouse with a wall around it, while his military force might consist of ten or twelve spear-carrying farm laborers. Such a knight had close and intimate connections with the towns in his local area. By blood and rank he was entitled to associate with the great lords, but their world and its concerns had little relevance for his. Furthermore, though under the British rule of primogeniture only the oldest son could inherit either land or title, the great lords for many generations possessed enough power to insure that other sons were well provided for. But the younger sons of a poor knight had little choice except to become priests, mercenary soldiers, or merchants—or, better yet, to marry into a wealthy merchant's family. The results of these last two alternatives were to merge the interests of the knights of the shire and the new town bourgeoisie.

Whether these were the compelling reasons or not, the fact remains that early in the reign of Edward III (1327–1377) the country knights began regularly to sit in Commons with the representatives of the towns and cities rather than with the lords. Originally the Great Council had been composed only of the first two estates, but beginning in 1265 the writ of summons for the meetings of Parliament, as the Great Council came to be called first colloquially and then officially, regularly came to include representatives of the third estate.

The king's reason for calling these meetings of Parliament had little to do with law-making. The idea that law is *made* as a new and fresh product is a modern concept. In medieval Europe as in all traditional societies, law was something that grew and developed over long centuries as matters of custom and precedent. The Magna Carta and other documents we consider landmarks in the development of modern democracy were regarded not as new and revolutionary statements, but as reassuring confirmations of rights and liberties which were felt to have been already established.

The king's reason was primarily to get financial support from his reluctant subjects in the form of new taxes or grants. In times of internal turmoil or foreign wars, such as the endless English campaigns against France, this was a particularly pressing need because of the absence of any type of organized revenue collections. It was for this reason alone that, as their prosperity increased, the reluctant representatives of the Commons found themselves regularly included in the calls to Parliament. Another important reason stemmed from the shaky eminence of the king on the top of the power pyramid. Only if he could keep himself reasonably aware of what his subjects, as represented by the three estates, were thinking and wanted could he hope to remain in power. The summoning of Parliament was a rudimentary but reasonably effective way of keeping in touch with the public opinion of those who counted in medieval society.

Meetings of the Great Council consisted of the king, seated on his throne and flanked by the benches of the lords spiritual and temporal, while the Commons stood respectfully behind a railing at some distance facing the king. English constitutional law still defines the term *parliament* in terms of this medieval arrangement. As one classic source expressed it: "Parliament means, in the mouth of a lawyer (though the word has often a difference sense in ordinary conversation), the King, the House of Lords, and the House of Commons; these three bodies acting together may be aptly described as the 'King in Parliament,' and constitute Parliament."[3]

After the king had outlined his latest financial needs, the Commons withdrew to a separate chamber to discuss the royal financial needs, with the understandable intention of trying to determine how the burden could be lessened. From this discussion of finances by the medieval Commons has developed the precedent, written into the American and other modern constitutions, that financial bills must originate with the lower house.

Some time in the course of the fourteenth century it became customary for the Commons to try to bargain with the king by offering him more subsidy in return for his reconfirmation of old charters or the granting of new rights of self-government to towns and cities. It was in this very rudimentary fashion that law-making by the king in Parliament first began. The often uncomfortable task of presenting the "humble" petition fell to the Commons's most prominent member who, for obvious reasons, at an early date became known as the speaker for the Commons. In the fourteenth century this was an office to be avoided, rather than sought after as it often is today. During this same formative period, the now widely accepted rights and immunities of legislators—especially freedom of speech in official debate—gradually became established. But service in the Commons was still so associated with the need to spar with the king over his financial demands that many towns and cities paid him lump sums to avoid having to send representatives to London.

[3]A. V. Dicey, *Introduction to the Study of the Law of the Constitution,* 7th ed. (London: Macmillan, 1908), p. 37.

The Privy Council

Like most other elements of British governmental structure, the Privy Council developed almost accidentally over a period of several centuries. In theory a medieval king consulted constantly with the members of the first two estates in the Great Council. But since all of them were men of affairs in their own rights with pressing business at considerable distance from the king's court, attendance ebbed and flowed. Normally only the king's most intimate personal advisors, aided by their monkly clerks and household stewards, remained at court. It was this group that gradually came to be regarded as an administrative entity separate from the Great Council and constituting the king's personal and private (privy) council. As improbable as it would have seemed in the fourteenth century, from this small group of perhaps a dozen or so key advisors and a few score clerks have developed the imposing administrative bureaucracies of today.

THE MODERN BEGINNINGS

Present in this simple medieval governmental structure are most of the elements of modern institutions. We turn now in our brief survey of the parliamentary system to about the year 1500 when it looked approximately like this:

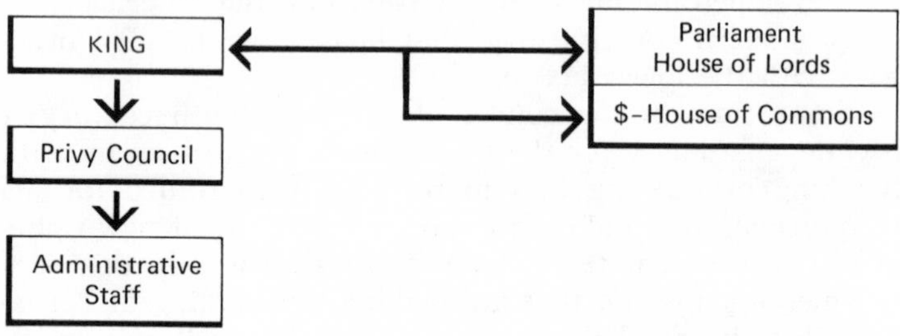

By 1500 the uncertain experiments and half-understood innovations of two centuries earlier had become hallowed precedents and constitutional traditions. The Privy Council, for example, had become a permanent group of officials who met regularly with the king, and each member of this policy-making group presided over a growing staff of career officials who administered the king's business. The monkly clerks of medieval times had given way to the new secularly educated members of the increasingly wealthy and influential middle class which already, not only in England but in France, had become advisors to kings and the strongest weapon for breaking the powers of the feudal nobility.

By this time there was no further reference, except in

constitutional treatises, to the Great Council. Instead, from its first use to describe a debate, then a formal conference, the term *parliament* had become the official designation for the official representatives of the king's subjects. Due to the insistence of the clergy on holding their own exclusive assemblies, the archbishops, bishops, and abbots (the lords spiritual) joined the secular holders of hereditary titles (the lords temporal) to form the House of Lords while the representatives of the towns and the small nobility of the countryside, the knights, continued to meet as the now well established House of Commons from which all financial grants had to originate. As the new middle class increased in power economically and became more confident, the Commons moved from the role of humble petitioners to that of representatives demanding their "immemorial rights and liberties." If the king can be described as the dominant factor in the fourteenth-century, by the sixteenth century the Commons, with which the term *parliament* had become interchangeable, had achieved an equilibrium.

CHECKS AND BALANCES APPEAR

By the late seventeenth century the king and Commons constituted the two major elements of the governmental structure, as the diagram makes clear. The most important

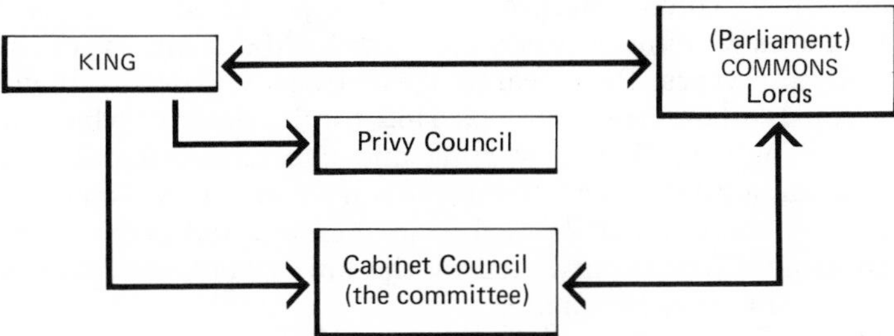

new development in the steady evolution toward the modern parliamentary system had been brought about, as usual, quite unintentionally and by the pragmatic requirements of daily administration.

As the power of the crown (the government) grew and its control over affairs became increasingly centralized, the divisions and subdivisions of administration of necessity became more complex and more numerous. The most important result of this was that the Privy Council, which had become too unwieldy a body to serve as the king's private advisory group, was broken up into committees. The so-called foreign committee, which actually dealt with all major policy matters, became so important that it was increasingly referred to simply as the Committee. On it served the king's most trusted advisors and closest friends. Because meetings of the Committee were held in a small chamber (a cabinet), it eventually became known as the Cabinet Council.

The Cabinet Council was unpopular, and its unpopularity arose from the fear and suspicion it aroused in the increasingly powerful House of Commons. In 1660 when the monarchy was restored after Britain's unhappy and short-lived experiment with republicanism, the nation had twenty dreadful years of civil war and social upheaval behind it. Not without reason, the Commons suspected that the ill-fated Charles I, who had been beheaded by the parliamentary party at the end of the civil war, had frequently been urged into rash and fatal policies by the members of his private Cabinet Council.

Under Charles II (1660–1685) the Cabinet Council was once again restored to its place of prominence in government administration with its members drawn from the closest cronies of the king and responsible only to him for their secret advice. Throughout Charles II's reign, the Commons tried to get some measure of control over the appointment of members and knowledge of what went on in the Cabinet Council's locked-door meetings.

The details of the struggle between king and Commons need not concern us here, fascinating as they are.[4] What is important for our broader survey is the system of delegating authority which emerged from this power struggle. Both king and Commons were haunted by the memory of the civil war years. Both feared fresh tragedy. The result was a constant but cautious sparring for hegemony, which resulted only in each thwarting and checking but not overwhelming the other. The Commons constantly sought to control the Cabinet Council's membership and policies, and constantly it was outwitted by the king's deft maneuvering. The result was stalemate.

In the years following the expulsion of the Stuarts from the throne in 1688, a move justified by Locke's classic treatise, it became increasingly the practice to select for membership in the king's Cabinet only those individuals, drawn from the Lords or Commons, who commanded sufficient trust and respect to insure the enactment of governmental programs by these two houses.

Although by mid-eighteenth century the reality of British government was otherwise, the idealized picture of the even balance of the last decades of the seventeenth century

[4]The old medieval legal procedure of impeachment was used extensively, for example, as a means of intimidating unpopular royal advisors and thus became a part of the American constitutional tradition.

had exerted unique and lasting influence. An aristocratic French scholar, the Baron de Montesquieu, who spent time in Great Britain, was impressed with the freedom and efficiency of British institutions in contrast to the despotism and incompetence of the rapidly decaying French absolute monarchy. In his classic *Spirit of the Laws* (1748), Montesquieu pondered the reasons for the British success story and concluded that it lay in the checks and balances provided by the division of powers, which he distinguished as being the legislative, the executive, and the judiciary powers, or as he defined it, "the executive in regard to matters that depend on the civil law."

Both in Great Britain and in the British colonies on the other side of the Atlantic, students of government, including Thomas Jefferson and James Madison, were deeply impressed with Montesquieu's praise of a structural division of shared authority as representing the best safeguard for political liberty. Other factors as well strengthened their high regard for a system of checks and balances, including the fact that when the fathers and grandfathers of the colonists had migrated from Great Britain the concept of shared authority was widely regarded as the most successful constitutional system since republican Rome.

The most distinguished of British constitutional authorities saw this sharing of authority as the basis for "the true excellence of the English government." In the mid-1760s the great British constitutional lawyer Sir William Blackstone published his *Commentaries on the Laws of England.* Until the end of the nineteenth century no other book exerted as much influence on British and American lawyers and legislators as Blackstone's *Commentaries.* In the United States in the late eighteenth and early nineteenth centuries, it was the chief source of the knowledge of English law.

Surveying the nature of authority in British constitutional structure, Blackstone observed:

> And herein indeed consists the true excellence of the English government, that all the parts of it form a mutual check upon the nobility, and the nobility a check upon the people; by the mutual privilege of rejecting what the other has resolved: While the king is a check upon both, which preserves the executive power from encroachments. And this very executive power is again checked and kept within due bounds by the two houses, through the privilege they have of inquiring into, impeaching and punishing the conduct (not indeed of the king . . . , which would destroy his constitutional independence; but which is more beneficial to the public) of his evil and pernicious counsellors. Thus every branch of our civil polity supports and is supported, regulates and is regulated by the rest: for the two houses naturally drawing in two directions of opposite interest, and the prerogative in another still different from them both, they mutually keep each other from exceeding their proper limits; while the whole is prevented from separation and arti-

ficially connected together by the mixed nature of the crown, which is a part of the legislative, and the sole executive magistrate. Like three distinct powers in mechanics, they jointly impel the machine of government in a direction different from what either, acting by itself, would have done; but at the same time in a direction partaking of each, and formed out of all; a direction which constitutes the true line of the liberty and happiness of the community.[5]

THE RISE OF THE PRIME MINISTER

But at the times when both Montesquieu and Blackstone believed they were describing the realities of the distribution of authority in the British parliamentary system, their descriptions no longer corresponded to the newest and most significant step in the emergence of the modern parliamentary system. For by the year 1730, a new element had been added to the pattern of British parliamentary development in the person of the king's first minister in the House of Commons. The prime minister fits into our diagram like this:

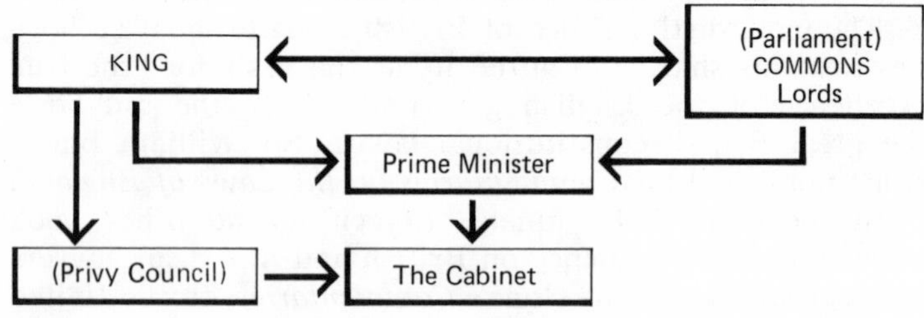

The emergence of this element in the development of the modern parliamentary system came about as the result of one of the oddest accidents in political history. When in 1714 Queen Anne died with no surviving children, the Elector of Hanover was brought to the British throne, and as George I, initiated the dynasty which still reigns over Great Britain in the person of Queen Elizabeth II.

The British sovereign, whether male or female, had always been very much the active executive head of government. The official constitutional definition of *parliament* did, and still does, include three elements: "the King, the House of Lords, and the House of Commons." From long before the Norman Conquest, the sovereign presided over the meetings of his advisors, whether Witangemoot, Great

[5]William Blackstone, *Commentaries on the Laws of England* (New York: W. E. Dean, 1847), Vol. 1 "Book the First," chap. 2, pp. 111–112. Notice how in the last sentence Blackstone draws on the technology of his time to illustrate his point.

Council, Privy Council, or cabinet, and with him rested the final decision on all matters of policy. When Britain acquired its new German king, there were a thousand years of history behind this tradition with all indications that it would continue unchanged into the indefinite future. But within two decades it was on its way to oblivion and an entirely new system, which was to become a global model, was in the process of emerging.

It came about from the fact that George I neither spoke any English nor, more important, cherished any affection for his new kingdom. Both he and his grandson, who ruled as George II, regarded Great Britain during the forty-five years of their combined reigns as simply a lucrative source of military and financial support for their beloved German kingdom of Hanover. Two years after he ascended the British throne, George I ceased to attend cabinet meetings or to pretend to any particular interest in the nation's affairs, except insofar as they contributed to his German interests.

But governmental administration, like physical nature, abhors a vacuum. It was another fortunate accident that during the first years of this new arrangement there was available a political leader almost ideally suited by temperament and personality to inaugurate the new office. Officially Sir Robert Walpole bore the title of first lord of the treasury, as have all British prime ministers since then. From 1721 to 1742 Walpole deputized for the king. With him began the custom of having the prime minister preside over the meetings of the cabinet and the establishment of the now-firm constitutional precedent that, although legally fully entitled to do so, the ruling sovereign never attends a cabinet meeting. Walpole's task was a difficult one. In fact, as well as theory, he was constantly answerable to two masters. As the king's personal appointee he had to keep the sovereign content with his performance; he was also under the necessity of pleasing a sufficient number of members of the House of Commons. Neither he nor his immediate successors cared for the title of prime minister, which was not applied as a compliment, but even in the early formative years of the slowly emerging office, Walpole executed many of the functions of a modern prime minister. He was in control of his colleagues in the cabinet, insisted they subscribe more or less to the same political viewpoint, and, most important, managed to maintain majority support in the House of Commons. For this latter purpose, since there were as yet no ties of party loyalty to utilize, Walpole found useful the access to the treasury afforded by his official position. Well into the nineteenth century prime ministers found their position as first lords of the treasury of very practical political use. With good reason the deputy undersecretary was known as the "patronage secretary."

THE INFLUENCE OF THE PARTY SYSTEM

It was not until after 1867 and the growth of the party system that parliamentary majorities could be created and precariously maintained except through bribery, patronage, and persuasion. The rapid transition to mass democracy which took place after the passage of the voting act of that year brought about an equally rapid development of the modern party organization. In the evolution of the modern parliamentary system, its effect was to add the last element necessary for its final development. The diagram shows the "chains" of party, added a few years after 1867; the relation of the other elements has remained the same up to the present time.

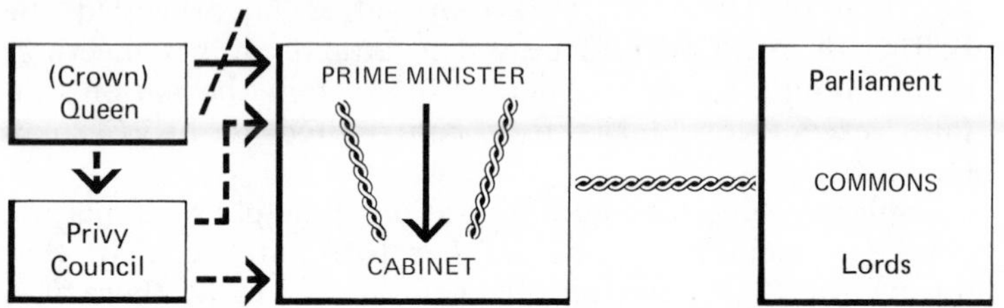

In the same year that the 1867 voting act was passed in Britain (and, incidentally, the same year that Karl Marx published the first volume of *Das Kapital*), a classic study, *The English Constitution*, was written. Its author, Walter Bagehot, was a skilled journalist as well as an informed scholar, and it continues to be a highly readable book even a century later.[6] Bagehot was the first to call attention to developments which were already more than a century old and which in some cases were, even as he described them, in transition to a new phase. He commented, for example:

> There are two descriptions of the English Constitution which have exercised immense influence, but which are erroneous. First, it is laid down as a principle of the English polity, that in it the legislative, the executive, and the judicial powers, are quite divided—that each is entrusted to a separate person or set of persons—that no one of these can at all interfere with the work of the other. . . .
>
> Secondly, it is insisted that the peculiar excellence of the British Constitution lies in a balanced union of three powers. . . . A great theory, called the theory of "Checks and Balances," pervades an immense part of political literature, and much of it is collected from or supported by English experience.

But the reality of British government, as of 1867, Bagehot went on, is very different:

[6]See the compact and well-edited Oxford University Press edition, 1955. The quotations which follow are taken from pages 2, 9–10, and 12 of this edition.

The efficient secret of the English Constitution may be described as the close union, the nearly complete fusion, of the executive and legislative powers. No doubt by the traditional theory, as it exists in all the books, the goodness of our constitution consists in the entire separation of the legislative and executive authorities, but in truth its merit consists in their singular approximation. The connection link is *the cabinet.* By that new word we mean a committee of the legislative body selected to be the executive body. The legislative has many committees but this is the greatest. It chooses for this, its main committee, the men in whom it has most confidence. . . . A century ago the Crown had a real choice of ministers, though it had no longer a choice on policy. During the long reign of Sir R. Walpole he was obliged not only to manage parliament, but to manage the palace. He was obliged to take care that some court intrigue did not expel him from his place. The nation then selected the English policy, but the Crown chose the English ministers. . . . [but now] There is nearly always some one man plainly selected by the voice of the legislature to head that party and consequently to rule the nation. We have in England an elective first magistrate as truly as the Americans have an elective first magistrate.

In one of his most often quoted phrases, Bagehot described the cabinet as "a combining committee—a *hyphen* which joins, a *buckle* which fastens the legislative part of the state to the executive part of the state." The importance of the cabinet continued to grow to the extent that by the 1930s the first edition of what is still regarded as the definitive study on British government could quite appropriately be entitled *Cabinet Government.*

CABINET DOMINANCE

In the years before World War II it was customary to refer to the prime minister, whose existence received belated official recognition in 1905, as being *primus inter pares* (first among equals).[7] It was an accurate description. In the nineteenth century the prime minister had ceased to be the king's (or queen's) minister in the House of Commons and there was no longer any need "to manage the palace." The day after a general election it was obvious to all who would be invited by Her Majesty to form Her next government. The feelings of the sovereign for the leader of the party which had just won a majority in the last election was immaterial. Linked by the chains of party to a majority in the House of Commons he was the only possible choice as the queen's first minister. It was also he, rather than the queen, who named those who would fill the cabinet posts. For the sovereign there remained only the ceremonial

[7]Official recognition came only in terms of a decree that at formal state affairs, the PM ranked after the Archbishop of York!

duty of issuing the formal decree which appointed the new prime minister and cabinet members to the Privy Council, thus giving them the official status necessary to enter on their duties.

But as important as the prime minister was, and as independent of the sovereign as he had become long before World War II, he was still far from being his own man. True, as a result of superior political skill and political qualities, he was the leader of his party which, after the early twentieth century, meant that he held a seat in the House of Commons.[8] But just a step, in some cases only a half step, below was a group of almost equally able and strong party leaders, each of whom had won his own spurs in the political wars and who, like the great feudal barons, often commanded political support almost the equal of the party leader's own strength. It was from among these leaders that the prime minister was required to choose his ministers.

The fact that the cabinet was composed of influential and experienced political figures, rather than the politically powerless and inexperienced individuals who so often compose an American presidential cabinet, has led to an entirely different pattern in administrative decision-making. Basic to cabinet government is the concept of *collective responsibility*. No British prime minister could say as Abraham Lincoln once did to his cabinet, "Gentlemen, the vote is seven noes and one aye. The ayes have it!" It was necessary for a prime minister to achieve a united front for public display to the outside world by persuasion or sheer force of personality. Very seldom could he, as President Truman did in 1947, summarily discharge a dissenting cabinet member. In recent times, however, the British prime minister has come to dominate his cabinet, a development which will be discussed later.

Characteristics of the Cabinet System

Because the British parliamentary system has been adopted around the world, we have traced its development in detail. Before discussing briefly the variations that have developed from the basic structure of the British system, let us summarize the major characteristics of governmental structure based on *monopolized authority*.

[8]A significant indication of the importance of the Commons and the loss of prestige by the Lords is that not since 1902 has a member of the Lords served as prime minister, and since World War I it has become a convention of the constitution that a member of the titled nobility must resign his title and sit for election to the House of Commons before he can become prime minister. In 1963, for example, the Conservative leader, the Earl of Home, resigned his title and as Sir Alexander Douglas-Home won election to the Commons in order to become prime minister.

1. The authority reserve is undivided. It is drawn on by all the institutional divisions of government in proportion to their predominance at the time. In the twentieth century, predominance has moved increasingly to the executive.

2. The executive is divided into, to use Bagehot's apt phrase, a "dignified" and an "active" part.

3. The dignified or ceremonial executive has extended permanent tenure and officially appoints the active executive to office.

4. The active executive achieves office as the leader of the party which has won majority control of the important house of the legislative branch. Office is retained for as long as majority control continues.

5. Within a stipulated time period (in Great Britain, five years), the active executive can ask the ceremonial head of state to order the dissolution of the elected legislative branch and bring about new elections. Since the timing for this is at the discretion of the active executive, a period when public-opinion polls show strong support for the party in power is most likely to be chosen.

6. The legislature can force the cabinet to resign by defeating it on important motions or by a formal vote of no-confidence. Under the British and other variations of the alternating-majority party situation, except at times of unusual national crisis, this almost never occurs. The last time that a cabinet was forced to resign in Great Britain, for example, for such a reason as this was in 1886. Such a development is frequent, however, under a fragmented-party system unless some unique convention of the constitution prevents the use of this power.[9]

THE BRITISH UNDIVIDED AUTHORITY SYSTEM AS A MODEL

It is difficult for Americans today to realize how very far behind Great Britain in both power and influence the United States was in the nineteenth century. British constitutional development was an unqualified success story in the organization of a modern democracy; American development was regarded as, at best, an interesting and unique experiment.

[9]During the period of the Third Republic in France, (1871–1940), the executive, i.e., the premier, technically possessed the constitutional right of asking the president to dissolve the legislative branch. In the late 1870s, however, such an action became associated with royalist efforts to overthrow the republic; thereafter no premier dared use this power. The result was to remove the most effective control the executive had over the legislative branch and to leave succeeding cabinets at the caprice of the shifting party coalitions. The result was 107 cabinets during the 65 years of the Third Republic's existence.

This was one of the basic reasons for the widespread imitation of the British parliamentary system elsewhere. It seemed to afford the perfect prototype for the other countries of Europe as they moved from monarchical absolutism and limited democracy to constitutional rule and mass participation in the political process. Certainly in part, at least, there was also an element of what has been termed "homeopathic or imitative magic" based on the "law of similarity" with its basic proposition "that like produces like, or that an effect resembles its cause."

If this proposition seems farfetched, recall that this is one of the basic psychological approaches in advertising. Although not explicitly stated, there is the clear inference that if you use a particular shaving lotion, your major problem will be fighting off beautiful women. Undoubtedly a major factor in the adoption of the British parliamentary system was the expectation that the adoption of the British structure and mechanics would somehow produce the same political prestige and material results.

For the European monarchies of the late nineteenth century, which were undergoing uneasy transition from absolutism to constitutional rule, British experience afforded reassuring guidelines as to the role of the monarchy under these new conditions, the organization of a legislative branch, and the function of political parties. The lessons were not always well understood or the knowledge creatively applied, but the British pattern afforded the only logical model, especially for such largely British-settled and culturally oriented new nations as Australia, Canada, and New Zealand, and for the British-trained new nation of India.

The reasons why India and other former British colonies adopted the parliamentary system were well summarized by an Indian constitutional scholar: (1) familiarity; (2) the ability of the parliamentary system to "provide effective leadership in emergencies"; (3) the insuring of "harmony between the Executive and the Legislature"; and (4) ". . . the American system gives more stability but less responsibility. . . . The daily assessment of responsibility, which is not available under the American system, was felt far more effective than the periodic assessment and far more necessary in a country like India."[10]

[10]R. N. Misra, *The President of the Indian Republic* (Bombay: Vora, 1965), p. 11. It is interesting that this Indian scholar is apparently thinking in terms of either the British alternating-majority system or the Indian smother-party system as it has operated for the first twenty years of independence. It is quite true that both these systems insure "harmony between the Executive and the Legislative." But as we are aware, under the conditions of a fragmented-party system the results can be anything else but that.

The ease with which the British parliamentary system could be adapted to local conditions was the main reason, however. The system worked equally well, in this respect at least, whether a reigning sovereign or an elected president, as in the case of India, provided the dignified part of the dual executive. In the older countries of the Commonwealth which still consider themselves kingdoms under the British crown—Canada, Australia, and New Zealand—a governor-general deputizes for the queen.

In many ways the spread of British parliamentary institutions was like the widening ripples from a stone tossed into a pool. The first imitators were the European neighbors and the self-governing colonies. In the period after World War II, as colonies emerged into independence and adopted the "modern" governmental forms of their former rulers, the circle of influence spread even wider. But the variations on the original British model were many and, in some cases, both in Europe and among the new nations, the traditions to make the parliamentary system workable were lacking. We now turn to a brief consideration of these.

THE DEPENDENT-VARIABLE ROLES OF THE PARLIAMENTARY SYSTEM

The type of party system involved is an influential factor in determining how a parliamentary structure will function, for it shapes the roles played by the prime minister and the cabinet on the one hand and the legislative branch on the other. In an alternating-majority party system, with the prime minister and the cabinet firmly in control of the majority in the legislature, the relative positions of the various elements in the governmental structure would look like the diagram.

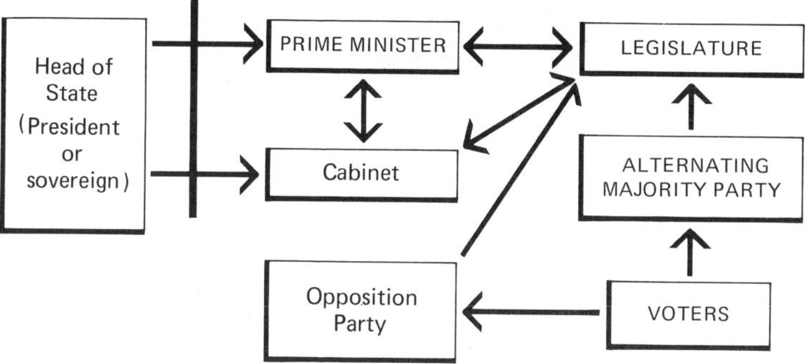

Note: The legislature is usually bicameral (two-house) with the executive branch responsible to the lower house alone.

Because under the alternating-majority system the head of state so rarely has any real option as to who the next prime minister will be, his appointment power has been shown with a solid line across the arrow. The relative position of the prime minister to his cabinet could vary, of course, according to the personalities involved. But given the high cohesion of a British-type party organization, the prime minister as the elected leader of his party always stands out above the members of his cabinet. Note that the arrows between prime minister and cabinet on the one hand and legislature on the other are all two-headed ones. Regardless of how high the degree of cohesion or how disciplined the party, its leaders, to remain leaders, must engage in a constant two-way exchange with the party's legislative representatives. However dominant or even at times arbitrary the leadership may be, failure to maintain communication either with the parliamentary majority or with interest groups and the voters at large is an invitation to political disaster. We can expand this from the alternating majority to all types of party leadership. Regardless of the amount of arbitrary power they may possess, no leaders can function for long in a communications vacuum.

Subject to these general conditions, the relationship of the different units of parliamentary organization under a fragmented-party system can also be diagrammed. Note the multiplicity of arrows both from voters to parties and from the parties to cabinet and legislature. Note also that there is only a broken line across the appointment arrow from head of state to premier and cabinet. As has happened on various occasions in the Netherlands, for example, it might well be that the head of state will exercise his constitutional prerogative of choosing among several party leaders in order to break a particularly difficult deadlock in negotiations among the parties.

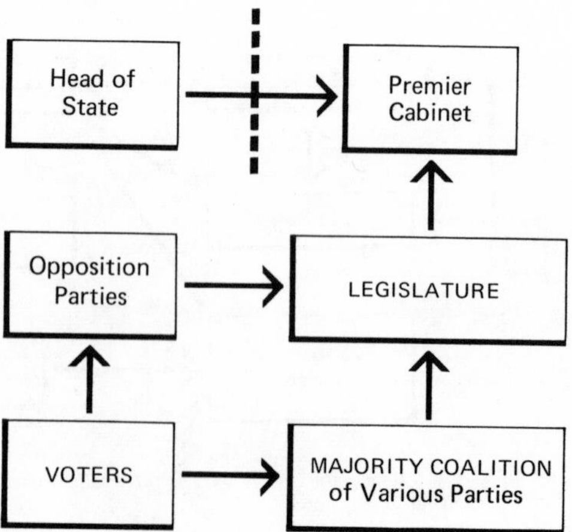

A fragmented-party system tends to make the premier or prime minister the persuader and reconciler of the varied viewpoints represented in his cabinet and among the often mutually suspicious members of the coalition which gives him his parliamentary majority. Regardless of his control over the legislative representatives of his own party, the leader of a fragmented-party coalition must negotiate with other party leaders as equals. In a political culture which regards them as competitors rather than ideological enemies, the aggregation of interests represented by the parties concerned can be combined into a hard-bargained but accepted program. Under these conditions a coalition cabinet is likely to enjoy the same degree of efficient functioning of the parliamentary system as would the cabinet of an alternating-majority party. Such fragmented-party countries as the Netherlands, Denmark, Switzerland, and Iceland are examples of this.

But with the same organizational structure present, the situation can be very different when the various fragmented parties regard each other not as mistaken but honorable political competitors but as ideological enemies intent on destroying their political opposition and leading the nation down a path of ruinous destruction. France, during the last hundred years, is the best (or worst) example of this. After the political and military debacle of 1870, repeated attempts were made under both the Third Republic (1871–1940) and the Fourth Republic (1946–1958) to establish a British-type parliamentary system. But the tragic inheritance of the unresolved and accumulated hatreds extending back to the revolution of 1789 produced a fragmented-party system bitterly divided not only among its major ideological currents but also within them. There was no French political culture as such. Instead there were a multiplicity of subcultures bitterly disagreeing not only on objectives but even on the fundamental rules of the game.

Under such conditions it proved impossible for parties to form long-enduring coalitions able to implement any program aggregating the interests of the coalition partners. Nor is it surprising that between 1875 and 1940 no less than 107 cabinets governed or attempted to govern the Third Republic. During the 12 years of its hectic existence the Fourth Republic saw 24 cabinets come and go.

French political history is perhaps the best illustration of the basically secondary role played by governmental structures in any political system. There need not exist one political culture with universally shared values. It is quite possible, as the Netherlands and other stable fragmented-party countries demonstrate, for a number of subcultures to exist, albeit in a state of aloofness and alert suspicion of one another. But, if the mechanics of the system are to function with any degree of reasonable efficiency, it is fundamental that the political parties accept the same rules of the game and, above all, regard opposition as normal and necessary rather than as a mortal threat.

One of the major reasons for the usual failure of efforts to transplant the parliamentary system to the new states of Asia and Africa is not so much inexperience in the mechanics of operating the system as the lack of any accepted tradition of political tolerance toward those who disagree with government policy. A case in point is the former British African colony of Lesotho (formerly Basutoland) which adopted the parliamentary system when it achieved independence in 1966 after having had two years experience in self-government and a theoretical knowledge of the British parliamentary system since becoming a British protectorate in 1867. But when in 1970 preliminary results of the first election since independence indicated a victory for the opposition, the ruling party declared a state of emergency and suspended the constitution on the not unusual grounds of alleged election frauds and the threat of communist subversion. As a result Lesotho joined that long list of countries where the parliamentary system has been rejected not because of inability to operate its mechanics but because the essential psychological and cultural framework was lacking.

It is important to note, however, that this lack of the proper framework applies only when the intent is truly to recreate the British model in spirit as well as in form. When there is either ignorance, indifference, or hostility to the spirit and intent of a parliamentary system, as understood in the British tradition, then the mechanics can be made to work very well. Indeed, under certain conditions, the machinery can be operated with a degree of efficiency which far surpasses that of the British prototype. Above all this is true of the way in which an order party in absolute control of every aspect of political activity can utilize the institutional arrangements of the parliamentary system to serve its own ideological goals. Let us turn then to an examination of the oldest and most successful example of this.

THE PARLIAMENTARY SYSTEM IN AN ORDER-PARTY FRAMEWORK

The Soviet system affords the best example of the way in which a parliamentary system operates under the total control of an order party. In reality, of course, under these conditions the theoretical constitutional relationships of premier, cabinets, and legislature are quite irrelevant. In theory, however, the supremacy of the legislative branch is spelled out even more explicitly than is the case for the British parliament. The 1936 Soviet constitution puts it bluntly, "The highest organ of state power in the U.S.S.R. is the Supreme Soviet of the U.S.S.R."

The official Soviet version of the parliamentary system looks like the diagram. The specific and sweeping authority of the Supreme Soviet is spelled out in a number of constitutional provisions. In relation to its role in the organization and control over the executive, here is the way a Soviet source describes it:

> The Council of Ministers of the U.S.S.R. is formed at a joint sitting of both Chambers of the Supreme Soviet of the U.S.S.R. At the first session of the Supreme Soviet held in March 1946, the Government of the Soviet Union was formed in the following way: J. V. Stalin, the head of the outgoing government, submitted a written statement to the Chairman of the joint sitting of the Chambers declaring that the Government "considers its duties at an end and surrenders its powers to the Supreme Soviet." This statement was read to the assembly by the Chairman. The floor was then taken by one of the Deputies who, amidst signs of general approval, said that the Supreme Soviet was unaminous in its complete confidence in the outgoing government. The Supreme Soviet accepted the Government's statement and unanimously commissioned J. V. Stalin to submit proposals for a new government. At the next joint sitting of the Chambers, the Chairman read the list of members of the new Government as proposed by J. V. Stalin. After statements by Deputies, the Chairman announced that no objection had been raised to any of the candidates for government office and that none of the Deputies insisted on a roll-call vote. The composition of the Council of Ministers of the U.S.S.R. as proposed by J. V. Stalin was then voted on as a whole and unanimously adopted. J. V. Stalin was elected Chairman of the Council of Ministers of the U.S.S.R.
>
> This illustrates the manner in which the Council of Ministers of the U.S.S.R. is formed. As we know already, individual ministers may be dismissed or appointed by the Presidium of the Supreme Soviet of the U.S.S.R.[11]

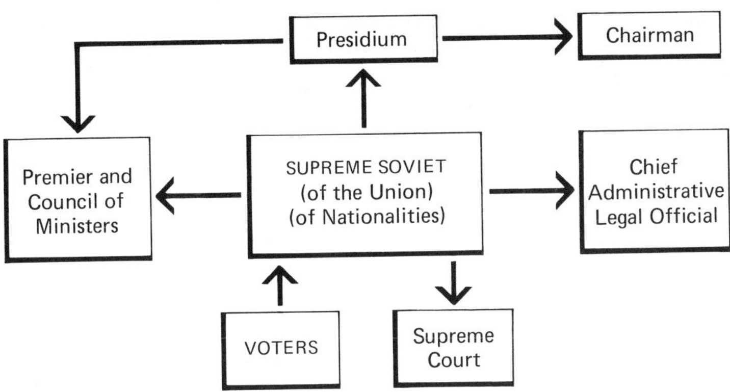

[11]A. L. Karpinsky, *How the Soviet Union Is Governed* (Moscow: Foreign Languages Press, 1954), pp. 52–53.

The theoretical doctrine of legislative supremacy is carried so far in the Soviet system that the appointment of the cabinet executive or any members is kept firmly in the hands of either the Supreme Soviet or the 33-member Presidium which exercises all of the Supreme Soviet's powers between its twice-annual meetings. The chairman of the Presidium, often referred to as the "president of the U.S.S.R.," comes the closest to being the equivalent of a reigning sovereign or a president under the usual Western-type functioning of the parliamentary system.

In terms of sheer output, the Supreme Soviet routinely compiles a record of impressive efficiency. In its four-week semiannual sessions, it not only accomplishes all of the legislative output over which the British Parliament or the U.S. Congress customarily struggle for so many weary weeks but also lays down comprehensive guidelines for social and economic policies which in the United States and Great Britain are the province of private business. And the same legislative efficiency is true of all the other order-party regimes which have adopted the Soviet model.

If we diagram the organization of the parliamentary system under order-party conditions, using the same format as for the alternating-majority and fragmented-party situations, the reason for this remarkable output efficiency become obvious.

The important conditioning factor is the party's total control of the whole political process. In each election district there is only one candidate who, three times out of four, is a party member. Any nonparty candidate has been carefully selected by the local party unit as a reward for loyalty and career achievement. Above the level of the Supreme Soviet all top government officials are 100 percent party members. Further the proposals which the Supreme Soviet approves with such dispatch have all previously been decided at the top level of party councils. Under these circumstances it is not surprising that in 1946, after almost 20 years of personal domination of the party machinery, Stalin was able to face his theoretically controlling legisla-

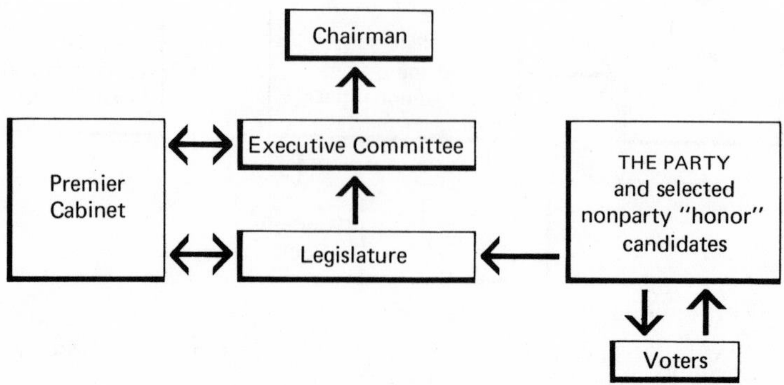

tive body with an equanimity which any government head outside an order-party regime could envy.

Government by Discussion

In this section we have surveyed the mechanics of the parliamentary system in both its actual and perverted forms. To whatever use it may be put, it is clear that institutionally the parliamentary system will continue as one of the two important modern types of governmental structure. Of the alternatives involved, Bagehot commented a century ago: "The practical choice of first-rate nations is between the Presidential Government and the Parliamentary; no State can be first-rate which has not a Government by discussion and those are the only two existing species of that Government."[12]

For Bagehot, government by discussion meant a functioning constitutional democracy. In his time, if a government described itself as parliamentary or presidential, it was safe to assume that this automatically implied government by discussion. But in the late twentieth century, quite the opposite is true. We have seen that the parliamentary system can operate in a variety of ways depending on the dominating factors of party systems and ideological intents and the same is true of the presidential system. But before we examine the variations on the original model, let us review briefly the characteristics of the American prototype.

AUTHORITY-SHARING OR THE AMERICAN PRESIDENTIAL SYSTEM

Just as the British parliamentary system is regarded as the prototype of a system of monopolized powers, the American presidential system has long been the model for institutional organizations based on the sharing or separation of powers. Yet one of the first objections raised against the constitution was that it failed to separate the various powers sufficiently.

In one of the *Federalist Papers,* James Madison, later fourth president of the United States, felt obliged to admit:

> One of the principal objections inculcated by the more respectable adversaries to the Constitution is its supposed violation of the political maxim that the legislative, executive and judicial departments ought to be separate and distinct. In the structure of the federal government, no regard, it is said, seems to have been paid to this essential precaution in favor of liberty.

Madison went on to comment:

[12]Walter Bagehot, *The English Constitution* (London: 1867), p. 311.

No political truth is certainly of greater intrinsic value, or is stamped with the authority of more enlightened patrons of liberty than that on which the objection is founded. The accumulation of all powers, legislative, executive and judiciary, in the same hands, whether of one, a few, or many, and whether hereditary, self-appointed, or elective, may justly be pronounced the very definition of tyranny. . . .

The oracle who is always consulted and cited on this subject is the celebrated Montesquieu. . . . Let us endeavor . . . to ascertain his meaning of this point.

The British Constitution was to Montesquieu what Homer has been to the didactic writers on epic poetry. As the latter have considered the works of the immortal bard as the perfect model . . . so this great political critic appears to have viewed the Constitution of England as the standard, or to use his own expression, as the mirror of political liberty; and to have delivered in the form of elementary truths, the several characteristic principles of that particular system.

With brilliant insight, Madison corrected Montesquieu by going on to point out:

On the slightest view of the British Constitution, we must perceive that the legislative, executive and judiciary departments are by no means totally separate and distinct from each other. The executive magistrate forms an integral part of the legislative authority. . . . One branch of the legislative department forms also a great constitutional council to the executive chief. . . . The judges, again, are so far connected with the legislative department as often to attend and participate in its deliberations, . . .

From these facts by which Montesquieu was guided, it may clearly be inferred that, in saying "There can be no liberty where the legislative and executive powers are united in the same person or body of magistrates" . . . he did not mean that these departments ought to have no *partial agency* in, or no *control* over, the acts of each other. His meaning . . . can amount to no more than this, that where the *whole* power of one department is exercised by the same hands which possess the *whole* power of another department, the fundamental principles of a free constitution are subverted.[13]

The view of the nature of the American institutional system held by its constitutional drafters was one based on a far more exact appreciation of the realities of British government in the eighteenth century than that held by either Montesquieu or Blackstone. It was this system which they sought to embody in the new constitution in terms of each department having a partial agency over the acts of the other two. This is why it seems more accurate to refer to the presidential system as based on the concept

[13]Alexander Hamilton, James Madison, and John Jay, *The Federalist*, ed. Paul Leicester Ford (New York: Holt, Rinehart & Winston, 1898), no. 47, pp. 319; 320–321; 321–322.

of the sharing or intermingling of authority rather than of separation.

Presidential System by Accident

There was no intent on the part of the founding fathers to create a presidential system. What they had in mind, rather, was an adaptation to American conditions of the British concept of legislative dominance. A seldom-mentioned but significant capsule illustration of this is that not only are the powers of the legislative branch dealt with in the first article of the Constitution, while the executive is relegated to second place, but they are detailed in more than twice the number of sections as is the executive. In *The Federalist* some 15 papers are devoted to discussing the legislative branch, whereas only seven are devoted to the executive. In terms of both the British constitutional heritage and the experiences of the prerevolutionary era, there was no desire to create a strong executive.

In a "comparison of the president with other executives as to powers," Hamilton with some satisfaction pointed out that the president's proposed control of the armed forces was not only less than that of the British king but of the governors of various states. Repeatedly in his discussion of the powers of the president, Hamilton emphasized how restricted they were. He noted, for example, "The President is to nominate and, *with the advice and consent of the Senate,* to appoint ambassadors and other public ministers." And contrasting the powers of the president with those of the king in control of legislation, he said that "the one would have a *qualified* negative upon the acts of the legislative body; the other has an *absolute* negative."

The original concept of the presidential system seems to have been as follows: Modeled directly on the idealized British pattern, there were to be three almost equal branches of government. Note that we said *almost equal,* for while the Congress was regulated by the judicial system and could momentarily be checked in its actions by the president's veto, its intended predominance in the system was obvious. The Senate, representing the "sovereign" states, on an equal basis was to be chosen by the state legislatures (and was until the Seventeenth Amendment in 1913), while the House was to represent the relative populations with its members elected on the same basis as state legislative representatives.

Again, modeled on the British pattern, each division of the legislature had power in its own right. The Senate could reject measures passed by the House and had the sole right to pass on important executive appointments and to ratify treaties. The House could reject Senate measures and had the sole power of initiating money bills, the life-blood of government. Together both divisions could repass a bill over the president's veto by a two-thirds majority. Except for limited powers to convene the legislative branch on extraordinary occasions and to adjourn its sessions when they were unable to agree on a time, the president was not to have any control remotely comparable to that of the British executive over the fate of the two houses. Instead each had its own separate and fixed terms of office, two for the House of Representatives and six for the Senate. The president was protected from the British necessity of insuring majority legislative support by having a fixed term of office for four years.

In his relations with Congress the president was *required* to provide it with information about "the state of the Union" at regular but undefined intervals and this almost immediately became the annual "State of the Union" message. He was permitted to *recommend* "to their consideration such measures as he shall judge necessary and expedient." But it was clearly intended that Congress was to be completely free to decide to accept or reject the recommendations. As Woodrow Wilson summarized it:

> The makers of the Constitution seem to have thought of the President as what the stricter Whig theorists wished the king to be: only the legal executive, the presiding and guiding authority in the application of law and the execution of policy. His veto upon legislation was his only "check" on Congress,—was a power to restraint, not of guidance. He was empowered to prevent bad laws, but he was not to be given an opportunity to make good ones.[14]

To use the title of Wilson's doctoral dissertation, the essence of the American system was clearly intended to be congressional government. Writing in the 1880s when the memory of the almost successful attempt to impeach President Johnson was still fresh and a series of weak presidents had abandoned national leadership to Congress, Wilson concluded: "Congress [is] the dominant, nay, the irresistible, power of the federal system, relegating some of the chief balances of the Constitution to an insignificant role in the 'literary theory' of our institutions." "Congress," he predicted, "is fast becoming the governing body of the nation."[15] But already in the nineteenth century two strong presidents, Jackson and Lincoln, had demonstrated, in Wilson's words, that for a strong leader the presidency "is anything he has the sagacity and force to make it." From the time of Andrew Jackson's administration (1829–1837), it was clear that the presidency could not occupy the num-

[14]Woodrow Wilson, *Constitutional Government in the United States* (New York: Columbia University Press, 1908), pp. 59–60.

[15]Woodrow Wilson, *Congressional Government* (New York: Meridian Books, 1956), p. 23.

ber two place in the American system and that inevitably it would come to dominate both the legislative and the judicial branches.

Characteristics of the American Presidential System

The modern American presidential system is shown in the diagram. The complexity of the arrows between the different branches of the American structural arrangement is an indication of the high degree of shared authority characteristic of the system.

In the same way that we summarized the characteristics of the British undivided authority system, we can note these important aspects of the American presidential system:

1. The authority reserve is shared. The first three articles of the Constitution carefully allocated the degree of participation. But, as in the case of the prime minister, authority in the twentieth century has moved more and more to the executive branch.
2. The president is both chief of state ("dignified") and head of government ("efficient").
3. He has independent tenure of office from the legislative branch but technically, though with great difficulty, could be removed by it.
4. The president seldom is the leader of his party in the way the prime minister in an alternating-majority system is. Even when he is, his leadership is likely to be both uncertain and short-lived.
5. Because of the independent terms of office, even the most powerful of presidents at his peak has scant ability to threaten the careers of his most persistent

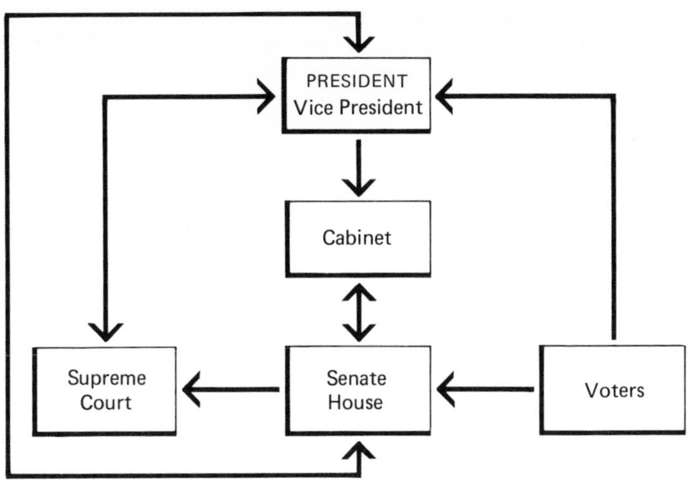

legislative opponents. Attempts to do so are highly likely to rally local support behind them.

6. Control over appropriations, the power of investigation and hearings, as in the case of the Senate Foreign Relations Committee on Vietnam and Laos, and refusal to approve the president's executive or Supreme Court appointments represent the major control levers available to the legislative branch.

The Potential of the Presidency

For an eloquent summary of the president's role let us turn once again to Wilson. Viewing the potential of the presidency in the light of Theodore Roosevelt's dynamic administration (1901–1909), some five years before his own career as the second in the long line of strong twentieth-century presidents, Wilson concluded about the modern president that:

> He cannot escape being the leader of his party except by incapacity and lack of personal force, because he is at once the choice of the party and of the nation.
>
> He can dominate his party by being spokesman for the real sentiment and purpose of the country, by giving direction to opinion, by giving the country at once the information and the statements of policy which will enable it to form its judgments alike of parties and of men.
>
> His is the only national voice in affairs. Let him once win the admiration and confidence of the country, and no other single force can withstand him, no combination of forces will easily overpower him. His position takes the imagination of the country. He is the representative of no constituency, but of the whole people.
>
> He may be both the leader of his party and the leader of the nation, or he may be one or the other. If he leads the nation, his party can hardly resist him. His office is anything he has the sagacity and force to make it. . . . The President is at liberty, both in law and conscience, to be as big a man as he can.
>
> His is the vital place of action in the system whether he accepts it as such or not, and the office is the measure of the man,—of his wisdom as well as of his force.[16]

The validity of Wilson's evaluation of the presidency as "the vital place of action in the system" was demonstrated by Franklin Roosevelt, Truman, Kennedy, Johnson, and Nixon, who has stated as his philosophy that "the days of a passive Presidency . . . belonged to a simpler past. . . . He must articulate the nation's values, define its goals and marshal its will." Indeed, the twentieth century has not only intensified all of the latent pressures for the dominance of the presidency but added some new ones, again because of the influence of technology on political developments.

[16]Wilson, *Constitutional Government*, pp. 67–73.

The same forces have transformed nineteenth century British cabinet government, as Bagehot described it, into what some students have termed a "quasi-presidential" system with the prime minister as the dominant power element. No prime minister, in theory, has the fixed tenure in office assured to a president. But in actuality this is really not very important. Under an alternating-majority system, as long as he maintains effective control of his party, a prime minister has virtually presidential security in office plus an effective control of the legislative branch that even the most popular presidents in the twentieth century have enjoyed only briefly, except in periods of war and national emergency.

Despite the fact that the American presidency has served as the broad prototype for the organization of nonparliamentary regimes, it still remains a unique product of a purely American political culture. With the possible exception of the Philippines, no other so-called presidential system follows the American pattern. An all-too-large number of so-called presidential regimes are merely the facade behind which a charismatic leader, a solidarity party, an oligarchic clique, or a military junta manipulates the levers of power. But, in the form of the Fifth Republic in France, a new and genuine type of presidential regime has been in existence since 1958 with no indication that it will soon end. To express the difference between the presidency of the Fifth Republic and that of the United States, French political scientists have coined the term *presidentialist.* It is under this heading that we examine the unique blending of an active parliamentary system with a strong president that is the contribution of the Fifth Republic to the standard alternatives for governmental organization.

THE FIFTH REPUBLIC AS PRESIDENTIALIST PROTOTYPE

The Fifth Republic was born in 1958 when France was faced with the very real possibility of both civil war and a military seizure of power. Aside from the five years of the dictatorial puppet regime of the Nazi occupation period of World War II, France had known more than 80 years of governmental instability. The constitutional structure of the Fifth Republic was designed to retain the parliamentary system but to avoid the chronic state of actual or threatening political crisis created by the antagonisms of the fragmented-party system. The solution was the creation of a president who not only performed the customary innocuous functions of a parliamentary "dignified" executive but, when emergency situations warranted, could exercise powers making him virtually a constitutional dictator.

So dominant in the shaping and application of this new

concept of the presidency was the Fifth Republic's first president (1958–1969) that it has been customary to refer to the regime as the de Gaulle Republic. Speaking of the Fifth Republic's constitution, one student of French government commented, "In a sense, the document was partially tailored to de Gaulle himself, and during his tenure as president he used it as an instrument rather than as a framework within which he had to act."[17]

Most of the presidential powers in the Fifth Republic are little different from those possessed by any parliamentary chief of state. The major difference in their exercise was the dominating influence exerted by de Gaulle's personality. However, the special powers granted to the president of the Fifth Republic are unique. With the safeguards intended to prevent their arbitrary use, they are as follows:

1. The president on his own authority may dissolve the National Assembly and thus force new elections; but he cannot do this more than once within any twelve-month period and thus use his power to rid himself immediately of a hostile majority;

2. The president may refer government bills to the voters at large for approval in a general referendum instead of risking their defeat by a hostile legislature; but this procedure is intended to apply only to draft legislation dealing with the organization of public powers or relations between France and members of the French community. Further, such a referendum is supposed to be proclaimed by the president only when the premier and the cabinet request it;

3. Article 16 provides that "in a situation where there is an immediate and serious threat to Republican institutions, national independence, territorial integrity, or the application of international agreements, and in which the regular functioning of the constitutional public authorities is interrupted," the president, after consultation with various other ranking officials, is authorized to assume sweeping emergency powers; but, "These measures, on which the Constitutional Council is consulted, must be inspired by the will to enable the constitutional public authorities to fulfill their mission with the minimum of delay.

Parliament meets as of right. The National Assembly cannot be dissolved during the period of the exercise of powers."[18]

In 1961 the threat of right-wing terrorist activity in what was then still French Algeria led de Gaulle to invoke these emergency powers. Characteristically he apparently

[17]Stanley Rothman, *European Society and Politics* (New York: Bobbs-Merrill, 1970), p. 509.

[18]*Ibid.*, pp. 510–512.

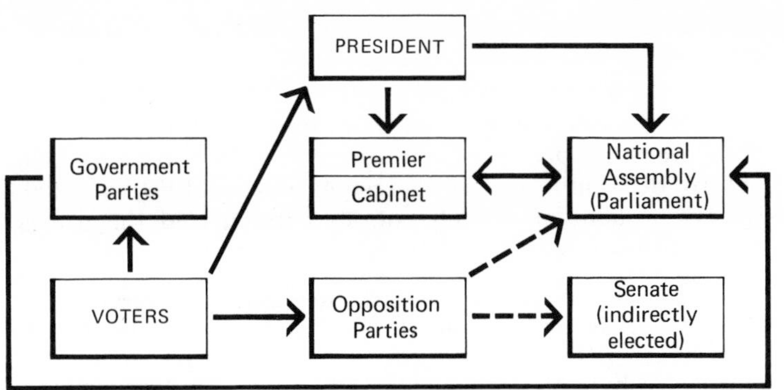

interpreted them in his own sweeping fashion and thus created precedents which some Frenchmen feared could be used to establish authoritarian rule under the guise of presidential emergency powers.

Though modifications may come in either style or constitutional amendment under Pompidou, elected as de Gaulle's successor for a full regular seven-year term in 1969, the constitutional structure of the Fifth Republic under de Gaulle was as appears in the diagram.

Until 1962 the president was elected indirectly through an electoral college composed in part by members of the National Assembly. In that year de Gaulle pushed through an amendment for direct election by the voters at large in order to strengthen presidential claims to speak for the nation at large. Under the Fifth Republic, while basic hostilities among political groups have certainly not diminished, the dominance achieved by the pro-government parties has prevented, at least so far, the political chaos of the fragmented-party systems of the Third and Fourth Republic. In 1968, for example, when the last elections were held for the new five-year parliamentary terms, the de Gaullist-oriented Democratic Union for the Republic won 292 of the 487 seats at stake while its Independent Republican allies won 61 seats, giving the government coalition an absolute majority. This compares with the 34 seats won by the Communist party and the 100 seats achieved by the splintered socialist movement and the democratic left.

But in addition to de Gaulle's appeal and the impotence of the opposition, a number of constitutional safeguards exist to prevent the political chaos of the last century. Unlike routine parliamentary procedure, a premier nominated by the president does not have to receive approval from the National Assembly. Since the inauguration of the Fifth Republic some premiers have and some have not taken advantage of this option. A second provision requires that an absolute majority be present to put a cabinet out of office. Other powers also strengthen the control of the premier over the legislature to an extent unprecedented in French political history.

For the reasons given above, the Fifth Republic continues to offer an interesting third possibility to the "pure" parliamentary or presidential alternatives. Writing two years before de Gaulle's abrupt resignation in 1969, an acute British student of French politics summarized the present and future possibilities:

> For a time, therefore, the Fifth Republic may survive in its present uneasy equilibrium. It is certainly no dictatorship, for Frenchmen enjoy freedom of speech and association and, having freely elected the Gaullists to power, still have regular opportunities to turn them out. It is not a government of separated powers like the United States, for France is a centralized country with no supreme court, where the Assembly is dominated by the cabinet and can be dissolved by the President. Yet neither is the government controlled, as in Britain, by the chosen leadership of the majority party. After de Gaulle the regime might evolve in the British direction, but even so it would remain something of an anomaly among the great democracies. For in that company France would still be the country in which the political executive, and the administrative technocracy behind it, have most autonomy in making decisions; and in which popular criticism, though not inaudible, finds expression least effectively through the nation's representative institutions. In the long run it will not be easy to reconcile this state of affairs with the historical traditions or current expectations of the French people.[19]

AFRICAN PRESIDENTIALIST SYSTEMS

The presidentialist system of the Fifth Republic has served as a model in the organization of the governmental systems of the former French African colonies. Not only was the French system the best known and most available for imitation, but the presidentialist concept has fitted well into the political culture of these new nations. In almost every case before independence in the early 1960s, there existed a solidarity type of movement-regime party headed by a charismatic leader. Under these conditions the presidentialist system offered the logical and easy pattern for constitutionally vesting both the solidarity party and its leader with the supreme authority which in actuality they already possessed. The presidentialist system made it possible to do this without resort to extralegal seizures of power or the need to flout world opinion by suspending any of the expected guarantees of citizens' rights or privileges.

Just as Guinea can serve as an example of a would-be

[19]Philip M. Williams, *The French Parliament* (New York: Praeger, 1968), p. 124.

order type of movement regime, the Ivory Coast and Senegal are good illustrations of the African presidentialist type. Although in both states the movement-regime solidarity parties monopolize the legislatures (Democratic party of the Ivory Coast and the Sengalese Progressive Union), the strong concentration of power in the executive branch would go far to insure a presidentialist system even if there were diversity of party representation. In both states the president is directly elected and is eligible for indefinite reelection. In both cases he appoints the ministers who are responsible only to him, not to the legislature. Constitutionally each president is "head of the administration and the armed forces" and can submit bills, following the French pattern, for approval by popular referendum. Following this popular approval, the president can then promulgate the new law within fifteen days without any need for action by any other governmental authority. In other former French colonial territories such as Chad, Gabon, Niger, and Upper Volta, similar constitutional provisions create the same type of presidentialist systems.

LATIN AMERICAN PRESIDENTIALIST SYSTEMS

For a much longer time than in Africa, presidentialist versions of the authority structure have functioned in Latin America. The difference between constitutional definitions and the actual power realities are demonstrated by an incident cited by Professor Harry Kantor, in a well-known text on Latin American politics. Kantor quotes a nineteenth-century Bolivian president-dictator who, standing before his thoroughly cowed congress and pointing respectively to his left and right pockets, is supposed to have said: "I want the gentleman who has just spoken and all the honorable deputies gathered here to know that I have put the Constitution of 1861, which was very good, in this pocket and that of 1868, which is even better in the opinion of these gentlemen, in this one and that nobody is going to rule Bolivia but me."[20] Kantor commented, "This may or may not be an apocryphal story, but that was indeed the way the governments of Bolivia treated its constitutions until 1952." The same was true, of course, of virtually all the other Latin American governments before 1952 and a substantial number of them since the Bolivian democratic revolution of 1952.

Characteristic of Latin American governmental organization since the declarations of independence against Spanish rule in the early nineteenth century has been a presidency

[20]*Patterns of Politics and Political Systems in Latin America* (Chicago: Rand-McNally, 1969), p. 520.

much stronger than the American version which allegedly furnished the prototype. In constitution after constitution, although lip service may be paid to the concept of shared authority, even the most liberal of chief executives has available to him strong emergency or "state of seige" powers to which he can turn when he considers that circumstances warrant. Typical of such powers is Article 29 of the Mexican constitution which provides:

> In cases of invasion, grave disturbance of the public peace, or any other emergency which may place society in grave danger or conflict, the President of the Republic of Mexico, and no one else, with the concurrence of the council of ministers and with the approval of Congress . . . shall have power to suspend throughout the entire Republic or in any part thereof, such guarantees as may be a hindrance in meeting the situation promptly and readily.

For any strong leader in control of the dominant smother party, this is, and has been, an open invitation to constitutionally authorized dictatorship.

But even where no such sweeping powers are constitutionally available, political realities over the decades have made a mockery of the theoretical restrictions on the Latin American executive. Oligarchic rule such as existed in Bolivia until 1952, the appeal of the leader, the ambitions of power-hungry generals, and, in recent years in some countries at least, the social concerns of the new military juntas, plus the political and social instability in general—all these elements have contributed to the reality of the presidentialist rather than presidential regimes of Latin America. There are few more graphic illustrations of the way in which the political culture of a society shapes the actual functioning of its governmental institutions, regardless of idealistic hopes or constitutional theory.

CONCLUSION

In this chapter we have tried to point out what a truly dependent variable any institutional structure actually is. The most significant aspect of this is the way in which political cultures and party systems mold institutional arrangements to express their needs. In long-range terms, the most important and striking development has been the changing power relationships between executive and legislative branches during the course of the twentieth century. A century ago Bagehot referred to the British cabinet as "a committee of the legislative body." Less than two decades later Woodrow Wilson thought it proper to write of congressional rather than presidential government. Now the central and dominating roles in both the American and the British systems are played by president and prime minister. Clearly something of vital significance has happened to executive-legislative relationships since either Bagehot or Wilson wrote.

EXECUTIVE-LEGISLATIVE SYMBIOSIS IN THE TWENTIETH CENTURY

The functions of the executive and legislative branches of government are customarily treated separately owing to the long-established assumption that there is an obvious and clear-cut distinction in their roles.

But in the twentieth century, both in systems of undivided authority and in systems of shared authority, there has developed between legislatures and executives an increasing symbiosis. It is no longer possible to make any sharp distinction between the activities of the legislative and executive branches of government. For that matter, even at the heights of nineteenth-century legislative supremacy, the distinction was never as clear-cut as theory alleged. If by law-making is meant the creation of official policy guidelines for future government action, then both courts and executive have long been involved in the process. Notable in this respect, for example, is the dominant role played by the U.S. Supreme Court in the development of an expansion of the application of civil rights legislation. But the complexity and the rapidly shifting character of the issues with which legislation must be concerned has led increasingly to the passage of broad enabling acts which provide the extensive constitutional framework within which the executive can take such action as seems necessary. Regardless of constitutional structure, the initiative in executive-legislative relations has passed inevitably, and permanently one would think, to the executive.

In this chapter we shall speculate a little as to why this instance of the crucial, indeed decisive, impact of technological development on political evolution has taken place.

LEGISLATURES: STRUCTURAL ORGANIZATION

The accident of historical development led to the emergence of the British Parliament as a bicameral (two-chamber) legislature. At a time when the aristocracy and the middle class were contenders for political power, it seemed to offer an equitable means for balancing them off against each other in both political and constitutional terms. For the American founding fathers, the concept of a bicameral legislature was not only familiar but necessary in order to provide both population and state representation within the framework of the federal system. In the nineteenth century, as constitutional governments developed, the bicameral system offered an ideal pattern either for the organization of federal systems or for finding governmental roles for both aristocracy and popular elements in the political community.

In the British pattern primacy was conceded to the lower house. But as the strength of popular democracy increased, the upper house played an increasingly vital role as a brake on too-hasty action. Indeed, the Conservative-dominated House of Lords played this role so effectively that a Liberal cabinet in 1911 and a Labor government in 1949 passed legislation substantially reducing the Lord's power to delay the passage of legislation. Today, for example, the House of Lords can delay the passage of ordinary legislation for up to twelve months, but it has no control over financial legislation.

The 950 members of the House of Lords are composed mostly of the approximately 820 hereditary peers and, since 1958, lifetime peers, plus the long-standing categories of the Scottish and Irish representative peers, the nine lifetime law lords who serve as the highest court of appeal and, the last remnant of the second of the medieval estates, three bishops and two archbishops. The purpose of the life peerage act was to make possible the appointment of distinguished authorities who could offer expert advice and guidance on important national problems. Under its provisions ten men and four women, although hereditary peeresses are ineligible, have been appointed to the Lords.

The political impotence of the Lords has long been a fact of British political life. No peer has been prime minister since 1902, and it is actually necessary to resign a title to become prime minister. So low is the political significance of the House of Lords that Winston Churchill, greatest of twentieth-century political leaders, preferred a simple knighthood and a continuing seat in the Commons to the high title a grateful nation was ready to give him for his wartime leadership. Many a promising career has been cut short when a member of the Commons has unhappily found himself suddenly elevated to the Lords by his father's death.

What purpose then does the House of Lords serve? Surprisingly, it is still a very useful one. For one thing, it provides an important link between past and present which has enabled Great Britain to achieve such a remarkable pattern of political evolution. The existence of the peerage, furthermore, offers a very tangible way to honor distinguished individuals who have contributed to the development or glory of their country. The Italian senate before the fascist period between the two world wars was organized in conscious imitation of the British House of Lords for this very reason, as is the Irish senate still. Both the Canadian and Indian upper houses provide for the equivalent of the lifetime peers, and the Indian constitution authorizes the president to appoint twelve members "having special knowledge or practical experience in respect of such matters as the following namely: Literature, science, art and social service."

Unhampered by the workload of the Commons, with only about 10 percent of its membership regularly in attendance, the Lords continue to serve as a highly useful national discussion forum to educate the nation on issues of vital public policy. The sweeping reforms in British laws regulating homosexuality, for example, occurred in the late 1960s largely as a result of the extended and searching discussion of the problem by the House of Lords. In varying degrees, most other upper houses serve much the same function.

In the United States and Australia the upper houses are unique in having powers virtually equal to the lower houses, although no upper house in the world enjoys as much power and prestige as the U.S. Senate. It is not without significance that the three most recent presidents all served as senators, although only one, John F. Kennedy, went directly from the Senate to the presidency. In contrast, the last state governor (the usual stepping-stone to the presidency in the late nineteenth and early twentieth centuries) to become president was Franklin Roosevelt, who had attained national prominence as governor of New York.

The size of the Senate's membership, the factor of direct election, and the extensive political power possessed by a long-established committee chairman like Senator Fulbright of Arkansas (Foreign Affairs) or Senator Stennis of Mississippi (Armed Services) are all factors adding to the prestige of the upper house. There is also the fact that in the U.S., as in other federal systems, the members of the upper house represent their states, which play so important a role in the federal system, and they are, in a sense, ambassadors to Washington for their particular geographical areas. But conflicts here have seldom been in terms of big state versus small state, the idea of which so disturbed the constitutional convention. Rather, they have been regional conflicts, the most serious of which culminated in the tragedy of the Civil War.

Bicameral legislatures, however weak the upper house,

are characteristic of those governmental structures which were organized prior to World War II. Very few have the prestige factor of direct election enjoyed by the American Senate. Upper houses are often indirectly elected, as is the senate of the Fifth Republic, or appointed by their state governments, like the members of the upper house (Bundesrat) of the Bonn Republic. Perhaps the ultimate in impotence as a source of authority is represented by the Ethiopian upper house, all of whose members are personally appointed by the emperor. However, it is worth noting that the same technique of executive appointment is found in such well-established constitutional democracies as Canada and Luxembourg. As in the U.S., where there is a genuine federal system with a considerable degree of state or regional autonomy, the upper house usually commands a comparable degree of prestige and influence.

Even in the Soviet Union, where the official structure is a very dependent variable, and where the governmental system is the prototype for unicameral assembly rule, it is a significant indication of the importance of regional feelings as a political factor that the Soviet of Nationalities, both in terms of authority and size, is given equal weight with what, in any other governmental system, would be referred to as the "popular" chamber, i.e., the Soviet of the People.

Since World War II, except for new nations like India or Nigeria which are organized on a federal basis, the trend has been for the establishment of unicameral legislative bodies, whether the system has a separate executive or is organized as a variation of the parliamentary type. All of the communist regimes, for example, including China, have unicameral legislatures as do most of the new states in Asia and Africa. Additionally, so do a number of Latin American States, plus Cyprus, Denmark, Finland, Israel, Lebanon, New Zealand, and, after a fashion, Norway.[1]

It is probable that the peak period of bicameral legislative bodies is past. There is the obvious argument of their powerlessness and the emphasis, in terms of people power, on locating all authority in the popularly elected house. For the overstrained budgets of many of the new nations, there is also the not unimportant factor of the considerable and possibly unnecessary cost of an upper house. But there is one further point in the realm of political psychology which is of more than minor importance. The new nations feel an intense need to build loyalty to an overall concept rather

[1]Under the 1814 constitution, Norway elects a unicameral legislature (the Storthing) which then nominates 25 percent of its membership to constitute a second house (the Lagthing) while the remaining original membership constitutes the Odelsthing. The Lagthing has the power to reject twice any bills passed by the Odelsthing. But the whole Storthing in a common sitting of its two component parts can then enact the legislation by a two-thirds majority.

than to cling to old regional and tribal loyalties. In a number of new nations it would be logical to provide for regional representation in a second legislative house. But their governments have opted against such an arrangement fearing that regional represenation would keep the old divisions alive. Instead, emphasis has been laid on a unitary legislative chamber with members elected in proportion to total population without any relation to regional or tribal groupings. These governments lack the efficient mechanism of an order party such as the Soviet regime possesses and dare not take the chance of offering any encouragement to continued divisiveness. This is unfortunate for several of these countries, like Congo Kinshasa (the former Belgian Congo) and the Republic of Indonesia, theoretically offer an ideal pattern for a federal system of organization.

REPRESENTATION BASIS

Since the eighteenth century the basis for representation has routinely been a geographical one, whether in terms of one or more representatives from a particular area. In societies with simply structured economic and social patterns this worked well enough. But increasingly in the twentieth century, as technological development produced complex and diverse occupational interests, there have been efforts to try to insure that these interests were represented as corporate entities in the legislative process. This effort to reformulate the status representation of the medieval period in modern guise has produced some interesting results. One of the earliest occurred in fascist Italy with the creation in 1930 of a National Council of Corporations. Twenty-two elaborately organized categories were set up to provide, theoretically at least, both political and economic represenation for both trade unions and industrial associations. This council existed simultaneously with the traditional chamber of deputies until 1939. In that year the chamber of deputies was abolished and the council was transformed into the Chamber of Fasces and Corporations, which theoretically became the representative body for the fascist state. But during the brief remaining years of the fascist regime (1939–1943) it continued to be as powerless as the old chamber, while all real power was exercised by the Fascist party headed by its Duce, Benito Mussolini.

In obvious imitation of the Italian regime, the semifascist Franco government adopted a new Spanish constitution in 1945 which provided for a substantial number of the members of the powerless legislative body (the Cortes) to be elected by various professional, trade, and business associations. Since World War II, the constitutions in Italy and France have provided for the existence of "economic and labor" or "economic and social" councils. But all these bodies have had only consultative powers, with the initiative for consultation on the side of the government. According to one Italian authority on representation, by the late 1960s, the Italian experiment could be said to have "definitely failed" although it was "relatively successful in France and in some smaller countries."[2]

The most interesting, and apparently most successful, experiment in occupational representation has been in Yugoslavia since the adoption of a new constitution in 1963. The federal assembly is composed of six legislative chambers including the federal chamber, based on a proportional population basis, the chamber of nationalities, and four functional chambers elected to give special interest and occupational representation. These chambers are: the economic; the educational and cultural; social-welfare and health; and organizational-political. Eligibility for election to this last chamber is possessed by "every member of an organ or management or a working organization or working community and every official of a social-political organization or association whose activities concern matters in the field of the social-political system."[3]

The 120 members of each of the chambers, with the exception of the federal chamber, are elected by majority vote in their respective local communal assemblies—"the basic social-political community." Members of the dominant federal chamber must be elected not only in the communal assemblies but also by "a majority vote of all the voters in the constituency." The election and removal of the president, other members of the federal executive council, judges, and other high officials is the prerogative of the federal chamber. Also reserved to its jurisdiction is the control of foreign affairs, national defense, and "affairs of general internal policy."

Though its structure is cumbersome, the Yugoslav sextuple legislative experiment apparently has not worked too badly, despite some difficulty in defining the jurisdictional areas of the various chambers. An influential element in making the system work has clearly been the guiding role of the League of Communists, Yugoslavia's variation of the order party. As we noted previously, when discussing the contrast between the apparent impressive efficiency of the assembly system under Soviet conditions and its dismal record in the political chaos of the Fourth Republic, it is the element of party which becomes the decisive factor in the success or failure of the functioning of any governmen-

[2]Giovanni Sartori, "Representative Systems," Part 2 of "Representation," *International Encyclopedia of the Social Sciences*, 13: 471.

[3]Amos J. Peaslee, *Constitutions of Nations* (rev. 3rd ed.), "Yugoslavia," art. 108, p. 1284.

tal structure, other than possibly in the judicial area, although here, too, the factor of party policy and ideology could play an important role.

PARTY INFLUENCE ON LEGISLATIVE ORGANIZATION

In the organization of any legislative branch of government, it is the factor of party, whether in a positive or a negative sense, which provides the frame of reference and the catalyst which makes possible its functioning. It is no exaggeration to say that the nature of the party defines the role of the Speaker of the House, in both the U.S. and Britain.

The British Speaker elected by the party in the majority at the time the vacancy occurs, serves for life with the opposition usually not contesting the Speaker's seat at any general election. Once elected, the British Speaker severs all party ties and presides over the delibrations of the House of Commons with majestic impartiality. So far is this carried that, on those very rare occasions when the Speaker must vote to break a tie, it has long been the custom that he will not vote to change the existing state of affairs, whether this benefits or frustrates his former party. One of the few resemblances between the role of the British Speaker and of the American vice-president, as presiding officers, is that neither ever participates in debate.

In contrast to the British Speaker's impartiality between the political parties is the intensely partisan position which the American Speaker is expected to take. He serves as the leader of the majority party in the House, but only for as long as his party commands a majority of the votes in the House. His task is to provide leadership for his party in the House to see that its program is enacted into law. This role obviously is of paramount importance when the White House is occupied by a representative of the Speaker's party. Until 1910 the American Speaker functioned as a virtually absolute ruler; but after the restrictions which a progressive coalition placed on the powers of "Czar Cannon" in that year, power has been centered in a fluctuating balance, largely dependent on the personalities of the Speaker, the Rules Committee, powerful committee chairmen, and the leaders of the majority party.

An often overlooked but a significant indication of the role of party is the fact that the modern status of the British Speaker did not emerge until the mid-eighteenth century when, in fact if not in constitutional theory, the roles of both party and the cabinet, headed by the prime minister, were becoming clearly defined. With members of the executive branch actively participating in the management and guidance of the House of Commons, there was increasingly less need for the Speaker to assume a partisan role and a continuing need for him to serve as the arbiter and expediter of proceedings. To do this he had to become the final authority on all matters of parliamentary procedure. Since the eighteenth century it has fallen to the Speaker to make parliamentary law by his interpretations in the same way that a judge makes law by his interpretations of existing statutes. But all this is possible because of the unique role which the British alternating-majority party system plays in the functioning of an institutional structure based on undivided authority.

As in America and Britain, any legislative body must be headed by a leader, although his power and prestige vary widely. Under a fragmented-party system like that of France during the Third and Fourth Republics, the president of the chamber of deputies possesses neither the judicial prestige of the British Speaker nor the political power as leader of the majority of his American counterpart. Often he is little more than a gavel-banger over the verbal and often physical turmoil raging beneath his dais.

In the general organization of the British and the American legislative bodies, as well as in the speakership, there is a similarity in titles and a difference in powers. Both legislative bodies possess majority and minority leaders, chief whips, and assistant whips. In Great Britain, of course, the majority leader is the prime minister, who sits on the front bench of the majority side of the Commons flanked by the other leading ministers of the government. Across the narrow gangway from him sits the leader of Her Majesty's Loyal Opposition flanked by the members of the shadow cabinet, those leaders of the minority party who, at the next election victory, will become ministers in the new cabinet. It is the job of the chief whip and the assistant whips to keep the members of their parties informed of upcoming business and to make sure, with varying degrees of emphasis, that they are present to vote on important measures.[4]

Unique to British practice is the payment of a salary to the leader of the opposition. The majority whips also receive salaries. The chief government whip is appointed as parliamentary secretary to the treasury and he and his opposite number across the aisle are influential figures in their parliamentary groups. It is they who serve as the chief channels of communication between the party leader-

[4]The term *whip* provides a capsule sociological analysis of the composition of the uncommon Commons in the eighteenth century. The gentry who sat in the Commons were much addicted to fox-hunting. An important role in the organization of a hunt was played by the chief whipper-in whose job it was to keep the hunting pack under control by a mixture of threat and cajolery in the same fashion that the party whip did in the Commons.

ship and the rank-and-file members. In this role they are in an excellent position to influence the party leadership and the careers of the average party representatives. Between them the government and the opposition chief whips decide the agenda for the parliamentary week, even to the amount of time to be allowed for debate on each topic. The American counterparts receive neither salaries for the work they do, nor in terms of the much weaker discipline of American parties are they in a position to exert the same degree of control. The difference in the authority exerted by British and American whips is illustrated by the fact that a British MP never votes with the opposite party while an American congressman may frequently do so without any party discipline being imposed on him.

The British Parliament is unique in the organization of its legislative committees. Most legislatures organize their committees on a particularized basis. Committees deal only with special subject matter, such as appropriations, armed services, foreign affairs, public works, agriculture, and so on. The chairmen and senior members of these committees come to be experts in their particular fields, and often wield more political influence over the activities of the executive departments with which their committees are concerned than do the cabinet officers who head them. In the U.S. Congress, for example, the chairman of an important committee may see five or six secretaries of his particular department come and go. Whenever there is lack of executive (which means party) control over the legislative branch, committee chairmen will play the powerful roles they do in the American system or did in the Third and Fourth Republic of France.

But neither in the roles played by the committee chairmen nor in the organization of the committees themselves is any of this true of the British legislative committee system. The standing committees of the Commons have the nomenclatures A through D, and regulations allow an E committee if needed. Between 20 and 50 members serve on each of these committees, with another 20 to 30 added temporarily depending on the draft legislation the committee is considering. The British committees have no subject specialization. A committee might, for example, turn from consideration of a bill to revise marriage laws to a measure concerned with agricultural subsidies. In addition to the standing committees there is also the Scottish committee composed of all 70-odd representatives from Scotland which considers all legislation relating to Scottish affairs.

In the Fifth Republic of France, the old specialized standing committees have been abolished and instead both assembly and senate are restricted to six large standing committees without area specialization. The constitutional dominance of the presidency and the political dominance of the Union for the New Republic (UNR) have served to put committees in a very secondary role indeed. In contrast the 19 specialized committees of the German Bundestag, corresponding to the important ministries of the government, seem to have acquired growing power in the consideration and control of legislation.

WHAT LEGISLATURES DO

In the early 1950s the clerk of the House of Commons estimated that the House spent its time approximately as follows: 50 percent on the passage of legislation, 10 percent on appropriations, and 40 percent on policy formulation and control. This division is probably about the same for any actually functioning legislative branch which is not simply an official rubber stamp for order-party or solidarity-party dictates.

The way in which legislatures are able to help formulate and control policy varies widely. While the type of party system plays an important role, the form of control is shaped by the differing organizational structure between parliamentary regimes with their undivided powers and presidential regimes based on shared powers.

POLICY FORMULATION AND CONTROL

Under the parliamentary system the legislature can have, quite literally, a face-to-face contact with the policy-makers of the executive branch. It has long been established procedure in the House of Commons, for example, that for four out of five days a week, the daily session is opened by the ministers on the front bench answering orally various questions which have been put to them. Usually the questions concern departmental policies and their relation to group or individual problems. Since supplemental questions can be raised on the spot, a successful minister must be able to think quickly on his feet and also be well briefed in advance by his staff on any embarrassing points that may come up. The opposition can exert constant pressure on the government administration during the oral question period, but not since 1895 has any British cabinet been forced to resign on a motion of no-confidence in the Commons by the opposition. Votes of confidence or no confidence today are registered by the voters at large at general elections. The question period is well recognized by everyone as the time when ammunition to sway the voters is being carefully accumulated.

In both the Third and Fourth Republics, however, the

oral question period often led to sudden votes of no-confidence which the parliamentarians felt free to engage in because of the government's reluctance to use its ultimate weapon of dissolution. Under the Fifth Republic's constitution, no-confidence votes as a result of the question period are not permitted. Nor, except under extremely limited circumstances, can censure votes be passed. But given the dominance of the Government coalition since the establishment of the Fifth Republic, these provisions have never actually been necessary to prevent political chaos.

Some variation of the question period is characteristic of all varieties of parliamentary organization. This is true even when, as in the case of the Netherlands and several other European systems, ministers either do not have to be or are specifically forbidden to be members of the legislative branch. In the Netherlands the ministers are permitted to sit in either or both legislative chambers with "only an advisory voice." Under these conditions they must be prepared to furnish information "either orally or in writing" and "may be invited by each of the chambers to attend the assembly for that purpose."

Currently, probably more use is made of investigating committees of one sort or another by the U.S. Congress than by any other legislative body. Under the Third and Fourth Republics, the *commissions,* both regular and special, carried on almost constant investigations into the affairs of the executive, but under the Fifth Republic both the power and the partisan incentive to do so has been drastically limited.

In Great Britain "select committees" of the House are appointed to inquire into the need for some particular type of legislation and to make recommendations as to how it can best be carried out. They can subpoena witnesses and government documents and conduct whatever investigations they consider necessary. A committee is disbanded when it makes its recommendations. "Royal commissions," on the other hand, seldom, if ever, include any Members of Parliament. Composed of distinguished public figures, frequently chosen for their expertise in the subject matter, a royal commisson holds hearings to solicit facts, opinions, recommendations, and suggestions from any interested individuals who wish to appear before it. Politically the appointment of these commissions has saved more than one government from the embarrassment of having to take a stand on a highly controversial issue. Although they are less important today, since the early nineteenth century royal commissions have been the inspiration for much important legislation, particularly of a remedial or reforming nature.

Similar to the British royal commissions are the committees of distinguished citizens appointed from time to time by American presidents. One of the best known of these and one whose recommendations have had the most lasting impact was the Commission on Organization of the Executive Branch of the Government, headed by former President Herbert Hoover, appointed by President Truman in 1947. The commission, after lengthy hearings and extensive staff research, made 270 recommendations for greater efficiency and economy in government operation. Of these it is estimated that approximately 70 percent were adopted. In 1953, a second Hoover commission was appointed which made 375 recommendations for administrative improvement with, once again, a high percentage of adoption. As in the case of the British royal commissions, the members of presidential commissions serve without compensation.

More routinely, however, it is the specialized standing committees of Congress which carry out the investigative function. In recent years the Senate Foreign Affairs Committee, for example, has held almost constant hearings on American policy in Southeast Asia in an effort to get information from the executive branch and to exert control over the conduct of that policy. As a result, the committee chairman, Senator William Fulbright of Arkansas, has become one of the best-known public figures in Washington. In the 1950s a prominent role was played by the House Committee on un-American Activities, now the Committee on Internal Subversion. These committees conduct extensive hearings, sometimes in the glare of national publicity, sometimes in secret sessions (*in camera*). Testifying before them is usually a long parade of witnesses, representing both official and private interests.

Out of such committee hearings and the research reports prepared by the committees' expert staffs often come publications that contain invaluable source material on the formation of governmental policy and background information not easily obtainable elsewhere. Question-and-answer periods in parliamentary bodies and congressional investigations and joint resolutions passed by both House and Senate in the U.S. are also important sources of information and a means of monitoring the activities of the legislative branch. In recent years many joint resolutions of Congress have been concerned with foreign affairs, as in the case of the so-called Tonkin Gulf Resolution of 1964, which was interpreted by President Johnson as congressional approval for military escalation in Vietnam.

Another power of the U.S. Senate is provided by the constitutional provision that the president "shall nominate, and *by and with the advice and consent of the Senate,* shall appoint ambassadors, other public ministers and consuls, judges of the Supreme Court, and all other officers of the United States whose appointments are not herein otherwise provided for." Customarily, presidential nominees are approved by the Senate after rather routine committee hearings. But recent years, as social and political tensions have mounted, have seen a reversal of this situation. In 1970 President Nixon achieved the unhappy distinction of being the only president in history to have two Supreme Court nominations in succession rejected by the Senate.

The power of the legislative branch to impeach government officials has been used so seldom and so unsuccessfully that it has become obsolete. Since the adoption of the U.S. Constitution in 1789, only 12 impeachment charges have been brought by the House of Representatives and only 4 of these resulted in Senate confirmation. The one attempt (1867) to use this legislative weapon against a president was so obviously politically motivated as to discredit its use completely.

THE CONTROL OF APPROPRIATIONS

Most bicameral and all unicameral legislative bodies give control over appropriations to the popularly elected lower house, but there is great dissimilarity of method from country to country. In some cases the legislature may simply approve the budget proposals of a dominant executive; in others it may be sufficiently powerful to use his proposals as the rough draft from which it then writes its own frequently very different financial legislation.

In the first instance two factors must be present: a parliamentary system with an alternating-majority situation and the majority party firmly in control of the mechanics of the legislative branch. The way in which financial legislation is handled in the British Parliament affords the best illustration of this situation.

The Dominant Executive

The outstanding aspect of the British budgetary process is the firm control which the leaders of the majority party have over it from start to finish. While the American financial year begins on July 1, the British fiscal year dates from April 1. In the Commons some time during April, the chancellor of the exchequer gives the annual budget speech, outlining the proposed expenditures and the government plan for financing them. The budget is intended not only to raise revenue but to serve as one of the government's most important means of managing the entire economy. In a "Background to the Budget Report," the British Information Service commented in 1970, "The Budget does more than raise revenue to meet expenditure; it is one of the . . . principal economic management tools." Needless to say the speech is always awaited with a considerable degree of nervous expectancy by the business and financial community. For that reason its contents are treated as top-secret information until the chancellor divulges them.

Budget preparations, of course, have been under way for months before the chancellor's annual speech. After cabinet policy discussions on the aims and objectives of the ruling party's program, treasury officials and representatives of the other government departments and agencies prepared the estimate of expenditures and the proposals on how to finance them.

Until 1967, following the chancellor's budget statement, the Commons then resolved itself into a Committee of the Whole with the Speaker out of the chair and relaxed rules of procedure. Now, however, the budget is initially referred to a standing committee of some fifty members. Over a period of weeks prior to general debate and discussion, the committee examines the budget proposals in sessions which may be attended by any interested governmental officials. It has been a long-standing rule in the consideration of the budget by the House of Commons that no increases can be moved in appropriations. The only way in which the opposition can attempt, always futilely, to bring down the government is by moving reductions in the appropriations. In the unlikely event that such a motion were successful, it would be interpreted by the cabinet as a clear indication that it had lost control of the legislative branch and therefore had to resign.

But this is precluded from happening by the very nature of the tight control over the legislative branch which the alternating-majority system makes possible. From the moment when the cabinet approves the draft budget proposed by the financial experts, there is little doubt in the minds of the heads of the various executive departments as to what their operating funds for the next fiscal year will be. The opposition may well use the budget debates to build up a case against the government for extravagance or poor allocation of priorities, but the government budget will be passed by the government majority as drafted by the government leaders. Nor is there any concern, as to what the other house may do. Ever since 1911 money bills have been sent to the Lords approximately a month prior to Parliament's adjournment. Whether it is accepted or not is immaterial. At the end of the annual session, it goes automatically to the queen (or king) for routine approval.

The Powerful Legislature

We can perhaps best illustrate the difference between the way in which financial legislation is handled under the British alternating-majority parliamentary system and the U.S. presidential system by an academic comparison. In Britain, once the cabinet has made its policy decisions on government finances, government administrators can then make firm plans for the forthcoming fiscal year. This is very similar to the pleasant situation in which the administrators of a well-endowed private college find themselves after the board of trustees has met and approved the next year's budget. Barring some financial or other catastrophe, it is then possible to plan the financing of the college's activities for the next year with confidence. Quite different is the unhappy situation of the administrators at a state-financed institution. Realistically, if grimly, they accept the fact that their proposals constitute merely an "asking" budget which, by the time it has been rewritten by various state fiscal agencies, revised in each house of the legislature, and finally patched together by a joint compromise committee, will emerge in final form, provided a hostile governor does not veto it, quite unrecognizable from the original proposal. This is the situation which the executive branch faces every fiscal year in the United States under the presidential system.

The budget message presented to Congress every year by the president represents as much careful and extensive planning as that of the British chancellor. But there the resemblance between the two budgetary processes ends. For in Washington, after extensive hearings before the appropriations committees of both houses, extensive floor debate which may drag on well into the new fiscal year, and a final hectic compromise on appropriations to reconcile House and Senate differences, what emerges may bear little resemblance to the blueprint offered by the chief executive.

The major reason lies in the functioning of the party structure. The chairmen and subchairmen of the appropriations committees are powerful political figures, invulnerable in their own states, who in many cases have seen three or four presidents come and go. Even at the peak of his influence, a president is seldom able to dominate those powerful political figures. Instead, it is they who call the tune in terms of appropriations calculated to aid their states or to conform to their philosophies of government. We might summarize the difference in the budgetary situation of a British prime minister and an American president by saying that the prime minister calmly plans for his appropriations, whereas the president nervously prays for them. (In both cases, of course, there is a great deal of behind-the-scenes action.)

THE PASSAGE OF LEGISLATION

Though the various legislative functions which we have just surveyed are important, the enactment of legislation is still more important. While the mechanics are not too different from one legislative body to another, the control over proposed legislation is very much influenced by the party system.

We commented that in connection with budget proposals, a British prime minister calmly plans while an American president nervously prays. The reason for this difference, of course, is the prime minister's confidence in his ability to exert effective control through party discipline; the American president knows, given the jealously nursed independence of the senior statesmen who head the key committees, that, along with a great deal of horse-trading and political manipulation, much good luck will be necessary to get even a major proportion of his proposals enacted, even when his own party is in effective control of the legislative branch. There is an essential distinction between what we can term the *law-assenting* legislative bodies of the world and the *law-making* ones.

Law-Assenting Bodies

Law-assenting describes those legislative bodies where the government, run either by the well-disciplined majority party or *the* party, is so firmly in control that there is no question about the enactment of its legislative program. In Great Britain, for example, over a period of years, it has been estimated that 85 percent of all bills introduced into Parliament were government inspired, with 95 percent of these being enacted. In the German Bundestag, 75 percent of all legislation enacted is government sponsored. Even more extreme are the percentages under either the smother-party or movement-regime systems, as in Mexico or the Soviet Union, where uniformly 100 percent of legislation is government inspired with virtually the same percentage of enactment.

Law-Making Bodies

In contrast are the law-making legislative bodies of the world with the U.S. Congress probably the outstanding example. As a popular current text on American government summarizes it, "Over the last ten years, presidential success scores have ranged from a low of 27 percent to a high of 69 percent, with the median lying well below 50 percent. . . . This is concrete evidence that Congress is no rubber stamp."[5] The times when an American president achieves the degree of success in getting his program enacted that a British prime minister would regard as routine are so few as to receive special note from political historians. In the last 40 years, the two most outstanding

[5]Thomas R. Dye, Lee S. Greene, George S. Parthemos, *American Government: Theory, Structure, Process* (Belmont, Calif.: Wadsworth, 1969), pp. 269–270.

examples of this are the famous "100 days" after Franklin Roosevelt took office in 1933 at the depth of the Depression and the first session of Congress after Lyndon Johnson's landslide victory over Barry Goldwater in 1964.

Comparable to the American situation was that of the French assembly under the Fourth Republic. Only 26 percent of bills introduced were government sponsored and of these only an average of 50 percent passed. Even more than in the United States, during the Third Republic and Fourth Republic, the French legislature was very much an independent law-making body in its own right. Under the Fifth Republic, because of the more restricted powers of the assembly and especially because of the smother-party role played by the UNR, the situation has come to resemble that of a typical law-assenting legislative body.

Where law-making legislatures exist, there are several possibilities for the origin of draft legislation rather than simply as part of the official governmental program. The proposed legislation might possibly originate as the bright idea of one particular legislator. More likely it would arise in the legislature either as a proposal by a party or coalition group or as a result of research carried on by the members or staff experts of one of the topical committees. But even more likely, an outside interest group will have convinced one or more legislators that it was either their moral duty or good political insurance to sponsor the proposed legislation.

Very probably prior to its introduction, committee experts or legislative drafting experts will have carefully edited the text for clarity and correctness of citations. After this, the formal steps in the passage of the draft legislation begin. They can be numbered as follows:

1. Introducing the Bill. This is the so-called first reading. In all cases, it is little more than the most formal and brief birth announcement of the proposed legislation; only the title and number of the bill are recited by the reading clerk.

2. Initial Consideration. Under the U.S. system, after its formal introduction, the bill is referred to the appropriate committee for consideration. The choice of the committee is not necessarily an automatic action. With equal appropriateness, the same bill might be referred to any of several different committees, one of which might be composed of members sympathetic to the bill while another might be hostile. Referral can well determine the life or death of a particular bill. After referral, the committee will hold limited or extended public hearings, depending on the importance of the bill. Open committee hearings are more characteristic of American procedure than any other. Elsewhere closed hearings seem to be the rule rather than the exception. In the open committee hearings various interest

groups, quite aside from their off-the-record efforts to influence individual legislators, have the opportunity to offer public testimony on the pending legislation. After hearing the testimony and discussing the bill, the committee may either vote to refer the bill for consideration by the whole legislature as it was originally introduced, or, more likely, extensively amend it in the light of the committee hearings, or kill it by a negative vote and thus "pigeonhole" it.

In British procedure, the initial consideration of the bill (the second reading) takes place in a one- or two-day plenary (full) session of the Commons where the general principles of the bill are discussed. If approved, it is then sent to one of the regular standing committees, or, if it deals with special matters, to a select committee, or, if it is concerned with fundamental changes of constitutional significance, it may then be discussed by the Committee of the Whole House, which is simply the entire House of Commons with the Speaker out of the chair and the members operating under more relaxed rules of procedure.

3. Further Consideration. In the U.S. Congress, after a bill has been "discharged" by a committee, it is discussed and debated in a regular session of the legislature. In those legislatures operating under the parliamentary system, the lead in discussion is taken by the government ministers and important members of the opposition.

In the U.S. Congress, those roles would be assumed by the floor managers for the bill, while the leadership of the opposition would likely come from those members of the committee which had voted against the bill being reported out and had released a minority report supporting their case.

Except in the case of the U.S. Senate with its jealously guarded right of unlimited debate, legislative bodies in order to get through their business regulate rigidly the amount of time allowed for debate. This regulation may be either in terms of the total time to be allotted, divided between proponents and opponents, or by such a device as the "guillotine closure" which divides up the total time among the various sections of the pending bill.

4. Final Consideration. In all cases this involves the quite routine third reading of the bill and a final vote on its acceptance or rejection as amended.

5. Bicameral Legislative Procedure. In those legislative bodies which have two chambers, notably in the U.S. and Britain, an identical bill will have been introduced in the other chamber unless constitutionally prohibited, or, after passage, the bill will be sent to the other house for consideration. Much the same procedure follows. In the United States and in India (and less so in Britain and Canada), the popularly elected house must give consideration to the changes made in the bill. Where it is not in a position

simply to brush aside, usually after a waiting period, the changes made, a conference committee of the two houses is customarily appointed. After the conference committee has reconciled the differences in the two versions, the amended bill can then be passed by each house in identical versions.

6. Executive Approval. In U.S. procedure this is a very real final hurdle. If the president vetoes a bill, and twentieth-century presidents have shown no reluctance to do so, it takes a two-thirds vote of both houses of Congress to repass the legislation. Also available to the U.S. president, and often used, is the so-called pocket veto. It could equally well be called the negative veto. To apply it, all any president has to do is *not* to take action on any bills reaching his desk, after their passage by Congress, within the last ten days of a congressional session. In theory the British sovereign has even more absolute veto power, but since it has not been used since 1707 this means little. The president of the French Fifth Republic has what might be called a reconsideration veto, since he has the power to "ask Parliament for a reconsideration of the law or of certain of its articles. This reconsideration may not be refused."

The procedures just described are used for what are termed *public bills,* that is, legislation which is of broad and general concern. A certain percentage of the time of any legislative body (only 2 percent for the British Commons) is reserved for consideration of what are known as *private bills.* An example of such a bill might be one entitled "An Act to Raise the Pensions of Minnie Jones and Eighteen Other Widows of the Spanish-American War." Such bills are obviously noncontroversial and receive very cursory treatment. They are usually referred to a committee on unopposed or private bills, given hearings there, and then reported out in batches for routine confirmation by the legislative body at large.

THE ROLES OF THE LEGISLATURE

Before we turn to a survey of the various roles which the individual legislator can play, it is appropriate to consider the basic roles of the legislature as a whole at the present time. It is a commonplace in the late twentieth century that legislative bodies seldom, if ever, either initiate or control policy the way they did in the nineteenth century. If legislative bodies are no longer the prime movers in governmental policy, what function do they perform? Or have they become to government what the appendix is to the human body, an interesting but useless survival? From the obvious respect which the British Parliament still inspires and the amount of attention, if frequently neither respectful nor friendly, which the U.S. Congress receives, it is clear that legislative bodies still play a vital role. For that matter, the extensive publicity which the Soviet Union gives to both the election of the members and the activities of the Supreme Soviet indicates that, even at its most powerless, the legislative body still fulfills several needs vital for the functioning of any political system. In tentative listing of these vital needs, we can mention the following:

1. The Legitimizing Function. Earlier we defined legitimate rule as those powers which are regarded by everyone as so right and proper for government to exercise that a minimum of coercion is needed for their enforcement. In the era of mass democracy, here is where legislatures, even of the most controlled sort, play an important role. For the basis of legitimacy in the late twentieth century is people power. An indication of this is the defensive posture always taken by a military group which has seized power. The purpose of the *coup d'etat* is invariably proclaimed to be the restoration of *real* democracy or one of the major reform goals, often in the vaguely indefinite future to be sure, is said to be the holding of free elections so that a truly representative body can legislate for the people.

In the U.S.S.R. and other order-party states, it would save money and bureaucratic waste motion if the Central Committee of the Communist party were simply to issue decrees embodying all of the measures duly passed by the Supreme Soviet in its semiannual sessions. But clearly something vital would be missing. The scrupulous care with which the all-powerful party nurtures the myth of the Supreme Soviet as the highest organ of state power in the U.S.S.R. is proof in itself.

2. Sense of Identification. It has long been accepted that one of the most important human needs is to feel part of a social unit, to have a sense of participating even vicariously, in its decision-making process. Even though this participation is very small indeed, it makes for a vast difference in attitude to feel that *we* rather than *they* had influence on policy. It may be remembered that among the problems of the developed nations is precisely this feeling of loss of identity and of individual worth.

It is difficult for the average citizen in any polity to identify with the most run-of-the-mill politician who has become president or prime minister let alone with an awesome supreme leader or "savior of the nation." But safely familiar and recognizable is the local lawyer or businessman (France, the United States, and Great Britain) or fellow tractor driver (the U.S.S.R.) who has asked for one's vote. Once elected, such an individual offers a familiar avenue of access to government in homely and reassuring terms. The existence of the representative offers a precise and understandable source to which complaints, proposals, and requests for governmental action or assistance can be sent, rather than sending off a letter to a vast and impersonal bureaucracy. Further, the fact that a representative is identified with a local area makes him accountable to the desires and wishes of its citizens which is not true of the national executive in even the most democractic states. Should he perform badly or fail to carry out the wishes and needs of his constituents, he either may be recalled at any time upon decision of a majority of the electors (in the Soviet system) or be punished by defeat at the next election.

The existence of a legislative body where there is at least one known or even familiar face serves to personalize the vast, impersonal mass of bureaucracy with its seemingly arbitrary rulings and often curt indifference to the plight of the individual citizen. This is one of the important roles played by the individual legislator.

3. As National Educational Soap Opera. One important role played by legislators is to lend some color to the often boring activities of government. The activities, both official and unofficial, of legislators provide a very human focus indeed for political interest and, at times, even instruction. For example, a state governor's grandstand political defiance of court actions serves to dramatize the authority conflict between executive and judicial as no sober constitutional discussion can do. The interplay of personality between a suavely evasive executive official and a relentlessly probing committee chairman demonstrates the struggle for dominance between executive and legislative. In the great policy debates of any democratic legislature, public issues are given an immediacy and a sense of meaning impossible in any other form. In both the official and unofficial activities of legislative bodies, the dynamic workings of the governmental system are personalized in terms that make them comprehensible to the average man.

THE ROLES OF THE INDIVIDUAL LEGISLATOR

We referred in Chapter 11 to Weber's comment that all "types" represent perfect models which are never actually realized. So it is with the roles which an individual contemporary legislator might play. It is doubtful if any legislator ever plays any one of these roles all the time. More likely in the course of any average week, perhaps in the course of a single typical day, he will function in several of them. Among his possible roles are:

1. "Ambassador" from a regional or social group
2. "Representative of the whole nation"
3. "Servant of the people" for his election district
4. Spokesman for a particular political or social group

In modern usage the first of these roles is probably the least played of any. This role is more characteristic of the representatives to the medieval estates who, quite literally, were ambassadors from their particular status-group, acting under strict instructions, unable to take action without referring it to their constituency, and subject to recall at any time. On an extensive basis probably only twice in U.S. history have representatives functioned in this fashion. Certainly the delegates to the Continental Congresses (1774–1788) were ambassadors from their several states, and the representatives to the Conferedate Congress (1861–1865) also played a similar role. At various times in U.S. political history, an individual prominent political figure has been regarded as the leading spokesman for a particular region such as, for example, John C. Calhoun for the South in the pre-Civil War period and William Jennings Bryan in the early twentieth century for the prairie states.

The second of the possible roles of the representative originated in the reforming zeal of the French Revolution. In an effort to get away from narrow, medieval status representation, the National Assembly asserted that its membership comprised *"the national representation, being one and indivisible. . . ."*

Ironically, the classic statement of the representative as having as his prime concern the affairs of the nation rather than of his own limited district was given by Edmund Burke who will be remembered as the leading contemporary opponent of the French Revolution and the founder of modern conservatism.

In 1774, some fifteen years before the beginning of the French Revolution, Burke wrote an often-quoted letter to the voters in the district of Bristol which he then represented in the House of Commons. Referring to the relationship which should exist between the voters and their legislative representative, he said:

> Their wishes ought to have great weight with him; their opinions high respect; *their business unremitted attention.* It is his duty to sacrifice his repose, his pleasures, his satisfaction, to theirs; and above all, ever, and in all cases, to prefer their interest to his own. But, his unbiased opinion, his mature judgment, his enlightened conscience, he ought not to sacrifice to you, to any man, or to any set of men living. These he does not derive from your pleasure; no, from the law and the Constitution. They are a trust from Providence, for the abuse of which he is deeply answerable. Your representative owes you, not his industry only, but his judgment; and he betrays, instead of serving you, if he sacrifices it to your opinion. . . . If government were a matter of will upon my side, yours, without question, ought to be superior. But government and legislation are matters of reason and judgment, and not of inclination; and what sort of reason is that, in which the determination precedes the discussion; in which one set of men deliberate, and another

decide; and where those who form the conclusion are perhaps three hundred miles distant from those who hear the arguments? . . .

Parliament is not a congress of ambassadors from different and hostile interests; which interests each must maintain, as an agent, and advocate against other agents and advocates; but Parliament is a deliberate assembly of one nation, with one interest, that of the whole; where, not local purposes, not local prejudices, ought to guide, but the general good, resulting from the general reason of the whole. You choose a member indeed: but when you have chosen him, he is not a member of Bristol, but he is a member of Parliament. If the local constituent should have an interest, or should form a hasty opinion, evidently opposite to the real good of the rest of the community, the member for that place ought to be as far as any other from any endeavor to give it effect.[6]

In his second paragraph Burke gives an excellent summary of the traditional role which a legislator was expected to play. Without any question, the "Address to the Electors of Bristol" is probably the most eloquent statement ever made of the duty of the representative to function on a broad and statesmanlike scale rather than in parochial and political terms. As a model it sets an idealistic goal which, in theory, cannot be challenged.

But the practical politics of it are something else again. It should not be forgotten that it was easier and safer for Burke to take such a high-minded attitude in 1774 than it would be for a modern politician. The eighteenth century was the period of property democracy in Great Britain when at most a few thousand voters participated in any parliamentary election and when the way in which their votes would be cast was usually determined by the highest bid made in terms either of cash or patronage. The typical parliamentarian or his noble patron so completely owned a particular constituency that its approval or disapproval of its representative's conduct made little difference.

An expression of the remarkable freedom which the eighteenth-century British legislator enjoyed was given by a Member of Parliament in a revealing letter in 1714 to his constituents who had urged him to change his vote on a pending tax measure. Giving vent to his honest indignation at such impertinence on their part, he wrote:

Gentlemen: I have received your letter about the excise, and I am surprised at your insolence in writing me at all.

You know, and I know, that I bought this constituency. You know, and I know, that I am now determined to sell it, and you know what you think I don't know, that you are now looking out for another buyer, and I know, what you certainly don't know, that I have now found another constituency to buy.

[6]Quoted by Herman Finer, *The Theory and Practice of Modern Government*, rev. ed. (New York: Holt, Rinehart & Winston, 1949), pp. 227–228. (Italics added.)

About what you said about the excise; may God's curse light upon you all, and may it make your homes as open and free to the excise officers as your wives and daughters have always been to me while I have represented your rascally constituency.[7]

While a contemporary legislator may on occasion act in direct opposition to the wishes of his constituents by taking a stand for what he considers to be the national interest, he does so at his peril. As President Kennedy pointed out in *Profiles in Courage,* it frequently has meant the destruction of a political career and severe financial and social penalties for a legislator to dare defy the voters.

Far more dominant in the American concept of the role of the legislator is that of the faithful servant of the people. His job is to take care of his district's interests in terms of federal appropriations and the establishment of installations with large payrolls. On a personal basis, his constituents expect help in everything from getting an increase in a veteran's pension to an appointment for a son to a service academy. In his position on pending bills the legislator is expected to serve as mouthpiece for the sentiments of his district. As we have noted before, the problem here, of course, is how to determine those sentiments. The role of interest groups in this connection needs no further comment.

This role-concept lacks the drama and color inherent in putting national interest ahead of local concerns and fearlessly speaking out on the basis of conscience instead of political appeal. But on precisely this basis many a legislator has built a long and successful career with reelection after reelection. It is an excellent formula for political survival if not fame.

Possibly U.S. legislators go the farthest in carrying out the servant-of-the-people role, but it is worth noting that there are aspects of this in the roles played by all legislators. On important policy matters, party discipline may well be observed. But when it comes to providing services and assistance for constituents, acting as servant of the people is one of the most essential elements in personal and party success.

The fourth and last of the roles the legislator may play is that of spokesman for a particular political or social group. In contemporary democratic legislative bodies, this is likely to be either a carefully concealed or very much a part-time role. In the age of mass democracy, there has to be at least a well-cultivated pretense of representing the masses of the people.

In the period of the limited franchise and indirect elec-

[7]Quoted by P. G. Richards in *Honorable Members* (London: Faber, 1959), p. 157.

tions it was quite otherwise. In the latter years of the nineteenth century, for example, the U.S. Senate with its members elected by state legislatures was known as a millionaire's club. As a cartoon of the time not inaccurately portrayed it, the members of the Senate represented the salt trust or the paper-bag trust or the copper interests or Standard Oil rather than the people of their states.

Much the same situation was true in the French legislative bodies of both the Third and Fourth Republic. In Great Britain many a Labour party MP is also a union official, and his Conservative counterpart, if not directly involved, is very likely to have close business ties of one sort or another which it would be folly to flaunt. Rather than performing full-time as the spokesman for a special interest group, in the nineteenth-century pattern, the twentieth-century legislator is far more likely to keep a protective eye peeled for the interests of the aircraft industry or insurance companies or the principal industry of his particular district. In terms of public relations, both the representative and the special interest are well aware of the need for caution.

In legislative bodies where either an alternating-majority or fragmented-party system exists, any legislator will very probably be playing any and all of these four roles at varying times. The degree to which any one of them is carried out will be greatly influenced by expediency and the pressures of the party system. In the U.S. Senate, for example, several prominent senators have demonstrated a high degree of skill in perceiving how to balance the several roles involved. Senator Fulbright of Arkansas, for example, is thought of in his role as chairman of the Foreign Relations Committee as largely concerned with being "not a member of Bristol, but . . . a member of Parliament." But, quite properly with the need to secure reelection every six years as the prime fact of political survival, Senator Fulbright has carefully and conscientiously promoted the interests of his state and his constituents. As a number of unhappy case histories demonstrate, those who forget entirely about Bristol and concern themselves only with the general good will sooner or later wake up in the cold, gray dawn of some postelection morning to discover they are now a defeated candidate.

The most obvious and clear-cut example of the legislator serving solely as mouthpiece of a particular political group is in a legislature either dominated by a smother party or completely controlled by some type of movement regime. Under these conditions the interests of the party and the nation are deemed to be one and the same so that there is no conflict between them. But even here, although the question of reelection does not enter into the picture, in the interest of cementing the party's influence, any individual representative must function to a degree at least as the member from Bristol. Apparently the Italian Communist party, the world's largest order party not in power, has largely based its success on the fact that its parliamentary representatives, however obviously dedicated they are to the party's ultimate ideological goals, have scrupulously functioned as servants of the people in their promotion and protection of the interests of their constituents and their districts.

WHY LEGISLATURES NOW PLAY SECOND FIDDLE

As we have commented before, nothing is more striking in the relationship between the executive and the legislature since the early nineteenth century than the shift which has taken place in the power balance between the two. From a position of unquestioned dominance, in the best liberal tradition of the late eighteenth century, legislatures now play a secondary role. For its part, the executive, particularly in the twentieth century, has increasingly become the dominant element. In no country is this more true than in the United States. In the 1950s when President Eisenhower sought to function as a proper nineteenth-century president and leave initiative to the legislative branch, he found himself under heavy criticism for his negative approach and his failure to provide adequate leadership.

It is impossible to make any authoritative list of the reasons why this change has come about, but we can at least suggest what seem to be some of the most important influences which have acted to increase the prestige and dominance of the chief executive. The ranking of these in order of importance is again a matter of choice.

1. The role of radio and television
2. The technologically influenced "age of anxiety" psychosis
3. The predominance of foreign affairs
4. The control of the armed forces
5. The rise of the positive state

1. The Role of Radio and Television. It is this factor more than any other which has made the modern chief executive a universal father image for millions of people. In the late nineteenth or the early twentieth century, a president or a prime minister was a dim and remote figure compared to the local legislative representative. Even in the course of a long political career, at most a few tens of thousands might hear him speak at a public meeting, while to 95 percent of his fellow countrymen he would be a face in a newspaper photograph, and his ideas merely columns of print in the accompanying articles.

Almost simultaneously in the 1930s, two very different world leaders, President Roosevelt and Adolf Hitler, discovered how to employ radio, which had been in general use only a scant 10 years, as a medium for establishing personal contact not merely with thousands or tens of thousands of individuals but millions and tens of millions. Roosevelt's "fireside chats" became a regular and tremendous factor in American politics. For his part, Hitler used radio to create that sense of mystical union between himself and his German *Volk* which, probably quite correctly, enabled Nazi propagandists to boast to the world that the Fuehrer's policies had virtually unaminous support from the German people.

In the 1960s and 1970s, the development of television offered new and more exciting possibilities for those political leaders able to use it effectively. There was not only the projection of voice and inflection but of eye and facial expression. Public leaders, such as de Gaulle of France, Trudeau of Canada and President Nixon, who understood television's possibilities were often able to use it to mobilize public opinion behind them regardless of the opposition or misgivings of the legislature.[8]

2. The "Age of Anxiety" Psychosis. The influence of radio and television on the developing predominance of the executive over the legislative branch has not been the only result of technology on political developments. In a generalized sense technology has also exerted much influence on the political expectations of the masses. With grim appropriateness, the late twentieth century has been termed "the age of anxiety." As never before, the masses of citizens in all countries feel threatened almost daily by the major crises which occur so regularly and by the overhanging threat of nuclear holocaust. Indeed, with new media advances bringing rapid and complete coverage of each incident, how could they feel otherwise?

Under these conditions there is a strong tendency, indeed a need, to look for a reassuring and protecting superfather. The most logical focus is the chief executive who stands at the pinnacle of power and is presumably better informed about the real state of affairs than anyone else. This need, created by the frightening technological development of weaponry, obviously serves to enhance the prestige and

[8]President Nixon, for example, in 1969 and 1970 made highly effective use of television to quiet public uneasiness over Vietnam policy and to blunt the impact of the antiwar movement. Probably no other prominent U.S. politician has better reason to be aware of television's power since it is generally accepted that the "bad image" projected by Nixon in the famous television debates with John Kennedy in 1960 goes far to explain his narrow defeat in that election. But in spite of Nixon's growing ability to utilize television adeptly, public opinion polls in 1971 revealed an increasing credibility gap of the dimensions which forced Lyndon Johnson from office.

influence of the chief executive. Coupled with the technological achievements of radio and television which make both voice and face familiar in every living room, it provides a potent catalyst for the rise in prestige of chief executives.

3. The Predominance of Foreign Affairs. As the Athenians discovered to their ruin, foreign affairs are ill-managed by either mass meetings or committees. Over a century ago, Tocqueville looking for those "accidental causes which may increase the influence of executive government," wrote:

> As for myself I have no hesitation in avowing my conviction that it is most especially in the conduct of foreign relations that democratic governments appear to me to be decidedly inferior to governments carried on upon different principles. . . . Good sense may suffice to direct the ordinary course of society; and among a people whose education has been provided for, the advantages of democratic liberty in the internal affairs of the country may more than compensate for the evils inherent in a democratic government. But such is not always the case in the mutual relations of foreign nations.
>
> Foreign politics demand scarcely any of those qualities which a democracy possesses; and they require, on the contrary, the perfect use of almost all those faculties in which it is deficient. . . . a democracy is unable to regulate the details of an important undertaking, to persevere in a design and to work out its execution in the presence of serious obstacles. It cannot combine its measures with secrecy, and it will not await their consequences with patience. These are qualities which more especially belong to an individual or to any aristocracy; and they are precisely the means by which an individual people attains to a predominant position.[9]

Woodrow Wilson while still a practicing political scientist wrote of the last years (1904–1908) of Theodore Roosevelt's administration, "It seems to be almost an axiom that the more a nation becomes involved in foreign affairs, the stronger its executive branch becomes."

From the very beginning of the republic, presidents have always taken a strong hand in foreign affairs. Virtually singlehandedly George Washington, by virtue of his prestige, kept the new United States from declaring war on Great Britain in the 1790s in support of revolutionary France. In 1803 Thomas Jefferson made the famous Louisiana Purchase by executive agreement, a device which has been much used since World War II to avoid the necessity of securing a two-thirds vote by the senate to ratify a formal treaty. On the basis of his power as the chief executive, a president simply makes an executive agreement with a foreign country and then, often much later, presents it to

[9]*Democracy in America* (London: Oxford University Press, 1952), pp. 160–161.

the Senate for majority ratification. By the time this occurs, the issue has been settled and there is no choice but to ratify the agreement, however reluctantly.

Texas was annexed in this way and in 1940 Franklin Roosevelt took the first important steps to align American power against Nazi Germany by trading Great Britain 50 destroyers for naval bases in the Caribbean. By virtue of his power to accept the credentials of foreign diplomats, a president can bring about a fundamental change in American policy, as Franklin Roosevelt did in 1933 when, without congressional action, he reversed 16 years of policy and formally recognized the Soviet Union.

In Great Britain, subject to parliamentary questions and debates, foreign policy has always been very much the prerogative of the executive and a source of influence over the legislative branch. Such superb political psychologists as Disraeli in the late nineteenth century and Churchill in the mid-twentieth knew how to use it to their advantage. During his ascendancy in the first years of the Fifth Republic (1958–1969), de Gaulle completely dominated French foreign policy as a result of his personal prestige and presidential powers. In all countries, the fact that the modern technological miracles of instant communications require instant answers has tended to intensify the impact of foreign affairs as a factor enhancing the power of the executive over the legislative.

4. Control of the Armed Forces. Particularly for the U.S. president, this same technologically created need for instant decisions has made already constitutionally granted power over the armed forces an important influence in his predominant role. Both Johnson and Nixon developed their use of U.S. armed forces in Southeast Asia almost at will regardless of their congressional critics. Even in 1970, at seemingly the peak of congressional criticism of his Southeast Asian policy, President Nixon's invulnerability to congressional control made it virtually impossible for his legislative critics to exert any effective checks.

In the broader area of foreign affairs, in the constant maneuvering between the two superpowers, the president's control of the armed forces gives him an unchallengeable hegemony over the legislative branch. With decision time, in the event of thermonuclear attack, reduced to thirty minutes or less, power has to be delegated to a single man. The very thought of declarations of war as a result of legislative debate is absurd. On a less grandiose scale, other chief executives have the same relative enhancement of their powers for the same reasons.

5. Rise of the Positive State. We discussed earlier the shift that has taken place in the twentieth century from the old liberal laissez-faire concept of the negative state to the emergence of the positive state. In the late twentieth

century, it is virtually axiomatic that it is the basic responsibility of government to guide the patterns of social and economic development. For more than 40 years diehard conservatives have railed against the menace of big government and creeping socialism. This has affected the course of events very little. The social and economic problems created by intensifying technological pressures have become the inevitable concern of government as the authoritative source for their control and regulation. Goldwater's crushing defeat in 1964 undoubtedly saw the last time that a presidential candidate of a major party would campaign on a platform urging a return to the era of the negative state.

Especially in the United States but elsewhere also, the chief executive has been the beneficiary of this development. Regardless of how many technical advisors are consulted or what departments or ministries make recommendations, the final responsibility rests upon the president or the prime minister. It is he who by one resort or another to executive action must assume the major responsibility for the regulation of economic and social development.

As we noted earlier, one of the major elements in this regulation is the annual budget. In the United States, in 1921, Congress handed over to the president the responsibility for making the annual budget proposals. From that time on, the annual budget has increasingly become an economic management tool which has increased the prestige of the president.

Here again the existence of such technological aids as radio and television has been of valuable assistance. In 1961, for example, the steel unions were persuaded to settle a strike with a wage increase far short of their initial demands on the grounds that it was their patriotic duty to do so in order to halt an inflationary spiral. Almost immediately after the settlement of the strike, all the major steel companies announced substantial price increases, thus making a mockery of the arguments used to persuade the unions. In a nationally televised address, an obviously angry President Kennedy made it very clear that in his opinion the steel companies had violated a tacit agreement and that he proposed to bring them into line by whatever means necessary. Since this could have meant expensive antitrust suits by the Department of Justice and the cancellation of millions of dollars in government contracts, it was no idle threat. In short order the steel companies capitulated and withdrew the proposed price increases. In the same way early in 1970, President Nixon used national television to announce his veto of a congressional appropriation for urban housing which he regarded as dangerously inflationary. Such special bodies as the Council of Economic Advisers give the modern chief executive a source of expert advice in his management of the positive state which no legislative body can equal.

The overwhelming complexity of the problems with which the executive ministries and departments must deal has led in recent years to yet another erosion of legislative authority in terms of so-called *delegated legislation.* The British term for this type of legislation is *statutory instruments.* Their purpose is to give broad discretionary powers to the executive branch in carrying out a wide variety of regulatory activities. But even when the enabling legislation only affects such matters as industrial safety regulations or rules for the collection of statistical material, the powers of the executive are still enhanced. In the same way, on the basis of very broadly delegated powers, the U.S. president in the course of any year issues hundreds of *executive orders* concerned with a wide variety of matters not only within the administrative structure of the government but also with the powers of the various departments, agencies, and bureaus to regulate and guide social and economic development.

CONCLUSION

The existence of a legislative body is an accepted aspect of a properly organized governmental system in the late twentieth century. In the Western constitutional democracies, the legislative branches play an important role, for they are the prime agency for the legitimization of policy decisions. The determination of policy takes place in the councils of the dominant party or parties, but only legislative authorization gives them proper legitimacy. It is an interesting paradox that although the U.S. chief executive has probably profited most from the power shift from legislative branch to executive, no other chief executive in the world is subject to more constant and frequently hostile scrutiny from an upper chamber. Both Johnson and Nixon have discovered this to their frustration.

LINKING THE PARTS TOGETHER: UNITARY, CONFEDERATE, FEDERAL

It is only a partial description of any governmental system to say that its authority is organized on a parliamentary or presidential basis, for this tells us nothing about how the various parts of these systems are related. There are three long-established ways of describing how the parts are linked together: the *unitary,* the *confederate,* and the *federal* linkage systems.

Assuming that all modern states organize their governmental systems in terms of a set of constitutional ground rules, we can diagram the way in which each of these systems links the parts together.

In a unitary governmental system, there is no sharing of authority. The regional governments exist for the purpose of administrative efficiency and convenience, and the central government represents the only source of allegiance and authority for its citizens. A confederate structure is almost the reverse of this. Here the central government exists for the convenience of the regional governments and to promote their efficient collaboration in certain important matters. The citizens owe their allegiance directly to their particular regional governments and quite indirectly to the central government, such as it is.

The unique character of the federal linkage system is the way in which it differs from the unitary and confederate systems while combining elements of both. Its outstanding features are the sharing of powers between the central and regional governments, both of which have direct authority over the citizens under their jurisdiction, although the element of regional citizenship is usually submerged under the encompassing hegemony of national authority.

The federal system is the one with the most direct interest for American students of government and also is the most complex. For that reason the major portion of this chapter is devoted to its analysis and discussion. But we will first take a brief look at the other two alternatives.

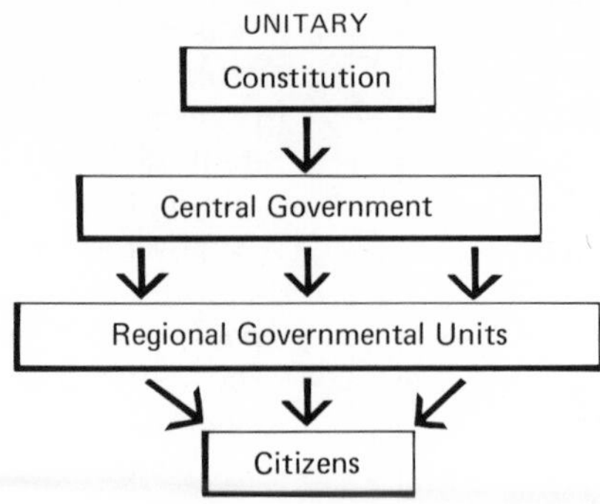

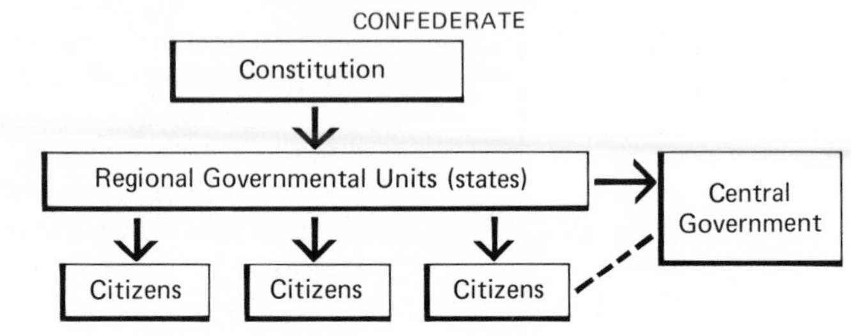

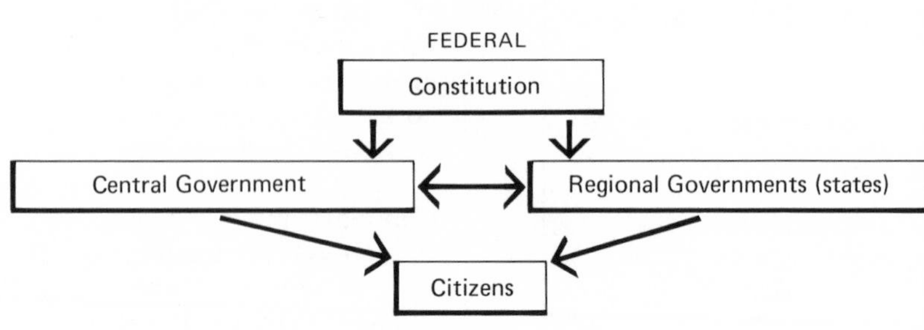

UNITARY AND CONFEDERATE LINKAGE SYSTEMS

The most obvious aspect of a unitary state is the fact that, in contrast to either confederate or federal systems, there are no important separate parts and all authority is focused in the central government. But here, too, there are parts which make up the whole. Even in unitary governmental systems, there have to be regional and local administrative subdivisions. Nor is the relationship between these subordinate units and the central government always the same. Both Great Britain and France, for example, are properly classified as unitary systems but there is much difference in the linkage involved. The British unitary system emphasizes *devolution,* which means "the transfer of power or authority from a central government to a local government." In contrast, the French variety of unitary control operates in a highly centralized and, in terms of the final authoritative decisions, unitary frame of reference.

As is usually the case, the explanation for this variation lies in the differing political heritages. In Great Britain the early and gradual development of nationalism made it possible for a considerable degree of local autonomy to develop without constituting either a challenge or impediment to national unity. Similarly, the almost spontaneous emergence of British industrialism made unnecessary the degree of governmental guidance and control that was characteristic of Continental development.

The basis of English devolution is the 58 administrative counties and the 82 county boroughs into which the country is organized. The administrative counties are further subdivided into such categories as noncounty boroughs, urban districts, and rural districts, which have as their final unit of semiautonomous local government, the parishes. At all of these levels there are elective councils with control over such matters as police, education, and government-sponsored housing developments. While there are, of course, a number of differences, any student familiar with the way in which county and municipal government operates in the United States will not have too inaccurate a picture of how devolution functions in Great Britain, even within the basic pattern of unitary linkage.

The French interpretation of the linkage between local government and the central authority, which means Paris, is quite different. As in other Continental countries, it was necessary to suppress local autonomy to promote both political unity and economic development. From the time of the Emperor Napoleon in the early nineteenth century, there has been strong centralized control and direction over local administration.

Even earlier the French revolutionary assembly had abolished the old provincial organization with its strong appeals to traditional regional royalties. Instead France was divided into departments deliberately organized to ignore any historical or sentimental boundaries. Contemporary France has 95 departments, with the ultimate unit of local administration the *commune,* of which there are approximately 38,000. This final administrative unit has a local town as its center and includes both urban and local territories, with populations that may range from a few hundred to tens of thousands.

But the key to the centralized linkage of the French system is provided by the Napoleonic institution of the *prefects* and *subprefects* on the departmental level. Appointed by the minister of the interior, they exercise *tutelage* over the decisions of the locally elected officials. Their approval is required before any programs can be initiated by local officials, and they can raise local taxes by decree in order to balance budgets or provide needed services.

Ironically it was an effort to reform local government rather than some dramatic foreign-policy issue which brought about the downfall of de Gaulle. Early in the 1960s, France had been divided into approximately 20 so-called program regions for the purpose of more effective economic planning. Under the supervision of the regional prefects, a series of economic development commissions were created. In 1969, for reasons best known to himself, de Gaulle chose to make the voters' acceptance or rejection of a proposed constitutional amendment to convert the economic regions into new political administrative units a question of confidence in his exercise of the presidential office. When the French voters rejected the proposed amendment, de Gaulle resigned. The result was that the basic linkage structure of French centralized unitary administration remained fundamentally unchanged.

In varying degrees, all unitary governmental systems follow either the British devolutionary pattern or that of French centralization. A unitary administrative system, in terms of both effective regional control and ease of administration, has much appeal. This is probably the major reason why the overwhelming majority of world governments are organized on a unitary basis even when theoretically a logical case can be made for a federal system.

Before we turn to a survey of federalism, it is necessary to mention briefly the confederate linkage system for regional organization. It is sufficient testimony to its ineffectiveness that no new government has chosen this system since the collapse of the Confederate States of America in 1865. As indicated in the diagram on p. 378, its most important aspect is the retention of all important powers by the various regional governments which come together to form the confederacy.

The philosophy of such a concept is well summarized in the Articles of Confederation under which the United States was more or less governed for its first eight years (1781–1789) as an independent nation. It is bluntly stipulated that "each State retains its sovereignty, freedom, and independence, and every power, jurisdiction and right which is not by this Confederation expressly delegated to the United States in Congress assembled." The powers so delegated were few indeed and largely negative in nature. No individual state, "without the consent of the United States in Congress assembled," was to engage in diplomatic relations or to wage war.

But in connection with any commercial treaties the powers of the central government, such as they were, had drastic limitations placed upon them, since it was provided that: "no treaty of commerce shall be made whereby the legislative power of the respective States shall be restrained from imposing such imports and duties as their own people are subjected to, or from prohibiting the exportation or importation of any species of goods or commodities whatsoever."[1]

Nor did the central government have any effective authority in such vital matters as either national defense or taxation. It could only request the states to furnish military forces and allocate governmental expenses among the states. They were left to their own devices to raise the necessary funds. Since there was no way of enforcing them, most of the time the various state legislatures simply ignored the requests of "the United States in Congress assembled" for financial support.

During its hectic four-year existence (1861–1865), the Confederacy suffered from the same inability to obtain either adequate revenue or military forces even when desperately needed.[2] The fatal flaw of a confederate system was the inability of the central government, whatever little there was of it, to exert any direct control over the individuals who lived within its territorial boundaries. It could neither tax them nor conscript them. It was always forced to go, hat in hand, to the regional governments that had brought it into existence and, often in vain, beg for the bare means to survive until the need for the next round of begging was again forced upon it.

Under these conditions it is not surprising that the confederate scheme for geographical linkage has had no proponents for over a century. Also, once again, the familiar factor of technological development weighs heavily in the negative against the adoption of confederate systems. Other influences aside, it is clear that in an era of split-second communication, whether of voices or missiles, there must exist the power for making possible life-or-death decisions on national policy in very short order rather than having to wait for the opinions of the country's component parts.

WHEN FEDERALISM IS LOGICAL

A unitary linkage system, however applied, is the most obvious and easiest way to administer any territorial unit. Under most conditions, operated with any reasonable degree

[1]Paul Leicester Ford, ed., *The Federalist* (New York: Holt, Rinehart & Winston, 1898).

[2]There are the well-known instances of state governors refusing to send reinforcements to fight Sherman on his march through the South on the grounds that they might be needed at home and the pathetic story of Lee's Army of northern Virginia, barefoot, shivering, and ill-fed in the last winter of the war, while the storage depots of the sovereign state of North Carolina bulged with supplies, which the governor declined to release even under the most desperate urgings—which were the only methods of enforcement available to the central government.

of efficiency, it can be not only acceptable but suitable. These facts explain why some version of unitary linkage is used by the overwhelming majority of the independent states of the world today.

But as satisfactory as the unitary system is, there are polities for which it does not offer the best solution for the uniquely difficult problems they face. Let us look at those special problems which make desirable some variation of the federal linkage system. The reasons why a federal system of governmental organization can be both logical and desirable usually are highly complex. One of the leading students of federalism, Professor Kenneth Wheare, lists the following reasons for the organization of a federal union[3]:

1. Sense of military insecurity
2. Desire to be independent of foreign powers
3. Hope of economic advantage
4. Some degree of political association prior to the effort at federal union
5. Similarity of political institutions
6. Effective leadership when needed

William P. Maddox gave these reasons for the formation of a federal system:[4]

1. "Fear, [which] may develop from direct attempts at intimidation, or from a sustained and profound feeling of insecurity"
2. Rational calculation of advantage
3. Response to some unifying idea, symbol, or myth
4. A reasonable approximation in size and in levels of cultural, social, and political development
5. Geographical contiguity

It is clear that both these lists, in slightly different words, express very much the same reasons. However defined, fear or a sense of military insecurity, was a very potent reason indeed for 12 of the 13 quarrelling and distrustful American states to link together in a federal system. Very much present also was the hope of economic advantage. It is worth remembering in this connection that the preliminary step to the Philadelphia meeting was a trade conference at Annapolis in 1786 attended by only five states. When they formed the world's first federal union, the American states had similar political institutions and were at similar levels of cultural, social, and political development, and they certainly had effective leadership at the Philadelphia convention of 1788 in the persons of Frank-

[3]Kenneth Wheare, *Federal Government*, 3rd ed. (London: Oxford University Press, 1953), p. 37.

[4]William P. Maddox, "The Political Basis of Federation," *American Political Science Review* 35 (December 1941): 1122–1124.

lin, Hamilton, Jay, Madison, and others. Without effective leadership to push matters to a conclusion, the other reasons are unlikely to be sufficient for success in organizing a federal system.

However expressed or defined, all of these factors obviously play a part in the formation of a federal system. But neither in the case of the American prototype nor in the emergence of later federal unions do they explain why this particular linkage system was preferred, for precisely the same reasons offer equally compelling justification for the adoption of the much more simple and easily administered unitary system.

The most compelling reason for the adoption of a federal system is a desire to combine all the possible advantages of complete independence as a separate political entity with the political and economic strength and prestige associated with large and powerful states. While the intent is to create "one from many," there is also the equally strong desire to permit each of the many to maintain as much as possible its own separate and unique political and social existence.

The key factor here is that prior to the federal union each of its component parts has had a separate and unique political and social existence. With the dubious exceptions of the Soviet Union and Yugoslavia, no unitary states, even in theory, have reorganized themselves as federations for over a half century.[5] By way of contrast, the three longest-lasting and most successful federal polities, the United States (1789), Canada (1867), and Australia (1901), all represented the coming together of previously separate political entities with their own traditions and special interests.

Even in terms of the American experience, it is easy to forget in the late twentieth century just how strong were the feelings of difference and separatism which made a federal system look desirable. Professor Wheare, for example, quotes a distinguished American historian as commenting that "most citizens of the United States in 1790, if asked their country or nation, would not have answered 'American' but Carolinian, Virginian, Pennsylvanian, New Yorker, or New Englander."[6] Seventy years after the formation of the American federal union, several million Americans, led by Robert E. Lee, considered that they owed their prime loyalty to their state rather than to the union.

[5]In theory the Soviet constitution of 1936 and the Yugoslav constitution of 1963 created federal systems. But quite aside from the constitutional restrictions, the continuing dominance in both cases of an order party insures no change in unitary control. Mexico in 1917 and what was left of Austria in 1920 adopted federal-type constitutions, although in both countries in practice there have always been strong centralist tendencies.

[6]Wheare, *Federal Government*, p. 39.

Aside from economic and geographical influences which have led to a desire to maintain a degree of independence within an over-all unity, divergence of nationality has been an important influence in such federal unions as Canada and Switzerland. In both cases, it was a sense of military insecurity and the fear of not-too-friendly powerful neighbors that overcame, to a degree, the divisiveness of the cultural, religious, and linguistic separation of British and French Canada and of the French, German, and Italian areas of Switzerland.

What Makes a Federal Union Work

So far we have surveyed briefly why federalism fits the paradoxical need for the maximum amount of independence within the same political frame of reference. But there is one further set of factors which needs to be considered. These are the elements which constitute what Wheare calls the "capacity" to make a "federal form of union" work. Included in this list are such factors as:

1. The desire to make it succeed
2. The existence of the same forces which led to union in the first place (i.e., fear of common outside enemies and a desire for economic advantage)
3. "Community of race, language, religion and nationality"
4. The factor which produces the desire for union and at the same time the capacity for union: similarity of social and particularly political institutions
5. "Possession of characteristics among these institutions usually associated with democracy or free government . . . particularly free elections and a party system, with its guarantee of a responsible opposition"
6. Differences, but not too great, in the areas, populations, and wealth of the individual units comprising the new federation
7. Sufficient economic resources and independent taxing powers to utilize them so that both the central government and each of the individual unit governments will have financial independence[7]

Of all these factors, perhaps the first and the last are the most essential, for without the will to succeed and the resources to do so, failure at any attempt at federation would be inevitable. Although the third point is highly desirable, Canada, for one, has survived in its present form since 1867 and seems likely to continue to do so, despite its divergent ethnic, linguistic, and religious backgrounds. The same is true of Switzerland since 1848. And the ina-

[7] *Ibid.*, pp. 45–48.

bility of the Quebec separatists to attract any significant support seems to indicate that the other factors outlined by Wheare far outweigh the lack of homogeneity in background.

The fourth and fifth points Wheare considers of particular importance since he believes that nondemocratic government in any part of a federation will eventually destroy "that equality of status and that independence which these governments must enjoy, each in its own sphere, if federal government is to exist at all." While less important, there is also need for a certain minimum degree of uniformity in social institutions. He concludes, "it must be emphasized that the capacity of states to form and work a federal union depends upon some agreement to differ but not to differ too much."

No true federal union can exist when one unit is so overwhelmingly dominant in both size and population that it can dominate the others as completely as Prussia did in the German imperial period (1871–1918) or as the Russian Soviet Federated Socialist Republic (75 percent of the land area and more than 50 percent of the population) dominates the other Soviet republics. Even without the factor of rigid party control, this disproportionate strength in itself would be enough to make difficult if not impossible the operation of a genuine federalist system.

But even if all of these factors are present, unless they are properly organized, there is not even a strong probability of the successful functioning of a federal union.

ORGANIZATION OF A FEDERAL SYSTEM

Three factors are important to the organization of a federal system: (1) a written constitution which is final and authoritative; (2) equal participation in amending the constitution by the central government and the component units of the federation; and (3) the existence of some type of supreme judicial authority which can arbitrate or decide disputes between the central authority and the regional governments.

The need for a written and authoritative constitution hardly needs comment. In the organization of a federal system there will obviously be a number of complicated arrangements necessary, all of which much be spelled out very specifically and very carefully. Without an authority to which to refer, it would be quite impossible to ascertain the jurisdictional divisions and lines of authority. To insure orderly administration the constitution must be the ultimate source of all authority.

The second point also is self-evident. The essence of a federal system is the sharing of powers by two independent authorities. Only if both participate in the amending process can these conditions be fulfilled. And nothing is more basic to the continued existence of the federal system than the way in which the constitution is modified. The American federal system has elaborate arrangements for constitutional amendment. First, a two-thirds vote of approval is required by both the Senate and the House of Representatives. Then either the state legislatures or specially elected state conventions can carry out the necessary ratification with approval by three-fourths of the states necessary.

The Australian constitution provides that any amendment "must be passed by an absolute majority of each House of the Parliament" and then within two to six months thereafter be approved by a majority of the general voters. Switzerland has a rather similar procedure. Constitutional amendments may be initiated by joint action of both houses of the legislature, or, under certain conditions, by one house alone, or by a "popular initiative" consisting of "a demand by fifty thousand Swiss voters for the adoption of a new constitutional article or for the repeal or modification of certain articles of the Constitution already in force." Final approval, however an amendment is initiated, must be by a majority not only of the total popular vote cast but also of the voters in a majority of cantons.

To settle disputes which arise as a result of the federal system, three of the leading federal states all have remarkably similar procedures. Canada and the United States provide for their supreme courts to be the final appeals agency. Australia, technically, has a provision that its high court can permit appeals to the judicial committee of the British Privy Council, but this apparently is almost never done. In all three cases, the personnel of these highest judicial bodies are appointed by the executive and are subject to dismissal, under highly restricted circumstances, by the legislative branches.

In contrast to the three English-speaking federal systems, Switzerland grants much less sweeping authority to its highest tribunal, which can pass on the constitutionality of cantonal laws but is excluded from ruling on acts by the national legislature. However, 30,000 voters distributed among eight cantons can force the calling of a popular referendum to pass on any legislative act.

The point is sometimes made of the American Constitution by so-called strict constructionists that, unlike Australia and Canada, in the U.S., the Supreme Court has no actual right to pass on the constitutionality of legislative acts and has really arbitrarily and improperly assumed such a power. It is true that there is no specific article or clause of the American Constitution which gives such authority to the Supreme Court in so many words, but there is little doubt that the drafters of the constitution took it for granted that it would be necessary for the Court to pass on the constitutionality of acts by the legislative and executive branches. Alexander Hamilton in *The Federalist* seems to put the case in unmistakable terms. He observes:

> Some perplexity respecting the rights of the courts to pronounce legislative acts void, because contrary to the Constitution, has arisen from an imagination that the doctrine would imply a superiority of the judiciary to the legislative power. It is argued that the authority which can declare the acts of another void must necessarily be superior to the one whose acts may be declared void. . . .
>
> There is no position which depends on clearer principles than that every act of a delegated authority, contrary to the tenor of the commission under which it is exercised, is void. No legislative act contrary to the Constitution, can be valid. . . . The interpretation of the laws is the proper and peculiar province of the courts. A constitution is, in fact, and must be regarded by the judges as a fundamental law. It therefore belongs to them to ascertain its meaning, as well as the meaning of any particular act proceeding from the legislative body. If there should happen to be an irreconcilable variance between the two, that which has the superior obligation and validity ought, of course, to be preferred; or, in other words, the Constitution ought to be preferred to the statute; the intention of the people to the intention of their agents.[8]

In the famous *Marbury* v. *Madison* case of 1803, Chief Justice John Marshall for the first time asserted this right of judicial review which Hamilton had outlined. Perhaps the fact that until after the Civil War there was only one other assertion of this power (the Dred Scott case of 1857) helped to establish the right of judicial review so firmly that now it is one of the unshakable pillars of the American constitutional system.

THE FEDERAL LINKAGE SYSTEM: AMERICAN VERSION

The modern concept of federalism emerged from the Constitutional Convention at Philadelphia in 1788. As Wheare, the leading British authority on federalism, puts it: "The modern idea of what federal government is has been determined by the United States of America. . . . Many consider it the most important and the most successful example. . . . It would seem sensible, therefore, in seeking a legitimate and convenient definition of federal government, to begin by examining the Constitution of the United States."[9]

[8]Ford, *The Federalist*, no. 78, pp. 520–521.
[9]Wheare, *Federal Government*, p. 1.

What are the essential aspects of the federal principle? A key to an understanding of American-type federalism lies in remembering that first there were the states, and then there was the federal government. Prior to the ratification of the Constitution, the states conducted themselves as independent and sovereign nations. Each one of them possessed inherent powers in the way that a human being possesses the inherent right of self-preservation. As a matter of course, an independent political entity has to defend itself from outside attack, maintain internal order, and raise the money to pay its administrators. All these are inherent powers.

The federal government, by virtue of the mere fact that it is the supreme national authority for the United States of America, has these same inherent powers, above all, as the Supreme Court has ruled, in the area of foreign affairs. But even more important, the federal government has both delegated powers and far-reaching implied powers; it has the authority "To make all Laws which shall be necessary and proper for carrying into Execution the foregoing Powers. . . ."

The delegated powers concern those matters necessary for the functioning of a governmental system. In external affairs, the United States is the sole authority in such matters as providing "for the common Defense," declaring war, and regulating "Commerce with foreign Nations." Internally it has authority to regulate commerce "among the several states" with the states themselves expressly forbidden to erect any trade barriers against each other. The federal government also has the exclusive power to coin money, establish a postal system, and coordinate with the existing state judicial systems "to constitute Tribunals inferior to the Supreme Court." The existence of a dual court system is only one example of the shared (concurrent) powers which exist in American federalism. Not only can both the central government and the states establish judicial systems; both can levy taxes and borrow money.

The Constitution is vague on what powers the states do have. The Tenth Amendment states in broad terms that "the powers not delegated to the United States by the Constitution, nor prohibited by it to the States, are reserved to the States respectively, or to the people." Only negatively does the Constitution itself deal with the subject by forbidding the states to engage in foreign affairs or warfare, to "lay any Imposts or Duties on Imports or Exports," to coin money, or to pass any "Law impairing the obligation of contract." In contrast to the exclusive powers given the national government and the restrictions placed upon the states, it is now accepted that the states themselves no longer have any exclusive powers, if they ever did. Virtually every area of state policy-making is now dominated by the influence of the federal government, above all in financial terms and in Article VI it stipulated that "the Supreme Law of the Land" is to be the Constitution and the laws "made in Pursuance thereof," regardless of any state laws to the contrary.

AMERICAN FEDERALISM IN PRACTICE

The relations between the central government and the states are often diagrammed in terms of two interlocking circles with the common area representing the concurrent powers shared by the two coordinate systems. In actuality the circles should be drawn to resemble an advanced partial eclipse of the sun, for there is no doubt that the central government possesses much more power than the states. Nor is there any uncertainty as to the considerable degree of shared powers. But, as we have commented, there is considerable uncertainty as to what, if any, exclusive powers the states have.

In recent decades this long-existing uncertainty has been increased by the steadily developing influence and intervention of the federal government in a large number of programs right down to the local level. Some of the more controversial of these are the programs for urban redevelopment and urban renewal and the intensified involvement in local policies of such government departments as those of Transportation and Health, Education and Welfare.

But these developments are far less a change in kind than in degree. Even during the nineteenth-century era of the negative state there was a considerable degree of intergovernmental cooperation. As one specialist on the development of American federalism puts it, "relative to what governments did, intergovernmental cooperating during the nineteenth century was comparable with that existing today."[10]

Financial Aspects of Intergovernmental Cooperation

Much of the influence exerted by the central government on state and local policies comes from a flexible use of the government's unquestionable powers to tax and to spend. Constitutionally, the federal government cannot directly intervene to bring about policy changes in affairs outside the range of its delegated powers. But lacking a stick, it has found that a carrot can be just as effective. As their problems have increased in number and complexity, state and local governments have eagerly sought financial assis-

[10]Morton Grodzins, "The Federal System," in *Goals for Americans: Programs for Action in the Cities,* U.S. President's Commission on National Goals (Englewood Cliffs, N.J.: Prentice-Hall, 1960), p. 269.

tance from the federal government. This the federal government has been willing to provide if the local polity was willing to accept its policy guidelines on such matters as school integration and municipal housing practices.

This not-so-indirect financial control has been exercised primarily by the use of *grants-in-aid.* The use of the grant-in-aid goes back to the early years of the federal union and in the area of education, it actually predates the adoption of the Constitution. Among the few constructive acts of the Confederation period were the passage in 1785 and 1787 by "the United States in Congress assembled" of land ordinances which donated nationally owned land in the new Northwest Territory for the development of a public education system. The government's huge tracts of land provided the chief source for grants-in-aid. One of the most notable of these was the Morrill Land Grant Act of 1862 which provided the basis for the establishment of state college systems in the West and Middle West. It is worth noting that despite the long-existent federal-state collaboration, in theory education is entirely within the area of state jurisdiction. The same is true of two other long-established areas of cooperation: the development of internal communications and the setting-up of sound state financial systems.

An indication of both the range of and the considerable amounts of money involved in the contemporary grants-in-aid programs is given in Table 14.

Note that 72.5 percent of the total grants-in-aid go to the two areas of health, labor, and welfare, and commerce and transportation. When education, and housing and community development, the third and fourth largest areas of federal assistance, are added to these first two, 93.4 percent of the total grants are accounted for. It would be difficult to

Table 14
Federal Grants-in-Aid by Function, 1969

Function	Grants (in millions)	Percent of total
National defense	32.5	.2
International affairs/finance	5.3	.06
Agricultural affairs	644.0	3.2
Natural resources	476.2	2.4
Commerce and transportation	4,806.0	23.9
Housing and community development	1,812.5	9.0
Health, labor, welfare	9,744.3	48.6
Education	2,398.2	11.9
Veterans' benefits and services	14.8	.14
General government	114.2	.6
Total	20,048.0	

SOURCE: This table has been adapted from Thomas R. Dye, Lee S. Greene, and George S. Parthemos, *American Government: Theory, Structure and Process* (Belmont, Calif.: Wadsworth, 1969), p. 82.

find any better illustration of either the high degree of involvement of the federal government in local matters or of the routine acceptance of the positive state as an active factor in molding social and economic development.

It is common to offer these agents on a so-called matching basis. This means that the state or local government involved must put up a proportionate amount of money—seldom as much as 50 percent—to match the federal grant. In large part this procedure is intended to make the state's commitment firm and to offer a strong inducement to the state to use local funds for the programs favored by federal agencies. Though less important, of course the matching system does reduce to some degree federal expenditures.

Judicial Influence on Federalism

In some sensitive areas, the federal government has intervened even more directly in the shaping of social and economic policies. Under an increasingly broadened interpretation by the courts of what constitutes "interstate commerce," for example, the 1964 civil rights act asserted the right of the federal government to regulate private employment practices to prevent discrimination based on race, creed, color, or national origin. In 1968 a second major civil rights act again used the most liberal interpretation possible of the term *commerce* as the basis for its open-housing policy, which gives government the authority to tell property owners that they must not refuse to rent or sell to anyone because of race or religion.

The courts have often been an important factor in the expansion of these powers. Basing their decisions on the need of the federal government to exercise effectively its commerce powers, the courts have consistently lent support to the expansion of control by the central government. An authority on the federal system commented, from the perspective of the early 1960s,

> In one imporant respect, the Constitution no longer operates to impede centralized government. The Supreme Court since 1937 has given Congress a relatively free hand. The federal government can build substantive programs in many areas on the taxation and commerce powers. Limitations of such central programs based on the argument, "it's unconstitutional," are no longer possible as long as Congress (in the Court's view) acts reasonably in the interest of the whole nation. The Court is unlikely to reverse this permissive view in the foreseeable future.[11]

It must be pointed out that there are still important influences which act to give the states a continuing role in the federal structure. The states, after all, are guaranteed

[11] *Ibid.*, p. 271.

important powers in their own right. They can tax, they can legislate, they can investigate pressing social and economic problems and mobilize public opinion to force national action. A striking example of this last recourse was the widespread publicity by various state health departments which in the late 1950s forced a reluctant Atomic Energy Commission to publicize information on fallout and radioactive contamination levels which it had tried to keep secret.

Politics and Federalism

Above all, the way in which the federal system has shaped the unique character of American political parties has given the states a continuingly important role. Only once every four years is there any national political focus. For the rest of the time the political parties must plan their programs for survival, let alone future growth, in terms of state and local elections. Significantly, political prognosticators often evaluate the state of health of a party on the basis of the governorships it controls and the number of state legislators and county officials it has elected rather than on the degree of success or failure in presidential elections. Success in presidential elections is possible only if the party has maintained and strengthened its state and local power bases.

On a personal basis, exactly the same inexorable law applies to the political careers of individual senators and representatives. Many a would-be national authority or world statesman has had a promising career cut short because he could no longer be bothered to take care of the home folks. It is notable that those members of Congress who have held office the longest and exercise the greatest power are those who have never forgotten to insure that Turkey Creek has its new post office, or that the old navy yard is kept open whether needed or not, or that the new airbase is announced just a month before election time.

Constantly working against all the *centripetal* forces tending to concentrate power in the central government is the *centrifugal* influence of the party system. As Professor Grodzins puts it:

> In summary, then, the party system functions to devolve power. The American parties, unlike any other, are highly responsive when directives move from the bottom to the top, highly unresponsive from top to bottom. Congressmen and senators can rarely ignore concerted demands from their home constituencies; but no party leader can expect the same kind of response from those below, whether he be a President asking for congressional support or a congressman seeking aid from local or state leaders.[12]

[12] *Ibid.*, p. 275.

Like congressmen, federal administrators constantly find themselves forced to take local wishes and feelings into account. Few important pieces of legislation are enacted without providing important roles for state and local governments in their administration. In the application of the regulations of any government department or agency, there is even stronger pressure for constant attention to state and local views.

We noted in the previous chapter the popular concept of the legislator as an effective channel of communications with the federal bureaucracy. The legislator's failure to transmit the desires and opinions of his constituents may well result in political oblivion. Not surprisingly legislators spend a considerable amount of time in negotiating the problems of their constituents with the various agencies, while an even greater proportion of the time of their administrative staffs is spent in telephoning and writing on behalf of constituents. The "important consequence" of these activities, writes Professor Grodzins, "is the comprehensive, day-to-day, even hour-by-hour, impact of local views on national programs. No point of substance or procedure is immune from congressional scrutiny. A substantial portion of the entire weight of this impact is on behalf of the state and local governments."

Because American parties "are without program and without discipline," the bureaucrat "is forced to seek support where he can find it," notes Grodzins. The result is the constant need to pay close and solicitous attention to the wishes and desires which congressmen are pushing on behalf of their constituents. The fulfillment of these requests means adequate appropriations for the bureaucrat and political survival for the politician. The obvious result is to insure an important influence for the state and local interests. This same dispersed character of the American party system "allows individuals, groups and institutions (including state and local governments) to attempt to influence national policy at every step of the legislative-administrative process." Barring the unlikely prospect of the development of a much more disciplined and centralized organization of its parties, the American version of federalism will probably continue with this sharing both of governmental functions and political power. In fact, with the contemporary concern over too-big government and too much power centralization, state and local influences almost certainly will continue as powerful forces.

THE NEW FEDERALISM

One of the most promising developments in federal-state relations on the American scene has been the enunciation of what has been termed the "new federalism" by President Nixon, although the phrase was first used by President Eisenhower. Its purpose was "to present a new set of reforms—a new set of proposals—a new and drastically different approach to the way in which government cares for those in need and to the way the responsibilities are shared between the state and federal governments."[13]

The need for this drastic restructuring of relations came about, according to the president, for the following reasons:

> A third of a century of centralizing power and responsibility in Washington has produced a bureaucratic monstrosity, cumbersome, unresponsive and ineffective.
>
> A third of a century of social experiment has left us a legacy of entrenched programs that have outlived their time or outlived their purpose.
>
> A third of a century of unprecedented growth and change has strained our institutions and raised serious questions about whether they are still adequate to the times.

To correct this situation the president proposed a three-part program involving reform of the welfare system, the streamlining of manpower-training programs and, most important of all, a far-reaching plan for revenue-sharing between state and federal governments. This "no-strings-attached" revenue-sharing program was to be based on income-tax collections increasing from one-sixth of 1 percent in fiscal 1971 (calculated to yield $500 million) to 1 percent in fiscal 1976 and thereafter, assuring approximately $5 billion for distribution. This annual "kickback" was to be divided among the states according to a complex formula based on each state's revenue-raising efforts. Within states, to prevent discrimination against any particular city or area, each city and county was to receive a share of funds proportionate to its tax contribution.

The president's proposal draws on a precedent of 1836 when the federal government found itself with a treasury surplus, which was liquidated by distributing it proportionately among the states. His proposals were clearly intended to strengthen the role of the states in respect to their big cities, for the desperate financial needs of some large cities had increasingly led them to by-pass impotent state governments and seek aid directly from Washington.

But more than a year after the president's call for the creation of the new federalism, the program remained a hopeful blueprint rather than a reality. This was due in part to the inevitable conflict between a Republican president and a Democratic Congress. But this aspect aside, congressional reluctance to enact the president's proposals also came from a desire to retain control over social and economic programs in the states. As Wilbur Mills, the

[13] *Congressional Quarterly Weekly Report* 27 (August 15, 1969): 1517.

powerful chairman of the House Ways and Means Committee, expressed it, "If it is just a block grant with no formula for ensuring Congressional objectives, I think it is a very bad thing. There would be no restraint on the state legislatures."[14] For that matter, reports from the 1970 governors' conference indicated a feeling among state executives that the administration itself had failed to push the new federalism with sufficient vigor. But in spite of this lack of progress, the sheer necessity of restructuring federal-state relations seemed to make the emergence of a new federalism an inevitable development in the decade of the seventies.

OTHER FEDERAL SYSTEMS

We have spoken of the United States, Canada, and Australia as the three most successful federal systems. But in the contemporary world other nations are also regarded as in the federal category. Sharing common roots in the Anglo-American political tradition with the three major federal systems are Cameroon, India, Malaysia, and Nigeria. Falling directly within the Hispanic political tradition are Argentina, Brazil, and Mexico, while Austria, West Germany, and Switzerland draw on a Germanic heritage. Of the Hispanic and Germanic backgrounds, Professor Elazar said:

> Both political traditions have been influential in stimulating federal inclinations in many of the non-federal nations, but they have been notably less successful in fostering lasting federal institutions; the Hispanic tradition has failed to combine federalism and stability, while the Germanic has tended more toward authoritarian centralization.[15]

To complete his count of 16 formally federal nations, Professor Elazar included Libya and the two communist federal states of the U.S.S.R. and Yugoslavia. But as of the early 1970s, revolutionary coups and military dictatorships in Argentina, Brazil, Libya, and Nigeria made it dubious whether these polities should be regarded as even "formally" federal. Then, too, given the dominance of the government machinery by their respective movement regimes, both the Soviet Union and Yugoslavia must be excluded. Rather than 16 countries, perhaps no more than 10 can be regarded as either federal or quasi-federal (Australia, Austria, Cameroon, Canada, India, Malaysia, Mexico, Switzerland, United States, and West Germany).

[14] *Ibid.*

[15] In this article on "Federalism" in the 1968 edition of the *International Encyclopedia of the Social Sciences,* from which this quotation is taken Professor David J. Elazar speaks of "16 formally federal nations" as of that time (vol. 5, p. 365).

In terms of his definition of a truly federal system as one where "the general and regional governments are each, within a sphere, coordinate and independent," Wheare regards only four countries as true federations: Australia, Canada, Switzerland, and the United States.

In a federal system, how is jurisdictional authority divided between the general and the regional governments? In addition to the limited categories of the jurisdictions exclusive to each, there is the much larger area of the concurrent jurisdictions. Notes Wheare,

> A concurrent jurisdiction is found in all modern federal governments, and with it a provision that when the laws of the general government upon matters in the concurrent field conflict with the laws of the regional governments in that field, then the regional laws must give way to the general laws to the extent of their repugnancy.[16]

In extent of concurrent field, Wheare ranks Canada as the least with only immigration and agriculture included, then Switzerland, followed by the United States and Australia with extensive concurrent areas. The Canadian constitution specifically lists the exclusive powers of the parliament and of the provincial legislature with a separate article providing for agriculture and immigration. The Swiss constitution also specifically enumerates the exclusive jurisdiction given to the federal assembly, while granting the right to the cantons to make "treaties with foreign states in respect of matters of public economy and neighborship and police relations."[17]

The U.S. Constitution not only specifically enumerates the delegated powers but concludes with that broad grant of authority which has been increasingly used in the twentieth century in connection with the "necessary and proper" clause.[18] The concurrent powers in the American federal system are not specified but are defined in terms of those which have been specifically delegated to the central legislative body, forbidden to the states, or "reserved to the States respectively, or to the people."

Similar to the reserved-powers provision of the Tenth Amendment to the U.S. Constitution is a stipulation in the Australian constitution which retains for the state legislatures all the powers which they possessed at the time of federation (1901) unless these powers are specifically dele-

[16]Wheare, *Federal Government*, p. 79.

[17]Its interesting that the Soviet Constitution gives the same technical right to the union republics.

[18]The final clause of Article I, section 8, provides that in addition to the enumerated powers, Congress shall have power "To make all Laws which shall be necessary and proper for carrying into Execution the foregoing Powers, and all other Powers vested by this Constitution in the Government of the United States. . . ." The courts have repeatedly resorted to the "necessary and proper" clause to justify new economic and social applications of governmental authority.

gated to the federal legislature. As in the U.S. Constitution, the concurrent field is defined by omission and covers a wide area.

Because of the basic predominance of the central government, Wheare does not include India in his classification of federal states. But, whether classified as federal or quasi-federal, the Indian constitution of 1959 does attempt to define the distribution of jusdictions as does no other federal or quasi-federal constitution. The "union list" of powers delegated specifically to the central government contains 97 items, with 66 on the "state list" and 47 on the "concurrent list."

The basic tenor of the provisions for dealing with a conflict between central and regional enactments on the concurrent topics is one reason why Wheare considers only a quasi-federal state. Initially, article 254 seems to defer more to the desires of state legislatures than is customary in a federal system, especially in the provision that regional legislative enactments must yield in proportion to the degree of their repugnancy. It then goes on to say that such a state law may receive "the consideration of the President" and, if it "has received his consent," can then prevail, in the state in question, over the national legislative enactment. Although this appears to provide a rather unusual degree of flexibility, Wheare considers it a violation of the basic federal concept of separate and equal powers. He comments, "Yet as it rests with the President to decide whether the general legislature is to be supreme, in this way a potentially exclusive control is vested with the general government."[19]

WHY SO FEW FEDERAL SYSTEMS?

Why is it that by even the most inclusive count only 16 sovereign states can be regarded as federal or quasi-federal? Clearly a federal system has much to offer. To restate the reasons, the federal system has these advantages:

1. It offers military security by creating one big nation instead of a number of small weak ones inviting military aggression.
2. By the same token it strengthens the possibility of independence from foreign interference.
3. It creates a sizable internal free market with consequent economic benefits.
4. It permits diversity within the framework of unity; the various regions, with all the advantages mentioned above, are still in a position "to do their own thing."

[19]Wheare, *Federal Government*, p. 81.

The Central American Experiment

But with all these advantages, still only about 10 percent of the world's states are organized on a federal basis. Obviously there are a number of states and regions of the world which would benefit from a federal type of association. Central America, for example, would seem to be a geopolitical region where the development of a federal union should be both logical and easy to achieve. The six small countries (Guatemala, Honduras, El Salvador, Nicaragua, Costa Rica, and Panama) which occupy the area have historically been unable to resist foreign military intervention, usually brought about by the constant political upheaval and social chaos which has characterized their individual histories. Federation would aid considerably in achieving political stability and economic development. In addition, there are traditional influences which would seem to offer strong inducements for federation. All of the countries involved came into existence as parts of the Spanish empire, and all have similar governmental institutions and a common background in terms of language, religion, and social customs.

After the end of Spanish colonial rule, the five states of Central America existing in 1823 formed the United Provinces of Central America which maintained an uneasy, strife-torn, and feeble unity until 1839 when it disintegrated. During the decade of the 1840s various efforts to reconstitute the union were equally unsuccessful and since that time the various countries have gone their separate ways. The creation of a United States of Central America continues to be in the realm of wishful political thinking. There now exists a hopeful degree of economic cooperation but this is only a modest first step.

The Central American failure at federalizing, when all the odds seemed to favor it, illustrates the difficulties that make federal systems so rare. Historically the negative factors have always outweighed what, on the surface, would seem to be strong positive forces for union. One of the important reasons for failure was the influence of those technological factors which have an important bearing on political developments, or the lack of them. Specifically in the case of the failure of Central American federation, poor communications between widely separated areas have proven an apparently insuperable handicap. Although it is true that all of the countries concerned shared a common political and cultural heritage, the original provinces were widely separated from each other, and even within limited areas communication was limited to mule pack trains over towering mountains and through virgin jungles. The result was that each area developed in isolation with purely provincial loyalties and customs and a profound sense of suspicion and hostility to the foreigners down the coast or over the mountains. Added to this was the isolation of a rural economy with widely scattered villages and an almost total lack of education except among the tiny social and economic elite.

Except for brief and fleeting periods, there has never existed in Central America either the strong desire for federation or the leadership to provide it. In each country the ruling elite has been too concerned with its own power position to wish to surrender its political control or yield any of its economic advantages in the interests of the region at large.

Possibly the end of the twentieth century will see the development of successful moves toward greater political and economic unity. But, although the technological barriers to closer contact may be considerably reduced, the traditional antagonisms and suspicions seem likely to continue unchanged. The border war in 1969 between El Salvador and Honduras was a significant indication of how strong the psychological barriers are to any kind of federation in spite of all the factors in favor of it.

Other Failures of Federal Union

Allowing for the obvious differences in geographical location, cultural heritage, and historical experience, the failure of attempts at Central American federation is the story in microcosm of similar efforts made during the past twenty years or so to bring about federation in the newly independent African states and in the Arab states of the Middle East, to cite two other equally unsuccessful efforts to achieve unity.

Perhaps the closest parallel to the Central American situation is found in the Arab states of the Middle East. Here, too, is a common colonial background (the Turkish empire for some four centuries), the same language, the same religion, and greatly similar social customs. The odds would seem to be heavily in favor of an Arab union which, in theory, could stretch from Egypt to Iraq. But every effort to accomplish this has failed.

The most ambitious attempt was Nasser's formation of the United Arab Republic in 1958, with Egypt and Syria as its two parts but with the obvious expectation of creating a federal pan-Arab state. In 1961, however, a Syrian military revolt dissolved the union, and Syria since then has followed its own independent course. In large part, the reasons for dissolution were similar to those which brought the first attempt at Central American federation to ruin. In that case, fear of Guatemalan domination had antagonized the other states. In the United Arab Republic, the Syrian military leaders charged, all important policy posts had been filled by Egyptians who used their offices solely for the benefit of Egypt, with Syria treated far more as an annexed province than as an equal partner. Here again the psychological barriers to union outweighed all the seemingly obvious and logical reasons for its success.

Psychological Barriers to Federal Union: The Indonesian Case

We conclude our illustrations of the way psychological barriers prevent the seemingly logical emergence of federal systems with a country, rather than a regional example. Among the nations of the world, few seem as obviously in need of a federal organization as the Republic of Indonesia.

For a country composed of some 3000 islands populated by 17 major language groups with widely varying cultural heritages and social customs, a federal system of organization would seem almost inevitable. But here again is an excellent illustration of the role played by psychological factors. In the late 1940s, the Dutch, who had governed Indonesia (the Dutch East Indies) for several centuries, sought to reorganize their colonial empire on a federal basis as a prelude to creating a Dutch-Indonesian Union.

The acceptance of this federal system was part of the bargain which the Indonesian nationalist movement had to accept in 1949 in return for Dutch acknowledgement of Indonesian independence. In theory the United States of Indonesia was a logical development. One of the major fears of the other Indonesian peoples had been of Javanese domination. Traditionally the island of Java had been the political and economic center of the archipelago, and the core of the nationalist movement had been centered there. A federal type of organization, with each area represented in the central government, seemed a logical way in which to alleviate these fears and make allowances for the diversity of Indonesia's peoples and regions.

But the dominant nationalists saw it quite otherwise. For them the whole Dutch-sponsored concept of federal organization represented a cunning plot on the part of the former imperialist rulers to weaken the unity of the new state and to continue a concealed influence through regional divisions. Within six months of Indonesian independence, the United States of Indonesia was abolished and a unitary republic established, with the various regions functioning simply as provinces administered from Djakarta. The price has not been small. Constant friction has continued between Java and the other regions. More than once, most seriously in the late 1950s, regional revolts have been stimulated by the apparent belief (often well justified) that Indonesia was being administered entirely too much by and for the Javanese. Here again the seemingly logical pattern of federal organization meant little when confronted with the formidable psychological and emotional barriers to its adoption.

SPECIAL REQUIREMENTS FOR A FEDERAL SYSTEM

Now that we have looked at these instances where federal systems were logical but unsuccessful, we can offer some tentative reasons why there are so few of them in the world. In no particular order of importance, here are some possible reasons for the limited number of federal systems:

1. The existence of a federal system calls for values peculiar to Anglo-American political culture.
2. Federalism as the embodiment of "an indestructible union of indestructible states" seems to threaten the precarious and dearly won unity of a new nation.
3. By its very nature, a federal system makes difficult, if not impossible, any kind of centralized economic and social planning.
4. A federal system depends on the existence of a large and well-trained pool of professional administrators.
5. A federal system is expensive to operate in view of its dual governmental organization.
6. A federal system cannot function in terms of any type of party organization based on the movement regime or any other type of highly centralized pattern.

The first point is certainly debatable and quite possibly is dubious. But, as Professor Elazar comments, "relatively few cultures have been able to utilize federal principles in government. Anglo-American civil societies have done so most successfully."[20] In part, the reason for this, he suggests, is "because both constitutionalism and noncentralization rate high on the scale of Anglo-American political values." Although this is implied in the concept of noncentralization, it is worth noting that the concept of pluralism is basic both to federalism and Anglo-American political culture. The philosophical climate which federalism needs in order to flourish is precisely what Anglo-American political culture regards as the only proper attitude to have.

In the post-Civil War period, Chief Justice Salmon P. Chase defined federalism as being "an indestructible Union, composed of indestructible States" (*Texas* v. *White*). Basic to this authoritative definition is the clear implication that both the oneness of the central government and the diversity of the states will continue indefinitely in a state of dynamic tension. Even in societies in which there is a

[20]"Federalism," *Encyclopedia of the Social Sciences* (1968), vol. 5, p. 365.

relatively high degree of consensus on values and objectives, this dual proposition can produce considerable conflict. It calls not only for much consensus but a very advanced degree of political sophistication in both theoretical and operational terms.

It is not surprising that few, if any, of these factors are present in the new nations just emerged from colonialism. Their desperate need is to emphasize unity and to break down regionalism, not to perpetuate it as an indestructible aspect of their future existence. The areas and peoples that compose a new nation often have little in common except the fact that by the accidents of international power politics they found themselves grouped together as a British or French or some other European colony.

Under these circumstances the encouragement of any kind of political diversity may not only be a dubious risk but, as the Indonesians and other nationalists have seen it, an outright exercise in subversive activity likely to disintegrate the fragile unity of the new nation. Further, such political values as compromise and pluralism are often little appreciated. All in all, it is not surprising that, in spite of its theoretical attractions, so few of the almost one hundred new nations created since World War II have adopted a federal system and those that have, notably India, have weighted it strongly in favor of the central authority.

The third objection to the adoption of a federal system clearly has little relevance for such long-established "free enterprise" economies as those of the United States, Canada, and Australia. In these societies, both economic and social life functions on a highly private and pluralist basis, although in the late twentieth century, myth and reality are frequently divergent. But even in these countries the rather modest attempts at governmental planning and direction of social and economic development have often been frustrated by the existence of dual and independent governmental systems. (In this connection, you will remember that one of the objections raised to President Nixon's no-strings-attached grants in the "new federalism" program was that this would make it impossible for the central government to exercise a sufficient degree of financial control to nudge the states into adopting federal guidelines for economic and social programs.)

For the new nations, virtually all of whom have adopted some type of centralized social and economic planning, the independent duality of a federal system might well prove an almost impossible hurdle to the achievement of an already too-difficult task. Here again, aside from the psychological and political barriers, is another potent argument against the adoption of a federal system.

The fourth and fifth reasons for the limited adoption of federal systems are clearly linked together. To operate a federal system calls for a comfortable surplus both in governmental budgets and trained personnel. A federal system is to governments in general what a Rolls Royce is to the automobile buyer—a luxury whch few can afford either to purchase or to maintain. Psychological factors aside, this cost in money and trained personnel tends to become a prohibitive factor in itself.

The sixth point needs little comment. This is why such theoretically federalist systems as those of the Soviet Union and Yugoslavia exist in name only. The movement regimes as the organizational embodiment of a "revealed" ideology are compelled by their most basic dynamics to insist constantly and forcefully on unity and centralized control. This type of party system is a powerful deterrent to the initial adoption, let alone successful functioning, of a federal union. But the reverse of this is that once a highly decentralized party system has emerged within the constitutional framework of federal government, it is a powerful influence for the continuance of a federal system. The influence of the decentralized American party system on the operations of government at all levels has already been commented on. Both the Democratic and Republican parties are often described as 50-state parties which coalesce, more or less, every four years in an effort to elect the president. For the rest of the time the jealously guarded autonomy of the state organizations acts as a highly effective check on centralizing tendencies in either the political or governmental spheres.

CONCLUSION

The existence of deeply rooted regional parties in such federal nations as the United States, Canada, and Australia goes far to explain the survival of federalism as a dynamic rather than merely theoretical concept. Federalism once established has demonstrated remarkable survival power, and no well-established federal system has ever evolved into a unitary regime. Rather, even though they cannot be classified as federal or even quasi-federal, a number of unitary regimes find it necessary and expedient to adopt various aspects of federal systems in efforts to cope with the problems of uneasy and explosive political diversity.

To attempt to forecast the future of any type of governmental system is folly. But we can make these statements about federalism:

1. For the reasons discussed in some detail, federal systems will always represent very much of a minority among the governments of the world.
2. Where established, they seem likely to continue indefinitely.

3. Quite probably even such self-consciously unitary-oriented regimes as the Indonesian will use various aspects of federal organization on a selective basis.
4. As a governmental concept, federalism will continue to exert an important and continuing influence on the reorganization of existing governments and the creation of new ones.
5. Possibly, the federal principle may offer a basis for new international or supranational organizations in the years to come.

14

THE NEED FOR GROUND RULES OR THE ROLE OF CONSTITUTIONS

Political action, except for short-lived anemic outbursts, is always defined by a frame of reference, a set of ground rules, which channels and structures it. A convenient term to describe these ground rules is to speak of them as the *constitution* of the country. Along with such symbols of national existence as a flag and an anthem, no country in the world today considers itself properly organized without a constitution.

Just what does the term *constitution* really describe? Has the meaning changed from one period to another? When did the idea of constitutions originate, and why is the idea so widely accepted today? What are the requirements for a satisfactory constitution? What changes have there been in the philosophy of constitution-making since 1789? How can we classify constitutions? The rest of this chapter will be devoted to answering these questions.

What does the term *constitution* mean? As always the Greeks have a word for it: *politeia*. Again, not surprisingly, it was Aristotle who made the first systematic study of constitutions. But the Greek word *politeia* had a far broader meaning than the word *constitution* does today. In the ancient world, the constitution of a political entity meant roughly what we mean today by the constitution of a human being. In short, in Aristotle's frame of reference, the constitution of a state was more than its by-laws, more even than its political culture. It was the seamless pattern of the life of the city-state, including what we now would regard as its economic, social, political, and organizational aspects. The Greek concept of the constitution was not only an organizational one; it also had normative implications since it was expected to provide the guidelines to being a good man by being a good citizen.

In addition to this ethical role which the constitution was to play, Aristotle had a realistic awareness of what is needed if any social arrangement is to endure for long. He notes in *Politics* that "a constitution is an organization of offices, which all the citizens distribute among themselves, according to the power which different classes possess." In contrast to Aristotle's realistic assessment, we often overlook today that a constitution is a creation of politics and has reality only if it reflects existing power relations. Unless this is the case, as various twentieth-century examples in Africa and Southeast Asia demonstrate, its influence is likely to be negligible and its duration brief.

At the opposite pole from Aristotle's concept of a constitution is the popularly held American idea of a constitution as composed of the words printed in a single document or set of documents. This, of course, no more comprises the whole constitution than does the one-eighth of an iceberg showing above water comprise the whole. A more realistic definition was given in 1733 by the English political scholar Lord Bolingbroke:

> By Constitution we mean, whenever we speak with propriety and exactness, that assemblage of laws, institutions and customs, derived from certain fixed principles of reason, directed to certain fixed objects of public good, that compose the general system, according to which the community hath agreed to be governed.[1]

A twentieth-century English constitutional scholar, C. F. Strong, in not too different terms describes a constitution as being "a collection of principles according to which the powers of the government, the rights of the governed and the relations between the two are adjusted."[2]

While broadly inclusive, such definitions as these are still more limited than the Greek concept of *politeia,* so, before we go on to define the requirements for a satisfactory contemporary constitution, let us survey briefly how the modern concepts of constitution have evolved from the original Greek understanding.

CONSTITUTIONS: FROM THE GREEKS TO THE EIGHTEENTH CENTURY

The Greek concept of a constitution represented a closed system. The *politeia* embodied the model, the paradigm, for the good life as conceived by the socioeconomic power group in control. Rational administration, law, and justice, all were there but were interpreted in one fixed pattern. The obligation of the good citizen was to conform. If he did not

[1]Lord Bolingbroke, *The Works of . . .* (London: Henry G. Bohn, 1844), 2:88.

[2]C. F. Strong, *Modern Political Constitutions,* rev. ed. (London: Sidgwick & Jackson, 1952).

do so, if he engaged in "agitation," then for the preservation of the harmony of the *politeia* it was necessary to eliminate him, even though he be Socrates. Without doubt the Greeks laid the foundations for modern constitutional development but it seems unlikely, given its introvertive nature, that their concepts would have developed any further. It was the Romans who created the basis for continuing growth.

What made this possible, more than any other single factor, was the Roman concept of law. Unlike the all-embracing totality of Greek political thought, for the Romans, law was divided into a private and a public sphere. There were the rights of the citizens, and the powers and responsibilities of the state. Among the responsibilities of the state was the protection of its citizens. Nor was this taken lightly by any parties concerned. Even though at the mercy of his jailers, the Apostle Paul, who typified for them a hated and dangerous subversive group, was able to protect himself from torture and mistreatment with the simple statement, "I am a Roman citizen."

This Roman concept of the rights of the citizen and the responsibilities of the state created a dual open-ended potential for growth. In contrast to the Greek version of citizenship, it made no demands for conformity to any ideal pattern. As long as the minimum of "rendering unto Caesar the things which are Caesar's" was accepted, the Roman citizen was secure in his rights and privileges. These minimum requirements permitted the interpretation of citizenship as implying "equal protection under the laws."

Significantly, this concept gave meaning to constitutionalism as a direct derivative of a constitution for the Roman pattern, much as it was deviated from at times, firmly established in the political thinking of Western man the principle that the purpose of a constitution was to guarantee certain rights and privileges to its citizens and place a check upon the powers of government.

The Roman contribution to the idea of a constitution limiting the powers of government has played an important role in the whole development of constitutions. We are indebted to the Greek writer Polybius, brought to Rome as a hostage in the second century B.C., for a description of the way in which the Roman constitution divided powers among the various organs of government. It was this division, according to Polybius, which explained the efficiency and power of the Roman state. Rome had, he observed, a "mixed constitution" which gave strong executive powers to its two annually elected consuls, who represented the monarchical element, while the aristocratic senate held the purse strings and the popular assemblies were the "sole fountain of honor and punishment." The strength of Rome lay in the fact that these three bodies were "accurately adjusted and in exact equilibrium."

Throughout the thousand years of the Middle Ages, Roman concepts of constitutionalism continued to be influential. Though often ignored in practice, the ideal of a rule of law was an important factor in medieval political thinking. Medieval society was organized on a status basis. The stratum into which a man was born determined both his rights and privileges and his duties and obligations. Even the most powerful rulers, although answerable only to God, were not above the law and were duty-bound to fulfill their obligations as well as to enjoy their privileges. This divine or natural law was the final source of all authority. A constant source of bitter dispute between the medieval church and the various rulers was the question of who was best qualified to interpret what natural law really meant in specific cases.

The highly pluralistic nature of medieval society and the lack of any effective means of enforcement made consent an important aspect of medieval constitutional development. Authority over other men came from the fact that they had freely pledged their fealty. But with this authority went the parallel obligation to govern properly and in accord with the wishes of the subjects concerned. Drawing partly on the Roman tradition, partly on established custom, it became customary constitutional practice for medieval rulers to convene great councils of their most important subjects to insure that there was consent for the proposed policies. From these medieval councils developed the modern belief that consent to acts of authority can come only through some sort of representative process.

The early modern period from the sixteenth to the eighteenth centuries seemed to represent an eclipse for constitutional development. Throughout continental Europe strong kings moved to consolidate their power. Eager to establish a more universal and uniform application of the rule of law and guaranteed rights, the newly emerged bourgeoisie, busily engaged in creating modern capitalist society, provided the financial and administrative support necessary. The dominant outlook of this age of "enlightened despotism" was never better summarized than in Louis XIV of France's famous statement, "I am the state." But in spite of this seemingly impervious layer of absolute despotism, just below the surface the forces of constitutional development were gathering strength for the revolutionary developments of the eighteenth and nineteenth centuries.

One of the most important of these influences was the widely held theory of social contract. While it is doubtful if any sophisticated political thinker accepted it literally, it did offer an ingenious explanation of how governmental authority had originated prior to the acceptance of evolutionary theory. Briefly, the social-contract theory hypothesized that a state of nature had existed prior to the establishment of any form of political organization or control. Depending on the particular interpretation, this state of nature was either a secular Garden of Eden without the serpent (John Locke) or a nightmarish condition where the life of man was "solitary, poor, nasty, brutish and short" (Thomas Hobbes).

In either case, so the political fiction ran, it was eventually ended by one or more social contracts which formally established social and political society. In Locke's popular version of the social-contract theory, government came into existence only as a result of the social contract and only as an affair of limited and delegated powers. It was obviously on this interpretation that Thomas Paine, the pamphleteer of the American Revolution, was drawing when he wrote, "A constitution is not the act of a government but of a people constituting a government and a people without a constitution is power without right. A constitution is a thing antecedent to a government and a government is only a creature of a constitution."[3]

The social-contract theory fitted neatly into the concept of popular sovereignty which traced its origins back to Roman constitutionalism. As pressure mounted in the eighteenth and nineteenth centuries for more popular control of government and extended political rights, the demands for a constitution became a convenient way to summarize the desire for more popular control of government and greater political liberties.

The first country in which a strong demand for a constitution appeared was England during the period of the 1640s when the Puritans were pushing for the adoption of the Instrument of the People, a surprisingly popularly oriented constitutional document for its time. Yet ironically Britain has never formally adopted such a document. For a brief period (1653–1660) during the protectorate of Oliver Cromwell, England was ruled under an Instrument of Government, but in 1660 it reverted to its previous and present state of what, in constitutional terms, has been called "happy anarchy."

Yet without any great basic document solemnly drafted by a special convention, Great Britain in the decades following the restoration of the monarchy in 1660 became the chief source of constitutional government in the world. Various court decisions, acts of Parliament, and ways of doing things became inviolable customs and conventions, and converged to create a pattern of limited government and the "rule of law" with its basic principle of the equality of all men before the law. Through this strange process of accident, blundering improvisation, and lucky circumstance,

[3]Thomas Paine, *Selected Works* (New York: Modern Library, 1945), p. 124.

Great Britain by the middle of the eighteenth century had become the world's first constitutional state.

But the first written constitutions developed from the American and French revolutions. Drawing on Locke's concept of limited government, the American Constitution of 1787 opened the age of mass democracy with its declaration that all authority and sovereign power comes from the people: "We the people of the United States . . ."

The French Revolution in its constitutional thinking drew partly on British and American inspiration but more directly on the writings of Rousseau who argued eloquently, if not always logically, for popular sovereignty with the masses as the final source of all power and authority. This was in contrast to Locke, who had so carefully evaded the question of where sovereignty lay. Acceptance of popular sovereignty, "the practical and imprescriptible rights of man," and the social-contract theory were the dominant themes of the Declaration of the Rights of Man and Citizen proclaimed by the French revolutionary assembly of 1789.

CONSTITUTION-MAKING IN THE NINETEENTH AND TWENTIETH CENTURIES

Since the American and French revolutions the formal drafting of a constitutional document has become an essential part of the creation of any new nation. From the failed Russian Decembrist revolt of 1825 to the successful revolt of the Young Turks in 1908, the adoption of a constitution has been linked with the establishment of constitutional government. It should be noted that this has had little to do with any concern for mass democracy. The constitutions of the early nineteenth century represented the most grudging acceptance possible of the revolutionary ideas of the American and French revolutions. Power was allowed to the aristocracy and the upper ranks of the new commercial classes, but the concept of power for "the people" was severely limited. The major role of the constitutional structures was to provide the framework within which the political power struggle was fought out.

In most cases the constitutional structures proved unequal to the task. It is startling to realize that only eight countries in the world, beginning with the United States in 1789 and ending with Canada in 1867, have been able to operate under the same constitution for more than a century.[4] In tune with the unromantic businesslike approach of the increasingly dominant middle class, nineteenth-century constitutions were little concerned with the abstract

[4]The other six oldest constitutions in the world are Sweden (1809), Norway (1814), Holland (1815), Belgium (1831), Switzerland (1848), and New Zealand (1852).

statements of political philosophy which had seemed so important in the eighteenth century. Matter-of-factly they outlined the division of powers, the duties of the various components of the governmental structure, and the political rights of citizens.

It was not until the Mexican constitution of January, 1917, that a new era opened in constitution-drafting. No longer is concern limited to the customary matters of the division of powers among the various parts of government and the traditional guarantees of civil liberties. In the third of 135 articles, the Mexican constitution provides that the aim of all types of education shall be "to develop harmoniously all the faculties of the human being and shall encourage in him at the same time love for the Country and the consciousness of international solidarity, in independence and justice." Land ownership was vested in the nation along with control over all mineral rights and the amount of rural property which might be owned by any one individual.

The Mexican constitution was quickly followed by others of similar type in the years after World War I. The Soviet constitution of 1918, the German Weimar constitution of 1919, and the constitution of the Czechoslovakian republic typified the coming of age of social politics. Also characteristic of these constitutions was an effort at a harmonious balancing of forces reminiscent of Woodrow Wilson's characterization of eighteenth-century constitutions as Newtonian in nature. It could be argued that the failure of most of these post-World War I constitutions to provide a durable framework for evolutionary constitutional development bore out Wilson's further warning that contemporary constitutions, rather than exhibiting the finely tuned static balance of a Newtonian world, needed to be Darwinian, i.e., organic in character.

This period of constitution drafting was brought to end with the Stalin constitution of 1936, which was widely trumpeted by communist propagandists as representing, to quote Stalin, "the only thoroughly democratic constitution in the world." In the pattern set by the Mexican constitution, it sought to define not only the political but also the social characteristics of the Soviet state, which it called "a socialist state of workers and peasants."

The most widely publicized section of the 1936 constitution is "Chapter 10: Fundamental Rights and Duties of Citizens." Among the rights specified are guaranteed employment with "payment for their work in accordance with its quantity and quality," rest and leisure, education, equal rights for women in all areas, the traditional civil liberties of speech, press, and assembly "in conformity with the interests of the working people and in order to strengthen the socialist system," "inviolability of the homes of citizens and privacy of correspondence," and "the right to unite in public organizations." Among other duties, citizens were "to safeguard and fortify public, socialist property," to accept universal military service, and to defend the country.

The constitution left unchanged the dominance of political life by the Community party, which in 1936 as in 1972 and probably in 2001 will continue to be "the leading core of all organizations of the working people, both public and state." The adoption of the world's "only thoroughly democratic constitution" preceded by only a few months the beginning of the great blood purges of the 1930s in which, as Khrushchev was to attest later, at least thousands of innocent Soviet citizens lost their lives or their liberty for periods of years. More than a generation later it is still difficult to assess the real influence of the Stalin constitution. In the late 1950s and early 1960s much was made of socialist legality, although the Communist party left no doubt of its intent to remain in firm control. In the 1970s there seem to be signs that a new Soviet generation is beginning to demand or, at least, expect a literal honoring by the regime of the "fundamental rights" as well as the duties of citizens. Regardless of this, the 1936 constitution does represent the culmination of social constitution-making prior to World War II.

Constitution-drafting since World War II has followed several different paths. In Western Europe, the constitutions of France, West Germany, and Italy represent, it has been suggested, "attempts to find foolproof answers to past mistakes." There is in them neither the soaring political philosophy of the eighteenth century, the self-confident matter-of-factness of the nineteenth, nor the hopeful idealism of the post-World War I period. The old divisions of power and enumeration of duties are once again run through as are all the proper references to the political and social rights of citizens. As one authority sums up the approach to constitution-making after World War II, "For the tired, neurotic, cynical, disenchanted society of the West . . . the importance of the written constitution had visibly faded."[5]

The constitutions of the new peoples' democracies of the Soviet orbit showed an understandable tendency to model themselves on the Stalin constitution. The statement of political and social guarantees in the constitution of the Polish People's Republic, for example, almost literally paraphrases the Soviet model. All these constitutions emphasize the rights of citizens on such matters as education, health, motherhood, labor, and social security.

One of the most interesting aspects of the Soviet-sphere constitutions is their universal selection of the assembly

[5]Karl Loewenstein in Arnold J. Zurcher, ed., *Constitutions and Constitutional Trends since World War II* (New York: New York University Press, 1951), p. 199.

system as the basis for the formal organization of governmental powers. The assemblies, East Germany, Outer Mongolia and Yugoslavia excepted, are all organized as unicameral bodies. Here again the Soviet pattern of "all power to the Soviets" has been closely followed.

We could speculate at length on what the Soviet-zone constitutions actually mean in terms of the rights of their citizens or the efficient organization of governmental functions. But, as in the case of the Soviet Union itself, it is sufficient to note that there is a discrepancy between promise and fulfillment. The constitutions of the Soviet zone are essentially public-relations gestures to the concept of people power and the influence of social politics.

The discrepancy between the ideal picture presented by these constitutions and the realities of political control is demonstrated by the East German constitution, which has been the longest-lasting of any of the satellite constitutions. In theory the constitution establishes a framework for the free operation of a multiparty system with rights of trade unions to strike, churches to give religious instruction in the public schools, and citizens to own private property. In actuality, of course, East Germany has been the most staunchly Stalinist of all the satellites and the least ready to permit any of these freedoms. In varying degrees, ranging from Albania and East Germany at one extreme and probably Yugoslavia at the other, the dominant factor in determining the functioning of the political systems of the communist states has been not the ground rules set forth in the constitutions but the policy needs of the order parties concerned.

In the new nations there has been an idealism and a sense of ideological purpose akin to that in the late eighteenth and early nineteenth centuries. In form and organizational principle the constitutions of the new nations have followed contemporary Western European patterns. Their most striking aspect has been their inclusion of sections in which, at greater length than in the Preamble to the U.S. Constitution, the basic philosophy of government is spelled out. This philosophy is usually a combination of Utopian socialism, liberal humanitarianism, and traditional communalism, and is frequently expressed in a marxist vocabulary. Such constitutions have been aptly termed "promissory notes on the future." In the 1960s all too many of these promissory notes came due and proved uncollectable. The glaring contrast between the promised achievements of independence and the disappointing results was all too clear and by undermining confidence, played a role in the replacing, often by military coups, of a number of the initial post-independence regimes.

The experience of the constitutions of the new nations illustrates in a negative sense some of the problems involved in the drafting of a constitution. But we need to examine this important problem in somewhat greater detail.

REQUIREMENTS FOR A SATISFACTORY CONSTITUTION

Probably the best short statement of what a satisfactory constitution should contain was given by the great Chief Justice John Marshall in 1819:

> A constitution, to contain an accurate detail of all the subdivisions of which its great powers will admit, and of all the means by which they may be carried into execution, would partake of the prolixity of a legal code and could scarcely be embraced by the human mind. It would probably never be understood by the public. Its nature, therefore, requires that only its great outlines should be marked, its important objects designated and the minor ingredients which compose those deduced from the nature of the objects themselves.[6]

In a list of requirements for a satisfactory constitution, Marshall's eloquent if involved prose could be summarized as the first point: A constitution should be confined strictly to fundamentals. One of the best examples of this is our own constitution, which is only about nine pages long, with another six or seven pages for all the amendments added in the course of almost two hundred years. The 1963 edition of the *Constitution of the United States Annotated*, listing all the various court cases to which the articles of the Constitution have given rise, is almost 1700 pages long, not including the index, but the basic document is short and simple. At the opposite extreme is the Indian constitution adopted in 1950. The 395 articles and schedules require 150 closely printed pages. But in spite of the effort made by the Indian constitutional drafters to cover every possible aspect of the relations between the central government and the states and among the states, problems of interpretation still continue to keep both lawyers and judges busy.

The second characteristic that a satisfactory constitution should have is some system of authoritative and final interpretation. Whether a constitution is as brief as the American or as lengthy as the Indian, problems of interpretation inevitably arise. The question is, how can they be settled? One answer to this is, by the American concept of judicial interpretation. It was Chief Justice Marshall who firmly established judicial review as an important aspect of American constitutional law. In the famous case of *Marbury* v. *Madison* (1803), Marshall argued that the Constitution was the supreme law of the land with which all other laws and legal acts must be in accord. If they

[6] *McCulloch* v. *Maryland*, 4 Wheaton 316 (1819).

were not, he said, then they were invalid and unenforceable. As to how the determination of the constitutionality of any law was to be made, Marshall said categorically that "it is emphatically the province and duty of the judicial department to say what the law is." While it is true that the Constitution does not specifically give the Supreme Court this power, there is general agreement among constitutional authorities that it was certainly intended to do so by the drafters of the Constitution. Particularly under a federal system, with its complicated and overlapping jurisdictions, final interpretation of rights and authority is a necessity. In the absence of a special body to do this, the courts were the only logical alternative.

Since the establishment of judicial review by Marshall, a number of other countries, mostly in Latin America, have specifically written it into their constitutions. One of the most interesting and creative variations on judicial review is found in the Irish Constitution, which provides that the president may request an advisory opinion from the supreme court as to the constitutionality of any legislative act. Should the court rule negatively, the president is empowered to refuse to sign the pending legislation into law.

Following the American precedent, Canada's supreme court has asserted the right to rule on the constitutionality of legislation, and India specifically grants this power to its supreme court.

The political impact of the power of constitutional review was dramatically demonstrated in India in December, 1970. By presidential decree, the Indian government attempted to abolish all privileges of rank and to eliminate the annual salaries which were awarded to 278 former princely rulers in 1948 for joining the Indian union. The court ruled, however, that the Indian president had no power to do so, and the ruling created a constitutional crisis for the government when it tried to push through a constitutional amendment to accomplish its original purpose. The Indian parliament was dissolved for the first special election in the nation's history and in March, 1971, Prime Minister Indira Gandhi's government obtained the two-thirds majority necessary to pass constitutional amendments to nullify the court's ruling.

Among the communist countries, there is either no provision for any final constitutional authority or, with the exception of Outer Mongolia, the power of final determination is given to the presidium (executive committee) of the ranking legislative body. Various countries as widely separated as Austria, France, South Korea, and Thailand have established special constitutional councils to serve as courts of final appeal on the propriety of executive and legislative actions. But a surprising number of countries have no constitutional provisions for any sort of final ruling. Broadly speaking, the establishment of some procedure for constitutional review seems to be a characteristic of those countries that accept constitutionalism as their political norm.

The third characteristic of a satisfactory constitution is tied closely to the need for a final source of interpretation. Indeed it is what makes interpretation possible. The constitution must be adaptable to changing conditions without the necessity of constantly amending it to bring it up to date. The ideal is to draft it in sufficiently broad and vague terms for it to be used for a variety of objectives over an extensive period of time. In this respect the vagueness of much of the phrasing of the U.S. Constitution, as compared to the attempted comprehensiveness of so many others, has been one of the major reasons for its success, since succeeding generations of judges have been able to interpret it as the times demanded. A classic example of such drafting is the final phrase of the enumeration of the specific powers of Congress: "To make all Laws which shall be necessary and proper for carrying into Execution the foregoing Powers, and all other Powers vested by this Constitution in the Government of the United States, or in any Department or Office thereof."

The U.S. Constitution also furnishes an equally classic example of the type of regulation which should never be included in so basic a document. This is the Eighteenth Amendment, prohibiting the sale of alcoholic beverages, which was adopted in 1919 and repealed by the Twenty-First Amendment in 1933. Experience has demonstrated that such matters as social custom or standards of personal conduct are too transitory for constitutional enactment. But where there is long-standing religious sanction for such practices, this does not necessarily apply. The Indian Constitution, for example, with many centuries of Hindu religious sanction behind it, prohibits "the slaughter of cows and calves and other milch and draught cattle."

The need for flexibility of statement is not only related to the problems of interpretation but also to the fourth characteristic of a satisfactory constitution: a formal method of amendment that will neither be impossibly difficult nor so easy as to place the constitution on a level with ordinary legislation. Generally, most constitutions require both action by the legislative branch, often by some such substantial majority as a two-thirds approval, and then popular ratification through a special referendum or special conventions.

Typical of Western European constitutions in connection with amendment is the French procedure. The Fifth Republic's constitution provides that after an amendment has been passed in identical form by both houses of the legislature, it must be approved in a popular referendum. Or, alternatively, the amendment can be approved without the referendum if it can obtain a three-fifths majority in each house of the legislature.

For a federal system, the Indian constitution provides perhaps the simplest procedure and the U.S. Constitution one of the most complicated. Most Indian constitutional amendments become effective when passed by two-thirds of the majority of the membership of each of the houses of parliament. Only certain amendments affecting state and central government relations have to be referred to state legislatures for concurrence, and even then approval by simple majority in only 50 percent of the legislatures involved is required.

In contrast to this uncomplicated Indian procedure are the several and complex methods outlined in the U.S. Constitution. Whatever procedure is used, ratification by the legislatures or specially called conventions in three-fourths of the states is necessary. A constitutional amendment can be initiated by its adoption by two-thirds majorities in both houses of Congress. The alternative procedure of the legislatures of two-thirds of the states requesting that Congress call a special convention to propose amendments is never used. From time to time efforts have been made to use this procedure, but to date these have always failed. Apparently there is a continuing feeling that any such special convention might find itself swept by the partisan prejudices of the moment and propose amendments disruptive to the basic philosophy of the Constitution. Nor is this an idle fear. A public opinion poll in the late 1960s, for example, documented the fact that a majority of the American people would have no objection to a drastic curtailment of the Bill of Rights.

In contrast to the French, the American, and the Indian amendment procedures, is the straightforward simplicity of the Soviet constitution which provides for amendment by a two-thirds vote in each house of the Supreme Soviet. Given party control of the legislative body, the effect is to place constitutional amendment on the same level as routine legislation.

The fifth and last requirement for a satisfactory constitution may seem obvious. The constitution must be suitable for the country in question. It must represent an organic growth from the political culture involved. The failure of a constitution to fulfill this simple and seemingly obvious requirement has been an important cause of much political turmoil in wide areas of the world where governmental patterns have been adopted with little regard to their relationship to the political cultures on which they have been summarily superimposed. Under these conditions, the constitutions outlining the particular set of ground rules either have been ignored or, as with Indonesia's short-lived experiment with federalism, dispensed with. It is reasonable to predict that Indonesia's 1945 constitution, reinstated in 1960, will continue to be that nation's basic document for the foreseeable future, for it represents a combination of all the diverse influences which were important in the shaping of the Indonesian nationalist movement. Further, it furnished the framework for political activity during the heroic independence struggle from 1945 to 1950. Thus the 1945 constitution acquired one of the most essential elements for an enduring constitution: loyalty.

Little loyalty is given an institution simply because it is efficient or well organized. Much more important is a feeling of emotional attachment to that institution. We know, for example, that a large section of American public opinion as of 1790 viewed the new constitution with emotions ranging from indifference to outright hostility. Now, from the perspective of almost 200 years, the U.S. Constitution is widely regarded as an almost sacred document. Following in the same pattern, the Indonesian 1945 constitution has already taken on a sufficiently emotional value in the national consciousness to insure its continued role as the basic framework for national development.

It is not unlikely that the 1970s will witness a new phase of constitution-drafting in the recently independent nations of Africa and Asia. Clearly the old imitative "white magic" period is over. Almost universally, the military regimes which seized power from the fumbling postindependence governments have proclaimed their intent, as has happened in Ghana for example, to return to constitutional rule. If this change is to be effective the new constitutions must represent organic development from the indigenous political cultures involved. The result may be that the 1970s will furnish a rich source of study for students of constitutional development. The results, let alone the durability of these constitutions, are likely to take some time to appear. As Walter Bagehot evaluated it more than a century ago:

> A new Constitution does not produce its full effect as long as all its subjects were reared under an old Constitution, as long as its statesmen were trained by that old Constitution. It is not really tested till it comes to be worked by statesmen and among a people neither of whom are guided by a different experience.[7]

THE CLASSIFICATION OF CONSTITUTIONS

From the time of Aristotle, one of the most popular branches of political morphology (the study of form and structure) has been concerned with constitutions. Longest

[7]Walter Bagehot, *The English Constitution* (London: Oxford University Press, 1955), pp. 260–261.

lasting and most famous has been Aristotle's own classification into the three good forms, monarchy, aristocracy, and limited democracy (polity) and the three bad forms, tyranny, oligarchy, and mobocracy. It should be remembered that Aristotle was not discussing constitutions in the limited modern sense but rather the basic distinguishing characteristics of whole societies.

Since the American and French revolutions established the contemporary meaning of constitution, there have been a number of efforts at classifying them. One of the most popular (and pointless) in the nineteenth century was to make the distinction between so-called written and unwritten constitutions. The pointlessness of this classification can be seen from the fact that the result was to place the British constitution in the unwritten category and all others in the written category, with the U.S. Constitution regarded as the prime example.

Yet in his monumental compilation of the *Constitutions of Nations,* Peaslee requires 62 pages to sample the principles of the unwritten British constitution and only 14 pages for the written American.[8] What is involved in this classification is obviously not stated in the misleading descriptions. The difference is really between those constitutions which state their concepts in one or, at most, several documents and those that have no one single authoritative and compact statement of these principles.

The written documents that make up the British constitution, for example, cover a span of 700 years from the Magna Carta of 1215 to the Statutes of Westminister of 1931 and the Ministers of the Crown Act of 1937. The statutes among these documents comprise one of the four major sources of the British constitution. Nothing distinguishes them from any other legislative statutes except the importance of the topics with which they are concerned. But, unlike standard constitutional documents, they are not protected by any special requirements for a two-thirds or three-fifths vote for their amendment or by the need for special judicial interpretation.

The second category of written documents includes the common-law cases which have provided the general rules of constitutional law. But like legislative enactments, they have no special status, and a routine parliamentary act can overturn any court decision in contrast to the American or Indian situations where only the formal process of constitutional amendment can do this.

The customs of Parliament and the conventions of the constitution are the actual unwritten sources which have been so influential in British constitutional developments. An outstanding example of the first of these is the status

[8]Peaslee, *Constitutions of Nations,* 3:509–571; 582–596.

of the Speaker of the House. Parliament as the supreme authority and the collective responsibility of the cabinet are examples of important constitutional conventions.

Custom and convention as important influences are by no means restricted specifically to the British constitution or unwritten constitutions in general. They play an important role in the actual application of all constitutional systems. Recall, for example, the unwritten but powerful prohibition against the use of the premier's constitutional powers of dissolution in the Third Republic in France. Or again, the long-established American tradition that presidential electors should exercise no independent judgment—quite contrary to the original intent of the Constitution.

In the British sense there have been only two other examples of unwritten constitutions during the last century. These are the accidental and nebulous system under which the Third Republic operated during the 65 years (1875–1940) of its existence and the interesting concept of a "constitution by evolution" which Israel voted itself in 1950. We can summarize this system of classification by saying that the only meaningful distinction which can be made between so-called written and unwritten constitutions is one of degree rather than of any distinctive difference as such.

There are various other customary classifications which, in varying degree, are equally unsatisfactory. One of these is the attempt to classify constitutions on the basis of whether they are difficult (rigid constitutions) or easy (flexible constitutions) to amend. The classification is based on the amending provisions in the constitution itself. Actually this system is worth comment only because it illustrates that absorption with institutional organization and procedures which was so characteristic of traditional political science. Obviously there are many factors in any political system which contribute far more to making a constitution either rigid or flexible than the mechanics of the technical procedures involved. The type of party system, the influence of interest groups, the degrees of social cohesion and consensus in the societies concerned—all these are likely to be far more important factors than any provisions.

Another traditional method of classifying constitutions also leans heavily on the mechanics of the governmental machinery. This is the classification of constitutions into unitary and federal types. Once again this offers but slight basis for any meaningful analysis or understanding of constitutions.

Is there any typology which might serve us better than these traditional methods? Perhaps the first step toward developing such a typology is to cease thinking of constitutions primarily within the frame of reference of traditional political science. Obviously it is important how authority is organized and how the powers of the various elements of government are distributed. It is important how the executive is balanced off against the legislative and what role the judiciary has. The details of the amendment process and the rights and duties of citizens all make up the character of a particular constitution. But there is still something missing, just as there is something missing when we have a detailed description of a human being's physiological characteristics but little meaningful insight into his actual personality. To understand the real nature of the individual, other standards of analysis are necessary. So it is with constitutions.

It might seem more logical to classify constitutions in terms of the political cultures that have produced them, but several objections can be raised to this method. First of all the content of any political culture is in a constant state of flux. To say that a constitution is a product of Western European political culture means little unless we specify which time period is involved and understand the frame of reference implied. In the second place, a number of constitutions, both past and present, represent borrowings from other political cultures, often on a wholesale basis. Under these circumstances, a classification system based on political culture criteria becomes complicated and cumbersome, if indeed it has any relevance at all.

A more meaningful basis for classifying constitutions might be in terms of an ideological-historical approach. Such a system would utilize such groupings as the political constitutions of the postrevolutionary period in France, the social-welfare constitutions of the period between wars in the twentieth century, the Stalinist constitutions of the Soviet sphere, the socialist-humanist constitutions of the new Afro-Asian states, and so on. This system would need much refinement and careful definition but in broad outline it should serve to organize constitutions into meaningful classifications.

THE SOURCE OF SOVEREIGN POWER IN CONSTITUTIONS

Earlier in this chapter we quoted Thomas Paine's comment that "a government is only a creature of a constitution." He also wrote that "a people without a constitution is power without right." It is certainly true that, aside from its role in organizing the allocation of governmental powers, one of the major functions performed by a constitution is to legitimize authority.

We take it for granted today that a constitution can do this. But why is this so? The answer, of course, is that a constitution is considered to embody the ultimate source of sovereign power in the political system. Any constitution is, as the U.S. Constitution puts it, "the supreme law of the land." In short, the constitution is sovereign, and we have already discussed the importance of the concept of sovereignty in the emergence of the modern state.

The major change brought about by the development of mass democracy since the American and French revolutions has been the drastically altered perception of the origins of sovereign power. In the Middle Ages it was God who represented the ultimate source of all sovereign power. In the sixteenth and seventeenth centuries, with a ritual genuflection toward divine sources, it was "our dread lord, the king." In the first period of constitution-making after the French Revolution, the source of sovereign power in a number of constitutions was delegated explicitly from the reigning monarch. As the French constitutional charter of 1814 put it, "We have voluntarily and by the free exercise of our royal authority, accorded and do accord, grant and concede to our subjects . . . the constitutional charter which follows."

Particularly for those countries where monarchial absolutism had a long-established tradition, the French 1814 charter was the pattern of the first phase of constitutional development. Probably the last of such constitutions was the imperial Russian constitution of 1905 which stated as its basis for sovereign power, "The Emperor of all the Russias wields the supreme autocratic power." But throughout the nineteenth century as the forces of mass democracy became ever stronger and the concept increasingly influential, the "we, the people" concept of the U.S. Constitution became accepted as the primary source for sovereign authority.

In the second edition of his *Constitutions of Nations*, Peaslee analyzed the sources of sovereign power in then-existing constitutions.[9] The results are revealing in terms of mid-twentieth-century political concepts. Approximately 60 percent (54) of the 89 nations with constitutions attribute the source of the government's sovereign power to "the people" or (peculiar to the Commonwealth countries) to "the crown and the people." As evidence of its regionalism, Switzerland adds the variation of "the cantons and the people." Various of the Soviet-zone states use some variation of "the working people" as their prime source. Rather interestingly, even in the mid-twentieth century five states, including such an odd combination as the Vatican state, Saudi Arabia, and Liechtenstein, still vest all sovereignty in the ruler. Only South Africa revives memories of medieval concepts by stating that the source of its sovereignty is "Almighty God." Nine states, echoing the Declaration of the

[9]*Ibid.,* 3: table 3, pp. 405–407.

Rights of Man, but not including France itself, give "the nation" as the source of sovereignty.

CONCLUSION

Beginning in the late eighteenth century, constitutions have become an established part of the symbolism of modern government along with the possession of a flag and a national anthem. Their philosophy and content have changed greatly in the last century. Undoubtedly they will change even more as the effort is made to adapt governmental structures and philosophies to the requirements of the problems of the age of thermonuclear power and cybernetics. But whatever their form or content, whatever the predominant system of international organization, it is clear that constitutions will continue to be important elements in the organization of political systems. Indeed, as suggested earlier, however ritualistic may be their use, however much their social and democratic provisions represent meaningless gestures of public relations, it seems almost inevitable that a generation reared under such constitutions will begin to question the difference between promise and reality and begin to demand substance instead of shadow. In this sense it is not impossible that constitutions may contribute constructively to the growth of popular control of various political systems.

INTERNATIONAL ORGANIZATION IN THE LATE TWENTIETH CENTURY

International organization is a descriptive term for the efforts by various states to structure important aspects of their relations in a continuing and formal fashion. There are two major goals concerned: (1) to provide the most efficient way of organizing recurring contacts of a nonpolitical nature such as the transmittal of mail, and (2) to prevent international conflicts from escalating into outright war. This latter goal has probably been the inspiration for more efforts at international organization than any other single cause. Usually it has taken the form of some sort of mutual-security league against a potential aggressor. Indeed history's earliest examples of international organization are of this type. In 478 B.C. the Greek city states, under the leadership of Athens, formed the Delian League for defense against Persian aggression. From that time until the North Atlantic Treaty Organization of 1948 the number of such international organizations has totaled in the hundreds, if not the thousands.

But in both the quantitative and qualitative sense, the nineteenth and twentieth centuries have witnessed substantial developments in both these goals of international organization. The nineteenth century saw the emergence of a number of organizations for international technical cooperation. In the twentieth century, although largely in vain, the states of the world have twice made history's most extensive efforts to create international organizations designed to maintain world peace and prevent the emergence of any potential aggressors, the League of Nations and the United Nations. This chapter is primarily concerned with twentieth-century developments, but first let us look at the nineteenth-century background.

DEVELOPMENT OF INTERNATIONAL ORGANIZATIONS IN THE NINETEENTH CENTURY

At the end of the Napoleonic wars in 1815, the first significant steps were taken toward a common world outlook on a mass basis. In the eighteenth century the dynastic rulers of Western Europe had shared a common outlook based largely on family ties and similar cultural backgrounds. But this was limited to a small and highly exclusive upper class. In the nineteenth century, the dominance of middle-class values, the common property of the newly dominant bourgeoisie in all the advanced nations, the development of mass education, and the growth of a communications network promoted an increasingly universal system of values and concepts of international organization.

In accord with the value system of bourgeois liberalism, the first approach to the problems of international association was one of laissez faire. Men felt neither the inclination nor the need to institutionalize international affairs. The dominant concept was that this was a civilized world run by men of reason who shared a common dedication to moderation and a common desire to insure that nothing prevented "business as usual." A belief in the negative state and the limited role which government should play in domestic affairs also contributed to the lack of interest in any type of international institutionalization.

Just as sensible businessmen gathered together, as the need arose, to negotiate their differences, the great powers of Europe became accustomed to meeting now and again to eliminate international friction through negotiation and compromise. At the end of the Napoleonic wars, an effort was made to organize a formal system to guarantee European peace. It was known initially as the Quadruple Alliance, and it was composed of the major victors of the Napoleonic wars (Great Britain, Austria, Russia, and Prussia). In 1818, when France was readmitted to the ranks of the great powers, it was expanded into the Quintuple Alliance.

For a brief period (1818–1822) the five great powers met regularly to discuss common interests and to consider threats to international harmony. It is fascinating to speculate on the course of events if these meetings had led to the establishment of a formal international organization for maintaining international peace a full century before the League of Nations was created in 1919. But such a development did not occur. In much the same way that the United States in the 1920s declined to support the League, the British government decided it wanted no involvement with the four Continental powers and brought the conference system to an end with the Congress of Verona in 1822.

In spite of this setback, the conference idea exerted a major influence on international affairs throughout the nineteenth century. Although there were no further efforts at formal organization, the operational concept for the regulation of international affairs emerged as the Concert of Europe. The Concert throughout its existence was an exclusive club. Its self-elected members were essentially those same great powers which had constituted the Quintuple Alliance. Their concept of Europe was not merely that of a geographical entity; they conceived of it as a political and social community with certain common standards and goals. One of the most important of the goals was "to maintain the equilibrium of Europe."

To implement this objective, the great powers convened as the occasion arose to decide such matters as the admission of Greece and Belgium to the European family in 1831 and of Turkey in 1856. Perhaps the most forceful example of positive action to maintain European equilibrium was the Crimean War in the mid-1850s when Great Britain and France intervened on behalf of Turkey to prevent its destruction by Russia and a resulting serious disruption of the power balance. Nor were the activities of the Concert confined solely to European matters. In 1884–1885, after mounting tension over colonial claims, the Berlin Colonial Conference partitioned Africa among the European powers with far-reaching results.

The enforcement of common standards of "social organization in all States of Europe" was demonstrated in 1878 when Serbia, just emerged as an independent state, was sternly admonished by the great powers that it could "enter the European family" only if it followed the generally accepted civilized custom of recognizing the religious liberty of its subjects. Throughout the century, the Concert of Europe was able to function with considerable success in regulating relations among the European states and in defining standards for international morality and proper conduct.

EARLY TWENTIETH-CENTURY DEVELOPMENTS

At the beginning of the twentieth century another important step toward an emerging world order was taken. The Czar of Russia in 1899 convened a conference at The Hague, the Netherlands, made up of 26 nations, primarily European, to discuss the growing problem of armaments. This was followed in 1907 by a second Hague conference with 44 states represented, including most of the Latin American nations. As the conference's president summarized it, "This is the first time that the representives of all constituted States have been gathered together to discuss interests which they have in common and which contemplate the good of all mankind."

Of "the Hague System," an authority on international organization commented, "If the Concert of Europe had been a Board of Directors of the European corporation, the Hague System, particularly in 1907, was a Stockholders Meeting of a much more extensive corporation."[1] For the first time the regulation of international affairs ceased to be in the hands of an elite group of great powers and became a matter of universal involvement.

At the conclusion of the second Hague conference in 1907, there were high hopes that this international assembly would become a regularly recurring aspect of world affairs. One of the American delegates commented: "Friends of peace, friends of arbitration, may now depend upon it that every seven or eight years there will be a similar conference, and that where the last conference left the work unfinished the new conference will take it up, and so progress from time to time be steadily made."[2]

Few expectations have ever been more quickly and brutally destroyed. In 1915, when the third Hague conference might well have met, World War I was already a year old.

In our time, when small wars are commonplace and universal wars are always in the offing, it is difficult to understand the shattering and traumatic impact of World War I on the men of the early twentieth century. You may remember that in Chapter 1 we cited the terms of the will by which Andrew Carnegie, one of the toughest and most ruthless business tycoons of the age, established the Carnegie Peace Foundation in 1911. Even to so cynically realistic and tough-minded a man as this, it was unthinkable that large-scale war could ever again occur.

THE LEAGUE OF NATIONS, 1919–1946

The unexpected and unbelievable catastrophe of World War I produced an intense determination to prevent a reoccurrence. This idealism found its leadership in Woodrow Wilson who personified all the strengths and weaknesses of the nineteenth-century liberal tradition. For Wilson and other liberal intellectuals, World War I had been a dreadful accident which occurred because there had been no opportunity for sensible and rational men to sit down and work out their differences together. Since men were sensible and rational except when hastily stampeded by blind emotion, it was only necessary to provide a frame-

[1]Claude L. Innis Jr., *Swords into Ploughshares: The Problems and Progress of International Organization*, 2nd ed. rev. (New York: Random House, 1959), p. 29.

[2]Quoted by Innis, *Swords into Ploughshares*, p. 31.

work for immediate consultation on world crises within which effective collective action could be taken against the unique international outlaw. That all decent and civilized men would come together to take such action was accepted as axiomatic.

But this naively optimistic view of human nature was not the only handicap from which the League of Nattions suffered when it came into being in 1919. It was organized not so much as a league of all nations but rather a league of the victor nations of World War I. In fact, its birthplace was the same Paris Peace Conference that laid down harsh terms to a defeated Germany. From the start it was clear that some of the members of the League, particularly France, regarded it, despite its general aim of world peace, primarily as a league to insure that there would be no changes in the balance of postwar power.

In its philosophic approach to the problem of maintaining world peace, the League concept drew upon the role played by the great powers in the Concert of Europe rather than upon the technical equality of the Hague System. The most immediate inspiration for this seems to have been the unarguable fact that it had been the great powers which had borne the principal burden of fighting and winning the war.

Organization of The League

This concept of renewed great-power domination of world affairs was embodied in the League Council, intended to be the most important of its organs. The League covenant provided for Council membership to consist "of Representatives of the Principal Allied and Associated Powers, together with Representatives of four other members of the League." However the refusal of the United States to join the world organization removed an important influence from the beginning, while increases in the number of elected members during the 1920s prevented there ever being a permanent great-power majority on the Council. Meeting at least three or four times a year, the Council was intended to serve as the executive committee of the League. It was anticipated that not only would it execute League policy, as the great powers saw fit to interpret it, but it also would be the principal means for the peaceful settlement of disputes and the enforcement of collective security.

From the start the Council was hampered by the requirement for unanimous agreement on all important substantive questions and the repeated reluctance of the great power members to accept the responsibilities and dangers of world leadership. As a result the Assembly assumed increasing importance in the functions of the League.

Initially the Assembly had been intended as little more

than a carefully limited opportunity for the small states of the world to let off steam at three- or four-year intervals. It was the organ of the League which drew its inspiration most directly from the Hague System. But included within its jurisdiction were very broad powers to "deal at its meetings with any matter within the sphere of action of the League or affecting the peace of the world." Increasingly over the years, as the Council proved unable to assert effective leadership and the small powers became accustomed to regular participation in the discussion of world affairs, the Assembly became the focal point of League activity.

As annual Assembly sessions became established practice, it became customary for the problems of the world to be aired in the September debates. Wilson expressed the hope that the League would serve as a "court of public opinion." "Nothing is going to keep this world fit to live in like exposing in public every crooked thing that is going on," he said. "A bad cause will fare ill, but a good cause is bound to be triumphant in such a forum. You dare not lay a bad cause before mankind."

The results fell far short of this, but at least for the first time in world history, an international forum had come into existence based on the propositions that all states of the world, regardless of size, had an equal right to discuss and register opinions on global problems and that it was possible to reach agreement by rational discussion rather than by brute force. The League failed, but it represented one small step toward the effective establishment of international order and a giant leap forward in man's vision of its potential.

The Council and the Assembly both had historical precedents, but the third important component of the League's organizational structure, the Secretariat, was an innovative development. For the first time a corps of international civil servants was created who owed their allegiance not to any one nation-state but to mankind at large.

Headed by a secretary-general, the Secretariat was officially intended to serve simply as the instrument for the routine housekeeping chores of the international organization. Record-keeping, technical research in the collection of statistical data, preparation of background reports for the committees of the Assembly and the Council, publicity, and physical maintenance of League property were the tasks envisaged for it.

But as the only League element constantly on the scene, week in and week out, the Secretariat, particularly the secretary-general, very quickly assumed a much more important role. Familiar with all aspects of League operation and the development of policy formulation, the Secretariat officials were in a unique position to influence policy determination. The first secretary-general, Sir Eric Drummond, established a pattern for a new type of international civil servant which furnished the precedent on which the Secretariat of the United Nations has built. In creating a vision of an international rather than a national loyalty, Drummond showed, if but fleetingly, that the nation-state could be regarded as a phase rather than an ultimate end in the long story of man's evolving political and ideological loyalties.

International Role of The League

The League covenant of 1919 outlined a revolutionary new concept for the ordering of international relations. Article eight charged the League with the responsibility for achieving the reduction of national armaments to the lowest point consistent with national safety and the enforcement by common action of international obligations.

But the very core of the new League approach to world order, and the source of its ultimate disintegration, was contained in Article sixteen. It provided that any League member who resorted to war should

> be deemed to have committed an act of war against all other Members of the League, which hereby undertake immediately to subject it to the severance of all trade or financial relations, the prohibition of all intercourse between their nationals and the nationals of the Covenant-breaking State, and the prevention of all . . . intercourse between the nationals of the Covenant-breaking State and the nationals of any other State.

Subsequent sections of Article sixteen authorized the Council to recommend to League members what military action should be taken to enforce sanctions and bound the members to "mutually support one another in the financial and economic measures which are taken under this article."

It was, of course, the failure to accept the obligation to prevent Italian aggression against Ethiopia in 1935 that destroyed the League as a moral or political force in world affairs. Had its members, above all Great Britain and France, fulfilled their obligations at that time, the history of the world might have been different.[3]

Had the League been in existence in 1914 it quite possibly could have prevented the unwanted war which no one knew how to stop. History seems to show that in the age of rationality before World War I no one actually wanted war. The League's nemesis lay in the fact that in the 1930s when it was put to the test there were great powers which saw war as desirable and others which

[3]But it must be admitted that probably nothing so weakened the League from the beginning as the failure of the United States to join.

shrank from the use of force until they belatedly realized that their very existence was at stake.

THE UNITED NATIONS

Formed with 41 members, the League had 63 member states at its peak and 46 when its tasks and physical properties were transferred at its final session in 1946 to the United Nations, which had come into existence at San Francisco the previous year. Even at the lowest ebb of the League's power and prestige, the majority of its members had retained their formal membership and, in spite of intense disillusionment with the League itself, hopefully planned for a more perfected international organization which, in the words of the United Nations charter, would "save succeeding generations from the scourge of war, which twice in our lifetime has brought untold sorrow to mankind."

The United Nations began its existence with 51 founding members. Twenty-six years later its membership included 131 of the then 146 sovereign nations of the world, with such countries as East and West Germany, North and South Korea, and the two Vietnams excluded not because of their lack of desire to join but because of ideological opposition to their admission. While the failures of the UN have been many and disillusion with its achievements is widespread, it is significant that the existence of such an organization and the desirability of membership in it is routinely accepted by the international community.

In neither its aims nor its organizational structure does the UN depart from the concepts of the League. Article one lists the purposes as being:

1. The maintenance of international peace and security through "effective collective measures"
2. The promotion of friendly international relations based on "equal rights and self-determination of peoples"
3. Fostering international cooperation on all types of problems
4. "To be a center for harmonizing the actions of nations in the attainment of these common ends."

In Article two the UN accepts as the basis for its existence "the sovereign equality of all its Members." From the start, the most important members of the UN, above all the United States, were aware of the gamble which sovereign equality represented. But, as Secretary of State Hull pointed out to President Roosevelt as early as 1943, only *if* the great powers, above all the United States and the Soviet Union, cooperated on an equal basis to preserve world peace, could the UN fulfill its obligations. The checkered history of the UN has demonstrated the correctness of this evaluation. When the United States and the Soviet Union have been in agreement, the UN has been quite effective in its efforts to maintain peace or to halt conflict. In 1956 in the Suez crisis and in 1960 in the Congo, for example, UN intervention was successful, and this was because the world's two superpowers, although from differing motives, wanted a speedy liquidation of the crisis. The reverse of this, of course, has been the inability of the UN to act as any more than a modestly successful buffer in the tragedy of the Middle East. Nor should it be forgotten that in the Cuban missile crisis of 1962, which was the greatest single confrontation between the United States and the Soviet Union, the UN was able to exert little or no influence, and the crisis was finally resolved on the basis of a direct American-Soviet agreement.

Both its greatest admirers and its bitterest enemies alike have overrated the UN. There is not the slightest prospect that it can ever develop into a world government as its admirers hope and its detractors fear. At best the UN represents a sophisticated and structured evolution of the nineteenth-century Concert of Europe concept. In and of itself, it has neither the necessary power nor the resources to shape international affairs. But as one commentator on its role in world affairs observed: "One of the main contributions of the United Nations is to serve as a place where, on the one hand, the statesmen of newly independent countries can learn better to appreciate political realities, and where, on the other hand, the statesmen of the West can gain a closer understanding of the new forces at work in the world."[4]

Military strategists often comment that the offense always seems to be one step ahead of the defense which, as in the case of the failure of the French Maginot line in World War II, is always prepared to win the last war but not the present one. So it seems is the case with international organizations.

The League, as we noted, would have been an excellent medium for stopping the helpless drift into the accidental war of 1914. It was not designed to cope with the deliberately planned aggression by the Axis powers (Germany, Italy, and Japan) in the early 1940s. This second great tragedy of the twentieth century occurred because of the disbelief that any effective coalition against aggression would emerge. The United Nations was designed to organize such a coalition well in advance. As one commentator summarized it, "The United Nations could be interpreted

[4]Geoffrey Godwin, "The Role of the United Nations in World Affairs," in *The United Nations Political System*, ed. David A. Kay (New York: Wiley, 1967), p. 15.

as an attempt to equip the world for dealing with Hitlers —after Hitler was already dead."[5]

With all its deficiencies, the fact remains that the UN has survived for more than a quarter of a century. Insofar as there is such a thing as a world conscience, the UN provides it. It is the one place where the statesmen of the world can meet regularly. That these meetings more often than not result in an exchange of attacks on each other's policies is not the fault of the UN. Perhaps it can even be recorded as an achievement that these attacks are merely verbal.

The great challenge which the UN must meet in the years ahead was realistically stated by the *Christian Science Monitor* on the occasion of the UN's twenty-fifth anniverary in 1970:

> Neither ceremonies nor congratulations nor a fresh declaration of purpose is what is needed from the United Nations as the latter begins the 25th anniversary session of the General Assembly. What is urgently required is a new series of accomplishments able to prove to mankind that the world body is a truly effective organization. . . .
>
> The danger with the United Nations (and at present this danger is far advanced) is that the world's power centers may be content merely to pat it on the head from time to time, give it their blessing, use it occasionally as a convenient platform for their own selfish purposes, and the rest of the time ignore it. . . .
>
> Yet the world body is there. Its potential for good is unlimited. It can be evoked at any time. It is up to men—and to the leaders of the great nations—to have the wisdom and inspiration to do so.

Since in theory at least the machinery of the UN provides the mechanism to carry out these objectives, let us now examine its organizational structure.

Organization of the United Nations

Basically the organizational structure of the UN has familiar outlines. Its major organs are the Security Council, the General Assembly, and a permanent Secretariat. The Council is composed of five permanent members (China, France, the Soviet Union, the United Kingdom, and the United States) and ten nonpermanent members elected by the General Assembly for two-year terms.[6] The Council's primary responsibility is the maintenance of international

[5]Innis, *Swords into Ploughshares,* p. 87.

[6]Originally the number of nonpermanent members was six. It is now customary for five members to be elected from the Afro-Asian group of states, one from East Europe, two from Latin America and two from Western Europe and other areas. Nonpermanent members can serve only one consecutive term.

peace and security. It is empowered to investigate disputes and situations potentially dangerous to world peace. But while it can recommend remedial action, including the use of armed forces, such action is voluntary on the part of its members.

It was not originally intended that the Security Council should be so completely dependent on the good will of UN members. Its charter provides that the members are to make armed forces available to the UN "on its call and in accordance with a special agreement or agreements" between the Security Council and the members. But the inability of the Soviet Union and the Western powers to reach agreement on the composition of any such military force has always prevented its creation.

Instead the Security Council, as in the Congo and the Middle East, has had to rely on the loan of military units from its members. It has become virtually routine for such temporary UN forces to be drawn from the smaller nations, such as the Scandinavian states, Ireland, or various of the African nations, since all these countries are small enough and neutral enough to be acceptable to both sides in any dispute. But it is obvious that should a major conflict erupt among the great powers, the UN would be powerless to cope with the situation.

The most criticized aspect of Security Council activity has come in connection with the right of each of the permanent members to veto any substantive decisions, provided it was not a party to the dispute in question. But if the application of military or economic sanctions is involved, a permanent member can veto a decision whether involved or not. At of 1971 the Soviet Union had used 107 vetoes, the United States one (as of 1970), and the other three permanent Council members approximately eight among them.

The mere existence of the veto power, aside from its obvious purpose of protecting the sovereign interests of the great powers, is a further indication of the way in which the UN was organized to prevent another international cataclysm occurring in the same way as had World War II. Operating in terms of the past, rather than the present, let alone the future, it was apparently assumed that major threats to world peace would come from a revival of German and Japanese power rather than from the actions of any present Security Council members. Hence there was no initial concern over a permanent member being able to block any effective action by the UN.

However, the frustration produced by the Soviet Union's constant use of its veto power led to an important change in the constitutional relationship between the Security Council and the General Assembly. On November 3, 1950, the General Assembly, under American urging, passed the

Uniting for Peace resolution. It provided for emergency meetings of the General Assembly to take jurisdiction on critical issues where Security Council action had been blocked by veto action. The Assembly was further empowered to reach its own conclusion as to when aggression had taken place and to recommend collective action by UN members to restore or maintain peace. Although concern had been mounting over the Soviet Union's constant use of the veto, frequently in policy matters of little importance, the major crisis of the Korean War had underlined the need for the UN to have the ability to act without the threat of paralysis by veto.

The Uniting for Peace resolution was, however, only one of the most prominent landmarks in the emergence of the Assembly, contrary to expectations, to a position of equality, if not predominance, as far as the Security Council was concerned. In 1959 Innis commented on the way in which the Assembly assumed this role: "It began by becoming a more frequently used alternative forum for the consideration of political disputes . . . it has in fact virtually replaced the Council as the agency bearing primary political responsibility within the United Nations."[7]

In the League pattern the UN Secretariat serves as an international civil service based on technical ability and geographical distribution. The secretary-general supervises more than 3000 technicians and administrators organized on a functional basis under various assistant secretaries and undersecretaries. Even more than was the case during the League period, the UN secretary-general has been called upon to play a key diplomatic role made particularly difficult by the U.S.-Soviet rivalry. It is probably because of the need for complete neutrality that the first three secretary-generals have come from the Scandinavian countries (Lie of Norway and Hammarskjold of Sweden) and a small neutral Asian country (U Thant of Burma).

Other Major Organs

Although it has not been overburdened with cases, the International Court of Justice is the successor to the League's Permanent Court of International Justice. Located in The Hague, the International Court, in theory, can make final judgments in cases brought before it; the Security Council is charged with enforcing the verdict. But, as we have noted, the Security Council lacks the force to make good on any such obligations. So powerless is the Court that in 1948 Albania was able to defy its verdict awarding damages to Great Britain in the Corfu Channel case.

As though the Court were not handicapped enough in the performance of its task, the United States agreed to

[7]Innis, *Swords into Ploughshares*, pp. 173–174.

accept its jurisdiction only on the basis of the Connally Amendment, which excludes from the Court's jurisdiction any case which the United States declares to be within its "domestic jurisdiction." Even in the realm of advisory opinions which the Court can be asked to render, both great and small powers have felt free to ignore them when it suited their purpose. As in the cases of the Security Council and the General Assembly, there is no lack of well-structured mechanisms available for pacific settlement of disputes. The lack of the desire to use them and the Court's lack of power to enforce decisions are the fatal flaws.

Two of the UN's most important specialized agencies are the Economic and Social Council (ECOSOC) and the Trusteeship Council, which by the early 1970s had almost worked itself out of a job. ECOSOC is rather unrealistically charged with the awesome responsibility of promoting every possible type of "economic and social progress and development" as well as seeking solutions for all the related problems and encouraging "universal respect for, and observance of, human rights and fundamental freedoms for all without distinction as to race, sex, language or religion."

Although constantly handicapped by lack of adequate funding, the ECOSOC, directed by a council of representatives from 26 states, has carried out a surprising number of valuable studies on world social and economic problems and has established a widespread network of regional and functional commissions, such as the economic commissions for Europe and for Asia and the Far East, and its commissions on human rights and social development. The work of ECOSOC and its commissions results in recommendations to the General Assembly, to various member states, and to the specialized agencies which have either been brought into the UN system or newly developed there. The specialized agencies comprise such bodies as the Universal Postal Union, originally established in 1874, the World Health Organization, the Food and Agricultural Organization, the International Civil Aviation Organization, and the International Monetary Fund, to name only a few. As Figure 8 shows, the specialized agencies are concerned with virtually every aspect of economic and social development.[8]

More in prospect than in achievement to date, the economic development assistance programs of the UN offer a great service to the world community. The International Bank for Reconstruction and Development, the International Monetary Fund, and the International Development Association are the leading agencies involved in economic development and technical assistance programs, and within their limits they have done well, although hampered by a lack of funds. Understandably but regrettably the wealthy

[8]U.S. Department of State, "The United Nations" International Organization Series, No. 6 (Washington, D.C.: GPO, 1970), p. 11.

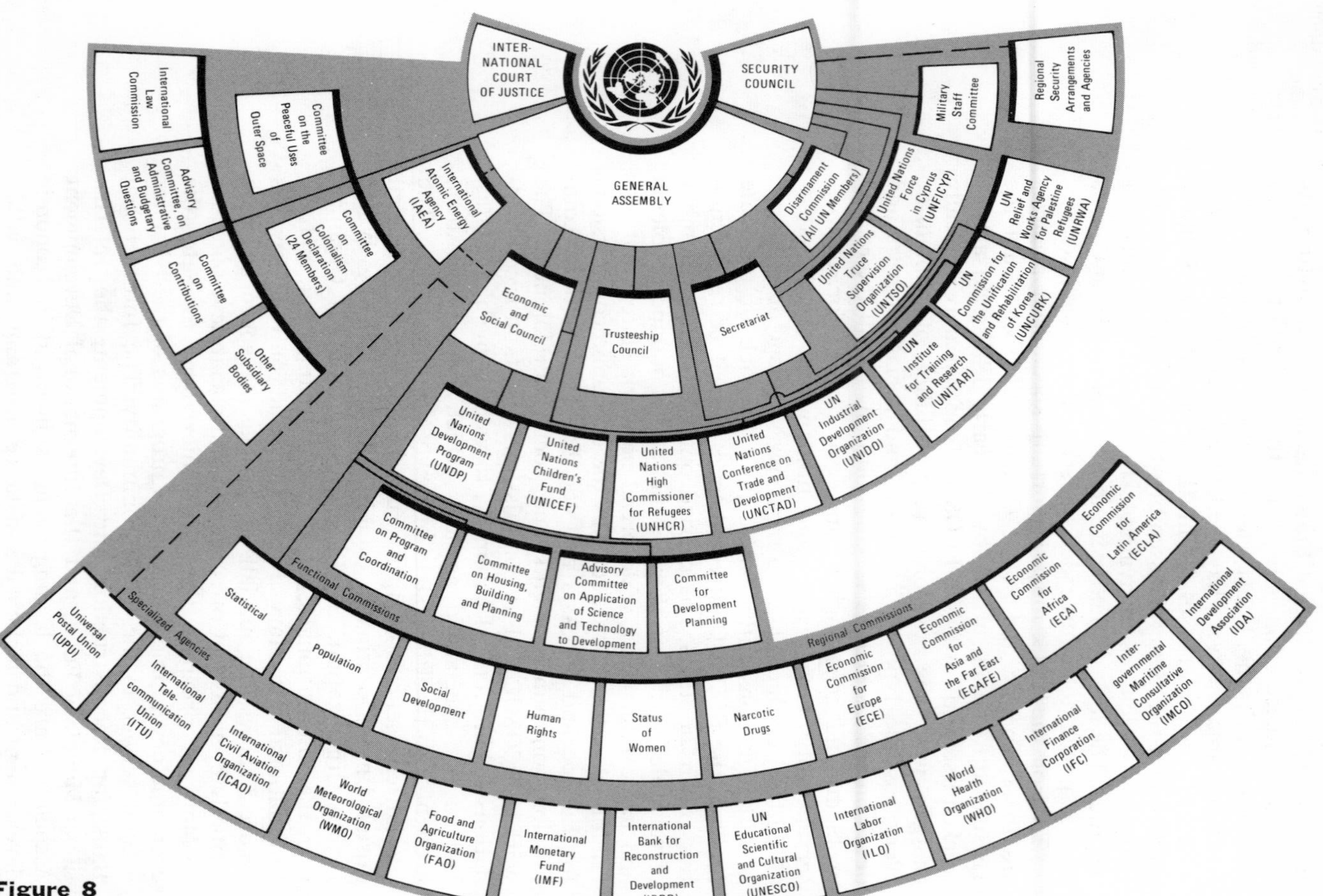

Figure 8
The United Nations System

countries of the world, such as the United States, the Soviet Union, Japan, and West Germany, have preferred to operate their own technical and economic assistance programs—with an eye, of course, to gaining political influence with the recipient country.

Probably one of the best known and most highly regarded of the specialized agencies, at least in academic circles, is the UN Educational, Scientific and Cultural Organization (UNESCO) which has as its goals the broadening of the base of world education, the promotion of science in all countries, and the encouragement of cultural exchange. In line with these objectives, UNESCO has tried to promote literacy throughout the world, encouraged international conferences for the exchange of cultural data, and sponsored an extensive book publishing program. In recent years it has undertaken programs designed to save important cultural monuments from destruction in areas as far apart as Egypt, Pakistan, and Italy.

FUTURE OF THE UNITED NATIONS

Perhaps the UN's most outstanding achievement is simply that it has survived. If this seems like very little, remember that within 15 years after its founding the League was a discredited organization. It survived until World War II in an atmosphere of contemptuous indifference from both its enemies and its members. The UN has had some success in the past, but its future prospects for continuing its modest successes are dubious. In the mid-1960s the UN experienced a severe financial crisis owing to the cost of its peace-keeping activities and the refusal of the communist nations and France, in connection with the Congo, to bear any of the costs. It has become clear since 1965 that the UN will be unable to perform any peace-keeping role against the opposition of one of the major powers, let alone in the absence of U.S. and Soviet concurrence.

In addition to its inability to establish its own military force, its constant lack of adequate funds seems likely to continue as a major handicap. In theory the UN's regular operating funds come from fixed assessments against its members based on ability to pay. Its charter provides that any member delinquent for a period of two years may be denied its right to vote in the General Assembly. But the Assembly declined to take such action against the Soviet Union and France in the 1965 financial crisis and even the United States made no effort to push the issue. The UN has suffered not only from its inability to collect regular dues but also from the refusal of various states to contribute to special funds of which they disapprove. Although the General Assembly has approved the principle that no nation should pay more than 30 percent of the UN's total operating expenses, American contributions continue to run at about 32 percent, and during the 12 years from 1946 to 1958, the U.S. paid 47.7 percent of the regular operating expenses.

Of its available funds, the UN has devoted 80 percent to economic and social activities and development assistance. These activities, along with its attempts to provide the framework for a relatively untroubled adjustment to technological development and its constant efforts to call attention to the urgent challenges of disarmament and the need for control of nuclear weapons, have been probably its major achievements.

The admission of communist China in October, 1971, was a fresh indication of the acceptance of the UN's role in world affairs by even one of its formerly most bitter critics. However powerless the UN seems likely to be, membership in it is still regarded as a status symbol of acceptance by the international community at large. But the expulsion of the Nationalist Chinese regime on Taiwan as an aspect of communist China's admission sets the dangerous precedent that in the future other nations may find themselves expelled because their internal regimes are unpopular in the world community. Future "two China" conflicts might well result in the UN tearing itself apart over ideological issues. In addition to all its other serious, possibly fatal, weaknesses, the UN now faces a new potential threat to its existence.

Under these circumstances, the contribution of the UN to the development of international organization is unlikely to be a dramatic one. While the UN may be able to prevent conflict between small powers, given American-Soviet accord, it obviously does not and will not have the resources or the authority to intervene effectively in any major power clashes. But if world catastrophe is avoided, it will be partly as a result of the UN, which, through the work of its specialized agencies, has laid the foundations for increasingly closer cooperation not only in economic and social terms but also in the political sphere. Commenting on the official American attitude towards the UN as of 1970, an authoritative newspaper observed, "the impression gained here from discussion with U.S. officials close to American policymaking is one of polite tolerance of the whole UN business—of the histrionic public debates, of the inflated rhetoric from all sides, and the confusion of 'bothersome minicountries.' "[9]

This last point has become a source of concern to the big powers. The General Assembly now includes a large number of small states with less population and often not much more area than any large Soviet or American city but each possessing, as do the Soviet Union and the U.S.,

[9]*Christian Science Monitor,* October 30, 1970.

one vote. The inability of these tiny states to pay even the minimum .04 percent of budget costs and their constant willingness to pass sweeping resolutions which the big powers must both finance and implement, if they are to be carried out at all, could sink the fragile UN boat.

Considering its obvious shortcomings and the official scepticism with which the UN is viewed by the U.S. and other official sources, it is interesting to find that for American public opinion at least the UN still is viewed as the world's best hope for peace. A Gallup poll taken in October, 1970, the UN's twenty-fifth anniversary, found that 75 percent of the American public thought it "very important" to have the UN succeed, 44 percent, in spite of all, thought that it was "doing a good job," and 67 percent favored the establishment of a permanent UN peace-keeping force. A similar Harris poll indicated that 66 percent of the public hoped the UN could become an effective force for peace, while 56 percent felt that it was doing only a "fair or poor" job in keeping the peace.

But in spite of these percentages and the scepticism of informed statesmen, the fact remains that, unlike the League's situation within two decades after its founding, no countries or world leaders call for the UN's destruction. Whatever it may or may not accomplish, it is clear that the general public and world statesmen alike feel the UN is needed and, with varying degrees of pessimism would like to see it succeed.

DEVELOPMENT OF REGIONAL ORGANIZATIONS SINCE WORLD WAR II

The period since World War II has seen the steady growth of the concepts of regional organization. Like most other aspects of international organization, organized regionalism has not developed as rapidly nor as extensively as its proponents had hoped. Nevertheless there has been progress compared with the past. As the foundations are laid and settle firmly, this may afford the basis for much more rapid development in the future. But for the present, let us simply note some of the more significant essays into regional organization.

Most, but not all, regional organizations have been limited in both geographical scope and function. Such extensive regional arrangements as the North Atlantic Treaty Organization or the South East Asia Treaty Organization, however, have been anything but regional in their membership although their function has been quite specific. On the other hand, while the Organization of American States (OAS), for example, has had an obvious regional focus, although a broad one, its objectives are the very broad ones of promoting the solidarity and defending the sovereignty of its members as well as providing them with social, political, economic, and technical services. Another example of the same type of broad-ranging association is the Organization of African Unity (OAU).

More typical of the way in which regional organization has developed since 1945 have been the efforts to foster European cooperation. These efforts achieved their first concrete results in 1948 in two separate moves towards developing greater European regionalism. The Organization for European Economic Cooperation (OEEC) was formed to coordinate American Marshall Plan aid for the countries of Western Europe. Almost simultaneously, Great Britain, France, Belgium, the Netherlands, and Luxembourg signed the Brussels pact pledging cooperation for the next 50 years in military economic and cultural areas. The following year saw the purpose of the Brussels pact widened by the creation of the North Atlantic Treaty Organization which, with political logic but geographical inconsistency, has come to include Portugal, Greece, and Turkey among its members. In 1949 also the Council of Europe was created. Composed of the Committee of Ministers and the Consultative Assembly, to represent the peoples and parliaments, the Council in many respects has served as a miniature version of the UN in terms of offering a continuing forum for debate and discussion among European leaders. As in the case of the UN, the Council of Europe has originated various statements of good intent and broad policy such as The European Convention for the Protection of Human Rights and Fundamental Freedoms.

But the really significant developments towards the emergence of European regionalism have come not in terms of new international organizations but in the emergence of supranational organization. In 1952, France, Italy, West Germany, and Western Europe's little three, Belgium, the Netherlands, and Luxembourg, officially launched the European Coal and Steel Community (ECSC) representing a new type of venture in economic cooperation. The ECSC brought under its authority the management of the coal and steel resources possessed by the six partners. Its administrative structure was composed of a high authority responsible to a community assembly, partly elected and partly appointed, and a court of justice to arbitrate disputes among the members. Initially the ECSC was intended to be the first phase of a new European unity which was to include both a defense and a political community. But the political community idea never moved beyond the vague planning state, and French refusal to ratify the defense pact ended that prospect.

Instead the ECSC has expanded, as a result of a treaty

signed in 1958, to include the European Economic Community (EEC) and the European Atomic Energy Community (Euratom). These three groups are organized on the basis of a shared plural executive responsible to a European assembly, with a European court of justice to interpret any treaty problems. The high authority by majority decision is able to implement policies intended to abolish tariffs and trade barriers among the members in order to creaate a single common market and to align the external trade policies of the members to create a common front.

The possibility of the EEC becoming an economic superpower was enhanced in October, 1971, when the British parliament voted to join the Economic Community. By January, 1973, Ireland, Denmark, and Norway are expected to join the original six EEC members and Great Britain to create an economic bloc of 265 million of the world's most technologically advanced peoples. Whether economic unity will be followed by political unity remains to be seen, but it is worth remembering that throughout history economic cooperation has always been a powerful incentive to political unity.

Elsewhere in the world other attempts at economic regional cooperation have not fared as well. A communist equivalent of the EEC formed in 1949, the Council for Mutual Economic Assistance (Comecon), has fallen afoul of the emergence of polycentric communism in recent years. Such independent communist states as Rumania have declined to accept the subsidiary role of suppliers of raw materials which the Soviet Union had assigned them and have insisted on pushing their own economic development.

One of the most successful ventures in regional economic cooperation has been the Central American Common Market (CACM) formed in 1960. In spite of the limited region it covers, CACM within nine years had increased trade within the area 700 percent and its members have accepted a common tariff schedule for 82 percent of outside imports. Even newer has been the formation of the Association of Southeast Asian Nations (ASEAN) which has moved little beyond the stage of promoting interregional cooperation.

Everywhere traditional rivalries and long-standing national independence form barriers to the development of regional associations. Yet their emergence in the era of the global village would seem inevitable. The failure of de Gaulle's herculean efforts of the 1960s to make France, as an old type of nation-state, the equal of the two superpowers seems to underline the inevitability of the emergence, in spite of all, of some form of United States of Europe.

This concept is no longer the exclusive property of

liberals or left-of-center thinkers. In a book published in 1970, one of the foremost spokesmen for conservative West German nationalism put it like this:

> We have arrived at Europe's crossroads. We must show whether we can make the transition from the nation state to the continental state. Those who fail to make the grade will be of no account in the space age, whose dawn we are approaching; they will not even have a say in deciding their own fate.[10]

THE ROLE OF INFORMAL PENETRATION

One more factor which needs to be commented on in discussing the emergence of regional cooperation and the increasingly accurate picture of the world as a global village. And that is the way in which technological development has increasingly brought about a new and significant element in the relations between nation states. Professor Andrew Scott, the originator of the term *informal penetration,* argues that a "revolution in statecraft" has altered "the functioning of the nation-state system." He comments:

> Throughout the history of the nation-state system, relations between nations have been predominantly of a formal nature—that is they have been confined to government-to-government contacts. In recent decades, however, national boundaries have become porous. Techniques have been fashioned to provide agents of one nation with direct access to the population and processes of another. . . . it is informal penetration that gives conflict and cooperation in this era their distinctive flavor. International politics in the twentieth century, in short, cannot be understood without a grasp of the role of informal access.[11]

By "informal access" or "penetration" Scott means "when one country's agents or instruments come into contact with the people or processes of another country in an effort to achieve certain objectives." The purposes may range from attack, such as the creation of subversive fifth columns within a country, to strong help in terms of intensive economic and military aid programs. In the middle of the spectrum would be such low-pressure activities as tours by cultural groups, the circulation of such publications as *Soviet Life* in the U.S. and *America* in the Soviet Union, and the establishment and subsidizing of friendship societies.

The beginning of the era of informal access Scott dates from the establishment of the Communist International in 1919 with its avowed purpose of using citizens of foreign countries to influence both internal and foreign policies.

[10]Franz Joseph Strauss, *Challenge and Response: A Program for Europe* (New York: Atheneum, 1970).

[11]Andrew M. Scott, *The Revolution in Statecraft: Informal Penetration* (New York: Random House, 1965).

A high point of such efforts at communist informal penetration came in the late 1940s when the communist parties of Western Europe, both on the governmental level and in terms of strikes and street riots, tried to prevent the success of the Marshall plan for economic aid.

While scattered examples of attempts at informal access can be found before 1919, it is only in the last half-century that it has become one of the standard techniques of international relations. There are various reasons for this. Since World War I public opinion has become an increasingly powerful force in the world. This is a direct result of the emergence of mass democracy with the constant need of government officials to be responsive to the general public. In the eighteenth century, Louis XIV could say quite accurately, "I am the state," and take what actions he wanted. Even for most of the nineteenth century, when property democracy was dominant, elected officials were accountable to a very limited section of the public who they could take for granted shared virtually the same social and economic views as their own. Now, however, with a large and often ill-informed and politically naive general public, whatever group is able to capture their interest and support can bring potent influence to bear on the shaping of government policy.

In addition, the achievements of modern technology have made possible the effective use of the techniques of informal penetration. One grimly negative technological factor has played an important role in the growing importance of informal penetration as a means of hostile action. This is the way in which the terrifying development of thermonuclear weaponry has rendered mutually suicidal the risks of open hostilities in the old sense.

In a less grim vein, technological development has affected all of communications. In the late eighteenth century, for example, the organizers of the American Revolution were limited to organizing public opinion by the tedious method of handwritten, horse- and sail-carried letters. Today, in this age of instantaneous communication, the possibilities for informal penetration as well as the highly developed technical skill in using them are virtually unlimited. Every country capable of doing so, either technologically or financially, endlessly beams radio programs to influence the citizens of other countries. It is no longer possible to protect one's own population against contamination by evil thoughts simply by forbidding the import of foreign books and publications. With the possible exception of communist China, not even the most authoritarian police states have been successful in preventing informal penetration by radio waves. To borrow a phrase from biology, frontiers have become "semiporous membranes"; no longer are they impermeable shells.

One of the most obvious examples of informal penetration is the widespread nature aid programs—economic, technical, educational, military and so on. Any country capable of organizing such a program now does so. Included in these activities are not only such obvious global competitors as the United States, the Soviet Union, and communist China; such countries as India, Saudi Arabia, and nationalist China are concerned with rallying regional or UN support from the nations they aid. The explosive expansion of the number of sovereign states from 50-odd at the end of World War I to the 146 extant in 1972 has greatly increased the possibilities for this type of informal penetration.

WORLD INTERDEPENDENCY

Few new countries have arrived on the world scene at a sufficient level of development to be able to carry on by themselves. Inevitably they have had to turn to outside sources for help. Given that perpetual state of financial anemia from which the UN suffers, this has meant accepting aid and assistance from other nation-states. But time and again, technical assistance programs have either been refused or summarily ended for ideological reasons. The Peace Corps was such a successful example of informal penetration that various other countries paid it the high compliment of creating their own versions. And the educational projects carried on by the Ford Foundation are perhaps the outstanding example of informal penetration by a nongovernmental organization for broadly humanitarian purposes. Yet the Peace Corps has been expelled from several African countries and the Burmese military dictatorship expelled the Ford Foundation in the early 1960s.

These actions and the acceptance or rejection of various aid programs are conditioned by another factor involved in the twentieth-century development of informal penetration. And this has been the inclination to accept or reject preferred aid programs on the basis of the ideology of the country offering them. The efforts of the United States to extend the Marshall Aid program to the countries of Eastern Europe and the desire of at least Czechoslovakia to participate were thwarted by stern Soviet refusal to let its client states participate.

In order to avoid ideological commitment, various African states have turned to harmless small powers with no global pretensions, such as Israel or nationalist China, for aid with their development programs. For countries deeply concerned with trying to find their own national social and cultural image, such an attitude is easily understandable. In recent years it has become clear that when a fragile and technologically backward society is exposed to informal penetration by one possessing an overwhelming dominance, the result is likely to be possession rather than penetration. Or, if not possession, then such a disintegration as has apparently occurred in South Vietnam.

Whatever the degree of its influence on the conduct of international affairs in the late twentieth century, it is clear that informal penetration represents one more disintegrative factor in the traditional organization of the nation-state world system. In the late twentieth century, not only in the technologically advanced countries but in many other nations, a generation will come to maturity with a knowledge of other peoples and cultures gained from television.

CONCLUSION

It would be naive to assume that knowledge will necessarily lead either to understanding or liking. Nor can we assume that it will produce any very sudden or startling results. But that this will occur in the long run cannot be doubted. Behind the emergence of informal penetration in international affairs, the emergence of articulate mass societies, and the dogged groping toward closer international association, and in spite of all the disappointments and heartbreak of this century, one factor is far more dominant than any other.

That is the fact that technology has literally expanded to the stars. If not quite yet, the moon shortly will become a way station in space. Technology has made universal the political problems of the various subdivisions of earth's global village. It offers the possibility for their successful solution or it can provide the means for world suicide. The political problems of the late twentieth century, let alone the twenty-first, will focus on whether man can learn the cooperative use of technology to attack his desperate problems, or whether technology will become a hungry dragon devouring him instead.

On the basis of four or five titles per chapter, this represents a minimum list indeed. It should be regarded as a launching pad for further exploration by the student rather than as a stopping place. Although this list represents the personal preferences of the compiler, I have tried to include generally accepted basic sources. (P) after a title means available in paperback.

Chapter 1. The Problems of the World We Live In

Boulding, Kenneth E. *The Meaning of the 20th Century: The Great Transition.* New York: Harper & Row, 1965. (P)

Science is the basis of the great twentieth-century transition from "civilized to post-civilized society" which will be possible if the war, population, and entropy traps can be avoided.

Heilbroner, Robert L. *The Great Ascent.* New York: Harper & Row, 1963. (P)

Perceptive and pessimistic analysis of the almost insurmountable difficulties facing the efforts of the new nations to achieve the "revolution of great expectations" and the grim political consequences of their probable failure.

Toffler, Alvin. *Future Shock.* New York: Random House, 1970. (P)

"This is a book about what happens to people when they are overwhelmed by change." It attempts to prepare the reader for the accelerating and intensifying rate of social and cultural change.

Weiner, Norbert. *The Human Use of Human Beings: Cybernetics and Society.* rev. ed. New York: Avon, 1964. (P)

The classic statement on the role of communications and the control of machines by machines in the creation of today's and tomorrow's technetronic society.

Chapter 2. Political Science Searches for Understanding

Charlesworth, James C., ed. *Contemporary Political Analysis.* New York: Free Press, 1967. (P)

A collection of essays by outstanding political scientists on the various methodological approaches to contemporary political analysis. At times difficult reading, but rewarding.

Easton, David. *A Systems Analysis of Political Life.* New York: Wiley, 1965.

The most comprehensive statement on the "input-output" version of systems analysis by its most eminent pioneer. This is the third volume of a detailed exposition. The others are *The Political System* (1953) and *A Framework for Political Analysis* (1965).

Freund, Julien. *The Sociology of Max Weber* (trans. from the French by Mary Ilford). New York: Random House, 1968.

An informed and detailed analysis of the sociological thought of the most important figure in the development of twentieth-century social science thought. The more political science has drawn on sociology, the more Weber's influence has become important.

Mackenzie, W. J. M. *Politics and Social Science.* Baltimore: Penguin Books, 1969. (P)

An excellent broad survey by a British scholar of the developments in the study of politics since World War II in a trans-Atlantic perspective. Highly recommended as a general introduction.

Somit, Albert and Tanenhaus, Joseph. *The Development of American Political Science.* Boston: Allyn & Bacon, 1967.

A highly readable and thorough survey of the development of American political science. Perhaps the best source to use for historical perspective.

Wiseman, H. V. *Political Systems: Some Sociological Approaches.* New York: Praeger, 1967. (P)

Another general survey by an English scholar with the "one simple, basic and unpretentious purpose" of providing "an introduction to some sociological approaches to a study of political systems." Not easy reading but worth the effort.

Young, Oran R. *Systems of Political Science.* Englewood Cliffs, N.J.: Prentice-Hall, 1968. (P)

This brief but brilliant monograph affords an excellent introduction to the contemporary methodological approaches. Along with Mackenzie, a basic book for both the advanced and beginning student.

Chapter 3. The Role of Interest Groups in the Political System

Almond, Gabriel and Coleman, James F. *The Politics of the Developing Areas.* Princeton, N.J.: Princeton University Press, 1960.

Although not primarily concerned with interest groups, it contains important material on their role in the political systems of the developing areas.

Bertley, Arthur F. *The Process of Government: A Study of Social Pressures.* Bloomington, Ind.: Principia Press, 1949.

Although its frame of reference is an advanced industrial society, this remains an important pioneering classic in the study of interest groups.

Ehrmann, Henry W., ed. *Interest Groups on Four Continents.* Pittsburgh, Pa.: University of Pittsburgh Press, 1958. (P)

Papers and the discussions on them from a symposium dealing with the role of interest groups in a number of nations. Somewhat dated but still an invaluable reference source.

Key, V. O. *Parties, Politics and Pressure Groups,* 5th ed. New York: Crowell Collier Macmillan, 1964.

Since its initial publication in 1942, this has stood as the fundamental study on American interest groups. Awareness of Key is basic to an understanding of the subject.

Truman, David B. *The Governmental Process: Political Interests and Public Opinion.* New York: Knopf, 1962.

No one is more responsible than Truman for rediscovering Bentley and bringing his methodology to bear on the contemporary scene. What Easton is to systems analysis, Truman is to modern group theory.

Chapter 4. The Political Party: Characteristics, Functions, Organization

Duverger, Maurice. *Political Parties: Their Organization and Activity in the Modern State,* 2nd English ed. rev. New York: Wiley, 1962.

While the 20 years since initial publication in 1950 have revealed faults in Duverger's analysis, this still remains a provocative and stimulating effort to create a typology for the organizational analysis of political parties.

La Palombara, Joseph G. and Weiner, Joseph G., eds. *Political Parties and Political Development.* Princeton, N.J.: Princeton University Press, 1966.

The chapters written by the two editors are particularly useful for their outline of the development of non-Western parties. The best general survey of non-Western political party development.

Leiserson, Avery. *Parties and Politics—An Institutional and Behavioral Approach.* New York: Knopf, 1958.

A successful combination of the two approaches by a knowledgeable scholar. It contains much useful historical material.

Michels, Robert. *Political Parties: A Sociological Study of the Oligarchical Tendencies of Modern Democracy.* New York: Crowell Collier Macmillan, 1962. (P)

A classic analysis which is constantly referred to by students. The thesis that power concentrates in few hands seems to have universal validity.

Milnor, Andrew J., ed. *Comparative Political Parties.* New York: T. Y. Crowell, 1969. (P)

A well-chosen group of readings which provides a good introduction to the study of parties. Focused, however, on Western European and American parties.

Chapter 5. The Movement-Regime Party and Other Party Systems

Armstrong, John A. *The Politics of Totalitarianism.* New York: Random House, 1961.

A scholarly and comprehensive survey of the development of the Soviet party from the Stalin period until the late 1950s. It contains an excellent discussion of the party organizational structure.

Dahl, Robert A., ed. *Political Opposition in Western Democracies.* New Haven: Yale University Press, 1966.

A collection of essays on various Western countries by specialists. Contains excellent bibliographical references.

Hodgkin, Thomas. *African Political Parties: An Introductory Guide.* Baltimore: Penguin Books, 1962.

An excellent survey of the origins and development of African parties. Might well be read in combination with Gwendolyn Carter's *African One-Party States* (Cornell University Press, 1962).

Schapiro, Leonard. *The Communist Party of the Soviet Union.* New York: Vintage Books, 1960.

A comprehensive history of the ideological and organizational evolution of the party. Covers through the important Twentieth Party Congress of 1956.

Neumann, Sigmund, ed. *Modern Political Parties: Approaches to Comparative Politics.* Chicago: University of Chicago Press, 1956.

The details are now dated but the various essays still are valuable. Neumann's own thoughts on the study of political parties have continuing importance.

Ostrogorskii, Moisei. *Democracy and the Organization of Political Parties,* 2 vols. New York: Macmillan, 1908.

The first great pioneering study on the origins and development of British and American parties. Still contains many pertinent insights into the functioning of party organization. There is a Quadrangle books abridged edition (paperback), published in 1964.

Chapter 6. Electoral Systems: How Voters Behave

Almond, Gabriel A. and Verba, Sidney. *The Civic Culture.* Boston: Little, Brown, 1965. (P)

Already regarded as a classic, this is a brilliant pioneering study of political attitudes in Great Britain, West Germany, Italy, Mexico, and the United States.

Gallup, George A. *A Guide to Public Opinion Polls.* 2nd ed. Princeton, N.J.: Princeton University Press, 1948.

As the leading commercial pollster, Gallup presents a case for the defense. Hardly objective but obviously authoritative in presentation.

Hennessy, Bernard C. *Public Opinion.* Belmont, Calif.: Wadsworth, 1965.

A good general survey written in readable style. Incorporates much recent research.

Key, V. O., Jr. *Public Opinion and American Democracy.* New York: Knopf, 1961.

An excellent introduction to the subject by a distinguished political scientist. It really has wider implications than just "American democracy."

Lippmann, Walter. *Public Opinion.* New York: Free Press, 1953. (P)

A pioneering study by the political columnist who exerted the major influence on opinion-makers and political leaders for more than 40 years. Still pertinent, and characterized by Lippman's lucid and brilliant style.

Chapter 7. Democracy: Concepts, Development, Characteristics

Aptheker, Herbert, ed. *Marxism and Democracy.* New York: Humanities Press, 1965.

A collection of essays by Marxist scholars, American, European, and African, dealing with this vital topic. Worth reading for its often trenchant criticism and a different methodological approach from the ordinary.

Dahl, Robert A. *A Preface to Democratic Theory.* Chicago: University of Chicago Press, 1956. (P)

A brilliant examination of various contrasting models of democratic systems which doesn't raise any normative frames of reference. It provides provocative criticism of traditional democratic theory.

Jefferson, Thomas. *On Democracy,* ed. by Saul K. Padover. New York: Mentor Books, 1952. (P)

A well-chosen selection of the writings of the greatest Anglo-American theorist. Without Jefferson, the development of modern democratic thought would have been far different.

Lindsay, A. D. *The Modern Democratic State vol. 1.* London: Oxford University Press, 1960.

An easily understood, objective, and stimulating analysis of the role and function of democratic theory in the development of the modern state. Particularly valuable for its relation to constitutional and political developments.

Mayo, Henry B. *An Introduction to Democratic Theory.* New York: Oxford University Press, 1960. (P)

A well-written and informed analysis of democratic theory. It could well serve as a good introduction to the liberal interpretation.

Chapter 8. The Alternative of Communism

Avineri, Shlomo. *The Social and Political Thought of Karl Marx.* London: Cambridge University Press, 1968.

This study by an Israeli scholar of the importance of alienation in Marx's writings is difficult but rewarding. It helps to understand Marx's contemporary appeal.

Bober, M. M. *Karl Marx's Interpretation of History.* 2nd ed. rev. New York: Norton, 1965. (P)

Originally published in 1927, this still remains as the best explanation and analysis of historical materialism. From the "dialectic" to "the significance of the theory," the coverage is lucid and authoritative.

Carew-Hunt, R. N. *The Theory and Practice of Communism.* 5th ed. rev. Baltimore: Penguin Books, 1963. (P)

Perhaps the best known and most readable of introductions to the theory and organizational development of Marxism. It uniquely combines exposition and analysis.

Daniels, Robert V., ed. *A Documentary History of Communism.* New York: Random House, 1960. (There is also a two-volume paperback edition in the Vintage Russian Library Series.)

An invaluable compilation of generously excerpted source material on the development of world communism from 1894 to 1960.

Feuer, Lewis S., ed. *Marx and Engels: Basic Writings on Politics and Philosophy.* Garden City, N.Y.: Doubleday, 1959. (P)

An excellent collection of sensitively edited excerpts from the most important writings, including revealing letters, of Marx and Engels. Basic for fundamental understanding.

Gay, Peter. *The Dilemma of Democratic Socialism: Eduard Bernstein's Challenge to Marx.* New York: Crowell Collier Macmillan, 1962.

The best survey of the often-neglected role of democratic socialism. It contains a comprehensive bibliography.

Gregor, A. James. *A Survey of Marxism.* New York: Random House, 1965.

In the words of the author, the book has two purposes: "to provide within the compass of a single, brief exposition a survey of the wealth and complexity of Marxism" and "to present not only the principal elements of Marxism as a philosophy and a theory of history but also to suggest some of the criticisms that have been or . . . should be leveled against it."

Wilson, Edmund. *To the Finland Station: A Study in the Writing and Acting of History.* Garden City, N.Y.: Doubleday, 1940. (P)

A superb literary stylist discusses the development of socialist thought and action from the utopians to Lenin's arrival in Russia on the eve of the 1917 revolution. The first reading will broaden anyone's horizons.

Chapter 9. The Nationalisms: Old and New

Deutsch, Karl W. *Nationalism and Social Communication: an Inquiry into the Foundations of Nationality.* Cambridge, Mass.: Massachusetts Institute of Technology Press, 1953.

A provocative and thoughtful insight into a new aspect of the foundations of nationalism. Important for a sophisticated understanding.

Emerson, Rupert. *From Empire to Nation.* Cambridge, Mass.: Harvard University Press, 1960. (P)

An excellent historical survey of the emergence of non-Western nationalism from colonial status. Not notable in methodological approach but good foundation reading.

Kautsky, John H. *Political Change in Underdeveloped Countries, Nationalism and Communism.* New York: Wiley, 1962. (P)

While the individual essays are now somewhat dated, Kautsky's own long introduction to this problem is still highly pertinent. Overall approach is essentially sociological rather than historical.

Kohn, Hans. *The Idea of Nationalism: A Study of its Origins and Background.* New York: Macmillan, 1961. (P)

A basic survey of the origins of Western nationalism which provides a solid basis for further study. Contains excerpts from important source material.

Snyder, Louis L., ed. *The Dynamics of Nationalism.* New York: Van Nostrand Reinhold, 1964.

A collection of essays concerned with attempting to explain the why and how of nationalism. Generally well written and contain good bibliographical references.

Chapter 10. Society, Government, and the State

Laski, Harold J. *The State in Theory and Practice.* London: Allen and Unwin, 1956.

A penetrating analysis by one of the foremost of Anglo-American political theorists.

Lenin, V. I. *State and Revolution.* New York: International Publishers, 1940. (P)

This is the classic statement of the Marxist theory of the origins and destiny of the state. It draws heavily on Engel's basic work, *The Origin of the Family, Private Property and the State.*

MacIver, Robert M. *The Modern State.* London: Oxford University Press, 1955.

A largely sociological analysis by a distinguished political scientist whose *Web of Government* is also valuable reading. Both perceptive and readable.

Mair, Lucy. *Primitive Government*. Baltimore: Penguin Books, 1962. (P)

A survey by a social anthropologist of "government without the state" in terms of African examples. Good as an introduction both to Dr. Mair's discipline and the government of non-Western societies.

Parsons, Talcott. *Societies: Evolutionary and Contemporary Perspectives*. Englewood Cliffs, N.J.: Prentice-Hall, 1966.

Valuable both for its own worth and as an introduction to the single most influential figure in the development of contemporary social science. Not easy reading but calculated to broaden the student's perspective.

Chapter 11. Governmental Structures as Dependent Variables

Bagehot, Walter. *The English Constitution*. New York: Oxford University Press, 1955.

Since its initial serial publication in 1865–1867, this collection of essays has been republished innumerable times. Its lively style and shrewd comments still make it relevant.

Beer, Samuel H., ed. *Patterns of Government*. 2nd ed. New York: Random House, 1962.

A high-level methodologically oriented approach to the governmental systems of Great Britain, France, West Germany, and the U.S.S.R. Notable for introductory essay and bibliography.

Bryce, James. *The American Commonwealth*. 2 vols., rev. and enl. ed. New York: Macmillan, 1918.

More institutional and less sociological in approach than the equally famous de Tocqueville's *Democracy in America*. Still one of the classic studies on the functioning of the American presidential system.

Burns, James MacGregor and Peltason, Jack. *Government by the People*. nat'l ed., 7th ed. Englewood Cliffs, N.J.: Prentice-Hall, 1969.

Perhaps the most highly regarded text on the institutional approach to American government. An excellent basic introduction.

Jennings, Sir William Ivor. *Cabinet Government*. 3rd ed. and *Parliament*. 2nd ed. New York: Cambridge University Press, 1959 and 1957.

Two authoritative and scholarly discussions by a distinguished British political scientist. Not easy reading but conclusive.

Chapter 12. Executive-Legislative Symbiosis in the Twentieth Century

Corwin, Edward S. *The President: Office and Powers, 1787–1957; History and Analysis of Practice and Opinion.* 4th ed. rev. New York: New York University Press, 1957.

An exhaustive and exhausting legal analysis. Not for leisure reading but the ultimate authority in its field.

Eden, Sir Anthony. *Memoirs: Full Circle (1951–1957)* and *The Reckoning.* Boston: Houghton Mifflin, 1960 and 1965.

No political figure ever looks bad in his memoirs. But this is lucidly written and gives interesting insight into the thinking of a distinguished member of the inner elite of the British establishment.

La Palombara, Joseph G., ed. *Bureaucracy and Political Development.* Princeton, N.J.: Princeton University Press, 1963.

Assessments by experts on the role of bureaucracy as the dominant factor in the stabilization and development of new governments.

Neustadt, Richard E. *Presidential Power: The Politics of Leadership.* New York: Wiley, 1960. (P)

President Kennedy is reputed to have kept a copy of this book always by him. In any case, an incisive and important analysis.

Rossister, Clinton L. *The American Presidency.* New York: Harcourt Brace Jovanovich, 1960. (P)

An excellently written and highly informative account by one of the most distinguished students of American politics. Makes obvious why power has had to gravitate to the executive.

Chapter 13. Linking the Parts Together: Unitary, Confederate, Federal

Hamilton, Alexander; Jay, John; and Madison, James. *The Federalist.* Garden City, N.Y.: Doubleday, 1966. (P)

As with every other aspect of American government, here is the classic statement of the thinking of the founding fathers on what a federal system meant.

Macmahon, Arthur W., ed. *Federalism: Mature and Emergent.* New York: Russell Publishing Co., 1955.

Well-rounded collection of essays on the theory and practice of federalism with primary focus on both the United States and Europe.

Mogei, Sobei. *The Problem of Federalism: A Study in the History of Political Theory.* 2 vols. London: Allen and Unwin, 1931.

Perhaps the best historical survey available of the various theories of federalism. Long and detailed, but the scholarship is impeccable and the information permanently valuable.

Wheare, Kenneth C. *Federal Government.* 4th ed. New York: Oxford University Press, 1964.

The outstanding study of the theory and practice of federalism by its most prominent student in the Anglo-American world. Wide-ranging and notable for bibliographical references.

Wilson, Woodrow. *Congressional Government: A Study in American Politics.* New York: Meridian, 1961.

Classic study of the dynamics of a legislatively centered federal system by a political scientist who went on to make good. Lucid in style, important in content.

Chapter 14. The Need for Ground Rules or the Role of Constitutions

Beard, Charles A. *The Republic: Conversations on Fundamentals.* New York: Viking, 1943.

In the form of platonic dialogues, an innovative political scientist of the early twentieth century discusses the nature of the American constitutional structure. Not only authoritative but fun to read. Probably for students of the 1970s, the concerns of their grandparents will be worth the trouble.

Friedrich, Carl J. *Constitutional Reasons of State: The Survival of the Constitutional Order.* Providence, R.I.: Brown University Press, 1957.

Not easy reading but very through. Well documented and worth pushing through.

McIlwain, Charles H. *Constitutionalism, Ancient and Modern.* Ithaca, N.Y.: Cornell University Press, 1958. (P)

Thorough survey of the history and development of constitutionalism. Basic for historical perspective.

Wheare, Kenneth C. *Modern Constitutions.* London: Oxford University Press, 1951.

Authoritative survey by a leading scholar on constitutional development. Good footnotes and bibliography.

Wormuth, Francis D. *The Origins of Modern Constitutionalism.* New York: Harper & Row, 1949.

An historical survey of the constitutional struggles over both religious and political issues of the important period of the English civil wars in the mid-seventeenth century. Important for an understanding of both British and American thought and their subsequent influence.

Chapter 15. International Organization in the Late Twentieth Century

Bloomfield, Lincoln P. *The United Nations and U.S. Foreign Policy.* Boston: Little, Brown, 1960.

Thoughtful, informed, and balanced account of the role of the United Nations in U.S. foreign policy planning.

Clark, Grenville, and Sohn, Louis B. *World Peace Through World Law.* 2nd ed. rev. Cambridge, Mass.: Harvard University Press, 1960.

Eloquently argued and deeply felt case for a highly desirable, if hopelessly utopian, cause. The best example of high-level idealism in thinking about world affairs.

Dallin, Alexander. *The Soviet Union at the United Nations.* New York: Praeger, 1962. (P)

Well-documented, well-written study of the use made by the Soviet Union of the United Nations and its probably future pattern.

Padelford, Norman J. and Goodrich, Leland M., eds. *The United Nations in the Balance: Accomplishments and Prospects.* New York: Praeger, 1965.

Surveys by well-known authorities of the present and probable future status of the United Nations. While on the optimistic side, there is a realistic outlook.

Walters, Francis P. *A History of the League of Nations.* London: Oxford University Press, 1960.

A well-balanced and dispassionate history of the tragedy of the League. If it is possible to learn from history, this study should offer insight.

Suggested Political Novel Reading List

Much fun and profit can be derived from reading political novels. In dramatic terms of human behavior they often give insight into political action that even the best textbooks can never achieve. The list below has been tested at various times on groups of students, all of whom reported that they had not only enjoyed the reading but had gained new insights into political action. All the books listed below are currently available in paperback editions. Unless otherwise indicated, New York is the place of publication.

Howe, Irving. *Politics and the Novel.* Meridian Books.

A well-written survey of the characteristics and development of the political novel. Contains helpful chapters on the different types of political novel which have developed.

Disraeli, Benjamin. *Sybil, or The Two Nations.* Baltimore: Penguin Books.

Originally published in 1845, *Sybil,* a love story of a young working girl and a proud aristocrat, gives a picture of the misery of the early industrial revolution and the bitter class struggle between rich and poor. Ironically, its crusading young author went on to become, as Lord Beaconsfield, the builder of Britain's new empire.

Drury, Allen. *Advise and Consent.* Pocket Books.

A gripping novel by an experienced political correspondent of the power struggle between an imperious president and his Senate opponents over the confirmation of the president's choice for Secretary of State. There are thinly veiled portraits of powerful Washington figures of two decades ago.

Greene, Graham. *The Quiet American.* Bantam.

A searing portrait, drawn in the late 1950s, of that self-righteous and naive American determination to save the world which has been responsible for so much of the tragedy of Vietnam. Pyle, blundering through the intricacies of Vietnamese politics in the late French period, epitomizes all the ineffective virtues and compulsive blunders of the years ahead.

Gheorghiu, C. Virgil. *The 25th Hour.* Pocket Books.

A nightmare picture of what happens to the little man caught in the machinery of the modern gargantuan state. The sufferings of Johann in the maelstrom of World War II have an even more uncomfortable contemporary application.

Golding, William. *Lord of the Flies.* Capricorn.

In the story of the lapse into barbarism of a group of small boys marooned on a tropic island, Golding gives a disturbingly convincing portrayal of the predatory nature of man and the fragility of the veneer of civilization.

Kafka, Franz. *The Trial.* Vintage Books.

First published in 1937, this book is one of the important novels of the twentieth century. For reasons he never understands, Joseph K. is tried by a mysterious tribunal and eventually executed. Marx's thesis of alienation in industrial society has never been more poignantly dramatized.

Kennedy, Jay Richard. *The Chairman.* Signet.

Tense espionage novel of China in the period of the proletarian Cultural Revolution offering insight both into Chinese communist society and Mao Tse-tung thought.

Knebel, Fletcher. *The ZinZin Road.* Bantam.

A skilled novelist writes of the trials and tribulations of a Peace Corps group in a somewhat mythical African country. Apparently the book has considerable factual basis.

Koestler, Arthur. *Darkness at Noon.* Bantam.

In terms of the downfall and death of Rubashov, the old bolshevik, Koestler offers insight into the still-haunting mystery of the purge trials of the 1930s. As a touching picture of a man enslaved by ideology it is unsurpassed.

Lopez, Hank. *Afro 6.* Dell.

The story of a doomed uprising by a Black nationalist group in New York City. Tensely written and disturbing in its contemporary applications.

Malraux, André. *Man's Fate.* Vintage.

In contrast to Rubashov as the epitome of world communism at its lowest moment of moral disintegration, Kyo personifies the intense idealism of the Chinese party at the time of its destruction by the nationalists in the Shanghai massacre of 1927. Politics aside, this is an expertly written novel.

O'Connor, Edwin. *The Last Hurrah.* Bantam.

An expertly written, thinly fictionalized account of the power and downfall of an Irish-American political boss. Offers excellent insight into political behavior and the management of men.

Orwell, George. *1984.* Signet.

Probably the most widely read political novel of this century. Its spine-chilling picture of a totalitarian world may not happen on time but, given modern technology and psychological manipulation, the possibility is there.

Solzhenitzyn, Alexander, *The First Circle.* Bantam.

Soviet Russia's most distinguished novelist pens a poignant picture of a group of political prisoners in the first circle of hell. Although laid in the last years of the Stalin period, Solzhenitzyn's own troubles seem to indicate that not too much has changed.

Stendhal (Henri Beyle). *The Red and the Black.* Baltimore: Penguin.

Although first published in 1830, this novel details the career of a superior political opportunist who would feel at home in contemporary politics. As a study in political behavior it is classic.

West, Morris L. *The Ambassador.* Dell.

A semifictionalized account of the U.S. role in the overthrow and murder of President Diem in 1963. A skillfully written story by an expert.

INDEX

72 73 74 75 76 9 8 7 6 5 4 3 2 1